Hurricane Katrina

Hurricane Katrina

The Mississippi Story

James Patterson Smith

University Press of Mississippi / *Jackson*

www.upress.state.ms.us

The University Press of Mississippi is a member
of the Association of American University Presses.

First printing 2012

∞

Library of Congress Cataloging-in-Publication Data

Smith, James Patterson.
Hurricane Katrina : the Mississippi story / James Patterson Smith.
p. cm.
Includes bibliographical references and index.
ISBN 978-1-61703-023-9 (cloth : alk. paper) — ISBN 978-1-61703-024-6 (ebook) 1. Hurricane Katrina, 2005—Personal narratives. 2. Disaster victims—Mississippi. 3. Disaster relief—Mississippi. 4. Hurricanes—Mississippi—Social aspects. I. Title.
HV636 2005 .M7 S65 2012
976.206'2—dc23 2011032598

British Library Cataloging-in-Publication Data available

For my granddaughter, Alice Marie Bradley,
and all of the children born since Katrina.

Contents

Acknowledgments

The completion of a project of this magnitude owes much to many people. This idea of a book that would give voice to the special experience of the people of Mississippi during and after Hurricane Katrina began as an inspiration from Seetha Srinivasan, the former director of the University Press of Mississippi. In December of 2006, it was Seetha's patient persuasions that made this historian and storm survivor believe that his own background had fitted him to make an effort to construct a credible scholarly account of the epic but neglected story of Mississippi's sojourn through the greatest natural disaster in American history.

I want to thank the Mississippi legislature for its visionary financial support of the Mississippi Humanities Council's Katrina Oral History Project, which enabled the Center for Oral History and Cultural Heritage at the University of Southern Mississippi to gather and transcribe over 400 interviews with local officials and Katrina survivors. Regardless of whether their names show up in the references and citations, each person who shared an oral history contributed to the collective insights which shaped this book. I and all future scholars who access this valuable collection owe a special debt of gratitude to Linda Van Zandt, Stephanie Millet-DeArmey, and Carol Short, who faithfully transcribed and processed these invaluable first-person accounts. I also owe a special thank-you to Rachel Swaykos, a graduate student in social work who worked with me in the summer of 2007 to help gather targeted interviews from school officials, mental health practitioners, and volunteer organizations involved in relief work in Mississippi.

A grant from the Community and Regional Resilience Institute at Oak Ridge National Laboratory supported the semester of release time from teaching which enabled me to finish the manuscript. Dr. Tom Lansford,

Dean of Instruction at USM Gulf Coast, and Associate Dean Dr. Mark Wrighton played major roles in helping me access those resources.

For their role in enabling our work in the Department of History at the University of Southern Mississippi Gulf Coast, I offer thanks to university president Dr. Martha Saunders, Dean Denise Von Herrmann of the College of Arts and Letters, and Dr. Phyllis Jestice, chairman of the Department of History. Dr. Jestice in particular supported my needs and requests at several critical junctures in the research and writing process.

Dr. Deanne Nuwer, my colleague at USM Gulf Coast, kindly shared with me her research on Katrina volunteers. Thus, I am happy to acknowledge Dr. Nuwer as a coauthor for chapter 6, "The Grace of Volunteers." Former Gulfport fire chief Pat Sullivan graciously allowed me to include in this volume selections from the thousands of photographs which he took during the response to Hurricane Katrina, and he added much to my understanding of disaster preparation and response in several in-depth conversations. Brian Martin and Steven Peranich on the staff of Congressman Gene Taylor provided me with a large number of documents, and through many long talks and e-mail exchanges, they led me to important insights on federal processes, insurance, and many other issues. To all of the Katrina survivors on the faculty and staff at USM Gulf Coast I owe thanks for sharing with me their stories, their special wisdom, and their constructive advice. Our common experiences in Katrina will shape the rest of our lives, and their availability as sounding boards has helped shape this book.

I owe a special thank-you to my daughter Jenny Elizabeth Benoit who patiently read the manuscript, offered insights, and helped purge many errors from its pages. In the time when the burden of this project seemed so very heavy, my daughter Amy Bradley and her husband, John, gave us the gift of a granddaughter who brought great joy and newfound purposefulness to days filled with the lonely job of writing. However, in this life I owe my greatest debt of gratitude to my wife, Jeanette Holcomb Smith. She guarded my time and delayed vacations and holidays in support of this effort. She read and offered corrections and advice on every chapter. For the past four decades she has stood beside me, endured my travails, and enriched every corner of my life. I consider her a gift from God, and as a person of faith, I acknowledge this and all of the other gifts of life that flow to us from a merciful Creator.

Notwithstanding the great help and support that others have so generously provided to me throughout this project, in the final analysis, any errors of fact or interpretation are my own.

Preface

The story of Hurricane Katrina in Mississippi is the story of unexpected strengths in unexpected people in the midst of the greatest natural disaster in American history. It is a dramatic but underreported story of the people along the 75 miles of the Mississippi Gulf Coast who, on August 29, 2005, suffered the full force of Katrina's deadly and unprecedented 30-foot tidal surge. The heroes of this saga are the local people and local leaders whose responses in a terrible time of testing bear witness to the compassion, strength, and creativity that arose in coastal Mississippians of all colors, creeds, and classes. Theirs is a story of resilience and perseverance in the face of overwhelming destruction.

Despite the great drama of this part of the Katrina story, within days of the catastrophe the main focus of national press coverage of the disaster shifted from the obliteration on the Mississippi Gulf Coast to the tragic flooding of New Orleans. At New Orleans, on the weak backside of the storm, man-made levees failed on the banks of the flood-swollen rivers and lakes around the city. In contrast, 60 miles away on the strong side of the storm, Katrina unleashed on the Mississippi Gulf Coast a brutal and shocking display of the raw destructive physical forces that nature acting alone can pack into tropical cyclones. On the Mississippi coast, homes, schools, and public buildings not only flooded, but were collapsed and literally swept away by the thousands in a powerful 30-foot surge of swirling water that pushed straight in from the sea. But for the calamities that befell New Orleans, the fate of almost 400,000 people of the Mississippi Gulf Coast would have stood forth on its own as an unparalleled national disaster epic.

Three months after Hurricane Katrina, in a lengthy front-page opinion piece, the executive editor of the Mississippi Gulf Coast's major newspaper complained about the lack of national press attention "to the plight of our

[Mississippi] region and its people." The Mississippi Gulf Coast's story, he lamented, had become a mere "add-on phrase to the news of Katrina and its effects on New Orleans." In most national news reports, the editorialist observed, the Mississippi sojourn had been "reduced to four words—'and the Gulf Coast.'" The neglect had in effect turned the area into "Mississippi's Invisible Coast." Four years later, in another long op-ed column entitled "Mississippi's STILL Invisible Coast," the same executive editor again protested that the tendency to underreport the Mississippi saga had become "virtually universal now," such that in fourth anniversary media assessments of Katrina, "the people of the [Mississippi] Gulf Coast have receded into the hazy status of non-people whose story is untold."[1] This book, with its focus on Mississippi, represents one effort to redress that imbalance through drawing together a fuller account of the suffering and resilience of the people caught at the very epicenter of the storm on the Gulf Coast.

Early in 2007, at the behest of Seetha Srinivasan, who was then the director of the University Press of Mississippi, I took on the project of researching and writing a book about the Mississippi Katrina experience. Seetha's proposal both surprised and humbled me. She stated that my experience in gathering and using oral histories had drawn her to me. I had coauthored with Dr. Gilbert Mason a successful book rooted in oral history and dealing with the desegregation of Mississippi's beaches. However, I was uncertain as to whether I could give the Mississippi Katrina story the telling it deserved. Quite frankly, I thought the epic potential of the Mississippi postdisaster struggle deserved the powers of a William Faulkner, a Eudora Welty, or a Shelby Foote. Nevertheless, I had to concede that no Faulkner, Welty, or Foote had yet appeared. I voiced other concerns. I had lived through the Katrina disaster and its aftermath on the Mississippi Gulf Coast, but even then, some 16 months after the storm, we—the faculty, staff, and students of the University of Southern Mississippi Gulf Coast—were still coping with serious side effects of the disaster both at work and in our personal lives.

However, Seetha knew that our USM Center for Oral History and Cultural Heritage housed one of the largest oral history collections in the nation and that with support from the Mississippi legislature, we had launched an ambitious effort to record and transcribe for posterity hundreds of personal stories from Mississippi Katrina survivors. Thus, over a period of several days, Seetha made me believe that despite my doubts and my deep personal involvement with Katrina I might be able to produce a credible professional account that in Seetha's words would "bring forth the voices of the

Mississippi people who experienced the disaster, lest the Mississippi disaster story be lost." These words struck a chord with me, and I have come back to them repeatedly as guiding concepts and inspirations.

There are a number of challenges in writing contemporary history. Many will point out that the perspectives of scholars on events through which they have lived can never be as complete or rise as far toward the goal of objectivity as those of a later generation. My goal in this has been to bring a balance to the story that arises from a solid research foundation. Balance, in my view, starts with a fuller account of Mississippi and Mississippians. However, while the ideal of balance has guided me in the treatment of government agencies and well-known political figures, my main focus and point of reference has been the travails of local people and local leaders on the Gulf Coast as they rose from the wreckage and dealt with the often-frustrating recovery rules and processes formulated and imposed by politicians and bureaucracies outside the stricken area.

Inevitably any effort to tell a story as far-reaching in its effects as this one must be selective. On the Tuesday following the storm an errand of mercy led this author on a personal drive through badly damaged sections of Gulfport and West Biloxi and far inland up Highway 49, where I witnessed the large numbers of downed trees and power lines, extensive power outages, closed gas stations, and the general business standstills which storm winds had inflicted on towns stretching north from Hattiesburg through Jackson and on to Madison. The winds of Katrina swept over great swaths of the state and left 70 percent of all utility customers in Mississippi without electricity for days or weeks after the storm. However, this study centers on the dramatic destruction and massive human dislocations visited on the people of the three Mississippi Gulf Coast counties and on the years of struggle for a return to normalcy which was their special ordeal.

It is inevitable that my own experiences in the storm and the long recovery effort have influenced me, though exactly how and to what extent I cannot say. Still, perhaps some further personal disclosure is in order. Along with those of almost every person in this region, my emotions run deep when I recall the volunteers from across the nation who came to our aid. The image of a cadre of students from Duke University working their way down the street to help us as we cleaned out my widowed sister-in-law's flooded house is still vivid in my mind. So is the epiphany that I experienced when I came to understand on a personal level how far a helping hand from a stranger can go in lifting one's morale in a moment of crisis. No matter how self-reliant we may be, in a deep spiritual sense people in distress have a profound need for other people with whom they can share their burdens.

Beyond the loss of my sister-in-law's house, our family dealt with the destruction of my aged parents' apartment and major roof and interior Sheetrock damage to my own house. The houses of two of my wife's elderly aunts, one in Hattiesburg and one in Columbia, also took major roof and structural damage when large trees were blown onto them. Still, our personal troubles looked small in comparison to the suffering of so many of our friends and neighbors on the coast. At work, due to catastrophic damage to our campuses in Long Beach and Ocean Springs, Mississippi, my colleagues and I on the faculty and staff at USM Gulf Coast put in long hours of extra duty in our effort to restore classes in alternate locations for our 2,500 students. At this writing neither of our USM Gulf Coast campuses has been fully restored. Such experiences may well have influenced me, but I will leave it to others to ponder whether it has been for good or ill in the telling of this story.

Beyond questions about their nearness to the events they study, scholars of contemporary affairs also face the challenge of a huge, even overabundant supply of government documents on the one hand, while, on the other hand, they are deprived of the kind of private letters, memos, and diaries that will be available to the next generation of researchers. In the age of the World Wide Web almost every federal and state agency maintains digital Web sites and archives filled with reams upon reams of readily accessible reports on every imaginable topic. Brian Martin on Congressman Taylor's staff pointed me to the many documents posted to their Web site. Both houses of Congress post committee testimony and speeches in searchable electronic collections discoverable through academic search engines such as LexisNexis, which is capable of unearthing and delivering hard copies of documents and testimony through title, author, and subject searches. This and other Web-based academic search vehicles can also find and deliver news media reports in staggering abundance. Although some government e-mail exchanges have come to light, the private troves of letters and personal e-mail that so often reveal the scaffolding behind the appearance of things will not come to light for another twenty years. Thus, when future archives finally obtain and grant access to the unpublished communications of the great, a more definitive account should be possible for the children born since Katrina.

This book describes the human and material impact of Katrina in Mississippi, the challenges of survival and emergency response in the wake of the storm, and the many trials and triumphs along the long road toward recovery. In this, the book makes significant use of oral histories in the USM Katrina Oral History collection. From a grassroots perspective, the narrative offers insights into the tangled disputes over recovery funding and the bureaucratic bungling and hubris that afflicted storm response and often delayed the work of recovery and rebuilding. However, several key contentions are supported. First, the people nearest a disaster must be prepared and given leeway to respond. In taking the initiative and inventing solutions in the midst of the most profound crisis, thousands of grassroots people in Mississippi proved their mettle. Ordinary people are willing and able to respond with determination and creativity, and in Mississippi they proved their capacity for endurance in a long recovery process. Secondly, if bureaucracies stumbled in Katrina, the American federal system also proved its genius and worth. The federal government enabled the deployment of vital state-level expertise and assistance in the early days of this disaster, and often the redundant capacities in neighboring states compensated for the widely publicized federal failures. Moreover, a generous nation provided billions to help rebuild everything from public buildings, roads, and bridges to private homes. However slow or frustrating the federal response, no Mississippian should ever doubt the tremendous advantages brought to the storm-stricken region through the pooled resources assembled and deployed through the federal government. Finally, anyone concerned about the moral fiber of American society will surely take note of the hundreds of thousands who dropped what they were doing in order to volunteer for sweated labor to help this region get back on its feet. This massive outpouring is surely a sign of health for the civic spirit of the nation.

It is the local people on the Mississippi Gulf Coast who, through their own stories, draw us to these insights and conclusions. Here, beyond the insurance companies, investment banks, and government bureaucracies that sometimes failed them, ordinary people, through many extraordinary acts of selfless service and perseverance, have revealed the foundations of the strength and resilience of a nation. It is a story worthy of its telling.

Hurricane Katrina

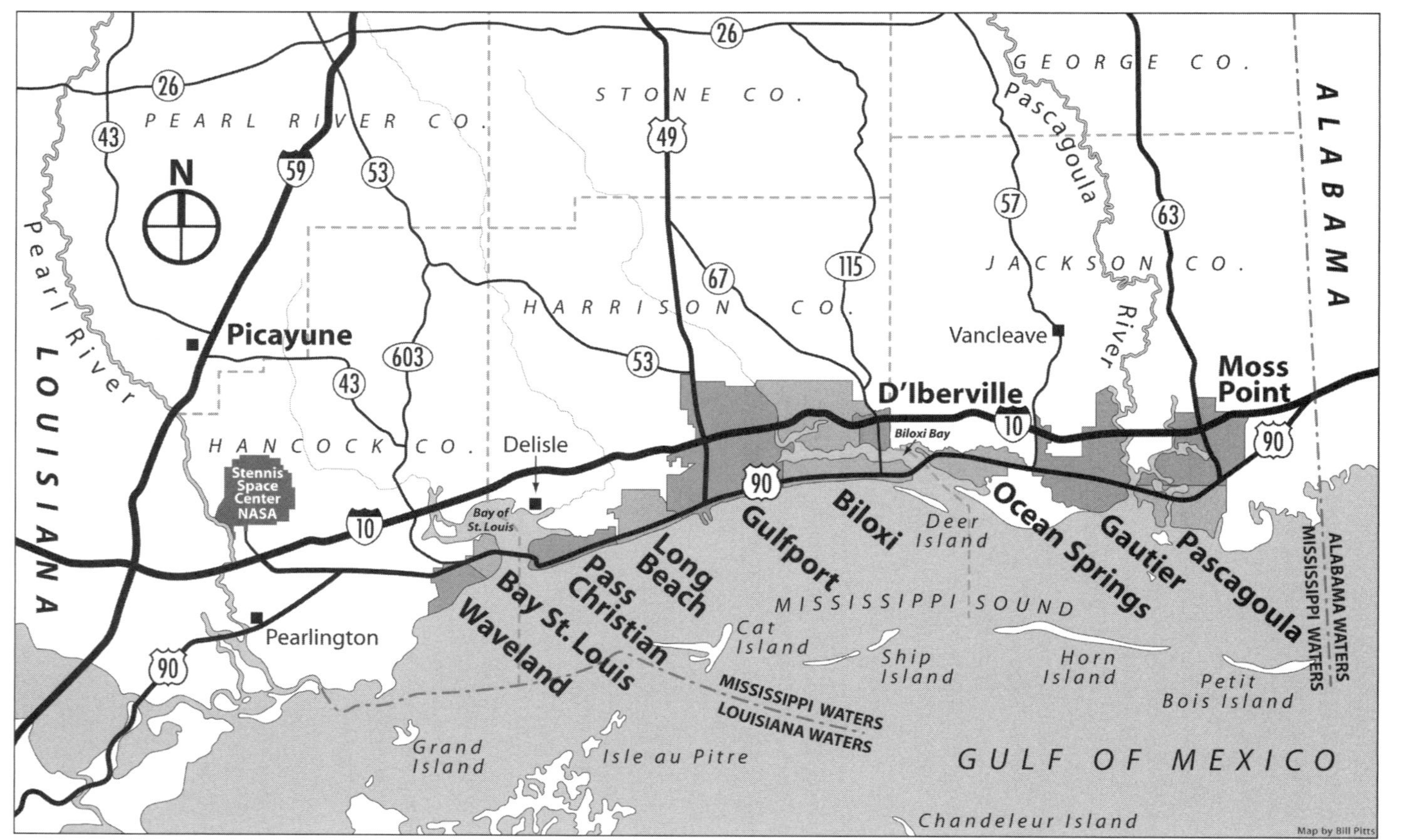

ALABAMA
LOUISIANA
GEORGE CO.
STONE CO.
PEARL RIVER CO.
JACKSON CO.
HARRISON CO.
HANCOCK CO.
Pascagoula River
Pearl River
N
Picayune
Vancleave
Delisle
Pearlington
Stennis Space Center NASA
Bay of St. Louis
Biloxi Bay
Moss Point
D'Iberville
Ocean Springs
Gautier
Pascagoula
Biloxi
Gulfport
Long Beach
Pass Christian
Bay St. Louis
Waveland
Deer Island
Cat Island
Ship Island
Horn Island
Petit Bois Island
Grand Island
Isle au Pitre
Chandeleur Island
MISSISSIPPI SOUND
GULF OF MEXICO
ALABAMA WATERS
MISSISSIPPI WATERS
MISSISSIPPI WATERS
LOUISIANA WATERS
26
43
59
53
49
67
115
57
63
603
10
90
Map by Bill Pitts

Chapter One

Katrina Impacts Mississippi

"This Is Our Tsunami"

I left the van . . . and walked . . . up the railroad . . . met some firemen . . . and I said, "What's happening?" They said, "It's bad, Father." I said, "Are the churches okay?" And they said, "The First Baptist Church is gone."

And I said, "No, you've got to be kidding." I said, "What about our church?" They said, "We don't know." . . . I honestly think that they did know, but they weren't able to tell me. So, I kept walking and made my way down into the church grounds. . . .

I couldn't believe what I saw. The awful destruction. Oh, you couldn't fathom what could have happened. Everything was ripped. I felt that the place was raped and thrown, just thrown there. . . . Everything had been destroyed.

—FATHER LOUIS LOHAN, PASTOR
St. Thomas Catholic Church
Long Beach, Mississippi[1]

Hurricanes pack a destructive power unrivaled by any other force known to the meteorological sciences. Tragic life-and-death struggles come with every hurricane landfall. Still, ordinary coastal citizens of every class, including well-informed veteran local leaders, often underestimate the danger. Such miscalculations are an unfortunate part of the story of Katrina in Mississippi and Louisiana. By 5:30 a.m. on the morning of Monday, August 29, 2005, hurricane-force winds extending 120 miles from the center of Hurricane Katrina reached the town of Waveland, Mississippi.[2] Behind

Shreveport
Monroe
Vicksburg
Jackson
Meridian
N
MISSISSIPPI
ALABAMA
LOUISIANA
TEXAS
FLA
Red River
Ouachita River
Mississippi River
Sabine River
Atchafalaya River
Pearl River
Chickasawhay River
Pascagoula River
Natchez
Laurel
Hattiesburg
Alexandria
McComb
Columbia
Lucedale
Wiggins
Mobile
Mobile Bay
Pensacola
Baton Rouge
Picayune
Long Beach
Gautier
Covington
Moss Point
Lake Charles
Lafayette
Lake Pontchartrain
Slidell
Waveland
Bay St. Louis
Pass Christian
Gulfport
Biloxi
Ocean Springs
Pascagoula
New Iberia
Lake Borgne
New Orleans
Chandeleur Island
Houma
GULF OF MEXICO
Buras
Venice
20
49
55
59
65
10
12
BILL PITTS

these winds the slow-moving eye wall of the dreaded northeast quadrant of the 400-mile-wide storm lumbered north toward the Mississippi Gulf Coast. The monster storm still packed winds reported at 145 miles per hour and pushed a storm surge predicted to be 18–22 feet above normal tides.[3] Unknown to Waveland city officials that morning, a NOAA data buoy located 64 nautical miles south of Dauphin Island and 73 nautical miles east of the storm center recorded a single wave height measurement of 16.9 meters, or 55.4 feet, making it the highest wave height ever recorded by a NOAA buoy in a tropical cyclone.[4] Hurricane Katrina, the most destructive natural disaster in American history,[5] was on its way to producing the unprecedented 30-foot onshore storm surge[6] that eventually killed 1,577 people,[7] including at least 238 in Mississippi.[8]

As the unmanned remote buoy took its deadly measure, Mayor Tommy Longo of Waveland stood on the second floor of a storm-hardened command center at the town wastewater plant. Longo's wife and five children, a number of city employees, and several last-minute elderly evacuees had taken refuge here with the mayor. All watched helplessly as furious winds and waters wiped huge parts of their city from the map. To the mayor's astonishment, water surrounded and flooded his own outpost. Sudden generator failure triggered a frantic life-and-death battle to free frail elderly refugees from a stalled elevator. A short distance away, water began seeping into the Waveland police headquarters. Here, 27 officers had gathered to ride out the storm. This building was located two miles from the Mississippi Sound, and no storm surge had ever reached it. By 8:30 a.m., water had risen three feet up the police department's boarded-up glass doors and jammed them shut. With the wind roaring and waters rising rapidly toward their ultimate eight-foot height, the trapped officers broke through the plywood-covered glass doors and pressed forward into the rushing water. Hanging onto each other in a single-file human chain, they fought and swam their way to some tall, sturdy hedges where they hung for several hours. Blocks away, staffers in the flooding Hancock County Emergency Operations Center wrote numbers on their hands to match names on a list to be used to identify their bodies in case their escape attempt failed.[9] Ten miles inland in Hancock County, flood waters crossed Interstate 10 and demolished homes in the upscale Diamondhead community. A 1,000-gallon aviation fuel tank from the Diamondhead airport floated onto the highway.[10] Across the Bay of St. Louis in scenic Pass Christian, floodwaters pushed a police cruiser through the storm-hardened doors of the emergency command center set up on high ground in the town library on Hearn Avenue. Here, in the midst of a sudden rush of water, Chief John Dubuisson led 13 trapped officers in a death-defying escape onto the roof of the building. On the east end of town, Pass Christian's fire fighters struggled with four feet of water in the station.[11]

At Pascagoula, 60 miles east of Waveland and the eye wall, a 7:10 a.m. observation reported a wind gust of 118 miles per hour. Later, a Pascagoula gauge clocked a gust of 137 miles per hour before stronger winds knocked it out.[12] Pascagoula city manager Kay Kell now found herself regretting her decision to allow her daughter and four grandchildren to take shelter with her at city hall. Though it was one of the highest points in town, five feet of floodwater quickly surrounded the building and began seeping in through the doors. Kell moved the children up onto the podiums in the council room to keep them safe. A short distance away in a third-floor office in the Jackson County Courthouse, District Attorney Tony Lawrence and Tom Illich watched as the waters rose to cover cars and pickup trucks in parking lots across the street. Nearby, the Jackson County Emergency Operations Center flooded. Director Butch Loper hurriedly relocated his staff to the upper floors of the courthouse. In the courthouse itself, in the heart of downtown Pascagoula, the sheriff's first-floor offices had already flooded. With waters waist-deep around First United Methodist Church and lapping the top step of Our Lady of Victories Catholic Church, rescue directed from the Jackson County Courthouse or Pascagoula City Hall had become impossible. Back to the west on Interstate 10 at the Biloxi River bridge, a point nine miles inland from the Gulf of Mexico and three miles upstream from Biloxi Bay, six feet of water covered the superhighway.[13] At D'Iberville, five deputies swam out of a sheriff's department substation in chest-deep water to reach a school bus sent to rescue them.[14] As far east as downtown Mobile, Alabama, Katrina's storm surge reached 11 feet, covering cars and matching flood records set in 1917.[15]

On the vulnerable east end of Biloxi, Captain Steve Scott and seven fellow firemen manned Biloxi Fire Station No. 3 on Elder Street, a station built on ground one foot higher than Hurricane Camille's 1969 high-water mark.[16] Captain Scott studiously logged the rising waters threatening the unit. He debated the wisdom of abandoning the post for higher ground. However, as the waters converged on the station, 20 weather-beaten local residents banged at the doors seeking safety. The group included an infant and a toddler. As the waters swamped the station, heroic firemen lifted the refugees to safety atop the largest truck. The firemen themselves swam for hours in the five feet of murky water that engulfed the station.[17] A few blocks away on the third floor of Biloxi City Hall, a haggard Mayor A. J. Holloway went before a battery-powered video camera to tape a message to citizens. Four feet of water surrounded Biloxi City Hall. Cars floated outside, churning in the waters alongside vending machines washed from nearby hotels. A gigantic 30-foot garbage dumpster drifted up the street, pummeling buildings in its path. Amidst this scene of devastation, Mayor Holloway looked into the camera and stated grimly, "This is our tsunami. Highway 90 is destroyed. It's something like I've never seen." In Biloxi alone, 53 people drowned that day in the costliest and one of the most deadly hurricanes ever to strike the United States.[18]

The Japanese word "tsunami" describes the awesome tidal waves which undersea volcanos or earthquakes set in motion. Technically speaking, Katrina was a hurricane, not a tsunami. However, months before Katrina, Mayor Holloway had seen televised pictures of the horrible tsunami devastation unleashed on the island of Sri Lanka, the coast of southern India, and Southeast Asia. For those who witnessed Katrina, the mayor's comparison seemed entirely appropriate. A 12-hour blast of wind and water from the northeast quadrant of Hurricane Katrina destroyed hundreds of thousands of homes and businesses across the Gulf South. Beyond New Orleans, on the Mississippi coast, Katrina destroyed more than 65,000 houses and threw more than 216,000 suddenly homeless individuals and families onto the mercy of their neighbors for shelter. In Louisiana, additional hundreds of thousands were likewise rendered suddenly homeless.[19]

In perhaps an understandable rush to cover the tragic flooding and larger body counts that failing levees visited upon the city of New Orleans, the national press left much of the story of the "Mississippi tsunami" untold. Quite apart from the heartbreaking New Orleans ordeal, Katrina reduced the Mississippi Gulf Coast from Pearlington to Pascagoula to a shambles of more than 46 million cubic yards of debris that matched in full the destructive force of Mayor Holloway's tsunami. *In Mississippi alone*, Katrina created a volume of debris equal to the combined destruction of Hurricane Andrew plus the 9/11 attack on New York. Katrina's trashing of Mississippi created enough rubble to fill 307,919 railroad boxcars, an amount which if stacked on a football field would produce a pile of broken dreams rising 4.9 miles high. In fact, Katrina's cataclysmic impact on *Mississippi alone* would rank this storm as the largest natural disaster ever to strike the United States.[20]

People along the northern Gulf Coast from Texas to the Florida panhandle have learned to respect and fear the northeast quadrant of winds whirling counterclockwise round the eye of these seaborne monster storms. Before the drag of land, trees, and buildings can cut their speed, it is the violent and forceful east and south winds of the northeast quadrant pushing massive volumes of water that cause the most damage to coastal communities of the northern gulf region. On August 29, 2005, three Mississippi coastal counties took the full-force impact of Katrina's terrible northeast quadrant. For New Orleans, on the weaker western side of the storm's eye, Katrina was a flood event occasioned by the nightmare-like failure of the city's man-made levee and pump systems. The raw destructive force of Katrina's northeast quadrant winds pushing a record 30-foot tidal surge enveloped Mississippi communities from Pearlington in the west to Pascagoula in the east and on into downtown Mobile, Alabama. In Mississippi, hurricane-force winds felled trees, destroyed buildings, and knocked out electrical power as far inland as Jackson and Meridian, some 160 miles from the coast. For Mayor Holloway, with over 60 years of coast storm experience, the impact was "something like I've never seen."[21] In a more scientific comparison, Ivor van Heernden, director of the Louisiana State University Hurricane Center, estimated that Hurricane Katrina brewed up an energy package equal to 100,000 atomic bombs.[22] Imagining such awesome destructive power emerging naturally over the course of a few days poses great difficulty for ordinary mortals. Yet, in 2005, 15 hurricanes emerged in the Atlantic and Gulf of Mexico.

To mortal minds, the vast fields of destruction spread over 93,000 square miles in Katrina's wake seem somehow logically disconnected from the inauspicious scientific descriptions of her origins as "a tropical wave" which "departed the west coast of Africa" on August 11. Eight days later, the "tropical wave" destined to become Katrina made its way through the Leeward Islands and produced a large area of showers and thunderstorms north of Puerto Rico. At 6:00 p.m. on August 22, the Tropical Prediction Center began analyzing the system. Just 24 hours later as it moved over the Bahamas, these meteorologists declared the system "Tropical Depression Twelve." Through the night of Tuesday–Wednesday, August 23–24, the storm became more organized. A well-defined band began to wrap the north side of a clear center of circulation. Thus, "Tropical Storm Katrina" was born and named at noon on August 24, as it spun 65 miles northeast of Nassau in the Bahamas. The storm graduated to full hurricane-force status with winds exceeding 70 miles per hour at around 9:00 p.m. that night. Two hours later, Hurricane Katrina made a landfall in Florida near the Miami-Dade and Broward County borderline with Category 1–sustained winds of 70 knots, or about 81 miles per hour. For six hours, Katrina moved slowly west across peninsular Florida. Here, 14 people died in her path. The friction of the Florida land mass reduced Katrina's winds to 69 miles per hour, briefly moving her back a grade to "tropical storm" status as she spun westward out into the Gulf of Mexico in the early hours of Friday, August 26.[23] Thus, the dispassionate language of meteorology chronicled a killer in the making.

For state and local emergency operations directors in Alabama, Mississippi, Louisiana, and Texas, the entry of a tropical storm into the Gulf of Mexico brings a heightened state of alert and triggers action on a list of routine emergency preparations. For Fire Chief and City Emergency Operations Director Pat Sullivan of Gulfport, Mississippi, "It's like watching a truck coming at you. . . . You can make decisions [so] as to speed up to get across the street," or if new information shows the storm slowing or veering away, "you don't have to speed up."[24] First responders on the Mississippi Gulf Coast began monitoring Katrina from 9:00 p.m. on Tuesday, August 23, when the National Hurricane Center issued its first advisory on "Tropical Depression Twelve" off the east coast of Florida headed in a northwesterly direction. When Katrina entered the Gulf of Mexico early on August 26, Chief Sullivan's "fast-moving truck" gave responders only 72 hours to finalize preparations. In regular daily meetings and continuous phone calls, state, city, and county officials reviewed emergency plans and procedures and considered appropriate timing for evacuation orders. Revised National Hurricane Center advisories every three to six hours helped emergency officials understand likely storm track, speed of movement, intensity, and size. These factors governed preparations and decisions whenever a storm entered the Gulf of Mexico. Local press briefings increased in order to alert the public to make family evacuation plans, secure items on private property that might become missiles in high winds, and lay in stocks of bottled water, cash, canned goods, fuel, and batteries. The public had to be prepared to cope with lost access to stores, gas stations, electric power, and water supplies in the aftermath of a major storm.[25]

Whenever hurricanes threaten Gulf Coast communities, firemen, police, and emergency operations employees labor steadily to top off fuel tanks in as many public vehicles as possible. Power failures inevitably render gas pumps inoperable for days after hurricanes. Government vehicles normally stationed in low-lying areas must be moved to higher ground. Tanker fire trucks are filled with water, anticipating loss of water pressure needed to fight fires. Police and fire departments as well as hospitals, nursing homes, and utility companies fuel and test backup generators and begin rearranging work shifts and deciding which employees to call in to ensure adequate staffing at the time of projected landfall. Police and fire departments operating on three-shift cycles go to two twelve-hour shifts.[26] Red Cross officials alert shelters—often inland schools—and check availability of shelter managers. Classrooms and teaching materials must be secured as part of the storm preparation ritual for teachers and principals at schools designated as shelters. Once rudimentary staffing plans are made, hospital and public service workers are notified to make arrangements for their families and report to work expecting to stay on the job for several days after the storm impacts.[27] Soon, Katrina would overwhelm even the best emergency response plans all across the region.

Hurricanes can build enormous power in stunningly short periods of time. While first responders in Louisiana, Mississippi, Alabama, and Florida methodically worked their storm checklists, the National Hurricane Center tracked Katrina through two periods of rapid intensification which included the collapse of the first eye wall and the formation of a second eye. During this same period, the time available for onshore preparation narrowed as the storm's speed of closure doubled from five to seven miles per hour on Friday–Saturday, August 26–27, to 10 to 13 miles per hour on Sunday, August 28. As time ran out in the wee hours of Monday morning, Katrina's forward speed increased to nearly 15 miles per hour. The storm also tripled in size on August 27–28. Tropical storm–force winds eventually extended a distance of 200 nautical miles from Katrina's center. Meanwhile, wind speed measured at 75 miles per hour (Saffir-Simpson Category 1) at 4:00 a.m. Friday, August 26, exploded to 175 miles per hour (Category 5) by 10:00 a.m. Sunday morning, when Katrina hovered about 200 miles southeast of the mouth of the Mississippi River. The U.S. Air Force Hurricane Hunter aircraft making that Sunday morning measurement reported flight level winds in Katrina of 191 miles per hour.[28] Meanwhile, Category 5 winds piled up a Category 5 wall of water on the shallow continental shelf off the coasts of Mississippi and Louisiana. The National Hurricane Center now predicted an onshore storm surge of at least 18 feet above normal tides. Sea walls along the Mississippi Coast stood at 12 feet. The levees surrounding New Orleans were at 17 feet. The numbers foretold the watery tragedy to come. With a projected landfall for Monday, August 29, even if the winds banked off to Category 4, there would be no time for the Category 5 volume of water to dissipate. There would be no place for the water to go but onshore in the coastal flat lands of Mississippi, Louisiana, and Alabama.[29]

Changing projections of Katrina's likely path also complicated local decision making. When the storm entered the gulf on the morning of Friday, August 26, National Weather Service National Hurricane Center (NHC) modeling pointed to the north Florida panhandle near Apalachicola as the likely landfall. That afternoon calculations changed dramatically. The NHC's 4 p.m. Friday, August 26, advisory shifted the storm track 170 miles west, projecting a Monday, August 29, landfall near Pascagoula, Mississippi. This prediction posed the first serious threat to the New Orleans levee system. Forecasts worsened at 4:00 a.m. on Saturday, August 27, when NHC Advisory 17 announced yet another adjustment in Katrina's course projecting a direct hit on New Orleans. This meant that the Mississippi Gulf Coast would stand in the dangerous northeast quadrant at landfall. In a short 24 hours, grave new urgencies had materialized involving the lives, safety, and property of more than 2,000,000 people on the Louisiana, Mississippi, and Alabama Gulf Coasts. Wind damage risks had increased, but the far greater risks of northeast quadrant Category 5 flood potential now forced costly evacuation decisions.[30]

Mississippians have a history with hurricanes. Thirty-six years earlier on August 17, 1969, Hurricane Camille had struck the Mississippi Gulf Coast with 200-mile-per-hour winds and a 25-foot storm surge. One of only three Category 5 hurricanes ever to hit the United States, Camille killed 335 persons and destroyed or seriously damaged 22,008 houses in Mississippi, Louisiana, and Virginia. New Orleans's own hurricane vulnerability also had a history. Hurricane Betsy, a 1965 Category 3 storm, overtopped the New Orleans levees, killed 75 people, and flooded 160,000 homes. In July of 2004, the Federal Emergency Management Agency (FEMA) exercise, Hurricane Pam, had demonstrated the overwhelming search and rescue, sheltering, and logistical nightmares that would befall New Orleans with a Category 4 or 5 direct hit if storm surge breached the levees. Little was done from July 2004 until August 2005 to address these problems.[31]

Even so, local evacuation decisions posed some troubling dilemmas. Hurricanes are notorious for their meandering paths and unpredictable last-minute changes in course. On the other hand, an evacuation order is guaranteed to be costly. Businesses shut down. Wages and business profits are lost. Tax revenues halt for days.[32] Individual families are pressed to buy fuel, flee inland in jammed traffic, find and pay for food and lodging, or

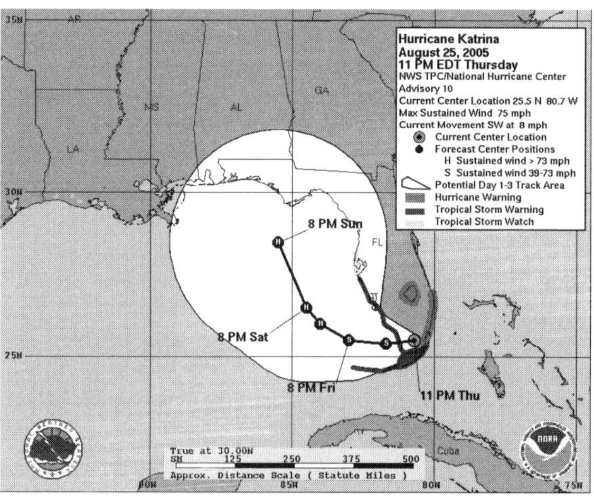

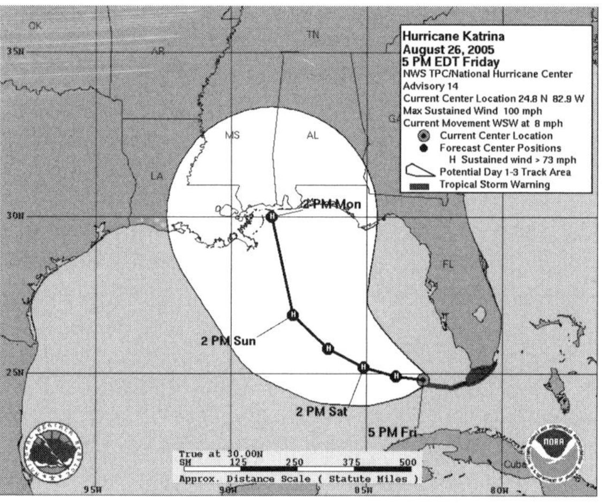

seek out and share unknown shelters in distant locations in the company of strangers. In addition, successful evacuation of the disabled, the elderly, or the poorest of the poor who have no automobiles requires a major, well-coordinated public effort. Before Katrina, authorities estimated that in New Orleans alone, 100,000 people did not own cars. Further, for families living from paycheck to paycheck, evacuation poses a serious personal financial

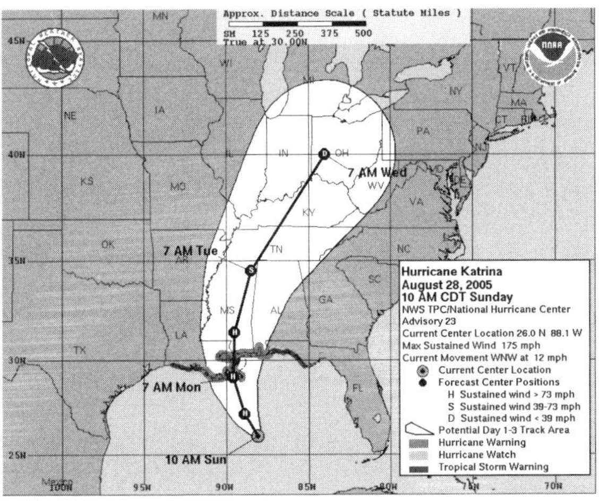

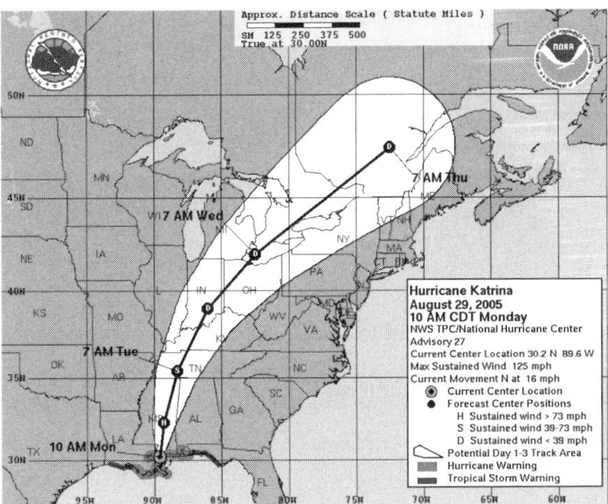

Changing Katrina Storm Track Predictions. National Weather Service National Hurricane Center, Katrina Graphics Archive, http://www.nhc.noaa.gov/archive/2005/Katrina-graphics.shtml (accessed October 29, 2008).

burden—particularly evacuations called as money runs low just before payday. With the lowest average wages and highest poverty rates in the nation, such concerns affect large numbers of people in the danger zones of Mississippi and Louisiana.[33]

Aside from monetary costs, an unnecessary evacuation order for a storm that changes course may cost emergency operations directors their credibility. As with the boy who cried wolf too often, later warnings and orders might not be heeded. In the summer of 2005, this concern was real. Just seven weeks before Katrina hit, local officials on the Mississippi Gulf Coast had ordered evacuations for Hurricane Dennis, a storm that ultimately went ashore to the east in Florida and produced little damage in Mississippi. There had been considerable expense and even a little embarrassment. On the other hand, gambling on forecasts or delaying evacuations could have cost hundreds or thousands of lives.[34] In the case of Katrina all forecasts from 4:00 p.m. Friday until landfall on Monday projected Category 4 or 5 winds and surge for New Orleans and the Mississippi Gulf Coast.

On Wednesday, August 24, while Katrina was bearing down on south Florida, the Mississippi Emergency Management Agency opened its Emergency Operations Center (EOC) in Jackson. At the same time, Mississippi Gulf Coast local emergency operations directors met to discuss potential evacuations of vulnerable hospitals, nursing homes, and assisted-living facilities. On Friday, August 26, local officials in Harrison County, Mississippi, implemented their evacuation plan for people in assisted living or with special needs.[35] On Thursday, August 25, Operations Commander Alan Weatherford of the Gulfport Police Department began evacuation discussions with state port officials in his jurisdiction. Unable to imagine a storm surge capable of floating loaded shipping containers, port tenants Crowley, Dole, and Chiquita delayed container evacuations until Sunday morning, leaving insufficient time to complete the task. This failure doomed scores of onshore buildings to collisions with moving-van-sized objects when Katrina made landfall.[36]

The Federal Emergency Management Agency (FEMA) headquarters in Washington, D.C., began monitoring Katrina on August 23 and went into Level 2 "partial activation" status at 7:00 a.m. on August 25. Daily video conferences linked FEMA regional managers, the National Hurricane Center, and representatives from the states in the storm's path. On Friday, August 26, Mississippi, Alabama, and Louisiana officials activated their state-level emergency plans. Ahead of the issuance of the 5 p.m. updated forecast, Max Mayfield, the director of the National Hurricane Center, and others on his staff telephoned state and local disaster managers in Mississippi and Louisiana with direct personal warnings of the likely catastrophic impact. The Louisiana National Guard mobilized 2,000 troops and set up its command center at the soon-to-be-flooded Jackson Barracks in New Orleans. In Mississippi, Governor Haley Barbour ordered the Mississippi National Guard to prepare for disaster operations. General Harold Cross activated just under 800 Mississippi troops with emphasis on military police and engineers.[37] The fact that large numbers of normally available units from both states were deployed in Iraq slowed and complicated response efforts in both Louisiana and Mississippi.[38]

Saturday, August 27, was a critical preparation day for Louisiana and Mississippi. At 7:30 a.m., a National Weather Service teleconference for Louisiana officials described Katrina's likely Monday landfall as taking the storm "smack dab through the metropolitan New Orleans area." Duly warned of the risk, Governor Kathleen Blanco quickly initiated the Louisiana Emergency Evacuation Plan. Its first phase focused on clearing areas south of New Orleans. Blanco immediately telephoned Governor Barbour to discuss implementation of traffic contra-flow agreements for interstate highways leading out of the New Orleans area into neighboring Mississippi counties. Throughout the day, the Louisiana parishes surrounding New Orleans issued local evacuation orders. Notably, the city of New Orleans itself did not order evacuation. Governor Blanco worried that Katrina's approach on a weekend might catch people unaware or still believing that the storm was targeting Florida. At 11:41 a.m. on Saturday, Blanco officially requested President Bush to issue a declaration of a federal state of emergency for Louisiana.[39]

By early Saturday afternoon, Governor Barbour joined in the call for a declaration of federal emergency for Mississippi. Local officials in Hancock, Harrison, and Jackson counties on the Mississippi Gulf Coast now issued mandatory evacuation orders for low-lying areas. These orders mandated that all coastal hotels and casinos in Mississippi close and totally evacuate their facilities by no later than noon the next day. The Louisiana-Mississippi interstate traffic contra-flow went into effect at 4:00 p.m. that Saturday, enforcing one-way traffic in all lanes for vehicles exiting greater New Orleans into Mississippi and Texas.[40]

Surprisingly, Mayor Ray Nagin of New Orleans lagged behind the other officials. Nagin waited until 1:00 p.m. Saturday before declaring a citywide state of emergency—a delay of almost 24 hours after his governor had declared a state emergency and a delay of almost two hours after Blanco made her plea to President Bush for a federal emergency declaration. By that time, the National Hurricane Center had warned repeatedly that New Orleans would likely suffer a dead hit from a Category 4 or 5 storm. Moreover, Nagin's 1:00 p.m. Saturday declaration fell short. Nagin only called for "voluntary" rather than mandatory evacuation of New Orleans. Powerful New Orleans business interests made sure that the mayor knew the high cost of any premature or unnecessary evacuation. Thus it was that Nagin continued a slow-down, wait-and-see approach. It was Sunday morning before Mayor Nagin issued a "mandatory evacuation" order for the city of New Orleans. Knowing the costs of evacuation for businesses and fearful of legal liability for lost tourism and hotel income, Mayor Nagin succumbed to a penny-wise but pound-foolish logic of delay.[41]

Forty-eight hours earlier on the previous Friday, Mayor A. J. Holloway of Biloxi, Mississippi, confronted the storm threat with strikingly different logic. In the matter of hurricanes, Mayor Holloway believed that Biloxi and the Mississippi coast had been "just too darn lucky over the years." Unlike Nagin, Holloway was unwilling to bet that Biloxi's luck would hold. Like New Orleans, Biloxi was a 300-year-old French settlement that had seen its share of economic woes in the 1970s and 1980s. In the 1990s, however, Biloxi transformed itself from a decaying second-rate beach resort into a major regional tourist destination. Legalized gaming drove Biloxi's revival. Nine of the Mississippi Gulf Coast's 12 new glistening shoreline casinos moored on the Biloxi peninsula at anchorages beside luxurious new high-rise hotels. The number of visitors had zoomed up from 1 million to 12 million per year. The casinos and hotels gave the area almost 20,000 guest rooms, 15,000 new jobs, and bountiful revenues to finance new schools, new streets, new parks, and new public housing—achievements of which Mayor Holloway was justifiably proud.[42]

However, for a year or more before Katrina, Mayor Holloway had carried an unusual sense of foreboding. In his mind a major hurricane hit on the Mississippi Gulf Coast was overdue. "Not just a hurricane," Holloway said, "we're going to get a *bad* hurricane." It was in Mayor Holloway's words "just a matter of time. . . . [It's] not if, it's when." The city's casino barges and the jobs and revenue that came with them were major concerns. Though their mooring systems were built to withstand 155-mile-per-hour winds and 15-foot tidal surges, any hurricane would test the casino barges' survivability. If the moorings failed, Biloxi had a lot to lose. In September of 2004, when Hurricane Ivan threatened in the Gulf of Mexico, Mayor Holloway told a reporter, "We're scared to death. Anybody that went through Camille, that's all we're thinking about now."[43] Hurricane Ivan's 130-mile-per-hour winds struck Gulf Shores, Alabama, 70 miles east of Biloxi—a landfall which had put Biloxi on the comparatively weak western side of that storm.[44] Still, Ivan had inflicted enough flood damage on three of Biloxi's casinos to close them for many weeks. Brian Richard of the Mississippi Gaming Commission told the Associated Press that forcing the 12 coast casinos to close for

Ivan had cost the casinos $10 million, and state and local governments lost $400,000 a day in taxes, a revenue loss which eventually totaled $6 million.[45] The Mississippi Gulf Coast's tourism business would be more at risk with a direct hurricane hit. On the other hand, for Biloxi as for New Orleans, the cost of any unnecessary evacuation order could also be staggering. The risk led Mayor Holloway and the Biloxi City Council to take the unprecedented step of buying a $10 million business interruption insurance policy in the spring of 2005. This protected the Biloxi tax base, at least for a time.[46]

Through the summer of 2005, the Biloxi mayor expressed fear that citizens were not taking hurricane warnings seriously enough. Biloxi had a resident population of 55,000 and could have another 55,000 visitors in town on any given summer day. Mayor Holloway worried about whether the casinos would close in time for hotel guests to evacuate safely ahead of a storm. With Hurricane Ivan the previous year, Mississippi casino evacuation orders had been delayed until just 24 hours ahead of projected landfall.[47] The Ivan experience had shown that it could take 12 hours just to close the casinos, secure them, and evacuate guests from the thousands of hotel rooms on the Biloxi peninsula. In Mayor Holloway's mind it was especially worrisome that Biloxi's casinos were only required to close if the Mississippi Gaming Commission ordered it. The gaming commission protocol allowed business as usual until the Harrison County Board of Supervisors declared a countywide evacuation for low-lying areas. The city did not control the evacuation decision.[48]

In the weeks before Katrina, issues of storm safety brought the Biloxi mayor into a small-scale shoving match with powerful business interests. Perhaps from a confidence that came from his recent reelection without opposition, or from stark memories of Hurricane Camille in 1969, Holloway held his ground. In July of 2005, under threat from Hurricane Dennis, Mayor Holloway had actively lobbied local casino managers, county officials, and the Mississippi Gaming Commission to close casinos and begin evacuating hotels ahead of the county's general evacuation orders. There was resistance to this idea. When one casino manager protested that he had to await close-down orders from the Mississippi Gaming Commission, Holloway's frustrated emissary asked bluntly, "If you have a fire are you going to call the gaming commission and ask if you should evacuate [for that]?" Holloway called the gaming commission and threatened to go on television to denounce the commission if it did not shut the casinos well ahead of official county evacuation orders. The mayor knew "they thought he was a son of a bitch." During this round, Connie Rocko, a member of the Harrison

County Board of Supervisors, sided with the Biloxi mayor. For her efforts, Rocko got an emphatic phone call from a prominent Gulfport businessman letting her know in no uncertain terms of his displeasure with early closures and evacuations. Rocko believed that if early closure saved one life, it would be worth it. Indeed, Mayor Holloway's calls produced earlier close and evacuate orders ahead of Hurricane Dennis. Then, as if to make the point about the gamble in any decision, Dennis suddenly veered off to a distant Pensacola, Florida, landfall, leaving egg on the faces of Holloway, Rocko, and the others they had persuaded to err on the side of caution.[49]

Biloxi's communications director, Vincent Creel, remembered some of the mayor's advisors worrying that the administration had overreacted and looked bad. However, egg on his face or not, the mayor's continued forward-leaning leadership got positive results in the run-up to Katrina in August. For Ivan in 2004, the county had given its casino close orders only 24 hours ahead of landfall. For Dennis, however, and again for Katrina in 2005, the Harrison County Board of Supervisors warned the casinos to start wind-down operations almost 48 hours ahead of landfall. As Katrina approached, all lodgers had to be out of Mississippi Gulf Coast hotels no later than noon on Sunday, August 28.[50] By the time Mayor Nagin in New Orleans finally got around to a Sunday morning mandatory evacuation order for his city, Biloxi had nearly finished clearing the thousands of hotel rooms on its vulnerable eastern peninsula.

Nonetheless, some, including Mayor Holloway, worried that the Hurricane Dennis false alarm might have made the public complacent about disaster warnings and forecasts. In an attempt to shake up that complacency, official city communications purposefully described Katrina as "a killer storm." The storm had in fact killed as it crossed south Florida and would kill again if warnings went unheeded. With the Dennis embarrassment in mind, at least one in the mayor's inner circle found this "killer storm" language excessive and "over the top." His friends did not want to see Mayor Holloway overreact or "cry wolf" again. However, for Mayor Holloway, the old sense of foreboding trumped all other considerations. Still believing that Biloxi had been "just too darn lucky over the years," Holloway opted to lean forward. Thus, he authorized the strongest possible "killer storm" language to urge evacuation on his evacuation-weary citizenry. With better-timed hotel and casino evacuations, Biloxi was better prepared for Hurricane Katrina than for any storm in its history.[51]

Mayor Brent Warr of Gulfport was also worried about the storm. He, too, had voiced concern that local emergency plans were inadequate. Biloxi and Gulfport were rivals whose city limits adjoined each other in Harrison County. Biloxi was 300 years old. Gulfport, an upstart by comparison, had grown up just west of Biloxi in the late 1890s with the coming of the north-south railway lines and a dredged deepwater harbor to export the first cuttings from Mississippi's virgin pine forests. Biloxi was an old, traditional, largely Catholic town. Gulfport was more Protestant and had less history, but soon after its founding, Gulfport had become the county seat. Though Gulfport had only two casinos (compared to Biloxi's nine) and perhaps a couple of thousand hotel rooms, Gulfport's industrial base gave Mayor Warr's city a population of over 71,000. In leadership longevity, Holloway had seniority on Warr. Just seven weeks prior to Katrina's arrival, Brent Warr, at age 41, had won a hard-fought election to his first term in any public office. At the same time, Holloway, a seasoned man in his 60s, had won re-election to a fourth mayoral term with no opposition. Holloway was then the longest serving mayor in the history of Biloxi.[52]

Holloway was a low-key, no-nonsense former school administrator and grandfather. He had been an Ole Miss football star and had coached for a short time before becoming a school administrator. Later, he owned a restaurant and a small mortgage company and worked as a regional agent for the Mississippi State Tax Commission. A slow-talking man with "an economy of words," Holloway lived by an old coach's advice—"don't trust a living soul," and "you don't have to explain what you don't say." His "economy of words" and unglamourous seriousness sometimes caused strangers to underestimate the Biloxi mayor, or, in the words of one close associate, to "make the mistake of thinking he was not the sharpest knife in the drawer." Nonetheless, those who worked with Holloway thought these qualities often worked to his advantage. They knew Holloway to be a shrewd man with real business smarts who was possessed of a devout Roman Catholic's deep sense of responsibility. These quiet qualities guided Holloway in such innovations as buying the business interruption insurance for the city in June of 2005.[53]

In contrast, Gulfport's Mayor Brent Warr was young, telegenic, and outgoing, but he was untested in office. Warr had earned a business degree from a Texas college and was father of two elementary-aged children. Warr's Men's Store, a successful haberdashery, earned the family a reputation for good business judgement and led a diverse list of Warr's local business and real estate interests. Warr displayed the winning retailer's friendly gift of gab. Moreover, as a choir-singing Southern Baptist, he did not mind telling others about his confident hope that his church would somehow help more people find their way to heaven. Within two weeks after his summer 2005 inauguration, Mayor Warr had declared a citywide emergency during the false alarm over Hurricane Dennis. He was uncomfortable with what he had seen, and resolved to rework Gulfport's emergency plans. Shortly after he reached this decision, Katrina confronted the new mayor.[54]

On Saturday morning, August 27, Brent Warr attended a combined meeting of the Harrison County Board of Supervisors and area mayors. The young mayor reflected on the contrast between the serious storm evacuation issues under discussion and the low-tech information system available to the group. Only "a telephone sitting in the middle of the table" linked the group to the State Emergency Operations director in Jackson who was relaying input from the Weather Service. This was decidedly not the high-powered firsthand information he had expected to receive as the mayor of a sizeable city trying to make costly decisions in the face of a monster storm.[55]

As the group debated casino closings and mandatory evacuation of low-lying areas, dissenting views emerged. Everyone understood the business costs of needless evacuations. However, these discussions frustrated Warr. The new Harrison County Emergency Operations director, General Joe Spraggins, had taken the job only days earlier. Though he was a respected former Air National Guard commander, Spraggins's inexperience with local storm response operations worried some of the mayors. Spraggins's reluctance to issue evacuation orders *unless this group was unanimous* especially disturbed Mayor Warr. Warr doubted that five mayors and five supervisors with different interests could ever reach unanimity.[56]

One very compelling piece of information came to the table. Already on Saturday morning, a NOAA buoy off the Alabama coast had measured waves in excess of 30 feet. In his typically self-deprecating style, Warr interjected, "You know, I wasn't the best [science] student in high school, but I do remember that water is not compressible." He explained that this meant that if 30 feet of water was there when the storm made landfall, all of that water would come up on land. The sea walls on the north side of Harrison County's 26 miles of beaches stood at only 12 to 14 feet above sea level. Mayor Warr was uncertain whether or not his science lesson carried the argument that day. However, these Mississippi Gulf Coast officials did in fact come to a *unanimous* mandatory evacuation decision on that Saturday morning, 48 hours ahead of Katrina's projected landfall.[57]

As Mayor Warr drove home along the Highway 90 beachfront, his cell phone rang with a call from the White House Intergovernmental Affairs Office in Washington, D.C. Like Mayor Holloway, Warr was a Republican, but having been on the job such a short time, he had no idea that anyone in Washington would know who he was or how to reach him. The voice on the other end of the line asked, "What do you think [about Katrina]?" Warr replied, "*We're toast*!" After an awkward pause, the voice asked, "What?" Then Warr explained, "You can go ahead and write us off. We're done for." Again, there seemed to be confusion. The voice on the Washington end of the line came back saying, "That's not the information . . . that we're getting. Why do you say this?" The mayor recounted the data about the 30-foot wave off the Alabama coast. Then grimly he reported, "There's not a lot down here within the first several miles of the beach that's 30 feet in elevation. . . . Our sea wall's about 12 feet," he continued. "So when that water comes in, *we're going down!*" Based on this conversation, the White House Intergovernmental Affairs Office decided to send a FEMA representative named Mike Beeman to Gulfport, rather than New Orleans or Mobile. Warr called Joe Spraggins to arrange quarters for Beeman at the Naval Construction Battalion Base in Gulfport. Beeman came to be known on the coast as "FEMA Mike." Mike Beeman became one of the few FEMA managers to be remembered locally with fond affection.[58]

While local mayors felt disconnected from top-tier storm information, at 7:30 p.m that Saturday, Dr. Max Mayfield, director of the National Hurricane Center, spoke again to Governor Barbour and Governor Blanco about the bleak scenarios forecasted for their states. At 10:00 p.m., the NHC released its first public storm surge assessment predicting that Katrina would bring flooding of 15 to 20 feet and locally as much as 25 feet above normal tides. On Sunday, President Bush, responding to Blanco's and Barbour's requests, issued an unprecedented prelandfall federal emergency declaration. The governors now asked Bush to take the additional step of issuing Presidential Major Disaster Declarations for their states as a means of speeding poststorm federal assistance under the Stafford Act. These additional declarations were signed Monday morning, as Katrina rolled ashore. By late morning on Sunday, in a video teleconference, Dr. Max Mayfield told President Bush, FEMA headquarters staff, FEMA regional officers, and representatives of Governor Blanco and Governor Barbour that the possible topping of the levees in New Orleans was "a very, very, grave concern." At this warning, FEMA Director Michael Brown ordered his employees to "keep jamming those lines full as much as you can with commodities."[59] Unfortunately, Brown's order did not energize his agency.

At home on Sunday morning at about 6:30 a.m., Mayor Holloway took a phone call. When he hung up, Holloway went to the bedroom and told his wife, "I got some bad news." Impatiently she asked, "Well, what, what?" He replied, "Jim Cantore's in town." They both knew this meant the Weather Channel had picked the Biloxi-Gulfport area as the likely zone of worst devastation. Cantore, the popular on-air Weather Channel meteorologist, wanted Mayor Holloway for an 8:00 a.m. interview at Biloxi's Emerald Beach Motel. Holloway did the morning interview, and at Cantore's request, he returned at 3:30 p.m. for another network feed. When Holloway arrived for the afternoon interview, he sensed that Cantore "was kind of upset. . . . You could tell it wasn't good." Soon enough, the meteorologist laid it out for the mayor. "I'll tell you," Cantore stated grimly, "this thing [Katrina] is bad. . . . The barometric pressure's down below where it was on Camille," the deadly 1969 storm that destroyed the beachfront in Harrison County. "It's huge," Cantore added. "It's covering the whole Gulf of Mexico, and there ain't no way . . . *no way* we can miss it. [There's] no way out of it." Then, Cantore added ominously, "Mayor, on your way home you ride around your city, because you won't see it like this tomorrow." Holloway knew it was true.[60]

That same Sunday afternoon, Mayor Warr attended a final Gulfport readiness meeting involving the city's entire management team. They reviewed Chief Pat Sullivan's flood graphics and agreed to meet to take stock of the damage at 4:00 p.m. Monday after the storm passed. They set the meeting for either city hall or around the corner at the downtown fire station. As they talked about the potential impact of a 15-to-25-foot mound of water, the mayor's emotions surged. A lump came to his throat. He hesitated, caught his breath, and said, "If . . . this building is not here, then we are going to meet at Station 12 in Orange Grove," located several miles inland.[61]

In Long Beach, a beachfront bedroom community of 17,300 just west of Gulfport, Mayor Billie Skellie had overseen the filling of every gas tank in every truck, car, or school bus the city owned. Long Beach also stored a seven-day water supply for first responders. As night fell, this mayor joined his officers in patrolling the vulnerable residential beachfront between Highway 90 and the railroad tracks. They looked for house lights that might indicate some poor soul who did not grasp the danger. One last time, they stopped to plead with people to evacuate. Ironically, Skellie's father had been the town's mayor in 1969, when Camille struck. Despite his father's personal pleas, some people had stayed. Camille took 36 lives in Long Beach. Now, 36 years later, that memory kept Mayor Billie Skellie and his police units on the streets pleading with stragglers until 9:30 or 10:00 p.m. on the eve of Katrina.[62]

For outsiders, it is hard to understand the reasoning that leads people to stay on their property to face a life-threatening event. In an era when satellite imagery and voluminous warnings fill the airwaves for days ahead of storms, it can look as if people play a kind of "hurricane roulette." However, looks are often deceiving. Better explanations lie in psychologically well-known human tendencies to make false judgements of risk based on prior personal experience.[63] For example, many 1969 Hurricane Camille survivors reported resisting evacuation because they had been successful in riding out the major unnamed 1947 hurricane that struck the Mississippi coast.[64] This false belief that safety in 1947 would guarantee safety in 1969 had cost many people their lives in Hurricane Camille, one of the few Category 5 storms to ever strike the U.S. This same logical error repeated itself in 2005, when even educated laymen assumed that Katrina could not be worse than Camille.

False analogies and false estimates of risk based on personal experience were common in August of 2005. Veteran Police Chief Frank McNeil of Bay St. Louis found that when he told people, "You got to leave," those who argued back "gauged everything on . . . Camille." They would say, "Well, we been here through Camille. . . . We'll be okay." If a house survived Camille in 1969 without flooding, the owner concluded that it would be safe in Katrina. At least 238 Mississippians died in Katrina. Thousands more misjudged the storm based on memories or reports of the Camille high water marks. Thus, as Biloxi spokesman Vincent Creel saw it, Camille was the storm that kept on killing.[65] Some lived to tell the story of water rising quickly in their homes, forcing them up to attics or out and into the branches of trees. Most had made common but faulty assessments of personal danger.

Strikingly, this type of reasoning based on history or memory went beyond the ranks of ordinary citizens. The same local officials who pressed the evacuations forward often misunderstood the risks to their own places of last refuge. Waveland's on-duty fire and police forces were washed out of their buildings, and the Hancock and Jackson County Emergency Operations Centers, as well as Pascagoula's city hall, all flooded. In Biloxi, Mayor Holloway's decision to stay in city hall with his wife and several family members was based on the fact that water did not reach that building during Camille. Katrina surrounded Biloxi City Hall with four feet of water and ruined the scores of city vehicles thought to be stored safely on high ground at Biloxi's Yankee Stadium.[66] At Pass Christian, city vehicles were sent to supposed safety at the Public Works Building a mile off the beach on Espy Avenue. This site flooded. Here, Pass Christian lost 17 vehicles, including all of its fire trucks and all but one of its police cars.[67] Even the most storm-wise utility, Mississippi Power Company, moved its senior management staff to Plant Jack Watson on the Harrison County Industrial Seaway. That facility did not take water or even lose power in Camille. Katrina flooded the ground floor of the plant, destroyed generators, ruined all of the vehicles on site, and marooned the management team in a second-floor room.[68] It was not a matter of class, race, education status, or a symptom of lack of character or purposeful recklessness. False estimates of security based on previous storms affected officialdom and citizenry alike.

The most heartrending stories involve those who were physically unable to cope with the rigors of evacuation. For Hurricane Ivan in 2004, Mrs. Harneitha Maxey, age 75, had evacuated with her feeble 92-year-old husband, retired plastic surgeon Dr. Louis Maxey. It had taken Mrs. Maxey eight hours of driving in heavy traffic to cover the 160 miles inland to Jackson for shelter. Dr. Louis Maxey had earned degrees in pharmacy, dentistry, and medicine and was one of the first black resident physicians at Cook County Hospital in Chicago. Yet, at age 92 and in poor health, Dr. Maxey needed help with everything. Just getting him in and out of the car was very difficult for his wife. When Ivan veered off to Florida, the Maxeys decided that for the very old, the rigors of evacuation were just too much. They were adamant that they would not evacuate again. Since no system of special needs shelters existed for Katrina, others with frail, elderly, or handicapped family members made similar choices. Harneitha Maxey, a lady of deep faith and endearing graciousness, died with her husband as Katrina's waters demolished their two-story home on seemingly high ground several hundred yards from the shore in Long Beach.[69]

Almost anything that people could love or be devoted to could keep them from evacuation. Mrs. Virginia Adolph, a social worker, saw people stay home out of fear of vandalism to their houses. Others stayed out of a sense of responsibility to somehow safeguard their neighborhood or community. Similarly, the safety of the family dog or cat kept some at home. In his May 2006 testimony before the U.S. Senate, Harrison County Emergency Operations Director Joe Spraggins spoke about pets. "Pets sometimes become more than just pets," he said. "They become a part of the family." Public shelters generally would not accept pets. Spraggins reported that several people who could not bring themselves to leave animals behind wound up dying with their pets in Katrina's fast-rising waters.[70]

The monetary cost of evacuation led others to stay. Reverend S.V. Adolph of First Missionary Baptist Church in Gulfport observed that it could easily cost a family of four a thousand dollars to evacuate for three days. Many people the preacher knew of just did not have the money to leave.[71] City Councilman Bill Stallworth, who represented East Biloxi's poorest and most flood-prone neighborhoods, spent the day before the storm "riding around and begging people . . . to leave." In 2005, East Biloxi's median household income was only 67 percent of the countywide median.[72] According to Stallworth, 40 percent of the people in his district earned under $15,000 per year. Stallworth found that Katrina's approach at the end of the month, just before payday, meant that many of his constituents lacked the money or credit to buy a tank of gas or pay for meals or hotel rooms.[73] Neither Louisiana nor Mississippi officials had allocated public resources for persons without cars, fuel, or the cash to comply with evacuation orders.

In reality, local evacuation orders had limited reach. All that local officials could do was plead or maybe arrest people on some trumped-up charge. Neither the jails nor county legal budgets could handle massive arrests.[74] Still, so-called mandatory orders went into effect in Mississippi Gulf Coast counties early enough to allow safe evacuations of low-lying areas. At least the casinos complied. They were all shut before noon Sunday. Every local official involved in that decision would have gladly accepted public embarrassment over evacuation orders if they could have avoided what Katrina brought on Monday morning.

At about 11:30 p.m. Sunday night, Mayor Warr joined Jim Cantore for a late Weather Channel broadcast from the high-rise Armed Forces Retirement Home near Warr's waterside home in Gulfport. When they finished the interview, Cantore and Warr walked outside to look at the water. The wind was already kicking up. Warr could hear the storm boards rattling on his nearby house. With a knot in his stomach he thought, "I hope they hold," though he knew "they probably wouldn't." By this time, the Gulfport mayor had sent his wife, Laura, to safety in Florida along with his mother, his daughter, Emma, and his son, Noah. With a police radio in hand to monitor emergency calls, Warr and his father put up in his grandmother's old house north of the railroad tracks in East Gulfport. They had not had time to board up the double sliding glass doors that faced south. Soon after dawn, strong winds began violently popping the unprotected glass and bowing it inward. Warr and his father braced their bodies against those large bowing panes of glass for what seemed like an eternity. Nearby, others prayed, and many fought for their lives.[75]

Not far north of where Mayor Warr hunkered down, 125 people had gathered Sunday night at First Missionary Baptist Church in Handsboro, a 144-year-old predominantly African American congregation. On the eve of a hurricane, in the coast's low-income minority neighborhoods with more than their fair share of old or substandard housing, some churches with strong buildings have a tradition of opening as unofficial storm refuges. Older folks in these communities seem particularly reluctant to bed down amongst strangers in Red Cross shelters. At First Missionary Baptist, Reverend S. V. Adolph had celebrated his fifteenth anniversary as pastor in an abbreviated 7:45 a.m. Sunday service. Remaining services for the day were cancelled. At the conclusion of the morning service, members asked the pastor to open the church as a storm refuge as was its age-old custom. Before dark on Sunday evening, people began arriving at First Missionary Baptist. Across town at Little Rock Baptist Church in the African American Gaston Point neighborhood, Reverend Lee Adams wrestled with the issue of whether to stay and open the church. His wife, Mrs. Ruby Adams, was especially disturbed about the Category 5 predictions on the airwaves on Sunday morning. Reverend Adams, however, was a Vietnam vet and a veteran of many hurricanes. He held a firm faith in God's providence. Moreover, he knew his neighborhood and knew that he had many elderly church members who probably would not go to a public shelter if the church were closed. Reverend Adams decided to stay and keep the church open so that he "would know that they would be all right."[76] As improbable as it may have seemed to those who gathered that night, both of these predominantly African American churches and many others on the Coast would soon morph into major centers for massive humanitarian relief operations.

Ahead of the storm on Sunday evening, neighbors brought pot luck dishes, radios, battery-powered televisions, and board games to church for distraction while the storm passed. In both churches, the fellowship atmosphere of a normal church social prevailed. At First Missionary Baptist, however, something different unfolded during the evening and through the better part of the next two days. There, in the center of the busy fellowship hall, a group of elderly ladies of the congregation sat at a table, focused, watchful, and praying. The old sisters refused to sleep or break their vigil midst the socializing of others around them. Young people walked in a wide path around the makeshift altar of the elders. The praying sisters seemed almost oblivious to the humming of activities in the corners of the room around them. The mood changed suddenly at 11:00 p.m., when the lights went off. A spontaneous large-group prayer meeting quickly began, adding its voices to those of the old sisters in the center of the room. In the dim emergency lights a hundred or more people sang "Jesus Keep Me Near the Cross" and "At the Cross, At the Cross, Where I First Saw the Light." As emotions subsided and others grew quiet, the old sisters of First Missionary

Baptist resumed their prayerful watch in the middle of the room. They prayed without ceasing Sunday night and on through Monday's long storm and its aftermath Monday night.[77]

Across town, the sound of shingles popping off the sanctuary roof rang out like rifle shots, "*patow, pow, pow, pow, pow,*" when the winds kicked up at Little Rock Baptist Church early Monday morning. In the education annex next door, Reverend Adams worked to lash together the big double doors to stop them from banging and blowing open. Just as it seemed as if the storm would never cease, a friend in Mobile reached the pastor by cell phone to relay a television weather report that "the worst is yet to come." At this dark moment, with fears rising, the fifty folks at Little Rock lifted spontaneous prayers and sang the familiar gospel songs "I Will Trust in the Lord" and "Hold to God's Unchanging Hand." Despite violent winds ripping the roofing off the sanctuary next door, Reverend Adams recalled that "A calm came over us. . . . Sometimes two people wanted to pray [aloud] at the same time." The pastor "didn't have to ask for volunteers" to lead prayer for almost an hour.[78]

On the Gulfport waterfront a mile away, just before high tide was due at 7:00 a.m., Harrison County Supervisor Connie Rocko and several other officials made a final survey of the situation near the harbor at the intersections of U.S. Highway 49 and U.S. 90. Boats had already washed onto U.S. 90, and the Copa Casino barge had broken its moorings. The little group of official sightseers concluded that they were seeing the last of the Mississippi coast as they knew it. They quickly retreated to the Harrison County EOC in the county courthouse north of the railroad tracks.[79] Before the morning was out, Gulfport Fire Chief Pat Sullivan reported downtown buildings "imploding" with the city's old business district "largely under water."[80] Further east at the Armed Forces Retirement Home where Jim Cantore's Weather Channel broadcasts originated, 21 volunteers from Gulfport's U.S. Navy Seabee Base worked to reinforce the structure. Despite their best efforts, the winds and waters breached the ground floor doors and knocked out the generator. In darkened halls and stairwells, "amidst rushing water, tidal pull and life-threatening debris," young Seabees moved 50 bedridden and wheelchair-bound veterans up flights of stairs to safety in the upper floors of the building.[81]

Retreat to safety had become impossible for 200 shrimp boat captains who, as usual, rode out the storm on board vessels tied off to trees or tied to other boats on the rivers and canals branching off Biloxi Bay. For self-employed shrimp captains, preserving the boat safeguards a lifetime investment and a future livelihood. Reverend Phan Duc Dong, better known as "Father Dominic," said mass on Sunday morning at Biloxi's Church of the Vietnamese Martyrs. The priest then joined several of his Vietnamese parishioners who took refuge on shrimp luggers that moved to supposed safety on Gulfport's industrial seaway. The winds picked up through the night. The bobbing of the boat made sleep impossible for Father Dominic, who was also afflicted with a queasy stomach. In the morning light, the large trees to which the boats were tied swayed violently. When the hurricane winds peaked, lashings broke, sending large steel-hulled boats colliding into each other, puncturing hulls, and sinking the weaker vessels. One heroic captain untied his own boat and, at great risk, motored to the rescue of the men thrown into the turbulent water.[82] Aboard another boat tied off on the Fort Bayou inlet behind Ocean Springs, Captain Ronald Baker "took a beating." Katrina's broadside winds banged together the raw hulls of boats to which his own, *The King Arthur*, was lashed. Baker worked frantically to tighten lines and secure buffers between boats. Looking ashore, he saw houses lose their roofs and walls and "go to pieces from the wind before the water came up."[83]

Accurate land-based measurements of wind speed at Katrina's landfall became impossible due to power outages and widespread destruction of weather instruments across the region before peak winds reached shore. The Gulfport/Biloxi National Weather Service office was out of commission by 6:00 a.m. The *Sun Herald* reported a 7:10 a.m. wind gust of 118 miles per hour in Pascagoula on the western edge of the storm. *The Mississippi Press* published a later reading of 137 miles per hour at Pascagoula. At 12:15 p.m., a National Weather Service spotter 30 miles inland at Wiggins, Mississippi, documented a gust of 120 miles per hour.[84] Aloft, mechanical trouble aboard an Air Force reconnaissance plane flying through the storm just before landfall prevented normal measurements in Katrina's powerful northeast quadrant. The only real-time storm data available to the Weather Service by 5:00 a.m. was extrapolated from Slidell, Louisiana-based Doppler radar. These estimates pointed to a surface wind speed of 145 miles per hour, or Category 4.[85] Months later, the Weather Service revised its landfall wind speed estimates downward to Category 3 (111 to 130 miles per hour) based on analysis of data from instruments dropped into the storm. One such device estimated wind speed from the speed of blowing sea foam.[86]

Whatever the maximum sustained winds may have been, poststorm studies conducted at the Naval Meteorology and Oceanography Command make clear that hurricane-force winds reached the Mississippi coast four hours ahead of significant storm surge. The Navy's analysis shows that from Waveland to Biloxi and Ocean Springs, hurricane-force winds arrived between 5:00 and 6:00 a.m. on Monday, August 29. Category 3 winds of 111 to 130 miles per hour pounded Gulfport and Biloxi from 9:00 a.m. onward. However, maximum storm surge was not seen until almost two hours later, just before 11:00 a.m.[87] This fact became important in many wind-versus-water insurance disputes. The Navy's poststorm analysis made it clear that the wind had time to do enormous damage before the surging waters arrived to add to the toll.

While incredible wind speeds get the hurricane headlines, it is the sudden waters of hurricane storm surges that kill. The Weather Service somehow underestimated the surge about to pile up on the Mississippi coast. On Monday, August 29, sometime between 6:00 and 7:00 a.m., Katrina had made its first landfall in extreme southeast Louisiana at the river town of Buras, 60 miles due south of the Mississippi Gulf Coast. Tidal surge overtopped the levees and flooded Buras. The storm then lumbered north, back out over water on a collision course with the Mississippi coast, pushing what proved to be a record 30-foot storm surge.

The massive campus of Memorial Hospital at Gulfport stands just four blocks east of Little Rock Baptist Church. At the hospital, another pastor, Reverend Rod Dickson-Rishel of Mississippi City United Methodist Church, took shelter with his family the evening before the storm for what the preacher thought would be "a big wait-for-this-one-not-to-happen hurricane party." Dr. Dorothy Dickson-Rishel, the minister's wife, was a clinical psychologist employed at the hospital. The hospital required its psychologists along with other emergency staff to be on duty throughout the storm. After a night spent in the medical office wing, Reverend Dickson-Rishel awoke Monday morning to the sounds of strong winds outside and decided to try to find his way to the cafeteria for coffee. Shattered glass from large windows in connecting walkways gave him his first clue that all would not be well that day. A security guard stopped the preacher and directed him back to the medical office wing. Here, the roof was now leaking. Saturated ceiling tiles bowed downward and fell in around the doctors and families gathered there. The minister recalled the bizarre and humorous confusion as doctors shouted orders at each other, which no one followed. The chaos subsided when a secretary to the medical staff arrived and began giving instructions. The staff and families now moved to a dry part of the facility.[88]

As the storm raged on, people who had floated or swum out of flooding houses three blocks south of the hospital began staggering in for treatment.

The number of swim-out survivors who walked to the hospital was huge—perhaps 100 to 150. This was way beyond the capacity of the emergency room. Hospital workers organized a temporary shelter with makeshift pallets in the large food court. However, the large south-facing windows in the food court had blown out. Piles of shattered glass and several inches of rainwater had to be cleaned up before people could be bedded down. Here, patients started telling the preacher stories of being trapped in houses, moving from "the ground floor . . . to second floors; going to the roof; . . . buildings floating from under them [and] collapsing; [people] jumping off buildings" onto floating vehicles or small boats drifting off of trailers. Many were physically exhausted from hours of swimming in churning water and violent winds. The pastor listened and prayed with them and provided any simple care that he could.[89]

Across 70 miles of coastal Mississippi, similar shocking visitations of racing waters laden with debris and sewerage brought life-and-death struggles to attics and hallways along the beachfront and in areas far inland that had never before flooded. Betty Smith and her neighbor Pearl Bozeman, widows in their late 50s and early 60s, decided to stay together in the Bozeman house to care for three dogs that would not be accepted in shelters. The ladies lived on Belmede Avenue in an older downscale section of the Bayou View neighborhood in Gulfport. On Belmede, small shingle-finished houses built in the 1950s stood on pilings three or four feet off the ground. This street was two miles from any sizeable body of water. It had not flooded in Camille nor at any other time in the 42 years Betty Smith had lived there. The wind had awakened the ladies at 3:00 a.m. Monday, so they stayed up to wait out the storm. In the morning light, they watched helplessly as winds toppled a giant pine tree onto the house next door, crushing the roof.[90]

There was no water in the street when the tree blew down. Sometime later, the sight of water seeping in under the back door surprised the two ladies. The water rose quickly. The seepage inside became a fast-rising swirl. The ladies retreated to a bedroom where an extra mattress piled high on a bed created an island for them and their three dogs. From the bedroom window they saw "waves and white caps rolling down the street just like at the beach." Inside, the water floated and tossed heavy pieces of furniture into heaps of disorder. Mrs. Smith recalled, "When water rose over the top mattress, we thought we were about to die." One Baptist, the other Pentecostal, "We prayed and quoted scriptures to each other," the widow explained, "but we stayed calm, and the dogs stayed calm, too."[91] Their houses churned into ruin as they sat soaking in the foul-smelling brine, but the water stopped rising, and they did not die.

Inevitably, the time had come that morning when police or fire rescuers could not be deployed into the hurricane-force winds and rising water. Hundreds had to be left on their own to live or die in violent contests with nature. Still, from attics and rooftops, cell phones connected the desperate and the dying to 911 operators all over the coast. Those taking the calls could only agonize and weep over the now hopeless pleas for help.[92] In the Harrison County Courthouse, county board member Connie Rockco and ten other operators took these frantic calls. As a former ambulance driver and EMT, Connie Rockco thought of herself as a tough trauma professional. Still, she found taking the Katrina emergency calls to be "the hardest . . . thing I've ever done." Rockco answered calls from families on roofs in East Biloxi with their children screaming for help. "I kept looking at the safety officers," she said, and asking, "Can't we do something?" By this point, the answer was always, "No, just take their name and address," for poststorm search and rescue.[93]

One of those calls came from Rockco's friend Beverly Martin. "Rock," she said, "I'm scared. I'm here on the second floor and water's rising and I'm scared." Then the phone went dead. Vincent Creel, Biloxi's public affairs manager, praised the professionalism of Biloxi's 911 operators. He listened to tapes of the calls they took and the calm advice they gave to those caught in the flood zone that Monday. A couple of days after the storm, Creel encountered one of those operators, a fire department employee, weeping openly as she heard firemen report the discovery of the bodies of people she had talked to in those desperate 911 calls. Callers often spoke of impending death or made pleas to just tell their relatives they loved them.[94] In Hancock County, Charlotte Favre reflected on taking emergency calls from people who were "out there drowning" when nothing could be done. "It would have been better," Favre said, "if the phones wouldn't have worked. Then you wouldn't have known."[95] As Rockco put it, emergency operators hear "the howl of the wind and . . . the screams—desperate sounds so piecing to one's heart and mind."[96]

Among those beyond reach of help were two caretakers who fought for their lives at Three Oaks Plaza, the former home of Blue Cliff Business College and a tourism office just off the beach near Tegarden Road in Gulfport. Here, 60-year-old Barry Jones and his best friend, the 55-year-old maintenance supervisor Rick Nagy, boarded up the place. Out of a sense of loyalty to owners George and Mike Rogers, they had spent Sunday night in the building watching TV, drinking beer, and eating steaks. They went to sleep listening to Jimmy Buffett's song "Mother, Mother Ocean." At 5:30 Monday morning, the wind awakened the men. Soon, the lights went out. Just after dawn, a good while before the water came up, they saw the roof fly off the motel next door. Shortly thereafter, the roof blew off a section of the Blue Cliff building itself. By cell phone, Nagy told the owner that this major breach meant that they would likely lose the structure. Nagy and Jones headed to the back of the building just in time to see a door blow off. When the water finally arrived, it rose with frightful speed. Trucks parked outside floated. As saltwater shorted circuits in the vehicles, a nerve-racking round of flashing lights and honking horns added to the surrealism of the moment. Meanwhile, the two men inside scrambled around in a futile search for safety.[97]

When the water-soaked interior walls started collapsing, Nagy and Jones first tried to secure themselves atop filing cabinets. This perch proved insecure. Rising water inside the building floated the cabinets. Next, they managed to pop acoustical tiles from the ceiling and hoist themselves onto air conditioning ducts in the crawl space. Jones, the older man, believed he lived through this maneuver only because Nagy jerked him upward as his own climbing strength failed. The men watched helplessly as whitecap waves gutted out the building. Nagy yelled at the older man, "This building is going to come down; we've got to get out." In an instant, the raging waters jerked Nagy away. When the unrelenting waves loosened the duct that Jones hugged, he grabbed an I-beam. Soon, even the I-beam weakened, and the remaining superstructure started to crumble. With water crashing over him, a fearful swim-or-die situation presented itself. Dangling there, Barry Jones held a one-man prayer meeting. "Lord, take care of me," he pleaded. "Please protect me. I'm turning loose."[98]

When Jones let go, the waves washed him clear of the building and smack into an oak tree. The impact broke his nose and blackened his eyes. Before he could take hold of the tree, another wave pulled him away, stripped the clothes off his body, washed his dentures out of his mouth, and nearly drowned him under a large floating section of the beach boardwalk. Even after securing himself in another tree, a huge wave swept over his head, prompting another one-man prayer meeting. "Lord, don't let me die naked and no teeth." On second thought, Jones amended his prayer. "Lord, I came in the world that way [naked]; I guess I can go out [that way]." For most of three hours, he gulped putrid brine and hugged tight as if he were "married to that tree." Then the water receded. Like some latter-day Noah, Jones lifted another prayer: "Oh, God, I've made it. I'm going to live. . . . Oh God, thank you Lord. Thank you Jesus."[99]

Wet, cold, and shivering in a wind that still pushed debris through the air, Jones climbed down, wrapped himself in a piece of plastic, and set out to hunt for the body of his friend Rick Nagy. As it turned out, Jones found Nagy alive. He, too, had miraculously survived the washout and took a battering of his own amongst trees and debris. Weeks later, Barry Jones, a decorated Vietnam veteran, would say, "I had lots of thoughts about Nam while everything was going on. [I thought] God, this is a nightmare, big time. . . . In that building, I was flashing back to Nam *over* and *over* and *over* through that whole six hours. . . . This was a lot worse than Nam to me. . . . It was so devastating, so scary, I just, I don't know. The Lord really took care of me and Rick; he's got a purpose for us."[100]

By the grace of God or the kindness of neighbors who risked themselves to save others, hundreds like Barry Jones and Rick Nagy survived to wonder at the meaning of it all. Some whose fate will never be known died making conscious sacrifices for others. At least one of these heros is known. Sgt. Joshua Russell of the Mississippi National Guard lost his own life trying to rescue an elderly couple in Harrison County. As his commander stated in tribute to Sgt. Russell, "He died facing forward to the enemy, in this case a natural disaster. . . . His last moments on this earth were spent helping others at the risk of his own life."[101]

From public officials to ordinary citizens, thousands had miscalculated Katrina's destructive potential on August 29, 2005. Places that intelligent people thought to be safe turned into watery traps. Hundreds endured life-threatening horrors or witnessed life-giving heroics that day. Prayers were lifted. Prayers were answered. However, from infants to old folks, 1,577 souls, including 238 Mississippians, did not live to tell of it.[102]

Chapter Two

Havoc in the Aftermath

It's the closest to an apocalyptic situation as you ever want to be in. It's the closest to how you would picture it to be after World War III.

You didn't have food. . . . You didn't have a place to go to buy food. . . . You didn't have electricity. . . . You didn't have fuel. You didn't know [how or when] fuel was coming.

. . . You didn't have emergency service. . . . It was as close to total anarchy as you can come to.

—FIRE CHIEF PAT SULLIVAN
Gulfport, Mississippi[1]

Bloodied, badly bruised, and naked but for pieces of plastic wrapped around them, Barry Jones and Rick Nagy, the survivors from the Blue Cliff Business College washout, looked like they had "been in some barroom fight or something." Still dazed from their ordeal and overwhelmed by the scenes of annihilation around them, the two men started walking north up Tegarden Road, working their way around and over pieces of buildings and fallen trees to Pass Road. Here, these walking wounded flagged down a fire rescue squad to ask for a ride to a hospital. The fireman's unexpected answer reflected a new reality. "I can't help you. . . . You're walking. . . . You're not critical. . . . Y'all lived. . . . Just keep moving."[2] For all first responders, rescuing people trapped in endless miles of ruins now took precedence. The 911 dispatchers' lists of persons trapped during the storm guided the initial efforts. Across the 70 miles of the Mississippi coastline, tens of thousands of flooded and wrecked buildings and homes had to be searched for the living and the dead. Beyond the 238 deaths, some 17,649 storm-related injuries were officially reported in the Mississippi storm–impact area alone. Additional thousands of injuries likely went unreported. Over 65,000 destroyed houses left at least 216,558 Mississippians officially qualified for FEMA housing assistance.[3]

As night fell, displaced persons moved toward the glow of generator-powered lights at hospitals, creating an overflow of people and security problems for overwhelmed medical personnel.[4] The critical needs of the tens of thousands of wounded and homeless Mississippians far exceeded the capacities of any normal police, fire, and medical forces in the region. As one fire chief put it, "We ceased being a fire department. Our one big thing was to find . . . people who were trapped, to get those folks out."[5] The national media focused on the levee breeches and the horrors unfolding for the tens of thousands stranded in flooded New Orleans. On the Mississippi Gulf Coast, where the storm's most powerful wind and wave action had pounded the shore for hours, death and suffering on an unprecedented scale also rose from limitless mounds of rubble. Mississippi officials had believed they were well prepared for Katrina. The sobering enormity of the destruction and the havoc that soon arose from critical supply and communications breakdowns quickly ended any residual illusions of storm readiness. Nothing could have prepared these beachfront communities for the challenges they confronted in the days following Katrina.

While rooftop rescues became the iconic images of Katrina in New Orleans, on the Mississippi coast, a surrealistic Hiroshima-like landscape presented itself. The cities of Waveland, Bay St. Louis, and Pass Christian were in total ruin. In Long Beach, as soon as winds fell below 70 miles per hour, Mayor Billie Skellie went out with the first teams of city firemen to try to locate people who had made desperate emergency 911 calls at the peak of the storm. It took this team an hour and a half to cut through fallen trees and other storm-blown obstructions to cover the three miles south from their Klondike Road command post to the railroad tracks. Here, a vision of total devastation presented itself. Long Beach City Hall, Harper McCaughan Elementary School, the First Baptist Church, and most of the shopping district lay in ruins along with 1,100 homes—a far larger physical toll than Camille had delivered in 1969 when 38 people died in the town. Six Long Beach residents died on August 29 in Katrina, an amazingly low figure given the enormous levels of destruction.[6]

Cognitive dissonance overwhelmed almost everyone with an inability to comprehend or a sense of being lost in one's own native environment. As far as the eye could see along the entire Mississippi beachfront from Bay St. Louis to Pascagoula, enormous piles of debris reeking with the overflow from broken sewers offended the senses and disoriented the mind. The old downtown district in Gulfport looked like an urban battlefield. Just east of Gulfport's new Russell Federal Courthouse, scores of the once elegant residences on Highway 90 and on fashionable Second Street had disappeared into heaps of rubbish. In East Biloxi, the old neighborhoods of shotgun houses and cottages were leveled or battered beyond recognition. Moss Point was flooded. In Ocean Springs and Gautier, beachfront homes as well as elevated homes built along the shores of rivers, inlets, and bayous lay in heaps of rubble. In Pascagoula, houses and businesses 25 blocks inland from the Gulf of Mexico had taken water. Humble bungalows belonging to Mississippi's working poor had exploded in the wind or washed away by the thousands along with hundreds of historic structures, antebellum mansions, and beachfront trophy homes of the nouveau riche. By FEMA's final accounting, first responders faced 46 million cubic yards of rubble in Mississippi outside of the totals from New Orleans.[7]

In Biloxi, the 911 dispatchers had taken more than 240 calls from people trapped and beyond help during the peak of the storm. As soon as the winds subsided, firefighters headed toward these addresses, which included Fire Station No. 3 on Elder Street in East Biloxi. Here, seven firemen and twenty residents had been trapped in the flooded building. They were found wet, but alive. As rescuers worked their way further into East Biloxi, they reported "running into people left and right who . . . were hung up in trees . . . [or] on their roofs," where they had climbed to escape the storm surge that had engulfed their homes.[8]

Search and rescue work in the August heat took its toll on local firemen and police who were already fatigued and running on adrenaline after days of overtime storm preparation. Now they were called on to work 18-hour shifts for days on end.[9] From dawn to dusk, daylight was a precious public commodity in the rescue and recovery effort. Many local first responders were themselves dealing with the loss of their own homes. Many did not know the fates of their own family members for days. Sleeplessness combined with unrelieved stress to induce uncharacteristic emotional eruptions, memory lapses, and even occasional instances of dreaming with eyes wide open or hallucination.[10]

Stretched to their very limits, local firemen and police kept working their way around and through the devastation searching for survivors. They also worked meticulously to cap off the thousands of broken residential gas and water lines that simultaneously zeroed out water pressure and created an explosive potential for catastrophic fire.[11] Computers and phone lines no longer worked. The few cell towers not blown down soon exhausted their generator fuel or gave only sporadic service. Moreover, because the storm knocked out water service and ruined many private food stocks, it created a risk of life-threatening dehydration and mass hunger. For Fire Chief Pat Sullivan, it was "how you would picture the aftermath of World War III, and "the closest to an apocalyptic situation" as you would ever want to experience.[12]

As local responders began their work, Gulfport Mayor Brent Warr and his father managed to make a quick tour of east Gulfport in a four-wheel-drive truck. Dodging power lines and limbs, Warr found Tegarden Road blocked by debris. From the Pass Road intersection with 28th Street, he saw people fleeing flooded apartments in waist-high water. The mayor then drove east on Pass Road to Debuys Road where he was able make it through to the beach. His truck made the first tracks through the sand and mud that covered Highway 90. The Olive Garden restaurant and Ryan's Steakhouse had been rendered a total loss. Along the beachfront, it appeared that almost every Gulfport landmark south of the CSX Railroad tracks was either gone or scarred beyond recognition. His own house near the Armed Forces Retirement Home had been badly damaged.[13]

When Warr approached the intersection of Highway 90 and Tegarden Road, he discovered looters already rummaging through the wreckage of his family-owned clothing store. Instinctively, he reached for the handgun that he carried in the truck. Wind and water had "just annihilated" Warr's building. Only the raw red steel support beams remained anchored in the concrete slab. He could see that saltwater and mud had covered what was left of his storm-ravaged stocks. A sudden new awareness struck him. "You know, there's nothing in there that's any good to me." He put the gun away and drove on, leaving the scavengers to their work.[14]

At Gulfport's 100-year-old city hall, he found a building "in terrible condition, but at least it was still there." The Greek-revival building stood several blocks inland from the beach, elevated three or four feet off the ground. The first floor had taken water.[15] Across the street, the domed sanctuary of First United Methodist Church stood intact, but like city hall this old sanctuary had taken water in its ground-level education building. A door had given way, allowing the murky saltwater to create a debris-strewn pool in the church basement. Every commercial building south of the CSX Railroad tracks in Gulfport had flooded. In the streets around city hall and First United Methodist Church, an array of broken church pews of three distinctive styles and colors adorned two-to-four-foot heaps of unholy rubble in testimony to the violence that had befallen other nearby church sanctuaries. Within two blocks of city hall three other houses of worship all stood in ruins. First Baptist Church had been totally gutted when the south wall of its huge worship center had collapsed. First Presbyterian Church stood as a washed-out ruin with its steeple missing and a live six-foot alligator as a new resident in the remains of its Fellowship Hall. The walls and windows of St. Peter's Episcopal Church had disappeared. The nearby Gulfport Public Library been washed through, distributing loads of books across the downtown wreckage piles. The small Christian Church up the street from city hall also flooded badly. The beauty of these buildings had graced the Gulfport harbor front for decades.[16] Now, they were ghastly hulks of ruination. On top of catastrophic flooding, tornados embedded in Katrina totally destroyed at least one Gulfport commercial building and heavily damaged several others.[17]

Soon after the mayor arrived at city hall, John Hairston, the chief operating officer of Hancock Bank, climbed to the top of the 17-story bank building in downtown Gulfport to assess the damage. In making his drive down Cowan-Lorraine Road to U.S. 90 and west into downtown Gulfport, Hairston went through several changing levels of awareness about the storm. As he drove past Bayou Oaks subdivision, Hairston saw people he knew "walking down the street." People "that had swum out of their houses" stopped to tell him about it. "That's when it hit me," he said. "This was a different storm than we thought it was going to be." At Floral Hills Cemetery, Hairston was shocked to see two boats, a thirty footer and a forty footer, sitting on dry land amongst the graves. Then it occurred to him that if the water was that high near Bayou Bernard, "good God, what must it have been in Pass Christian and Bay St. Louis and Waveland. . . ." South of the railroad tracks, he saw rooftops in the middle of the road that did not match nearby houses. The sides of a nearby fire station had been blown out. A condo and a little amusement park were destroyed. Sitting at an intersection, John Hairston realized that the community in which he had grown up had utterly changed. "I became aware that all those landmarks" along the beach "were probably damaged," Hairston said. Then, a new realization struck. "They're not damaged," he thought, "they're gone. They're *gone*." Heading west on Highway 90 at Courthouse Road, the banker noted that all of the businesses were "slabbed." "Slabbed"—a new verb used only in the past tense—entered the coast's post-Katrina vernacular. "Slabbed" came to describe the vacant lots which Katrina had cleared of all of their structures on August 29. Only the concrete foundation slabs remained as evidence of previous human usage.[18]

When John Hairston reached downtown Gulfport, the condition of his bank's limestone and glass corporate headquarters building shocked him. Until gaming was legalized in the 1990s, the 17-story Hancock Bank edifice had been the tallest building on the Gulf Coast waterfront between Tampa and Galveston. Four feet of surging water had ruined the ground floor lobby and offices. A tornado had blown the east wall out of the computer center, peeled off the inch-thick steel roof, and exposed all 17 floors to catastrophic leakage. With Norman McDonald, another Hancock Bank officer, Hairston climbed to the top of the building. From this vantage point, they could look out over many miles. The men could see the giant Grand Casino and Copa Casino barges sitting on Highway 90 and hundreds of van-sized shipping containers from the Port of Gulfport scattered among the businesses and neighborhoods far to the west. In this setting, John Hairston reached a new awareness—an awful awareness, an awareness "that people had died. A lot of people had died."[19]

Prior to the storm, port employees had surrounded the shipping container storage yard with the heaviest of the loaded containers in an effort to secure the lighter-loaded and empty vans. Operations managers for Dole, Crowley, and Chiquita, the companies who owned the containers, believed that loaded containers weighing 26 tons could not possibly float. The 22.5-foot storm surge depth at the Port of Gulfport, combined with wind-driven waves, defeated this strategy. Engineering reports showed that the hundreds of van-sized shipping containers floated as far as 1.5 miles west of the port and up to 0.3 miles inland, scrubbing bark from trees and demolishing waterlogged houses and office buildings in their path. U.S. Coast and Geologic Survey photos show port containers onshore far west of Broad Avenue and beyond the Long Beach city limits. The washout at the Port of Gulfport destroyed nearly 1,000,000 square feet of warehouse space. Here, tons of frozen chicken stored in massive refrigerated units had been awaiting shipment overseas. Wind and wave spread more than 3,000,000 thawing and rotting chicken carcasses[20] and pork bellies into West Gulfport neighborhoods, where they mixed in a surrealistic scene with 2,000 heavy rolls of paper and building rubble west of the port as far as the eye could see.[21]

In the banker's mind, the destruction at the port and the sight of casino barges shipwrecked on Highway 90 represented an immediate threat to tens of thousands of jobs. The coast's twelve operating casinos alone took in almost $1.3 billion in calendar year 2004 and produced approximately $47.3

million in local taxes in addition to $100 million for the state budget.[22] The New Hard Rock Casino in Biloxi, which had been scheduled to open the week Katrina struck, would have added a thirteenth lucrative property to the mix. State regulation limited gambling to floating dockside barges. In the early 1990s, the casinos with their new luxury hotels had revived a dying coast tourism sector. Moored beside posh hotels, the barge-mounted gaming facilities often stood three or four stories high above the water. In effect, the casino superstructures acted like gigantic sails able to propel the barges long distances if the moorings failed.

During the storm, 10 of the 13 Mississippi coast casinos broke their tie-down systems and suffered irreparable damage. At Bay St. Louis, hurricane winds drove a Casino Magic barge two miles north across the bay where it came to rest near the Dupont Chemical Plant.[23] One section of the Grand Casino at Gulfport wound up astraddle four lanes of Highway 90, nearly a half mile west of its dock. The Copa Casino at Gulfport floated into a parking lot 1,500 feet from its pier. Back up the beach, opposite the Broadwater Resort in Biloxi, the President Casino had been anchored inside a marina about 1,500 feet from the shore. It broke moorings and came onshore 2,000 feet from its berth, where it struck a low-rise Holiday Inn Hotel. Nearby to the east, the Treasure Bay pirate-ship barge was pushed onto the beach. The luxurious high-rise Beau Rivage Hotel suffered major storm surge damage to its first two floors, but the Beau's gaming barge held steady in its anchorage where it was tied to the bottom with a unique system of driven piles and steel cables. On casino row in East Biloxi, the two-barge configuration of the Biloxi Grand Casino came to rest on the north side of Highway 90. The Hard Rock Casino barge took catastrophic damage but stayed moored dockside. The Biloxi Casino Magic gaming structure floated over its tie-down pilings and landed 800 feet inland, while the Isle of Capri barge sank at its mooring. On the easternmost point of the Biloxi peninsula, Katrina's wind and surge propelled one of the two barges of the Palace Casino complex 2,900 feet from its dock before it came to rest in a large parking lot 1,100 feet from the water.[24]

On the protected north side of the Biloxi peninsula, three miles from the front beach, two Back Bay casinos, the Imperial Palace and Boomtown, held their moorings in an estimated 20-foot storm surge and suffered comparatively minor damage.[25] Still, it would be three months before the gaming floors of either of these establishments could reopen.[26] It was clear that thousands of jobs and millions in revenue had been lost. Given the vulnerability of waterfront gaming, no one could be certain that the lost jobs and revenue would ever be restored.

The enormity of the utter destruction spread out over a 70-mile-wide corridor in southeastern Mississippi dwarfed available state and local response forces. Fortunately, U.S. Coast Guard helicopters from Mobile joined the local search and rescue efforts as soon as winds subsided. A grateful Governor Haley Barbour described that first evening of Coast Guard action. "Fearless young men," Barbour said, "hung from helicopters on ropes dangling through the air" to pull people off of roofs and out of trees. By Friday, according to the Mississippi governor's congressional testimony, "these Coast Guard daredevils had lifted 1,700 Mississippians to safety."[27]

Other specialists rushed in to help carry the burden. The Federal Emergency Management Agency (FEMA) had pre-positioned 7 of its 28 specialized Urban Search and Rescue (USAR) teams from throughout the nation.[28] When the scale of the destruction in Mississippi and Louisiana became clear, all 28 USAR teams were mobilized. Eleven of these teams served in Mississippi.[29] FEMA's Urban Search and Rescue teams won uniform praise from the Mississippi first responders who worked alongside them.[30] In addition, the Mississippi Emergency Management Agency (MEMA) mobilized 19 light search and rescue teams of its own at Camp Shelby. These units moved to the coast on Monday evening. In his congressional testimony MEMA Director Robert Latham estimated that state and local forces, along with USAR teams, units from Florida and Alabama, and the U.S. Coast Guard made more than 5,000 rescues from the massive Mississippi rubble in the days immediately following Katrina.[31]

The sudden demand for this huge effort came at a time when 40 percent of Mississippi's National Guard force was on station in Iraq.[32] From the remaining units, an 800-man Mississippi National Guard rapid response force had been assembled at Camp Shelby near Hattiesburg the day before the storm. It was 5:00 p.m. on Monday before Katrina's winds subsided enough in the Hattiesburg area to allow the force to begin moving south into the coastal zone of greatest devastation. Storm-blown obstacles impaired all movement. On its line from Meridian, Mississippi, passing through Hattiesburg and on to New Orleans, Norfolk Southern Railroad officials reported that on average there were 150 trees per mile blocking the track. Highway 49 presented similar difficulties. Moving south on U.S. Highway 49, cutting their way through downed trees, utility poles, and debris, the leading National Guard elements took five hours to cover the

60 miles from their base to the coast. South of I-10 in Jackson, Harrison, and Hancock counties, debris piles sometimes several blocks wide choked off the normal local avenues of commerce. Meanwhile, before floodwaters had receded in downtown Mobile, the state of Alabama sent two Alabama National Guard Military Police units to Mississippi.[33]

Across the coast, many local first responders recall the arrival of police officers and emergency operations specialists from Florida as their first significant relief. Florida officials managed to deploy search and rescue teams into Mississippi by 6:00 a.m. Tuesday. Scarcely 24 hours after the storm struck, the Florida teams made their first Mississippi rescue.[34] That afternoon some 250 Florida police and rescue personnel began staging at the Mississippi Gulf Coast Coliseum.[35] For search and rescue purposes, Florida emergency management officials treated the hardest-hit Mississippi counties as if they were extensions of the Sunshine State—a level of support that saved countless lives and earned genuine appreciation at the time.[36] It took large quantities of fuel to power the time-sensitive rescue efforts. If fuel supplies dried up the response would be halted in its tracks. Forty-eight hours into the disaster, the first signs of a serious fuel shortage appeared. Memorial Hospital in Gulfport informed the Harrison County Incident Management Team that the hospital's emergency generators had less than a two-hour supply of diesel remaining in the tanks. If the generators failed, life support equipment and surgical suites in the Mississippi Gulf Coast's largest hospital would fail. Needless deaths would follow. Bobby Weaver, the county Incident Management Team's newly designated operations officer, quickly dispatched a truck from the Harrison County Sand Beach Maintenance Department with 200 gallons of diesel to keep the hospital generators running. However, county fuel reserves were rapidly running out.[37]

The hospital fuel pinch was a harbinger of a major fuel supply crisis that caught every state, local, and federal emergency manager by surprise. Many Mississippi municipalities had reduced their use of large underground fuel storage tanks in the 1990s in favor of working through local retail gas stations with fleet credit cards. Now, without electricity, the private station pumps could not access their tanks. Cities relied on county supplies to tide them over in an emergency. Unfortunately, Harrison County's prestorm backup fuel orders did not arrive as promised. Many truck drivers refused to venture into the disaster zone without armed escort.[38] However, state-level Mississippi and Louisiana law enforcement officials with unknown priorities also intercepted and diverted fuel trucks away from the Mississippi coast.[39] WLOX-TV saw its privately ordered generator fuel shipments confiscated twice before reaching the station. This vital emergency media outlet whose teams broadcasted the only around-the-clock local disaster information came near to shutting down.[40] At the end of the week the *Houston Chronicle* reported that local municipalities had been reduced to siphoning fuel from school buses and nonessential vehicles. Gen. Joe Spraggins of Harrison County Emergency Operations confirmed that authorities in Long Beach, just west of Gulfport, were "dead out of gas."[41]

Uncoordinated fuel confiscations introduced a new level of chaos. Heavy debris-removal equipment had to be refueled along with fire, police, and rescue vehicles. Just as the response built momentum, emergency workers arrived in the impact area only to find that the lack of fuel kept them idle.[42] When alert local responders thought to salvage stocks of bottled drinking water from devastated hotels and casinos, lack of fuel prevented its distribution. With the regular electric grid down, diesel-fueled generators powered everything from sewage lift stations and municipal water pumps to local emergency operations centers. Moreover, as generators at remaining cell phone towers died, already massive communications problems worsened. Even the refrigerator trucks drafted into use as temporary morgues required fuel to run the cooling units.[43]

With the sudden fuel crisis threatening to halt all emergency operations, Harrison County officials set out to determine whether the Chevron Oil Refinery on the Pascagoula waterfront in Jackson County had survived the storm. Communications outages required the dispatch of two Harrison County employees to physically inspect the plant. Though the refinery had flooded, it had plenty of gasoline and diesel fuel in storage. However, the refinery had no way to truck the product out. Harrison County employees spent nearly a day securing tanker trucks from Mobile to enable an around-the-clock daily emergency fuel operation for Harrison and Hancock counties. To make sure that some other agency did not confiscate the loaded tankers, two carloads of Indiana state troopers on emergency duty in Harrison County escorted the first shipments.[44] Because local officials invented a solution to their own problem, the rescue work could move forward. It did so amidst several other critical emergency supply and logistics failures that were also to require innovative local leadership and locally crafted solutions to avert the real threat of a secondary humanitarian disaster.

In East Biloxi and in Hancock County, serious food and water shortages loomed. Before Katrina, the humble wood-frame bungalows and shotgun houses of Biloxi's fishermen, seafood canners, and casino workers created a stunning visual contrast with the luxurious waterfront casino hotels towering over the Biloxi waterfront. In these low-income neighborhoods, Katrina exacted an especially heavy toll. Bill Stallworth's predominantly African American city council district covered most of the old East Biloxi neighborhoods. After riding through his district to urge evacuation on the afternoon before the storm, Councilman Stallworth and his wife retreated to his mother's house two miles north of Biloxi Bay. As soon as the worst of the storm had passed, Stallworth drove down I-110 to assess the situation. Driving south, he saw that water still enveloped much of the town of D'Iberville across the bay from Biloxi. On the East Biloxi peninsula itself, subsiding waters revealed a community in "total devastation." Downed power lines and traffic lights webbed over and around "cars, trucks, . . . trees, [and] homes washed into the middle of the street." It appeared that not a single house or store on that end of town had escaped flooding. Later surveys showed that over 3,000 homes were lost in his East Biloxi district. Stallworth's own house on Bohn Street just south of Division still stood, but it had flooded. Like so many others, his furniture and appliances had been turned into a topsy-turvy mass covered with stinking mud and muck. As the sun went down, people stumbled out of what was left of their soggy houses "absolutely in shock," looking for someplace—anyplace—dry enough to bed down for the night. It took three hours for the councilman to get back to his mother's house. When his wife asked what he had seen, the only words he could muster were, "It was really bad. Really, really bad."[45]

On the Tuesday after the storm, Bill Stallworth rose early and ventured back south across the bay to see what he could do. In broad daylight the real extent and implications of the devastation hit him. Beyond the living who ventured out of torn-up houses, he now saw dead bodies. Among the dead were some whom he had personally urged to evacuate. In the living he saw "a blankness in people's eyes" that masked a gnawing fear that food and water supplies in stores and private homes had been destroyed. "Councilman," one man pleaded, "there's a body over there. What are we going to do? How are we going to get food?" In fact, Stallworth's riding survey revealed that every grocery store had flooded. There was precious little salvageable food left. The windows on the Dollar Store on Division Street had been blown out. People were already scavenging for food there. Further compounding the sense of desperation, the storm surge appeared to have disabled every private automobile in East Biloxi. Moreover, the storm had floated the concrete decking off the Highway 90 bridge to Ocean Springs, leaving the bridge in ruins and blocking any easy access to help from the east. When

Stallworth rolled to a stop, "just sitting there, . . . looking around," an abrupt realization struck. "We don't have anything," he thought, "nothing at all." A sinking feeling came over him.[46]

At this moment an older lady, possibly 60 years old, waved vigorously to draw the councilman's attention to the place where her family sat under some trees. Her husband was diabetic, she explained. He needed food to keep from going into diabetic shock. Stallworth headed back to the Dollar Store where he had seen people scavenging for food. There, someone produced a liter bottle of Coke and a bag of cookies which the storm surge had spared.[47]

When he brought these offerings back to the people waiting at the tree, Stallworth asked, "Why are you sitting here?" The reply drove home the new reality. "We're waiting on the coroner." Their elderly wheelchair-bound aunt had drowned before their eyes. As the waters rose, this couple in their 60s had climbed onto a table and pulled themselves up into the attic. However, despite all of their tugging they lacked the strength to pull up their aunt. They had to sit and watch her drown in the filthy storm waters. Now, like so many others in East Biloxi with no food, no house, no phone, and no transportation, this bereaved family could only sit and wait for the coroner. With no sign of FEMA or the Red Cross, the utter helplessness of the situation struck Bill Stallworth in the core of his being.[48]

Just then, Stallworth encountered someone with a cell phone that still worked. He immediately called his brother Jeff, the pastor of Word of Worship Church in Jackson. The message was simple, "Brother, we need . . . some help, there is nothing, no food, no water." The councilman begged his brother to organize his community to send something down. Soon after making this call, Stallworth discovered that members of the Main Street Baptist Church had managed to set up a little feeding kitchen, serving up broth with a few vegetables on a plate. Like everything else in East Biloxi, the sanctuary of this predominantly African American congregation had flooded. However, the second floor of Main Street Baptist's Sunday school wing had stayed dry and saved the lives of people who had taken refuge there. Bill Stallworth was overwhelmed at the sight of these storm-blown local saints striving valiantly to meet a desperate need. The councilman climbed the church steps "just crying like a baby" because the pitifully thin soup "was all that there was, but at least someone was trying to do something."[49]

Both humbled and inspired, Stallworth now focused his own effort on a search for any food stocks that might extend the Main Street Baptist

Church's fledgling effort. Employees at the Save-A-Lot Grocery Store told him they were ordered to allow no one inside. Nonetheless, after considering the situation, they decided to let their councilman take anything he could salvage from the flood-ravaged stocks which they guarded. He loaded up muddy canned goods and took them back to Main Street Baptist where the cans were washed and their contents added to makeshift stews. Next, he thought of the nearby seafood-packing companies. Without electricity to run freezers, their stocks would thaw and go to waste. Stallworth was able to get the packing companies to donate frozen fish and shrimp to the grassroots community survival effort. Sometime in those first three days, representatives of Oxfam America, an international relief organization, appeared and had $10,000 wired into an account to support and expand the Main Street Baptist Church soup kitchen. James Crowell, the president of the Biloxi NAACP, drove in from Atlanta with a van loaded with food and other relief supplies that Wal-Mart and the National Board of the NAACP had donated. The soup stocks multiplied. Stallworth believed that prayers were answered. Main Street Baptist Church became the place where anyone in need could find food. Stallworth recalled that the National Guard managed to get water and ice deliveries going on the third or fourth day after the storm, and the Salvation Army got two feeding trucks on the streets a day or two later.[50]

Storm survivors in hard-hit Hancock County did not see Red Cross representatives on the ground until two weeks after the storm had passed. When the cavalry did not show up in force, a few hardy souls, including Bonnie Page of Bay St. Louis, set up their own relief operation in the gymnasium of Second Street Elementary School where faith-based groups sent supplies and volunteers from outside the region to help.[51] In a miracle of faith, entrepreneurship, and will power, local people in devastated Hancock County and in impoverished East Biloxi rose up to craft a disaster response of their own. Leaders like Bill Stallworth, James Crowell, the Biloxi seafood processors, Reverend Kenneth Haynes of Main Street Baptist Church, and scores of local church members saw a need and just started cooking and scavenging for food. In Bay St. Louis, Bonnie Page, who lost her rented home and lived in a tent at her makeshift Second Street relief center, stepped into the breach and mobilized self-help resources. Page said she did it because the Red Cross and FEMA had "not gotten their act together to come feed these people."[52]

For the poor in East Biloxi, a *Sun Herald* banner headline summed it up: "FORGOTTEN: Poor Residents of Coast Seem to Wait the Longest for

Supplies, Assistance."[53] Both the Red Cross and FEMA were absent without leave in East Biloxi. These agencies, the only ones with federal statutory disaster mandates, initially ensconced themselves in less-damaged middle-class neighborhoods well beyond walking range for Biloxi's most desperate storm victims. Moreover, the Red Cross did not seek county input and did not accept county direction in targeting its mobile feeding effort. The Harrison County Incident Management Team found that the Red Cross, with a logic of its own, set its own priorities for mobile feeding van operations each day and merely informed local officials.[54] The East Biloxi poor were not on the Red Cross radar screens. Fortunately, the Salvation Army made its mobile kitchens available to cover any areas deemed high priority to county officials.[55] The Salvation Army served East Biloxi when the Red Cross could not or would not. Official press releases show that FEMA finally set up in East Biloxi at Yankee Stadium on October 6, some 38 days after the disaster struck.[56] A somber Bill Stallworth recalled that "the Red Cross arrived three days after" FEMA.[57]

The Red Cross absence in East Biloxi was part of a much bigger problem. In the largest mobilization in the organization's history, the Red Cross also initially declined to send volunteers into the city of New Orleans.[58] In October of 2005, investigators for the U.S. Government Accountability Office reported a general pattern in which Red Cross officials had invoked agency safety policies as an excuse to bow out of providing "relief in certain areas." Unfortunately, large numbers of victims remained in areas where the Red Cross would not work. Thus, the Salvation Army or smaller church-based groups were left to carry this load alone.[59] Other expert national assessments of the American Red Cross's performance in Katrina pointed to the legacy of past racial discrimination as a factor in a general pattern of Red Cross neglect of minority communities. Before Katrina, the Red Cross had failed to recruit and train sympathetic minority volunteers who would have been willing to reach out to low-income communities such as East Biloxi or New Orleans without reservation.[60] Beyond the coast, volunteer shortages generated complaints of poorly run shelters and neglect of rural communities.[61] These failures led to the forced resignation of National Red Cross President Marsha Evans in December of 2005.[62]

Despite these glaring organizational failings, Red Cross volunteers worked tirelessly. In Mississippi alone Red Cross volunteers manned over 120 shelters, housing and feeding more than 17,000 refugees in the days following the storm.[63] Across the nation in the two weeks after the storm, the Red Cross opened 700 shelters in which 63,000 volunteers served

7 million meals to Katrina refugees and paid for hotel rooms for nearly 100,000 evacuees scattered across 46 states.[64] Moreover, many Red Cross volunteers from Mississippi and Louisiana continued heroically in the relief work despite heavy personal losses. Paige Roberts, the executive director of the Southeastern Mississippi Chapter, lost both her home and her office in Katrina. Roberts was certainly a local hero.[65] To its credit, in the months after Katrina, the Red Cross worked to increase its volunteer base in rural Mississippi[66] and launched significant new efforts to recruit minority volunteers on the Mississippi Gulf Coast.[67]

FEMA's failures in the Katrina aftermath were laid out in several federal investigations. No one was more outspoken in criticizing FEMA's initial bungling than Mississippi's Fourth District U.S. Congressman, Gene Taylor. Congressman Taylor worked disaster relief for two weeks in hard-hit Hancock County, the Katrina eye wall's ground-zero impact zone 27 miles west of Biloxi. Here the congressman had boarded up his own waterfront home the weekend before the storm. Taylor later stated that he had an unusual sense of foreboding about this storm. He knew that his own hundred-year-old house had taken water during Hurricane Camille in 1969. Thus before Katrina, the congressman took time to move cherished items upstairs to the second floor and cover them with plastic as protection against potential roof leakage. With their house boarded up and valuables protected from rising water, Gene Taylor, his wife, Margaret, and their teenage son, Gary, evacuated inland ten miles to his brother's house which stood safely at sixty feet above sea level. Tornados, however, threatened even inland shelters. During the storm the congressman's family heard the classic freight train–like tornado sound. Suddenly, windows bursted out on opposite sides of his brother's home. This sent the men scurrying to stuff mattresses into the breaches to prevent catastrophic structural failure. Somehow the roof and walls held firm and safe.[68]

When the winds subsided, Congressman Taylor and his son, Gary, ventured out to check on his Bay St. Louis house. They slowly made their way south in an old Jeep weaving around and through downed trees and power lines. A fire unit stopped them to warn that six feet of water covered Highway 603 along the Jourdan River several miles north of Interstate 10. Taylor and his son launched a small boat on the road about a half mile north of the Jourdan River bridge. Boating down the roadway, they encountered a surreal assortment of displaced clutter—couches adrift in the water, boats in treetops, and a pool table floating across the highway with balls in the rack, ready for a game to start. Taylor said that "it still hadn't sunk in that whatever house that pool table came out of was probably long gone." They cruised under the Interstate 10 overpass and noticed one of the Casino Magic barges adrift at the Dupont Chemical Plant far north of its normal moorings. The men steered into the river bed and followed it to the bay. The wind was still gusting from the south creating "a hell of a chop." Still, they continued on toward the mouth of the Bay of St. Louis. The rough ride through high waters disoriented the two wayfarers. They made it all the way to the draw span of the old Highway 90 Bay St. Louis Bridge before they realized that the rest of the two-mile-long structure was gone. The congressman had lived near the end of that bridge for over 35 years and did not recognize the place. The experience brought to mind "those *Planet of the Apes* movies where they come back and . . . find the Statue of Liberty sticking out of the sand."[69]

When they turned north to head back up the east side of the bay, Taylor began a methodical survey of the shoreline. One by one, he named families and looked for their homes. One by one, he realized that they were gone—all gone, including his own house and the house nearby where he had grown up. At this point, nothing in the scene made any sense to him. Clothing, curtains, and rugs hung high in trees as if the furies had "toilet-papered the town" to add visual insult to the total devastation. Taylor "could see a good half mile inland. There [wasn't] a leaf on a tree, . . . [nor] house standing, . . . dog barking, . . . [or] bird flying." As a former Coast Guard Search and Rescue skipper, he thought there would be someone to rescue, "and there was just nothing." The seeming "total absence of life" provoked the eery thought that "this is what Hiroshima looked like." As Congressman Taylor cruised back upriver the enormity of what had happened struck home. Then the thought came to him: "If it had to happen to this many other people, it's probably for the best that it happened to me, too." With his own house gone, at least as he encountered other victims he would now "fully comprehend" what it meant to them and "fully understand" what needed to be done.[70]

As in Biloxi, the massive storm surge that inundated most of Hancock County ruined or disabled most of the remaining cars. The collapse of the Highway 90 bridge over the Bay of St. Louis along with damage to secondary bridges to the north and east left Taylor's hometown isolated. It was without power, without working gas pumps, and could muster only sporadic cell phone communication to the outside world. Moreover, Hancock Medical Center had experienced first-floor flooding that contaminated most of its linens and emergency medical supplies. At the height of the storm its staff had worked heroically to save critically ill patients from rising water.[71] Now, in what remained of the only hospital west of Gulfport, there was no power and nothing could be sterilized. At Hancock Medical Center, 850 injured survivors walked in for treatment during the first two days after the storm. They found the hospital staff manning a makeshift triage station outside the building. Still, surgeon Brian Anthony managed to repair a man's severed radial artery while a technician held a flashlight overhead. A FEMA Disaster Medical Assistance Team prestaged in Memphis could not get to the scene until Wednesday evening.[72]

No one knew when outside help might arrive. In the midst of mass destruction of housing and private food stocks, Bay St. Louis Mayor Eddie Favre and Waveland Mayor Tommy Longo decided to commandeer commodities in the local Wal-Mart, Winn-Dixie, and Sav-A-Center supermarkets. All three stores had flooded, but the remaining canned goods were salvageable. Local police officers stationed at each store allowed people to take only the food items they could individually carry plus one change of clothes. Police were instructed to arrest anyone who tried to take more. Despite the utter desperation of the situation, Bay St. Louis Fire Chief Robert Gavagnie remembered it as "a fairly orderly" process with "everybody helping everyone."[73]

FEMA's slow response disturbed Congressman Taylor. When he encountered Eric Gentry, FEMA's point man for Hancock County, the local FEMA manager's insistence on full compliance with preestablished FEMA procedures struck the congressman as "incompetent" and "out of touch with reality." When the congressman urged that "You have to get food in right now," Gentry cited FEMA policy guidelines that insisted that victims ought to be able to take care of themselves for three days. Taylor insisted that this would not work for this disaster. Thousands of people had lost everything. The congressman pointed out that he personally had a hundred pounds of frozen fish in his freezer. However, his house had been wiped off the map, and he could not find his freezer. Taylor grew emphatic: "You have to get food in right now." Congressman Gene Taylor was a ranking member of the House Armed Services Committee. He was convinced that the destruction of local food stocks had created a real danger of starvation. On Tuesday afternoon, Taylor found a working satellite phone and placed calls to General Steven Blum, who headed up the National Guard Bureau in Washington, and to Chief of Naval Operations Admiral Mike Mullin. The congressman apprised them of the dire situation in Hancock County. Alarmed at FEMA's foot-dragging, Taylor's message to General Blum and Admiral Mullin was simple: "People are going to die; I need your help."[74]

The sluggishness of the FEMA relief effort in the hardest-hit East Biloxi and Bay St. Louis–Waveland areas was emblematic of the major FEMA system failure unfolding in both New Orleans and on the Mississippi coast. Unbeknownst to Congressman Taylor at the time of his encounter with Eric Gentry, FEMA's supply system for Mississippi had all but collapsed. FEMA could not find the food and water trucks it had set in motion toward Mississippi and Louisiana before the storm. Truck drivers did not know where to go. Emergency officials did not know what was on the road or when it might show up. In fact, the little that did show up gave the impression that FEMA's Washington offices had mysteriously cut Mississippi emergency relief orders by as much as 80 to 90 percent.

On Saturday, August 27, FEMA's Mississippi coordinator, William Carwile, had placed orders for adequate supplies of food and water in the FEMA Region IV office in Atlanta. Officials on the scene had no way of knowing that FEMA's Washington logistics center either could not or would not deliver more than a small fraction of these vital requests.[75] On Sunday, the day before landfall, the reported Category 5 intensity of Katrina prompted Carwile to increase the order. However, by late Sunday, Carwile's e-mails already expressed concern about food and water supply issues. Carwile had ordered 400 truckloads of water, 400 truckloads of ice, plus 250 truckloads of military-style ready-to-eat meals (MREs) to be staged at the Meridian, Mississippi, Naval Air Station. It alarmed Carwile that he was unable to determine which, if any, of these life-sustaining commodities had arrived. On Monday evening, after Katrina hit, Carwile found that only 30 truckloads of water, 30 truckloads of ice, and 15 truckloads of MREs had arrived.

Both MEMA and FEMA officials in Mississippi complained that supply orders disappeared as if into "a black hole." U.S. Senate investigators found that FEMA's inability to locate or direct commodities in transit was a source of much behind-the-scenes friction in Mississippi, because it left state and local officials "totally in the dark." Tom McAllister, the Mississippi Emergency Management Agency's Response and Recovery director, quickly realized that the system had failed, leaving Mississippi's food and water situation "critically" short. FEMA's deliveries were "nowhere near what we had asked for," McAllister complained.[76] Unless remedied quickly the huge shortfall would pose an immediate survival threat to thousands of Mississippi storm victims. In desperation, Mississippi officials turned to the

Department of Defense and the state of Florida for emergency food, water, and ice supplies.[77] The gravity of Mississippi's looming food and water crisis received little publicity at the time, as the media focused on the simultaneous horrors unfolding in New Orleans.

Safe drinking water was now a life-or-death issue. Given the heavy destruction in the populous urban areas of the Gulf Coast, the Mississippi Emergency Management Agency made a puzzling decision in the first deployments of the few available water and ice trucks. Of the 27 water and ice distribution points set up on Wednesday, August 31, only three were placed in the devastated coastal counties. Further, only one of the three coastal delivery points, the Jackson County Fair Grounds, was within a municipal boundary. In Harrison and Hancock counties a 10-to-12-mile trip inland was required to find MEMA's first water supplies.[78] Given fuel shortages and the large-scale destruction of automobiles on the Gulf Coast, the neglect of the coast's urban centers in that first-day water distribution plan is mystifying.

On the same day, Wednesday, August 31, Scott Morris in the Florida Recovery Office bluntly told FEMA's Washington headquarters that "Gulfport, MS, only has enough commodities for roughly 3 hours' distribution tomorrow." Florida responders deployed in Mississippi had become very alarmed about the shortages. Morris, a former FEMA deputy chief of staff, warned that the situation invited civil disturbances. He worried that local officials' decision to allow evacuees back into town would further strain water and food supplies.[79]

In the late summer Mississippi heat, the threat of dehydration from lack of water weighed heavily in everyone's calculations. Municipal water supplies were either disabled due to system leaks, contamination, and lack of pressure, or due to electrical outages and pump failures. Commodity shortages also threatened the lives and safety of refugees in shelters. A week after the storm, emergency officials reported that 17,374 refugees were housed in the 113 Red Cross shelters and evacuation centers in Mississippi.[80] The 72-hour personal supplies of food and water that refugees were urged to bring to shelters were long gone. Water rationing became necessary. On Friday, September 2, the *Houston Chronicle* reported that water distribution was limited to half a cup per refugee per day at the Harrison Central Elementary School shelter in Gulfport. The Houston paper found "a tense crowd" on hand with "officers holding rifles" when the first loads of potable water arrived for distribution at Milner Stadium in a low-income area of West Gulfport. When told that they could take as much water as they could carry "they made a fast but orderly rush toward five large truckloads of ice and water."[81] In a front-page editorial on Thursday, the Biloxi-Gulfport *Sun Herald* issued an urgent plea. "The essentials . . . are simply not getting here fast enough. We are not calling on the nation and the state to make life more comfortable in South Mississippi. We are calling on the nation and the state to make life here possible."[82]

Water system outages also meant that toilets could not be flushed in shelters and homes. This alone posed a serious health threat on top of the more obvious hazard from the 40 tons of chicken and shrimp washed out of the docks and spread across neighborhoods in Gulfport and Biloxi. On Thursday, Harrison County Emergency Management Director Joe Spraggins made a press appeal for portable toilets. The county had ordered 2,500, but they had not arrived. In a public statement, Spraggins worried that truck drivers were not delivering supplies because of uncertainties about conditions in the disaster zone. "Please help us," Spraggins pleaded. "Bring the gas and the food and we will make it as good for you as we possibly can."[83]

The basic food and water supply situation in Mississippi had deteriorated so much that by Thursday, September 1, FEMA Regional Response Officer Robert Fenton angrily warned FEMA's Washington Logistical Resource Center (LRC) that "if we get [no more than] the quantities in your report, tomorrow we will have serious riots."[84] Fenton had discovered that the levels of water and ice reported in pipe to Mississippi even four days into the disaster were still far below minimum requirements. From the front lines, FEMA's Mississippi coordinator, Bill Carwile, supported Fenton's grave assessment: "It turns out that this report is true, Bob. . . . There seems no way we will get commodities in amounts beyond those indicated. . . . Will need big time law enforcement reinforcements tomorrow. All goodwill here in Mississippi will be seriously impacted by noon tomorrow. Been holding it together as it is. Can no longer afford to rely on LRC. Fully intend to take independent measures to address huge shortfalls."[85]

In a separate communication, a frustrated Bill Carwile informed his Washington superiors that the system was broken. "Sense of urgency demonstrated yesterday by LRC personnel unacceptable," Carwile wrote. "Will now attempt to get product in alternate ways."[86] Months later in his U.S. Senate testimony, the normally reserved Mississippi Emergency Management Agency director, Robert Latham, pronounced the FEMA emergency commodity supply system a total failure in Mississippi.[87] With only 10 to 20 percent of their FEMA commodity orders filled, Mississippi officials had no choice but to beg supplies from the state of Florida and the U.S.

military, or else to purchase stocks on the open market in competition with FEMA. In the critical days when life hung in the balance, the state of Florida stepped up to provide $28 million worth of its own emergency reserves of bottled water and ice for Mississippi.[88] According to Mississippi officials, Florida response teams "basically circumvented" the FEMA logistics system. From Florida state stocks, they brought in truckload after truckload of food, water, and ice and staged them at Stennis Space Center in Hancock County. Still, the Florida contribution could only raise Mississippi supplies to a level that was 40 to 50 percent of what was needed.[89]

Despite feverish scrambling over several days "to get product in alternate ways," on Tuesday, September 6, FEMA's Bill Carwile again warned his Washington supervisors that life-sustaining commodity deliveries in Mississippi were still "totally unacceptable."[90] "We're ordering 425 trucks of ice, [and] 425 trucks of water a day," Carwile protested, "and you are giving us 40." The fact that there continued to be a gigantic gap between what Mississippi officials required and what was actually sent made Carwile, a retired Army colonel and a senior FEMA manager, doubt whether anyone in FEMA's Washington office even looked at the Mississippi emergency requests.[91] The Louisiana FEMA food and water delivery effort suffered similar huge, life-threatening breakdowns.[92]

Working through a new and highly centralized procurement system, the FEMA Logistics Resource Center in Washington appeared to use a top-down cookie-cutter approach which moved supplies forward at a predetermined rate. Trucks sent forward could not be tracked. Somehow the system did not change in response to feedback from the field or in reaction to readily available news reports of the catastrophic nature of the emergencies in Mississippi and Louisiana. At the top of the organization, FEMA Director Michael Brown conceded his agency's failure in one of its core disaster responsibilities. On Thursday, September 1, Brown requested the Department of Defense to take over full logistics operations in Louisiana and Mississippi.[93] The resort to military commodity stores confirmed the complete failure of FEMA logistics. A few days later, FEMA Director Michael Brown was forced to resign.

The FEMA logistics failure presented the real potential for a secondary humanitarian disaster in Mississippi. Ahead of Michael Brown's admission of FEMA's failure, Major General Harold Cross, commander of the Mississippi National Guard, had on August 31 forwarded a formal request for Department of Defense supplies from U.S. Army stocks. On September 1, military aircraft loaded with MREs and water began arriving at the Air

National Guard Training Center at Gulfport-Biloxi International Airport.[94] Air transport was an expensive alternative. Over the next several days, the Department of Defense airlifted 1.7 million meals to south Mississippi to help replace critical survival supplies that could not be tracked in the FEMA system.[95]

In Mississippi's pre-Katrina disaster recovery plan, National Guard troops were tasked with manning locally designated points of distribution (PODs) for water, ice, and food in each county. Both Congressman Taylor and General Cross had concluded that any storm victims lucky enough to still have a working automobile would find debris blocking many roads and preventing them from converging on the planned points of distribution.[96] Taylor advocated helicopters to supplement ground delivery. General Cross quickly assigned National Guard helicopters to air-deliver critical supplies of water and food once they became available. Mississippi Public Safety Commissioner George Phillips also committed his agency's helicopters to the relief mission. Phillips was deeply disturbed when "the minute people heard helicopters, . . . they came, people came running out, holding up signs [saying] SOS and NEED HELP and FOOD AND WATER." In locations too tight for helicopters to land, crews dropped water and MREs. In Mississippi, 62 Army National Guard helicopters worked these missions. They included units from neighboring states as well as Mississippi. Each crew averaged as many as 15 missions per day. The Mississippi National Guard estimated that 1.2 million MREs and more than 1 million gallons of water went out via helicopter from September 1 through September 9.[97]

Beyond FEMA's gross failure to provide adequate supplies in the first place, its truck distribution broke down for the limited supplies that FEMA did put into the pipeline. Mike Beeman, the FEMA representative assigned to Harrison County, reported finding trucks parked along Highway 49, the main north-south access route to the coast. Beeman testified that he personally went over to "find out who he was and what he had in the back end, . . . because many times [we] knew items were sent to us, but we didn't know where they were. Some of them sat sometimes two or three days." Beeman "found 25 trucks one day. . . . They were just sitting there, waiting for somebody to tell them where to go." Neither Beeman nor any local officials ever got information on the supply trucks' point of origin or estimated time of arrival.[98] FEMA's difficulty tracking its orders led to duplicate requests and lost or wrongly deployed supplies. Trucks bypassed the staging area at Meridian Naval Air Station. At Stennis Space Center in Hancock County, which became the forward supply base, there were no truck terminal management capabilities. This left trucks standing idle or in long lines waiting to unload.[99] All of these factors led MEMA Director Robert Latham to assert months later in written testimony that Mississippi did not receive "adequate supplies" of food and water until September 9, or some 12 days after Katrina smashed the Mississippi Gulf Coast.[100]

On Sunday, September 4, long lines of people were left waiting when a priority FEMA commodity shipment failed to show up in Pearl River County, an inland county housing large numbers of Louisiana and Mississippi refugees.[101] Normally reticent pastors and priests spoke out. On Friday, Catholic Bishop Thomas Rodi visited the offices of the *Sun Herald* to express his disappointment, frustration, and anger at the sluggishness of the federal response.[102] Sunday worshipers who gathered in damaged buildings or in the open air on the Mississippi coast voiced concerns to pastors. By Sunday, it was apparent to Reverend Chuck Register of First Baptist Church in Gulfport that despite the spontaneous volunteer groups dropping supplies at the doorsteps of churches, "the community had exhausted its three-day supply, . . . and people were looking for food and water." Register knew that the Southern Baptist Convention had an impressive disaster response network. However, no denominational effort was evident in Gulfport. In phone calls to the Mississippi Baptist Disaster Relief coordinator, Register learned that one large Baptist emergency kitchen had been sent to suburban North Biloxi where it was to service Red Cross and Salvation Army mobile feeding units. Register's concern was that without gasoline people from across the coast could not get to North Biloxi. His pleas for more feeding capacity led to deployment of an additional large Baptist kitchen unit for Gulfport. Reverend Register's efforts also produced a long-term relief and recovery relationship with the North Carolina Baptist Men. This group eventually spent $5,000,000 on disaster relief and housing on the Mississippi Gulf Coast.[103]

Once supplies started trickling into Hancock County, Congressman Taylor again confronted what seemed to be an irrational FEMA do-it-by-the-book insistance on National Guard escorts for any FEMA food and water deliveries. With 40 percent of its forces deployed to Iraq, the Mississippi National Guard was stretched too thin to cover a disaster of this size. It took many days to mobilize and assemble reinforcements from other states. Rigid application of the FEMA guard rule meant that for many days only one National Guard commodity distribution point could be manned in Hancock County. To Congressman Taylor, this FEMA limitation in itself appeared to be another threat to the lives of survivors.[104]

Again, it was FEMA representative Eric Gentry who roused the congressman's ire. Gentry had worked in the Florida hurricanes the previous year. In Congressman Taylor's view, the massive loss of household food stocks and automobiles in the storm surge rendered much of FEMA's Florida model inapplicable to post-Katrina realities in Pearlington, Waveland, Bay St. Louis, and much of the rest of Hancock County. Taylor confronted Gentry about the single point of water and food distribution located at the intersection of Highway 90 and Highway 603. "You have to have multiple points of delivery," Taylor argued. "The people in Pearlington are 20 miles from here; the people in Kiln are 15 miles [away]. You have got to bring the food to the people," Taylor insisted, "because they don't have vehicles, and they don't have fuel." Gentry's FEMA-rule-book style retort angered the congressman. "No, no, no," Gentry asserted. "Based on my Florida experience, if we don't have the National Guard there when we distribute food, there'll be rioting."[105]

Given the few National Guardsmen available on the ground in Hancock County, Taylor believed that such a rule would create the violence that FEMA agents feared. He insisted on proactive water and food distribution. However, in a later interview Taylor stated that the very imputation that his neighbors would cause trouble so infuriated him that he grabbed Gentry by the collar and in coarse language stated words to the effect that "this isn't Florida; this is South Mississippi. We all know each other. . . . If someone gets out of line, his neighbors will tell him, 'Get back in line.'" Taylor turned to the local National Guard commander, Colonel Melton, and persuaded him to put the four or five Humvees then available out on the roads to give out food and water to people unable to get to the distribution point.[106]

FEMA could never say if or when more food and water was coming. Thus, Hancock County authorities decided to carefully ration vital commodities. The impact was heartrending. At dusk on the third or fourth day, after working with his first responders around the clock shutting off leaking gas and water lines, Mayor Tommy Longo of Waveland drove back toward his storm-ravaged office. Off in the distance, he saw a woman with children walking beside the road. As he drew near, he found it was his own wife and five children, ages 2 to 19. They were pushing a grocery basket, making their six-mile round trip back from that single Hancock County FEMA distribution point. There, the family had been given two gallon-sized bottles of water. The water ration, Longo thought, was hardly enough to sustain those five kids for the long walk, let alone do them for the next day. Each child also got one prepackaged military meal. Longo testified that for the first month after the storm in Hancock County provisions were not adequate. However, in the mayor's view, there was never a danger of rioting. People were too busy helping each other. "They weren't going to riot," he told the House Select Committee. "Our people aren't that way." Longo pointed out that Marsha Barbour, the governor's wife, had fearlessly made 24 personal trips to Waveland to drop privately raised provisions.[107]

The arrival of military desalinization units finally brought the drinking water situation under control in Bay St. Louis, Waveland, and East Biloxi. Feeding tents run by various charities eventually contributed 7,000 meals per day in Hancock County. However, despite the critical role of the charitable soup kitchens, at the end of 30 days, FEMA began to pressure the volunteer-run feeding tents to shut down. FEMA wanted to encourage people to eat in restaurants to help revive the local economy. Longo observed that closing the soup kitchens in Waveland would have meant that "7,000 meals go unfed . . . because there's no restaurant open." With 5,000 homes obliterated in Waveland and 5,000 private kitchens lost, the stereotypical approach that FEMA brought to bear did not fit the magnitude of the disaster.[108]

If the FEMA supply system failed the living, it also failed the dead. In anticipation of large numbers of deaths in a Category 4 or 5 storm, FEMA mobilized a mortuary team with refrigerated temporary mortuary trucks and body bags sufficient to deal with the situation. The mortuary trucks and body bags disappeared in the FEMA logistics system and could not be tracked. Thus, to the distress and anguish of their loved ones, there was delay in the respectful handling of the dead in the late summer heat in Hancock County. Congressman Taylor told his colleagues on the House Select Committee that "probably the most troubling thing" he saw "was a local undertaker in tears approaching Mr. Latham, begging for a DMORT, . . . because the bodies were stacking up at his funeral home, . . . and there was no hope of getting electricity for about ten days." With the funeral director's building full, search and rescue teams would have to lay out additional bodies in public view on the parking lot.[109]

Congressman Taylor recalled that as he stood with MEMA Director Robert Latham and FEMA's Bill Carwile, listening to the tearful description of this morbid situation, a refrigerated tractor-trailor loaded with ice pulled up. Latham immediately approached the driver with an offer to rent the truck for use as a temporary morgue. The driver, an independent trucker, protested that the truck and trailer were his livelihood, and if dead bodies were placed in the trailer, he would be banned from ever hauling ice or food products in it again. Latham then offered to buy the trailer. With Carwile's on-the-spot approval, Latham negotiated a price. Dead bodies from the sweltering funeral home were immediately loaded. Five days later, the mortuary trucks ordered through FEMA finally appeared on the scene.[110]

Thirty-six years had passed from Hurricane Camille's legendary impact on the Mississippi Gulf Coast until the fury of Katrina laid waste to the beachfront cities on a far grander scale. Before Katrina, there was sometimes observed to be an air of worldly wisdom and pride in those who had survived Camille. Coast natives to some degree owned the Camille experience as a kind of red badge of courage. The Camille experience nurtured an unrealistic belief that its survivors had seen it all and could cope with anything Mother Mature had to offer. Katrina burst all illusions and drained away any such hubris. Institutions, plans, preparations, bureaucratic processes, buildings, and people failed. Beyond New Orleans, the limitations of all human endeavors revealed themselves as hundreds stood naked and thousands stood homeless and beyond the reach of ordinary civilized supports. The forces of nature demanded and won a new level of respect. For a while, at least, a healthy humility replaced any pride in mere survivorship.[111]

In the months and years since Katrina, the tragedy of the New Orleans levee failures has tended to become the metaphor for Katrina. Yet, the full power of nature's fury was visited in the northeast quadrant of the storm which struck far to the east of the river city. On the Mississippi Gulf Coast, 238 lives were lost, thousands of dreams were shattered, businesses employing tens of thousands were obliterated, and over 216,000 individuals and families lost housing. Bureaucratic systems failed Mississippians in their hour of need. Here amidst the chaos, people often crafted life-saving responses on their own. The importance of individual ingenuity and local initiative in times of crisis is a key part of the Katrina story from the Mississippi Gulf Coast.

However, there were other lessons. Katrina certainly revealed the limits of the nation's underfunded and understaffed lead disaster agency. FEMA was in reality a small organization with only 2,000 employees spread across the nation. Katrina revealed that the Federal Emergency Management Agency had suffered from serious mismanagement and neglect after the 9/11 attacks when it was buried within the newly organized Department of Homeland Security. However, Katrina also displayed the strength and resilience of the nation. A wealth of redundant capabilities within the American federal system and the abundant goodwill and generosity of the American people ultimately made up for the failures of the Federal Emergency Management Agency. The capacities of the American military supply system and the resources of neighboring states were available and quickly tapped when FEMA stumbled. Moreover, once the initial shock passed, Mississippi local governments proved to be surprisingly agile in their response operations.

As the life-and-death struggles of the days immediately following the storm subsided, another struggle emerged—the struggle to salvage and re-create the destroyed economic and social support structures necessary for the rebuilding of these communities.

Chapter Three

Hitching Up Our Britches

Strength at the Bottom in a World Turned Upside Down

> *Sometimes I'm scared, too. But we're going to hitch up our britches, and we're going to get this done.*
>
> —HALEY BARBOUR
>
> Governor of Mississippi[1]

> *There are so many to thank. . . . And we must not let those South Mississippians among us who are doing so much for their neighbors go any longer without knowing how much their efforts are appreciated. . . .*
>
> *We wish we could walk up to every person on their feet in South Mississippi and say thank you. Because we know—and they certainly know—that they are doing quite a bit to be thanked for.*
>
> —EDITORIAL, *Sun Herald*
>
> September 6, 2005[2]

Moments of great crisis can reveal strengths and weaknesses which in lesser times lie hidden behind facades of mundane busyness or the glitter of status and rank. It has now become almost legendary that while Katrina churned, top-tier Washington-based FEMA officials jousted over political turf, and Director Michael Brown quipped with aides about wardrobe selections for his televised emergency briefings.[3] One of the tragedies of the human condition is the tendency of the powerful to fall victim to hidden sins of the spirit—hubris, complacency, and bureaucratic indifference. On the other hand, in a strange inversion of expectations, times of trouble show us that unbelievable capacities for work, sacrificial devotion to duty, and heroism sometimes reside in even the most unassuming among us. Hundreds of testimonials document the unexpected heroism that emerged in people of every age, race, and class at the time of Katrina. They speak of amazing problem solving in the midst of horror. They speak of compassion and courage. They speak of strengths of spirit in ordinary people that touched friends and neighbors and bred hope in the midst of ruin.[4] Individual commitment powered the businesses and local governments that somehow got back on their feet. Those Mississippi businesses that had planned and trained for disaster and empowered front-line leaders to make needed decisions tapped the spirit of the people most effectively and proved surprisingly resilient.

Dave Elliot, a Minnesota native, began working as a reporter at WLOX-TV in Biloxi in 1985. In the 20 years before Katrina, he had become a well-known and popular coanchor of the station's *Five O'Clock News* and host of the station's Saturday half-hour *News Watch This Week* interview program. In preparing for Hurricane Katrina, Elliot sent his wife and son to Florida, and beginning Sunday afternoon, he spent 48 hours hunkered down at the station to help broadcast "wall-to-wall" emergency information to south Mississippi. Dave Elliot was on the air when the roof blew off the newsroom at the height of the storm on Monday morning. Crews quickly relocated equipment to a secure corner of the building and continued broadcasting. On Tuesday afternoon, the anchorman was finally able to get away from the station to discover the fate of his own home. Nine feet of water had washed through and ruined his house and all the houses on the Gulfport cul-de-sac where he lived. When Elliot got there, he found neighbors, some in their 70s, still dazed and wandering in the street. He discovered that 10 out of the 22 people on his block had stayed through the storm and survived in their attics "with water lapping at the attic door." In the midst of this doomsday scene, one of those attic survivors, a woman about 75 years old who had lost everything, called to him. "Dave," she said, "let me know if there's anything I can do for you." For the successful 48-year-old anchorman, this was one of the most moving personal experiences of Katrina. "Here I was an . . . able-bodied . . . man," Elliot recalled, "and this 75-year old woman who looked like she had just been through it all—*she* had asked *me* if there was anything she could do for me."[5]

Katrina presented a great paradox. Michael Brown's Washington-based FEMA logistics center failed under pressure, yet at the grassroots level, Mississippi storm victims who had lost everything were reaching beyond their personal tragedies to seek out and help neighbors whose plight was worse than their own. On the Mississippi Gulf Coast, Katrina was a great social leveler—an equal-opportunity disaster that took away the beachfront mansions of the rich and the shotgun houses of the working poor. Barriers came down; social roles were inverted. People who normally ignored each other now shared their stories. Neighbor helped neighbor. Strangers brought water and comfort to those in need. The dark side of human nature did not disappear. Tempers sometimes flared in the long, hot lines where people waited for commodities or filled out forms.[6] And there was some looting on the Mississippi Gulf Coast.[7] However, in this odd juxtaposition of human nature and "a disaster of Biblical proportions," unexpected outbreaks of brotherly love and sacrificial giving produced help and mercy on a grand scale that far exceeded the impact of the few thieves who exploited the misery.[8]

The outpouring of compassion surprised Father Louis Lohan, pastor of St. Thomas Catholic Church in Long Beach. A graying and much-loved Irish priest with a melodious Irish accent, Father Louis conducted three services on Sunday morning before the Monday storm. St. Thomas stood on a bluff overlooking the beachfront. Beside the sanctuary, the priest's residence, built on 10-foot pilings, appeared safe from any storm. Nonetheless, despite a fleeting temptation to stay, on Sunday afternoon Father Louis gathered a change of clothes and evacuated to a parishioner's home on the north side of town where he safely rode out the storm. St. Thomas, the parish elementary school, and the adjoining rectory house were all utterly destroyed in the storm. In the days following Katrina, Father Louis Lohan conducted the funerals of three members of his church who perished in Katrina, but his most vivid memories were of people pulling together. As Father Louis put it, "I mean they bonded together, and they worked together, and you lived out of everybody's grocery bag, and it was wonderful." With the rectory totally gone, a local family, Jerry and Cindy Levins, shared their home with their pastor for three months. Thousands of others rendered suddenly homeless also found friends and family opening their homes to them. When at one point the 58-year-old priest was reduced to using a bicycle for errands, he recalled that "people that I did not know came out to me; they brought water out to me." One hot day on Pineville Road an unknown man brought out a cap and said, "Sir, you need a cap."[9]

With tears welling up in his eyes, Father Louis Lohan brought back a special memory of wheeling into a store parking lot to check out some suspicious-looking men sitting in the back of a pickup truck with an ice chest and a load of sandwiches. Thinking they were likely "a bunch of rascals" come to "rip people off," he decided to confront them. In a thick Irish brogue he asked, "How much are your sandwiches?" The answer stunned him. They said, "What do you *mean,* how much? They're *free*!" Young men from Florida had brought bread and meat and water, and "they just sat in the back of the pickup truck and said, 'Y'all come take whatever you want.'" It was an emotional encounter and a moment of learning for the priest who had doubted their motives. "They were so wide open," Father Louis observed, "and I thought, . . . there is so much good in people if they are given the opportunity to present good." As a seasoned man of faith who had suffered loss along with everyone else in his community, there were few things about which Louis Lohan could be certain. "One of them," he said, "is that God is a loving God."[10]

Still, as he circulated through scenes of overwhelming material loss Father Louis was surprised to discover a spiritual strength and longing in the laity. Homes and businesses, churches and schools had been destroyed. Yet, large numbers of people of all denominations expressed a desire "to gather and pray in some form or other." So it was that on the Sunday following Katrina, drawn together by word of mouth, a crowd of 3,000 people[11] of all faiths assembled on the grounds of Quarles Elementary School for an open-air mass. In Father Louis's words, "walls of prejudice were taken down." A Lutheran pastor joined the Catholic priest to bring words of inspiration. "It was made very clear to us," Father Louis said, "that there's only one God, and He's the God of all. You can divide yourself up into any kind of pie that you want to," he observed, "but God says, 'I am your God, God of everyone.'" As the priest consecrated wine and bread and offered communion, the inescapable message of the moment was "that God is God, and these are God's people, regardless of color, creed, or culture." Grace Lutheran Church quickly offered to share its facilities with the St. Thomas Catholic congregation.[12]

On that same Sunday, worshipers gathered seeking solace and giving thanks beside the ruins of dozens of churches all over south Mississippi.[13] Beside the rubble of the Episcopal Church of the Redeemer in Biloxi, Rev. Harold Roberts conducted services with a borrowed Bible. The roar of a U.S. Navy hovercraft bringing emergency equipment ashore accompanied the distribution of communion. Nearby, in East Biloxi, members of Lighthouse Apostolic Holiness Church set up folding chairs on one lane of Division Street and praised God for lives saved. Rev. Debruce Nelson reminded them that the Lord's deliverance had shown itself "more than once, from the Red Sea to Division Street." In Gulfport, members of First Baptist

Church and First Presbyterian Church, whose harbor-front sanctuaries lay destroyed, joined with members of Cross Point Church for worship. Quoting the words of Job, "The Lord giveth and the Lord taketh away. Blessed be the name of the Lord," Rev. Chuck Register reminded the congregation of God's providence and urged them to "love one another." The pastor called Gulfport Mayor Brent Warr and his wife to the altar, and, with a symbolic laying on of hands, he prayed for strength and wisdom for them in the hour of crisis. Bishop Thomas Rodi of the Catholic Diocese of Biloxi quoted the same passage from the Old Testament book of Job in sermons at Our Lady of Lourdes Church in Pass Christian and at St. Rose de Lima in Bay St. Louis. "Those who suffer," said the Catholic bishop, "can become bitter and cynical," or they can "become generous and their heart expands." On a hot Mississippi Sunday when food and water were still scarce, Rodi reminded the faithful that the Gospel says that "not even [the gift of] a glass of cold water will be forgotten in God's eyes."[14] In the days of crisis, many saw hearts expanded in their own neighborhoods and in the volunteers who poured in from across the nation.

For awhile at least, the common plight of loss and suffering drew people together across religious, socioeconomic, and racial lines. Methodists and Baptists helped Catholics, and Catholics helped Jews and Protestants. White volunteers helped black families. Black churches helped elderly white people. When the predominantly white faculty at William Carey College searched for classrooms to replace their devastated facilities, the predominately black congregation at First Missionary Baptist in Handsboro opened their Sunday school facilities for college classes to resume. African American congregations like Little Rock Baptist in Gulfport, First Missionary Baptist in Handsboro, and St. Mark's Methodist in Gulfport opened their facilities to house thousands of white relief workers and volunteers.[15] The open-hearted responsiveness of neighbors stood in welcome contrast to the sometimes unethical behavior of insurance adjustors or the impatience of the itinerant functionaries who reigned over the paperwork grind required for FEMA trailer applications and/or the state housing grant program which followed.

The recovery of the St. Thomas Parish Elementary School in Long Beach offers a glimpse into the way local people came together, invented solutions, and supported each other's efforts. Prior to Katrina, 280 children were enrolled in the St. Thomas school, and there were another 100 on a waiting list. The storm totally destroyed the one-story brick building which sat amongst the oaks just north of the church. About a week into the disaster, the principal, Mrs. Elizabeth Fortenberry, announced to the pastor and several of the parish school board members, "We'll be opening school on October third." At first, the plucky announcement was met with laughter. Father Louis Lohan half-jokingly asked just where it was that the principal intended to open the school. Mrs. Fortenberry's determined reply set a process in motion. "I don't know," she said. "You're the pastor; I'm the principal. It's up to you to find the place, and I'll run the school."[16]

The principal's bold refusal to accept the loss of the school struck a chord with the priest and with board members who knew the value of the school in the lives of the children and in the life of the parish. The pastor formed a committee to locate a suitable facility. Even though St. Thomas was a parochial school, Dr. Carolyn Hamilton, the Long Beach public school superintendent, helped in every way possible. At first, nothing they investigated seemed suitable. After much frustration, someone finally suggested that with business activity so disrupted, perhaps the local skating rink might be available. Indeed, the owners were willing to talk about renting the property. However, considering the necessary renovations, the rental price was beyond what the school could pay. In a final bid to get the school back in business, the committee sent one of its members, Mrs. Jimmy Macken, to see if the owners would consider selling the building. Two or three days later, Mrs. Macken announced to her pastor, "I bought the building for you." The sale price was $250,000. The news stunned the priest who could not see how they would pay for it. "Don't worry," Mrs. Macken said. "We'll work this out. I am going to ask ten people to put up $25,000 each, and we'll pay them a dividend. This is a business deal." She was certain that the church would use the property for awhile, resell it for a profit, and then pay the individual lenders a dividend. Within a short time, six people had each made $25,000 pledges. The seventh person the committee approached turned out to be Mr. Elvis Gates, the grand master of the local Knights of Columbus Lodge. The lodge hall had been destroyed, and an insurance company had just written its board a check for exactly $250,000. Mr. Gates proposed that the lodge buy the skating rink and rent it to the church and school for a dollar per year. The lodge board agreed to the deal. Parents, grandparents, and students immediately went to work to renovate the facility. Naval Construction Battalion volunteers joined volunteers from Iowa, New York, and Ohio in the effort. An impossible task became a feasible project. The school opened on October 3, the plucky principal's original target date.[17]

In their mobilization of commitment and shared values at the neighborhood level—in their clear sense of mission and willingness to accept personal responsibility—the St. Thomas Parish Elementary School community displayed an important element in the recovery. It was initiative and resourcefulness at the bottom that got the little Catholic school back into business. In a world turned upside down, it was local people, local businesses, and Mississippi's local governments that often demonstrated the most unexpected strengths.

Grassroots initiative and clarity of mission distinguished many resilient organizations in this crisis. Stephen Peranich, Congressman Gene Taylor's chief of staff, noted the striking difference in performance between what he called "mission-driven" versus "compliance-driven" federal agencies in the aftermath of Katrina. Bureaucracies or officials lacking a clear, passionate sense of mission often made, delayed, or reversed decisions based on fear that the "wrong" thing would be done. Fear of failure to comply with complicated rules slowed or paralyzed the response and recovery operations in "compliance-driven" organizations.[18] In a respected post-Katrina review, the U.S. Government Accountability Office pointed to the United States Coast Guard as an example of effective disaster response. Behind the Coast Guard's effectiveness, the GAO found an agency permeated with a few basic operational principles. Mission clarity, unity of effort, careful planning, and constant training headed the list. However, it was the Coast Guard's practice of "on-scene initiative" and "flexibility" that stood out in explaining the success of its Katrina disaster operations. The Coast Guard relied on the strengths of the men and women in its bottom ranks. As the GAO put it, Coast Guard personnel were "given latitude to act quickly and decisively within the scope of their authority, without waiting for direction from higher levels in the chain of command."[19] The Coast Guard is not unique in this. The management literature on effective organizations and "high-reliability" military units is filled with examples of such paradoxes of devolved decision-making within otherwise hierarchical military and corporate cultures. This characteristic was a key part of successful disaster response in many civilian organizations.[20]

On Congressman Taylor's staff, both Stephen Peranich and Brian Martin praised the military services in general for their "forward-leaning" and "mission-driven" Katrina responses. Both congressional staffers pointed to a similar forward-leaning, mission-driven attitude in the culture of the local electric power companies whose employees set a record for speed and efficiency in restoring service.[21] Stephen Peranich's father, John Peranich, was a career Mississippi Power employee, but accolades for utility companies also radiated from many sources including local newspapers and the U.S.

Senate committee investigating Katrina.[22] Across four states, Katrina left 2.7 million customers without power. Seventy percent of all utility customers in the state of Mississippi lost power for some period of time.[23] In south Mississippi, providers faced the gargantuan task of rebuilding an electric grid that had taken almost a century to create.

Mississippi Power was the largest supplier for the 23 hardest-hit counties in southeast Mississippi. Alongside Mississippi Power, two rural electric cooperatives—Coast Electric with 70,000 customers and Singing River Electric with 65,000 customer—operated complementary networks in the coastal counties. The utility companies faced thousands of downed poles, transformers, and transmission structures and thousands of miles of wire on the ground or needing repair. The nearer the coast, the greater the damage was to the grid. From Bay St. Louis to Gulfport and Pascagoula, from Biloxi to Hattiesburg and Meridian, Katrina left all 195,000 of Mississippi Power's customers and all 135,000 Coast Electric and Singing River Co-op members without service. These total grid knockouts were unprecedented. Between the three companies serving coastal Mississippi, 49,950 poles had to be repaired or replaced, and before it was all over the three companies had strung enough wire to cover the distance from Biloxi to Vancouver, British Columbia.[24]

Moreover, in the case of Mississippi Power, Katrina struck at the core of the company. The storm took away the homes of hundreds of company employees,[25] and it destroyed one of the company's major generating facilities, Plant Jack Watson, in Gulfport. Initially, Mississippi Power estimated that it would take at least a solid month to restore its system. However, the company mustered a response that got its system back up in less than two weeks. The two neighboring electric power associations were able to complete their restorations by the end of the third week after the disaster. Mississippi Power Company's enormous comeback won for it the Edison Electric Institute's prestigious Emergency Response Award and the Franklin-Covey Leadership Greatness Award.[26]

Ahead of the storm, Mississippi Power had staged reserve manpower and equipment in Alabama at Montgomery and Birmingham. Because no one utility can afford the army of technicians needed to restore power quickly after a major disaster, companies routinely share line crews with neighboring providers when needed. Within Mississippi Power, the insights gained from their blue-collar line crews' rich and varied emergency experience in working across the nation provided a constant flow of ideas which the company used to refine its home-area storm operations. In the months before Katrina, Mississippi Power had revised many aspects of its own disaster plan based on Gulf Power Company's response to Hurricane Ivan in 2004.[27] From planning to execution of the disaster response itself, it was the strength of rank-and-file utility workers that propelled electric grid recovery every step of the way.

Although Mississippi Power's disaster recovery plan was based on what was thought to be a worst-case scenario, it did not take into account devastation on the scale of Katrina. The company's top managers had identified the Watson generating plant as a safe storm center because it had withstood Hurricane Camille in 1969. Katrina, however, flooded Plant Jack Watson in Gulfport with 16 million gallons of saltwater that reached a depth of 20 feet in the facility's lower levels and severely damaged all six of the plant's generating units. Beyond this unexpected loss, the unprecedented line damage from Gulfport to Meridian created a demand for poles, wire, transformers, labor, food, fuel, and water that was beyond anything anticipated in the company plan.[28] Initial assessments showed that 5,600 miles of wire in Mississippi Power's 8,000-mile network was either on the ground or needing repair.[29] Furthermore, 119 of its 122 massive main transmission lines were knocked out due to the destruction of 300 transmission structures, including 47 metal towers. At the local neighborhood level, 9,000 wooden poles and 2,300 transformers had to be replaced.[30] Beyond all of this, Katrina flooded out nearly 140,000 square feet of company office space and forced dispersal of headquarters employees all over the region for many months.[31] Thus, Katrina struck Mississippi Power harder than any other Mississippi utility and inflicted the greatest losses in company history.[32]

Each of the 1,500 Mississippi Power employees had a distinct disaster recovery assignment. Individual emergency response functions were assigned and rehearsed each year before hurricane season. Thus, when Katrina struck, line crews reported for duty knowing that they would be asked to work long hours for an indefinite period before they could attend to personal losses. Power plant workers focused on restoring generation capacity. Office staffers became logistics workers, food service helpers, or laundry specialists. Reserve specialists like John Peranich knew that their experience and expertise would be needed to expand the company's management backbone for effective supervision of visiting workers from other regions. Every employee understood the absolute seriousness of the mission. Hospitals, police and fire stations, banks, supermarkets, and every other enterprise essential to the restoration of civil society required power. No part of the recovery could get under way without electricity.[33] When Katrina put Mississippi Power to the test, it was the mettle of the men and women in the bottom ranks that proved to be the decisive factor.

One story reveals much about the sense of mission ingrained in utility workers. On August 30, 2005, John Peranich, a retired line manager, returned to temporary Mississippi Power Company service to manage the restoration of the many miles of transmission lines branching off from a substation in Pass Christian. "I know this area like the back of my hand," John Peranich told an interviewer. He had lived most of his life in this zone in a house built on land that had been in his family for three generations. Like hundreds of Mississippi Power Company's active employees, John Peranich lost his home in Katrina. His son and his mother-in-law also lost homes in the storm. Despite these losses and despite his retirement from full-time work in 1997, John Peranich returned to company service the day after the storm with a sense of urgency about the work. Hundreds of Mississippi Power Company employees did the same. The level of commitment that stands an employee back up for service the day after they have lost everything they own speaks volumes about the source of the strength and resilience of this company in particular and of the Mississippi communities beyond. In a career that spanned over 35 years, John Peranich had worked his way from apprentice lineman to lead lineman, and on to jobs as a troubleshooter, an engineering technician, a foreman, and finally to the post of Supervisor of Electric Operation Services for Mississippi Power's Coast Division. Like many other retired utility workers at the time of Katrina, John Peranich still worked storm recovery projects on a regular basis all over the nation. Now he and every Mississippi Power employee faced the overwhelming needs of their own communities, friends, and families. There could be no greater basis for building a personal sense of urgency in the work.

Pass Christian, like Biloxi, is a 300-year-old community built on a scenic oak-covered peninsula. Katrina demolished large sections of the town and flooded much of the surrounding area. The day after the storm, John Peranich reported to a preassigned center where he picked up a company-supplied rental car and an emergency packet of maps and procedures for his recovery zone. He immediately began riding the area to count downed poles and to estimate the amount of line and the number of transformers and substation mechanisms that would need replacing. Peranich and other substation restoration coordinators then calculated the man-hours needed to get each section of the system back into service. Such estimates from each substation section coordinator across 23 counties guided the purchase and distribution of equipment and manpower.[34]

When line crews arrived from other states, field recovery coordinators like John Peranich directed their work in each substation service area. The company erected large tent cities with mess halls and laundry facilities to house the visiting crews. In the late summer heat, line crews and their supervisors worked long hours to take advantage of every hour of daylight. With his own house reduced to shambles, Peranich sometimes slept in the company's Bay St. Louis office building or in his company-provided rental car. In large numbers, local utility workers joined the local policemen, firemen, and thousands of other essential but less visible blue-collar workers who found unsuspected inner wellsprings of strength that enabled unexpected perseverance in unbelievably difficult but vital missions.[35]

The task ahead was monumental and labor intensive. The company's pre-Katrina worst-case scenario estimated that at the most, it could muster the logistics to support its own 1,500 workers and a maximum of 5,000 emergency linemen from other companies. According to post-Katrina company man-hour calculations, with 5,000 visiting workers it would take at least a month to restore power to all customers.[36] The only way to change this restoration time line was to find a way to feed, fuel, house, equip, and supply more linemen. With a strong mission focus, the company did just that.

Twenty-four hours after the storm ended, the company reported 2,500 outside crewmen had arrived, and it expected 5,000 by Thursday, September 1, or 72 hours after the storm.[37] The speed of these deployments exceeded that of the National Guard. Refusing to accept the inevitability of a four-week repair period, company managers began scavenging the country for materials, tents, bedding, and food service contractors to build capacity for more line crews and a shorter time to restoration of service. Somehow, the company found a way to support a near doubling of its line crew support capacity. Eight days after the storm, in camps and staging areas all over its 23-county service area, Mississippi Power alone was successfully housing and supplying 9,200 crew members from roughly two dozen companies from as far away as Canada working along with its own 1,500 employees. Beyond Mississippi Power, the various electric power cooperatives around the state brought in an additional 7,605 workers from 14 other states.[38]

This huge pool of manpower would have stood idle and useless without fuel for vehicles. By itself, Mississippi Power's fuel consumption for 5,000 utility trucks reached 40,000 gallons per day. In the midst of the unexpected first-week fuel crisis when preordered fuel shipments failed to arrive, the Chevron Pascagoula refinery became the direct supplier for this huge force. By September 9, line crews had delivered 6,000 poles and over

1,000 miles of wire through the Mississippi Power service area alone.[39] This unprecedented effort cut the company's four-week restoration time line in half. At the end of work on September 11, thirteen days after the storm, Mississippi Power alone had spent $277.4 million and successfully restored power to all of its customers still able to accept service.[40] Mississippi Power and other utilities were reimbursed through the federal appropriations in the Community Development Block Grant program passed in December of 2005.[41] However, the work was accomplished with a speed and efficiency that greatly boosted morale for hundreds of thousands of storm victims. With a simple and clear mission and with well-trained crews and supervisors, the company had vastly exceeded its own restoration time estimates.

At Plant Jack Watson, another massive job remained. Thousands of switches, meters, pumps, motors, and cables that had been inundated in saltwater had to be repaired and tested. After 46 days of 24-hour-per-day effort, Mississippi Power employees and outside crews brought the first of the damaged generators back online. A second large generator was up and running by the end of the year, and remaining generating capacity at the plant was recovered by the end of May in 2006.[42]

Beyond the electric companies, it seemed that unsuspected inner strength awakened within tens of thousands of ordinary Mississippians who powered every facet of the recovery in the community at large. Within a week of the storm the *Sun Herald* remarked on the enormous debt of gratitude owed to so many who had already exceeded the call of duty in rendering service to a community in ruins. It was "not just those wonderful men and women" seen "out in the street and at the distribution centers and shelters" to whom "unending thanks and appreciation" were owed. It was, as the newspaper said, "the men and women behind the scenes" who made it "possible for those front-line personnel to be on the front line." The emergency workers were the most obvious heros of the hour, but as the newspaper pointed out, so were "the men and women willing and able to get some of our businesses up and running." Local journalists saw and reported many things. An opinion column simply titled "Thank You, Thank You, Thank You" closed with the wish that "we could walk up to every person on their feet in South Mississippi and say thank you. Because we know, and they know, that they are doing quite a bit to be thanked for."[43]

The harried workers in the local news media were certainly among those whose long hours should have earned a thank-you. It was reported that only four of the 90 radio stations from Mobile to New Orleans were able to remain on the air in the immediate aftermath of the storm. Some broadcasters put their lives on the line to bring vital information to the public. The staff and technical crews at WLOX-TV in Biloxi continued broadcasting after the roof blew off their newsroom and the guy wire from a falling tower threw a multiton piece of concrete onto another part of the building. In Hancock County, WQRZ, a low-power, nonprofit FM station, kept operating after storm surge floated the home studio of Brice Phillips, the tiny station's owner. When the eye wall passed, Phillips salvaged his transmitter and moved it to the county Emergency Operations Center where Brian Adam, the county's EOC director, had been left without any means of communication with the outside world. In rising water, Phillips rigged car batteries to power the station for search and rescue broadcasts. Brian Adam believed that after the storm, when FEMA logistics failures posed their greatest danger in Hancock County, Brice Phillips saved many lives with low-power broadcasts of the locations for scarce water and food supplies. In a creative adjustment, MEMA and FEMA officials quickly bought and distributed 3,500 battery radios so that those who had lost everything could receive the WQRZ signal.[44] To the east in Jackson County, when Tim Lee, the owner-operator of WPMP-AM, was knocked off the air, he moved his operation to the LaFont Inn. Lee's broadcasts let local people know where to find food, water, and ice. Two years later, Wanda Comello of Pascagoula made a special effort to thank Tim Lee for his efforts, because "when we were thirsty and hungry, it meant a good deal."[45]

Katrina also elicited unprecedented cooperation between local news outlets. Four local radio media groups carried the WLOX-TV sound signal, and the *Sun Herald* shared its staff with WLOX to augment disaster coverage. With their offices located across the street from each other, the TV station and the newspaper also shared generator fuel and port-o-lets. WLOX-TV gave up 12 solid days of network advertising revenue to broadcast emergency information 24 hours per day. The devastation of area businesses left the pages of the *Sun Herald* virtually denuded of advertising. Still, the paper never missed a day of publication. In the post-Katrina world without cell phones, electricity, or cable service, the newspaper became an information mainstay for thousands of people. In runs far beyond the normal 47,000 daily total, the *Sun Herald* distributed up to 80,000 free copies each day on street corners, in shelters, and anywhere people gathered and needed basic news about when and where to get the help they needed. Free newspaper distribution continued until October 10, some six seeks after the storm. To their credit, parent corporations, Liberty Broadcasting and Knight Ridder, stood behind local decisions at WLOX and the *Sun Herald* to provide emergency media services regardless of bottom-line financial considerations. Both companies brought in supplies and additional staff to make sure that the *Sun Herald* and WLOX kept serving their communities in their hour of greatest need.[46]

In Hancock County, Randy Ponder, the editor and publisher of the weekly *Sea Coast Echo,* lost his office and press to the Katrina storm surge. Working from computers set up in his house, four days after the storm Ponder produced an issue that was printed in Pikeville, Kentucky, and shipped back to Bay St. Louis. Using a beat-up Jeep to distribute free copies across devastated Hancock County, Randy Ponder met his readers in the kind of desperate circumstances that most publishers never see. Ponder's description of the "tearful appreciation" he encountered speaks to the value of journalistic efforts in a crisis. "I had people come up and cry, absolutely cry, just because I am handing them a newspaper," he said. "It was something they could see and hold in their hands. It was a comfort to them."[47] Regular news created a bit of order in the chaos and held out the promise of a return to normalcy. In 2006, the *Sun Herald* won the Pulitzer Gold Medal for Public Service for its exemplary work in the aftermath of Katrina. That same year WLOX-TV won a Peabody, a Dupont, and a Southern Emmy for its Katrina coverage.[48]

The commitment of their reporting and support staffs enabled these media outlets to keep information flowing. At WLOX, anchorwoman Rebecca Powers came back to work in borrowed clothes after she and her husband narrowly escaped death when their flooding house collapsed, forcing them to swim for their lives. Readers of the *Sun Herald* took heart from the personal accounts of veteran local reporters like Kat Bergeron and Lisa Monti who lost their homes and worked through the struggle for recovery just like so many of their neighbors in Biloxi and Bay St. Louis.[49] Twenty percent of Powers's colleagues at WLOX and 25 percent of Bergeron's cohorts at the *Sun Herald* also continued working after losing everything. In both news organizations some homeless staffers slept at the office for many days or weeks. For reporters and support staff alike, the mission of getting information to the public became a way to find meaning in what was for them a very personal disaster.[50]

Beyond the news spotlights, other businesses also somehow picked themselves up and got to work on tasks vital to community life. The morning after Katrina, a handful of employees of The People's Bank pushed the water out of their flooded main office in downtown Biloxi and opened for business. The People's Bank was a 109-year-old Biloxi-based institution with 17 branches in four south Mississippi counties. The morning after the storm, only 18 of the bank's 230 employees were able to get to work. Forty percent of the bank's workforce had lost their homes and 20 people, including third-generation bank president Chevis Swetman, were now forced to live in the bank headquarters building. From Waveland to D'Iberville, 7 of the bank's 17 branch facilities were destroyed.[51] Beyond the difficulties for bank employees, the fate of the banks had a deeper meaning for the community. Katrina had struck on August 29—the day before payday for the hourly workers whose labor would be needed to jumpstart the recovery. With power outages, there were no ATMs or credit card machines. For tens of thousands of families, access to cash became an immediate issue. Restoration of the most basic commerce depended on weather-beaten banks and devastated bank employees clawing their way back into business.

The People's Bank president, Chevis Swetman, had believed that his operation was prepared for this hurricane. The bank's thick disaster preparedness plan had addressed every conceivable storm preparation task down to the teller level in every branch office. However, the plan had not anticipated the flooding of the main office or the computer center and did not mention sandbagging these critical facilities. After all, the bank's headquarters and nearby computer center on Lameuse Street had never before flooded—not even in Camille in 1969. One employee's initiative saved the bank's Biloxi computer center. Water in the computer center would have been catastrophic. Despite the plan's silence on the matter, on the weekend before Katrina, a rookie employee insisted on going beyond the plan and sandbagging the computer center. As a result of this decisive action, when the storm unexpectedly piled water deep enough to float cars in the street outside, the computer center stayed dry enough to support bank operations after the storm. More ingenuity was required to open and stay functional. The storm plan had not anticipated disrupted fuel deliveries. The Biloxi-based bank had to find 300 gallons of diesel fuel each day to feed the emergency generators that powered its main office and computer center. As the tanks neared empty, the bank staff turned to longtime customers in the local seafood industry. Stored diesel fuel intended for the shrimp trawlers wound up keeping the computer center running and The People's Bank open for business.[52]

The gravest threat to regional banking and commerce came from the utter ruin of the Hancock Bank's 17-story, 300,000-square-foot headquarters building and computer hub in downtown Gulfport. Whereas The People's Bank operated 17 branches in four Mississippi counties, Hancock Bank with over five times the assets operated 155 branches spread across

Louisiana, Mississippi, Alabama, and Florida. During the storm, 20 Hancock Bank employees, including 80-year-old board chairman Leo Seal, Jr., had taken refuge in the bank's high-rise Gulfport fortress. Katrina's 30-foot storm surge had pushed four feet of water through the bank's ground floor lobby and offices. A tornado had spun off the main storm and propelled roofing, debris, and furniture from other buildings through the glass facade of the massive bank building, damaging or shattering 1,300 windowpanes. Interior spaces were laid open to a salty spray of wind-driven water. Atop the 17-story tower, the inch-thick steel roof had been peeled back and blown off, exposing all 17 floors of the building to catastrophic leakage down the hollow columns and shafts between floors. Interior walls were waterlogged on every floor such that the slightest pressure would send Sheetrock crashing to the floor or down elevator shafts. Worst of all, tornado winds had blasted out the east wall of the critical fifth-floor data center.[53]

Located on the north side of the building, the Hancock Bank's main computer operations facility was the only part of the building with brick walls and no windows. Because it had no windows, it was considered storm safe. For this reason, the 20 employees who rode out the storm at the company headquarters had taken refuge in the fifth-floor data center. When the exterior brick wall collapsed, Sheetrock quickly gave way and the floors lifted. Only the massive wire network behind the facade had saved the employees sheltered there from plunging to their deaths. It was obvious to John Hairston that the computer center and the rest of the iconic Gulfport building could not be brought back to use for months or even years, if ever.[54]

The loss of the massive Hancock Bank building and all that was housed there represented an unprecedented threat to banking in the region. Corporate computer operations, the technology hub, check processing, loan servicing, and all other critical elements of the banking operation across four states were located in the destroyed building. Like its Biloxi-based competitor, Hancock Bank maintained a thick disaster plan. However, as Norman McDonald, the bank's business recovery manager, explained, "We were ready for a Camille. We were not ready for this."[55] The storm put the very survival of the business in jeopardy. Yet somehow, on the morning after the storm, without electricity, and without computers or working ATMs, Hancock Bank managed to open several of its branches for business.[56]

As fate would have it, early in 2005, the bank's chairman of the board, Leo Seal, Jr., had expressed worry about the possibility of a catastrophic storm and voiced concern that people on the coast in general had let their guard down. Seal urged Hancock executives, "You make sure this bank is ready." In the spring of 2005, Leo Seal's worries led to a major new bank exercise that simulated the loss of the downtown building. In the immediate aftermath of Katrina when the actual survival of this multibillion-dollar bank hung in the balance, that exercise proved its worth. For many decades, under Mr. Seal's leadership, Hancock Bank had been known for its bottom-up strategic planning processes. Bank officers always had a clear set of objectives and goals in normal business operations.[57] Moreover, for years, every time a hurricane entered the gulf, the multistate bank had downloaded its electronic account files and sent teams with duplicate copies to Chicago and Atlanta where the files were to be uploaded onto rented mainframes if a storm knocked out the Gulfport headquarters. On August 29, 2005, that worst-case scenario became a reality.[58]

Hancock Bank's response began late Monday afternoon with 40-mile-an-hour winds still blowing over the wrecked headquarters building. In that scene of devastation in downtown Gulfport, Chief Operating Officer John Hairston managed to get a cell-phone call through to his Chicago team leader, Jeff Andrews, who had flown out with back-up computer data 48 hours earlier. The message to Jeff Andrews was simple. "Jeff, the building's a total loss," Hairston said. "You've got to move the flag. Bring up the data center in Chicago." On the other end of the line, even though the routine had been tested many times before, Jeff Andrews could not believe what he was hearing. "It can't be; Hancock Plaza can't be damaged that badly," he implored. Having just climbed 15 flights of stairs and a two-story exterior ladder on the Gulfport building, Hairston stated emphatically, "That's what I said, Jeff. Trust me. Move the flag. We won't be in this building for a long time. . . . What is important right now is . . . to bring those systems up in Chicago." Sitting in Chicago and still stunned, Andrews protested, "You know, we've never done this before." At this point Hairston interjected what was to become a theme in this organization. "We've tested it every year, and it's worked every year. I believe in you. I believe in the team. Y'all will get it done."[59]

With the wind still blowing, Hairston uttered the words that amounted to a huge devolution of authority and responsibility to the Chicago team. "You've got four days. Bring it up, get it current. I may not be able to talk to you again for awhile. You remember, you bring it up." After pledging to take care of the homes of the deployed technical team and committing to fly families to Chicago and put them up for the duration of the crisis, Hairston reemphasized the mission. "You guys stay the course. Your job is to get those systems up. If we cannot get the systems up, we don't have a company. Get them up." Their disaster plan called for a four-day window to have the systems operational from the remote location. The mission was clear. It had been rehearsed many times. Now, facing a corporate crisis of unbelievable dimensions, the deployed team stepped into the arena. Working 24 hours a day in Chicago with little to no communications from the Gulfport headquarters, Hancock Bank's skeleton-force iTech group got alternate technology operations up in three days.[60]

After making this call from the ruins of downtown Gulfport, John Hairston and Business Recovery Manager Norman McDonald tried to think out the course for the bank employees who would be making their way to work the next day. In a disaster of this magnitude it was hard to know just where to start. Standing in the debris, the men quickly committed to just start working the thick emergency plan. Thinking of the exercises the previous spring, Hairston summed it up. "We've been through this," he said. "We know how to do it. We know the plan will work." The next morning, the Hancock Bank employees "executed the plan from page one." A cleanup contractor with 200 workers was set working immediately to remove debris from the streets and lobby of the headquarters building. All available employees were organized into a human chain stretching up 15 stories of stairs to begin the salvage of tons of confidential paper files. With a few glitches the massive salvage operation went according to plan. Key headquarters functions were devolved around the region to Baton Rouge, Louisiana, Purvis, Mississippi, and Tallahassee, Florida.[61]

Because people need extra cash during emergencies, for a hundred years Hancock Bank had taken pride in its commitment to being the last bank to close before a hurricane and the first to reopen in the aftermath. Thus, the Hancock Bank emergency plan called for branches to be opened immediately after a hurricane with available employees and facilities. Nonetheless, as they huddled over the hood of a car on the morning after the storm, key executives confronted stark issues for basic banking. The destruction of the central data system that serviced all Hancock branches across four states was unprecedented. There were no phones, no electricity, and no computers for 50 of its Louisiana and Mississippi branch facilities. Some branch buildings were totally destroyed, and others had lost roofs. The contents of vaults had been saturated with floodwater. In the Mississippi and Louisiana markets, police and fire departments were overwhelmed with search and rescue duty and could not provide protection. Would it be realistic to reopen immediately given these levels of destruction? How would you know who your customers were? What about storm victims who presented themselves asking for cash but who had lost everything, including checkbooks, wallets, and identification? How would you check balances to guard against overdrafts or fraud? What about people who would need cash but banked with another institution? The risk was clear. Yet, credit cards would not work for gas, food, or any other basic need, and it was August 30—payday. People would need cash.[62]

In that moment of worried consideration, the core executive group went back to the bank charter and asked basic questions about institutional values and mission. They noted that there was no mention of the word "profit" in the Hancock Bank's 1899 charter. The old charter mandated that the bank serve people and communities. Supplying people with money and keeping it safe was their basic service. What about risk? Over the years, chairman Leo Seal, Jr., had drilled into their heads the concept that banking would be an impossible business if 99.9 percent of the people were not honest. With this precept beckoning them, and with documents spread on the hood of a car, bank officials made a tough decision to stick with the charter and provide money to the community—even, or especially, in this crisis where security was not guaranteed. In their time of trial, an almost obsessive mission focus emerged in the bank's officers. Disaster-ravaged people needed cash.[63]

In a gutsy move for a bank that had just lost its data center, Hancock Bank officers decided to allow people—whether Hancock customers or not—to draw up to $200 cash if they could simply write out their name, address, or social security number on a scrap of paper, or as George Schloegel put it, "if they seemed halfway identifiable."[64] Across town at The People's Bank where a computer center was still intact, Chevis Swetman also decided to distribute cash on an IOU basis.[65]

On the Tuesday after the storm 10 of the 50 offline branches of the Hancock Bank opened without power in the disaster zone. Three days later, 30 of the company's 50 offline branches were back doing business without lights, phones, and in some cases without roofs or buildings. In Pass Christian and Waveland, they opened behind card tables under tarps or from vans or repossessed mobile homes. Within ten days, The People's Bank managed to set up modular trailers to replace destroyed branches in D'Iberville, Bay St. Louis, and Pass Christian. For both institutions, banking was reduced to Post-it Note IOUs that were tossed into boxes to be processed later. Because both Hancock Bank and The People's Bank opened up amidst such uncertainty and ruin, tens of millions of dollars flowed into the community. A powerful message was sent that the local bankers believed in a future for their devastated region. Much-needed cash was salvaged from flooded and waterlogged vaults and ATMs. Unable to determine when Federal Reserve funds might arrive, Hancock Bank set up a system that literally washed, dried, and ironed massive hoards of contaminated and foul-smelling cash. Beyond the cash sent moving through disabled branch locations, both banks managed to deliver cash in vans to cover payrolls on the spot for various businesses in the region.[66]

Moving massive amounts of cash into an economy that ordinarily worked on checks and credit cards involved tremendous federal documentation requirements in the post-9/11 world. Federal agencies ignored bank pleas for emergency waivers. Overburdened bank employees had to wrangle with Homeland Security paperwork in order to supply the cash needed to run the post-Katrina cash economy.[67] However, with a strong sense of mission and hundreds of bank employees willing to return to work with their own homes in shambles, banks that were so vital to the poststorm response and recovery got back on their feet.[68]

In the week after the storm, Hancock Bank, by itself, went through more than $42 million in cash—cash supplied whether or not the person had an account with Hancock. Before normal operations could resume, Hancock Bank secured millions more in additional cash from the Federal Reserve Bank in Nashville to feed its own operations and those of other banks in the region. The risks that Hancock Bank and The People's Bank took for their community could have opened them to massive losses. In the case of Hancock Bank, at least $3.5 million went out the door to people who could not later be linked to any account or working phone. In a profit-and-loss organization like a bank, the wisdom of "trusting people" might be questioned. For the community, though, the decision taken over the hood of a car the morning after Katrina was the right decision. Three years later, George Schloegel reported that of the millions of dollars given to people for a signature on a Post-it Note, all but $200,000 had come back to the bank. As people returned to the area and got on their feet, the majority remembered that Hancock Bank IOU and paid it back. Moreover, he noted, employee morale at the banks soared to historic highs.[69]

In time, the right decision for the community paid great dividends for both of the locally based institutions. As insurance payouts and housing grants began to flow, new banks from outside the community attempted to establish themselves in the coast market. However, in the year after Katrina hit, total assets at The People's Bank grew by 45 percent.[70] Hancock Bank assets grew similarly, and in the five months following the storm, Hancock Bank opened 13,000 new accounts. Despite increased competition in the rebuilding phase after the storm, people turned to the long-established local banks that had put themselves on the line for their customers and said in the words of George Schloegel, "You were there when I needed you; you're going to be my bank."[71]

For a banker like John Hairston, the Katrina experience was important for what it revealed about the spirit of the people of Mississippi—"their sense of being bound together and willing to help each other." The negative history of the state—slavery, racial conflict, high poverty levels, low education attainment—all set up negative expectations of Mississippi in the nation. "Then comes Katrina," as Hairston saw it, and Mississippians "did it right." The nation took pause and said, "What an amount of character these people have! How resilient they must be!"[72] Katrina revealed a power derived from personal caring and commitment which history seldom glimpses and statistics cannot quantify. It was a power seen in white and black, poor and rich, and in both blue collars and white collars. It was a power whose potential was often overlooked or unappreciated before the crisis. Far away the mighty may have faltered, but in setting after setting, local people "hitched up their britches" and plodded forward in the hard tasks of recovery.

Chapter Four

Rising from Shell Shock

Sources of Resilience in State and Local Government

An entire swath of coastal Mississippi was totally eradicated by Hurricane Katrina. But we focused exclusively on New Orleans tonight because in Mississippi, for the most part, the system seemed to work. At least it didn't fail as miserably as in New Orleans.

—TED KOPPEL, ANCHOR
ABC News *Nightline*
September 15, 2005[1]

The teamwork of the various state and federal agencies and local governments working within the Unified Command System which was established very early, has been a critical part of our success. . . . It requires strong leadership, . . . and there is no time for turf battles.

—ROBERT·LATHAM, Executive Director
Mississippi Emergency Management Agency[2]

In the United States, standard practice vests responsibility for initial disaster response at the local government level. If the disaster overwhelms local capacities, local governments request state support, with the federal government providing financial support and assets upon the request of the state.[3] Katrina overwhelmed local government on the Mississippi Gulf Coast. Dr. Marlin Ladner, who represented the wrecked towns of Pass Christian and Long Beach on the Harrison County Board of Supervisors, thought that the unbelievable devastation in Mississippi had left most local officials "stunned" for the first day or two. "We were . . . shell shocked," Ladner recalled, " . . . in the state of confusion where you don't know where to go . . . [or] where to turn around."[4] Despite this early distress, and against all expectations of the poorest state in the union, one month after Katrina, Acting FEMA Director David Paulison singled out Mississippi's state and local emergency operations as "a model" disaster response. While accusations still whirled about FEMA's national-level logistics failure, Director Paulison told reporters that he had "not seen in a long time a system that worked as well as the one in Mississippi."[5]

Two weeks earlier, at the end of an ABC News *Nightline* broadcast that had focused on ills of the Katrina response, reporter Ted Koppel had also concluded that in contrast to New Orleans, "the system seemed to work in Mississippi."[6] The fact that credible national-level leaders and respected journalists found positive things to say about Mississippi's state and local government disaster response surprised and heartened community leaders like John Hairston, the chief operating officer at Hancock Bank. Hairston had grown up in Mississippi. He believed that there was more to the people and communities that he knew and loved than could be accounted for in the measures of education, health, and per capita income that tended to create low expectations of the state and its people. In a certain sense, John Hairston's own career had defied expectations. His father had dropped out of school to join the Navy during World War II. The fact that the elder Hairston had never finished high school showed in the state's poor statistics. What it did not show was his father's capacity for hard work and idealism. After the war, Hairston's father had run a gas station before taking up sales work for Sears and later for United Insurance. Along the way he sold real estate and owned a shrimp boat. John Hairston's first job in high school was aboard that shrimp boat. From a father who regretted his lack of formal education, John Hairston learned to work hard, and the younger Hairston worked his way through engineering school at Mississippi State University. John Hairston began his professional career doing engineering consulting work that led him to Texas. However, soon thereafter, he took an improbable turn that put him working in the field of bank liquidations and mergers which then led John Hairston to a promising position in a major bank in North Carolina. Hairston knew that statistics could not measure a person's work ethic or their commitment to community—things he had learned from his father's example. Statistics, too, were poor measures of the family values which led John Hairston back home to Gulfport and a job at Hancock Bank at age 29. In short, Hairston believed that statistical measures missed something very important about the spirit of the place he called home. Certainly, Katrina was a tragedy that one would not wish on anyone else, but one of the ironies of that tragedy for Hairston was the fact that it gave the people of Mississippi a chance to prove their mettle. That his fellow Mississippians got credit for basic competence in digging out of what many called the greatest natural disaster in American history was a major positive in the banker's mind.[7]

Paulison's positive evaluation of Mississippi's state and local government performance was really praise for their quick adoption of the so-called "Unified Command" crisis management system. Still, some discounted Secretary Paulison's praise for Mississippi as an example of partisan Republicans straining to find something good in a dysfunctional and incompetent federal Katrina response. Others claimed it as evidence that Mississippi Governor Haley Barbour's refusal to criticize the Bush administration was paying a political dividend.[8] In fact, just six days before Paulison's positive evaluation of the Mississippi disaster response, press reports quoted Governor Barbour's remarks to a Washington GOP gathering to the effect that the Bush administration had "done . . . much more right than wrong." Haley Barbour's background fed the speculations that Paulison's praise for Mississippi might have been simple GOP political back-scratching. A former chairman of the Republican National Committee, Barbour had come to the Mississippi governor's mansion after a long career at the helm of a highly successful Washington-based corporate lobbying firm. He had a well-earned reputation as a fierce partisan competitor. In his dealings with the Democratic majority in the state legislature, Barbour had proven to be an exceptionally strong "hands-on" governor who left no stone unturned in his efforts to impose his agenda on resistant lawmakers. On many occasions his adversaries had labeled the governor's approach "dictatorial."[9] Therefore, no one was surprised that Barbour joined Governor Blanco of Louisiana in refusing President Bush's proposed federalization of the National Guard and the whole emergency response and relief operation. The Mississippi governor told the president bluntly that "we need help," but "we don't need somebody coming around telling us what to do." In Barbour's view, emergency response decisions, or "incident command," belonged in state hands.[10] Such states' rights assertions also polished the political image that made Haley Barbour an icon for southern Republicans.

Whatever the political spin put on Paulison's comments, within Mississippi itself, even Governor Barbour's political adversaries gave him credit for skillful handling of the Katrina disaster. Much of the comparative success of the state-level response in Mississippi stemmed from Barbour's early decision to delegate significant authority to the qualified emergency specialists on his team for the duration of the crisis. In testimony before the House Select Bipartisan Committee in December of 2005, the Mississippi governor outlined his role in the Unified Command structure which Mississippi adopted. Pointing to MEMA Director Robert Latham, State Health Officer Dr. Brian Amy, and former Federal Coordinating Officer Bill Carwile, who were all seated beside him, Barbour stated firmly, "I delegated authority to these guys right here. I don't try to run things day-to-day. I'm not competent to do it. I haven't got time to do it. They come to me," the governor stated, "when they need decisions made. . . . We operated on a chain of command, through the unified structure. They looked to me when they needed direction, and they ran it."[11] Though he delegated authority to his emergency professionals, Barbour met with them often during the crisis period,[12] and he established a strong public presence through daily press briefings and constant travel through the disaster zone. Ironically, this delegation of authority allowed the Mississippi governor to quickly shift his focus to the daunting issues of long-term recovery.

Ten days after the hurricane, Barbour appointed a high-profile commission to chart a path for reconstructing the debris-strewn towns and cities of the Mississippi coast. As a result, even a strong Democrat such as Representative Bobby Moak, who had fought Barbour tooth and nail over education and Medicaid funding, praised Governor Barbour for doing a "pretty good job of putting his arms around" the Katrina issue.[13] At the time, local political analysts believed that Barbour had managed to "at least look authoritative." On the national scene he came to be seen as "the only political figure to gain" from the Katrina ordeal.[14]

The Unified Command System which Director Paulison lauded was not a Mississippi invention. Unified Command concepts evolved to fight California wildfires in the 1990s. After the 9/11 terror attacks, this approach became part of the National Incident Management System and the Incident Command Systems which federal experts urged state and local responders to adopt as their principle crisis management tool. In a disaster, Unified Command requires a high level of cooperation and coordination across a wide array of normally separate state, local, and federal agencies. It was this system of cooperation that Paulison commended in Mississippi. In so doing he echoed Bill Carwile, the federal coordinating officer in Mississippi during the Katrina crisis. Carwile had worked as a FEMA section chief in New York after 9/11 and served as federal coordinating officer for the California wildfires in 2003 and for each of the four Florida hurricanes in 2004. Carwile believed that in the Katrina aftermath in Mississippi he had witnessed the most thorough state implementation of the Unified Command concept in his experience.[15] It was the high degree of cooperation across state and local agencies and jurisdictions which distinguished the Mississippi response and made it stand out in contrast to the public struggles between city, state, and federal authorities in Louisiana.[16]

Carwile, however, was reluctant to cast stones at Louisiana. The very idea of Unified Command is extremely challenging in a federal system where a multiplicity of state and local elected officials and federal agencies share responsibility for response, resources, and personnel. Successful Unified Command scenarios require that state and local policymakers be willing to delegate authority for day-to-day operations to incident command teams who set disaster response priorities, allocate resources, and interface seamlessly with each other at the state and local level.[17] Devolving such responsibilities is a lot to ask of an elected official who will be blamed or praised for the results at the next election. The success of Unified Command at the state level in Mississippi stemmed from Governor Haley Barbour's willingness to place substantial authority in the hands of those most able to deal with the various aspects of the hurricane emergency. Barbour set the example for others.[18]

As fate would have it, in the months before Katrina hit, the state-level incident command team and many of Mississippi's county emergency managers had undergone training on the National Incident Management System and Unified Command doctrines.[19] Once the governor declared an emergency, his designation of MEMA Director Robert Latham as his authorized representative enabled a Unified Command System to become operational at the state level 48 hours before Katrina's landfall. Mike Womack became the state coordinating officer and Mississippi Adjutant General Harold Cross, Public Safety Commissioner George Phillips, along with FEMA's Bill Carwile, filled out the state-level Incident Command Team. Colonel Damon Penn also joined them as defense coordinating officer.[20] Disaster-related nongovernmental groups such as the Red Cross, Salvation Army, and Southern Baptist Disaster Services provided representatives at the Emergency Operations Center to work with the Mississippi Department of Human Services on sheltering and mass care issues.[21] Once the storm passed, Robert Latham and Bill Carwile went south to establish a field command center in the parking lot of the Harrison County Courthouse in Gulfport. From here the two senior officials forwarded assistance requests from the three devastated coast counties, while their deputies in Jackson handled requests from other storm-affected areas of the state.[22]

On the coast, local officials in all three counties somehow sorted their way through the poststorm chaos to establish local unified command structures which reported to each county's emergency operations director—Butch Loper in Jackson County, Joe Spraggins in Harrison County, and Brian Adam in Hancock County. At the state level, there were morning strategy meetings to formulate daily objectives. On the county level, joint county-municipal daily strategy sessions also became a ritual for city and county managers, members of the county boards of supervisors, and state and federal liaisons. After each morning strategy meeting, joint operations and logistics officers met to coordinate the manpower, equipment, and supplies needed for that day's objectives. Each evening, managers met to report progress, assess new problems, and formulate recommendations for the next day.[23] All responders in all municipalities reported to the countywide Incident Command Team and worked priorities and tasks which the County Unified Command established across municipal jurisdictions. If the National Guard or other federally supplied assets were needed, federal law (the Stafford Act) required local officials to draft formal requests or task orders. The law mandated that Robert Latham and his state-level team validate local requests before they could be passed on to Bill Carwile for federal approval and forwarding on through the FEMA bureaucracy to be tasked to appropriate federal agencies.[24] In all of this, FEMA's national logistics and tasking were seriously deficient and frustrating. When promised federal assistance was delayed or did not materialize, it left local officials embarrassed and feeling like they were lying or misleading their constituents at a sensitive moment.[25]

However, the systems for establishing priorities through the Unified Command process earned across-the-board praise from normally skeptical Mississippi local officials.[26] At first, Pascagoula's no-nonsense city manager, Kay Kell, doubted the usefulness of Unified Command. Pascagoula's city hall, Kell's own home, and her daughter's home had all flooded. When called to the first Jackson County Unified Command session her thought was "I don't need to go to another meeting. I had to be dragged kicking and screaming," she said. Kell recalled that the process made leaders from across the county sit and talk and form joint municipal-county teams to "deal with issues together." Countywide teams worked problems ranging from debris and housing to public safety and health. Despite her initial skepticism, in retrospect Kell described Unified Command as "one of the best things that . . . Jackson County did." Four years later, Kell stepped up to be a FEMA recovery mentor for the southeast Texas communities recovering from Hurricane Ike. She credited the spirit of teamwork that emerged in the Unified Command structure as "keeping Jackson County on track" in the aftermath of Katrina.[27]

Getting "on track" was no small task given the untold numbers of city and county workers who had been rendered homeless, the countless emergency vehicles that had been ruined, and the numbers of local government buildings that had been heavily damaged or destroyed. In these chaotic circumstances the Unified Command System that drew praise in Mississippi owed much to the responders and trained local emergency managers who poured in from Florida. Florida responders worked under the auspices of the FEMA-financed Emergency Management Assistance Compact (EMAC). Before the storm hit, Florida had offered aid, but Mississippi officials, at that time, had declined to accept.[28] However, in a tremendous act of leadership immediately after the storm, Florida officials moved assets and manpower into Mississippi before the chain of paper approvals that guaranteed federal reimbursement could even be initiated. At first glance the federal Stafford Act looks generous in its disaster financial-aid provisions and promises. However, its implementation involves a multilayered system by which localities must formally declare the need for specific assets, which the state must verify before a request can be forwarded to FEMA for approval and assignment to an appropriate agency. Brian Martin of Congressman Taylor's staff saw instances in which local officials' fears about the paper processes required for federal reimbursement "started to paralyze some of the recovery."[29] Fortunately, such fears did not impair Florida's response to the Mississippi disaster.

As Katrina came ashore on the morning of Monday, August 29, it became apparent that Florida would not need the state forces assembled in the Panhandle area. Col. Julie Jones, Director of Law Enforcement for the Florida Fish and Wildlife Conservation Commission, called the Mississippi Emergency Management Agency to offer help. With the storm in progress, MEMA officials had no idea what requests to make. On Monday night, after the storm passed, Jones again contacted MEMA. Mississippi officials again reported that they were unable to evaluate the damage or state their specific requirements as mandated in the FEMA reimbursement process. However, at this time they told Florida officials to send whatever they could send. According to Col. Jones, by this time, Florida emergency response units were already "at the border ready to go, and we were in Mississippi by 6:00 a.m. Tuesday." Jones reported that "before Mississippi could wake up and say, 'Okay, we have to start doing assessments,'" Florida emergency response units were already operating in Jackson and Harrison counties.[30]

The importance of the Florida presence in Mississippi in the early hours of the poststorm crisis cannot be overstated. Florida teams schooled in Unified Command helped their overwhelmed Mississippi counterparts prioritize the response and organize their own countywide Unified Command Systems. As Harrison County Supervisor Marlin Ladner described it, "The first day or two (after the storm) local officials, even our EOC was stunned. . . . I think we were in a state of confusion . . . shell shocked," not knowing where to turn. Ladner recalled that "the folks from Florida . . . sat us down at the table and said, 'We're here to help you. We're not here to take over, but we have these suggestions.'" According to Ladner, "They brought organizational charts and a step-by-step outline of what needed to be done and in what order."[31]

For Robert "Bobby" Weaver, the director of the Harrison County Sand Beach Authority, when Florida emergency operations managers showed up on Tuesday afternoon, it was as if "the cavalry" had arrived. The Harrison County Board of Supervisors had just drafted Weaver into the job of county response operations chief with responsibility for identifying and supplying the people needed to implement county response decisions. It was a job Weaver had never done. Weaver remembered sitting in a meeting with Rupert Lacey, the newly appointed emergency logistics chief, when two leaders from a Florida Incident Management Team walked into the room. The Florida responders had worked four or five storms over the preceding 24 months. They knew what they were doing. The Floridians announced their availability to help and tactfully asked for five minutes just to explain something. "After we're done," their leader said, "we'll do whatever you want us to do." The seasoned Florida managers immediately clarified the tasks at hand. "Everybody in this county is emotionally attached to this disaster," the Florida team leader said. "You have the desire to take care of all your citizens' needs right away, [but] that will not happen. You do *not* have the mental or physical capacity to do that today. So, . . . you need to focus on one or two or three priorities, . . . and when you achieve that goal, then focus on the next one and then the next. You're not going to take care of everybody tonight."[32]

That clear perspective helped Weaver and Lacey to quickly clarify their goals. Search and rescue was at the top of the list. Local fire and police and

USAR teams were already on that task. Water and ice was next, so they concentrated on identifying distribution sites and identifying the personnel to man them. With the help of the Florida team, order started to emerge from the chaos. By 9:00 p.m. on the evening after the storm, cities in Harrison County knew where and by what means water would be distributed whenever the trucks arrived.[33]

As Harrison County Supervisor Connie Rockco saw it, the Florida first responders and emergency operations advisors "saved our lives absolutely." They brought technical expertise of every type. They rescued victims from collapsed buildings. Florida vehicles stood in for destroyed Mississippi police cars and fire trucks. In Harrison and Hancock counties, the rapid deployment of Florida state and local emergency forces within 24 to 48 hours of the storm met a critical need for organizational advice, manpower, and equipment. Storm-battered and physically exhausted local police and fire units that had lost many (and in some cases all) of their vehicles absolutely needed the help.[34] Appearing unexpectedly as they did in the middle of a disaster scene of unprecedented scale, it was easy for Connie Rockco to conclude that the Florida teams were our "white knights in shining armor."[35] However, it was Mississippi local officials across three counties who made the decisions to adopt the Unified Command structures that the Florida responders recommended.

By the end of the first full week following Katrina, the state of Florida had committed assistance to Mississippi valued at $68 million, including 701 state and local law enforcement officers, 424 National Guardsmen, plus almost 1,000 other emergency responders including firemen, search and rescue teams, ambulance teams, bridge and infrastructure inspectors, emergency management leadership teams, and an array of health and environmental specialists.[36] For many weeks after the storm, 600 Florida law enforcement officers provided "indispensable support" to Mississippi Gulf Coast local law enforcement. Over the first few weeks of the disaster the state of Florida sent 100 ambulances, a mobile 911 call center, 170 emergency generators, plus traffic control equipment including 1,300 rubber safety cones, 1,000 barricades, and a supply of mud pumps. In addition, Florida provided 2,000 truckloads of water and ice that saved countless lives when FEMA's central logistics system failed during the week after the storm.[37] At one point, Governor Barbour told Governor Jeb Bush of Florida that he could be "elected king" of the Mississippi Gulf Coast "for all that Florida's done to help us."[38] The Emergency Management Assistance Compact made possible the quick exploitation of state-level strengths dispersed across the region and nation.

State-level EMAC assistance proved itself in every sector of the disaster response. With 40 percent of the Mississippi National Guard force on station in Iraq, the widespread devastation dwarfed the 3,800-man Mississippi force that could be assembled for disaster duty. Again, state-to-state aid saved the day. By Wednesday, Florida and Alabama Guard units had added 1,100 men to the Mississippi force. As Arkansas, Tennessee, Indiana, Ohio, Maryland, and others responded, the out-of-state National Guard forces on duty assisting the Mississippi Guard swelled to 9,400 on Sunday, September 4. Ten days after the storm, on September 8, out-of-state National Guard forces in Mississippi peaked at 11,500 soldiers. Sixty-two Army National Guard helicopters flew an average of 300 missions per day to support Mississippi relief and recovery operations.[39] Beyond supplemental National Guard units, the EMAC program provided police officers, firemen, medical teams, and a wide array of other specialists. Some of the New York fire and rescue units that came to Mississippi had worked ground zero at the World Trade Center on 9/11. In December of 2005, MEMA Director Robert Latham testified that 48 states had sent 24,791 men and women for 892 specific EMAC missions in Mississippi, all of which were tasked and coordinated under local Unified Command teams. This enabled Mississippi to tap the expertise of other states at federal expense, which Latham valued at $193 million.[40] The vital local community public safety backbone was strained to the breaking point in the days after the storm. Harrison County Supervisor Marlin Ladner concluded that without assistance from other states, the Katrina aftermath "would have been an impossible task for local agencies to handle."[41]

In a disaster that struck down the mighty and overwhelmed local institutions, essential help poured in from other states. This outpouring demonstrated anew the genius of the federal system with its multiple centers of strength and innovation. FEMA stumbled; yet even skeptical Mississippians saw the beauty of the nation in the strengths that the different states deployed to good effect through EMAC and federal financing. Katrina was thus an occasion when Mississippians saw the nation in a new light, and, with the national disaster spotlight focused on them, Mississippians were themselves seen anew. Before Katrina, those who looked at Mississippi from the outside or through the lens of its troubled past would have sorely doubted its leaders' ability to bury egos and abandon political turf wars to concentrate on the crying human needs of the region. However, Katrina demonstrated that a state known for its stubbornly independent-minded leaders had in fact produced officials who had the wisdom to follow good advice and delegate the prioritization of the disaster response to local incident command teams. This was asking much of officials who would be held accountable at election time. Moreover, local people learned that they could depend on each other and that they could depend on the collaborative processes behind the Unified Command concept.

Furthermore, state and county employees who had often lost everything demonstrated the same strengths of spirit that propelled ordinary citizens to lend a helping hand to their neighbors. Perhaps Katrina simply drove everyone into the same cave where there was no choice but cooperation. Banker John Hairston observed that "as bad as Katrina was, there were some wonderful gifts out of that experience. . . . People here care about each other more than they did before the storm. . . . We're a more giving people than we were before the storm." Hairston believed that "even the most cynical heart is a little bit more willing to help other people than they were before the storm."[42] Thousands emerged from the rubble of their own homes to begin rebuilding local government services, local businesses, and local institutions. In a time of great testing for a state burdened by a tragic history, elected leaders won national acclaim for effective delegation of authority to the Unified Command teams that coordinated the state and local response. For an America in doubt of itself and for a state with a troubled past, these unexpected strengths pointed to wellsprings of caring, commitment, and capacity for service that will forever remain beyond the scope of mortal ledger books.

Chapter Five

Digging Out in a Whirlwind of Contract Controversy

Television pictures show glimpses of the destruction: the gutted antebellum homes, the rows of pancaked houses, the mangled gas stations and fast-food joints, the casinos that float no more. But it's the shear mass of Katrina's fury—the decimation of entire coastal towns, the jarring pockets of odor that bespeak animal or human death . . . that leave hurricane hardened residents and experienced relief workers awestruck.

—REPORTER JOHN SIMERMAN
Contra Coasta Times (California)
September 11, 2005[1]

America is being threatened by a Category 5 hurricane of peculation. All the elements are in place: $200 billion or so in federal cash, a large helping of government guilt about its failures to prepare for Hurricane Katrina, an atmosphere rife with cronyism and fueled by public and private corruption. . . . That much money spent that fast . . . by so many firms with no, or limited, bids cannot be monitored closely.

—EDITORIAL, *St. Louis Post-Dispatch*
September 28, 2005[2]

The massive volume of the destruction left in the wake of Katrina dwarfed all previous records of disaster wreckage in American history. Spread over a 90,000-square-mile area in three states, the storm left 118 million cubic yards of debris, a volume many times greater than the previous record set by Hurricane Andrew.[3] Frank Reddish, manager of the Bureau of Recovery and Mitigation for Miami–Dade County, believed that it might take as long as five years to clear the Katrina destruction. He speculated that in the near term, the job was "more than all of the debris companies in the world could handle."[4] Apart from its Louisiana and Alabama impacts, just within the state of Mississippi Katrina left 46 million cubic yards of destruction lying on the ground, mired in a stinking sludge. In Mississippi's bottom six counties, the debris load was initially estimated to be six times the solid waste that the entire state generated in an ordinary year. The local property tax base was largely gone. No recovery could begin until local governments and private citizens alike faced up to the daunting task of digging out. On one level, the cleanup involved the finality of personal loss and pain. On a second level it was an engineering marvel. At the end of the first month after the storm, 10,000 truckloads of debris were moving off Mississippi streets each day.[5] However, before the bills were paid and the last loads hauled away, the technological triumph had become ensnared in a political tangle. While Mississippi's disaster response and local Unified Command System drew national accolades, the removal of Katrina's massive mounds of destruction spawned tentacles of Washington-based second-guessing that reached forward for years to frustrate, distract, and dismay many of the local leaders who spearheaded the recovery.

There was urgency at all levels in attacking the debris problem. Unnecessary delays in removing putrefying waste could spread disease, attract rodents, and present unmanageable fire hazards. Thus, in the midst of FEMA's massive logistics failures, Mississippi officials had to make quick decisions on how to execute the cleanup. As if health and safety concerns were not enough to get them started, the initial 60-day time limits set for 100 percent federal cleanup support presented additional pressure. Fuel and food shortages or not, an army of equipment and a bevy of disposal sites had to be located and engaged. Federal help with the task of digging out was essential and much appreciated. However, clouds of suspicion soon gathered over the Army Corps of Engineers contracts that had been awarded on an expedited, limited competition or "no-bid" basis. The charged atmosphere of distrust surrounding corps contracting generated pledges of heightened federal auditing attention for all Katrina contracts. Increased scrutiny produced ex post facto auditing standards, which in turn underscored the clumsiness and insensitivity of the FEMA and Army Corps of Engineers processes.

Local governments had the option to openly bid their own cleanup contract. Those that did so found that they could get the job done more cheaply and employ more local workers by going outside the Army Corps of Engineers "no-bid" arrangements. However, cost-effective bargains were of little concern to the swarms of auditors sent to second-guess these decisions and their execution. Even before the furor over Katrina contracts came to a head in Washington, FEMA functionaries cautioned local governments that exercising the option to contract debris removal on their own would necessitate a large commitment to careful record keeping for the federal audits that could be expected whenever reimbursement requests were filed. The specter of the paperwork burden led the smallest of the hard-hit Mississippi entities to choose to do the debris work through the Army Corps of Engineers. There would be no debris removal audits for cities and counties that elected the corps for cleanup.

On a personal level, every storm victim wrestled with debris on his or her own property. When Katrina's surge waters subsided on Belmede Avenue in Gulfport on Monday evening, Betty Smith and Pearl Bozeman, the two widows who had perched atop mattresses to escape drowning, somehow managed to clear a path through the topsy-turvy wreckage which the invading waters of the Katrina storm surge left inside the Bozeman house. With the life-and-death struggle of the day behind them, the ladies, both in their 60s, fell asleep exhausted on waterlogged sofas and mattresses oblivious to the foul stench that now enveloped everything that the surge had touched. The next morning, Betty Smith walked down the debris-strewn street to check on her own small house. The structure had lost some shingles, but it was still standing. However, the door was jammed and would barely budge. Four feet of water had penetrated the house and turned its contents into a slimy, odorous mass of disarray. The waters of Katrina had floated, overturned, saturated, warped, or otherwise ruined everything inside. From waterlogged chests of drawers and bedding to furniture, appliances, and curios collected over a lifetime, it was all a total loss. Outside, Betty Smith's late-model Honda had also been enveloped in water and would not start. The car and virtually all of the contents of her house now counted as part of the 46 million cubic yards of debris which Katrina left behind in Mississippi. With only the clothes on her back to call her own, Betty Smith took up residence with her sister 10 miles inland.

Over the next two weeks, friends and family members salvaged a few precious photos and mementos and dragged the rest of the widow's worldly goods to the street. Soon thereafter, unknown contractors operating cranes with huge claws ripped load after load from the ground and slung it over the side of a dump truck to be hauled away. Over the coming year, debris piles and dump trucks became the defining feature of the local scenery. Trucks and tractors clogged streets, created massive traffic jams, and pulverized the pavement. For months on end, everything on the Mississippi Gulf Coast seemed to move in slow motion behind a debris truck.[6] Never-ending streams of ragged cargo headed toward one of the 340 temporary disposal sites across the state. Behind the scenes, a federal-state Joint Debris Task Force set rules, identified appropriate permanent dumping grounds with suitable clay-based soils, and resolved a litany of problems related to the disposal of unprecedented mountains of rubbish contaminated with household chemicals, rotting food, and sewage.[7]

The Mississippi Department of Environmental Quality, various local governments, and the Army Corps of Engineers identified locations for temporary storage, staging, sorting, and final disposal of the various types of debris. In the three Mississippi Gulf Coast counties, 65 to 70 percent of the load was made up of household items and construction waste from tens of thousands of building demolitions. In Harrison, Hancock, and Jackson counties, over 450,000 appliances—washers, refrigerators, hot water heaters, and the like—were separated out for pulverizing. This enabled the recycling of more than 24,000 tons of metal. In addition, 1,500 pounds of refrigerant were extracted from air conditioners, freezers, and refrigerators. Specialized sites were developed for concrete crushing and the staging of tens of thousands of ruined automobiles and boats. Even though these efforts allowed considerable volume reduction, 13 new disposal sites were opened on the Mississippi Gulf Coast in addition to the six permitted sites in operation before the storm.[8]

As the hurricane moved north off the coast, the debris left in its wake changed from 70 percent structural and household in makeup to one that was 85 percent tree limbs and logs. Of the 340 temporary sites across the state, 250 were chip or burn sites for vegetative debris. This type of green waste could be recycled as boiler fuel or used as mulch for blueberry farms, playgrounds, or live oak recovery efforts. However, by January, the threat of spontaneous combustion in mulch heaps reaching 40 feet high combined with the lack of sufficient markets meant that much of the vegetative waste wound up being burned on site and the ash reused for soil enrichment.[9]

For engineers, the waste disposal effort was a marvel to behold. However, behind every ton that was crushed, burned, recycled, or buried there stood personal stories of loss. Seeing the contents of family homes go to the street was one of the more painful memories of the storm for Rev. Guss Shelly, age 60. Rev. Shelly had been the pastor of First United Methodist Church in Gulfport for eight years when Katrina hit. After 37 years in the ministry, Pastor Guss and his wife, Sarah, had bought their first home just three years earlier. Located on Second Street in Gulfport, the Shelly residence was a modest old wood-frame bungalow built off the ground on three-foot pillars. When they returned to their Gulfport home the day after the storm, the Shellys found that four feet of water had entered the house and taken its toll. Once-beautiful hardwood floors had buckled. When he took his first step inside, Guss Shelly's foot slipped on the slimy gunk that covered the floor. Never one for foul language himself, the preacher quoted his country cousins. "Slicker than greased owl s–t," he was sure they would have said. The phrase encompassed both the consistency and the smell of the mud that Katrina deposited on the floors inside and on the yard outside. With two changes of clothes to call their own, the Shellys pulled a few salvageable items from the house and took up residence a short distance away in the Sunday school wing of the church. Here, over the next several days, they dined on a seemingly endless buffet of canned tuna and made themselves available to meet the needs of others.[10]

In the Shellys' congregation, 128 families had lost their homes. Ten or twelve days passed before a large volunteer group from Oxford insisted that it was time to clean out the preacher's house. Mrs. Shelly did not want to watch, but as Rev. Shelly recalled, "I really thought I was big boy enough that [cleaning out the house] wasn't going to be a problem." He had spent a lifetime helping people place value on matters of the spirit. "After all," he said, "things are just things." Nonetheless, when the moment came, his tears betrayed him. Guss Shelly "discovered right away" that he "wasn't nearly prepared to watch" the family's clothing and furniture—"the things we had worked to buy and were proud to have"—be thrown out into the street. The Shellys' personal pain made them one with tens of thousands of others who saw their clothes and furniture heaped before their eyes. Katrina reminded the preacher that sometimes things are not *just* things. For things and places can evoke powerful memories of the people and events connected with them—people and events that have shaped our lives.[11]

For the Shellys, resilience in the face of overwhelming loss owed much to personal faith and to the supportive presence of others. Somehow the sharing of simple tasks could transform moments of heartache into times of renewal. Unexpected armies of volunteers descended upon the region in a flood of compassion that pushed aside, at least for a time, much of the despair normal to such scenes of loss and desolation. "I know that we are taught that we are born into sin, and that we are of a sinful nature," the pastor observed, but "I've always believed that there's more good in humanity than there is evil," or at least "the good overwhelms" the evil. Through the eyes of faith, the proof was seen in the action of the thousands of people who saw "others suffering and wanted to do whatever . . . they could to make a difference." Rev. Shelly recalled that even shipments of supplies and clothing from strangers far away brought an unspoken encouragement "that was worth more than what was in the boxes . . . ten times over."[12] Crosses and flags sprang from the rubble as both symbols of determination and as witnesses to the sacred value attached to feelings of connection to community and nation in the time of crisis.

There were flags, but there were also frustrations. Federal disaster recovery programs held the promise of financial relief in one hand, while spinning a web of bureaucratic red tape and indifference with the other. Yet, there was another reality. FEMA might stumble, but in the bodies of a countless army of volunteers, the nation reached beyond its flawed bureaucracies to assert its compassion and manifest a will to redeem a devastated region. The nation's compassion could not be doubted. It helped that President George W. Bush made 11 trips to the Gulf Coast in the 12 months after the storm.[13] This power, the power of simple human caring multiplied hundreds of thousands of times, propelled the personal recovery of countless thousands of Katrina's victims as they navigated through their darkest hours of loss.[14]

Beyond the personal, the removal of the debris presented a challenge of unimaginable proportions for the local officials who, under duress, had to make the complicated contracting decisions that got the ruins cleared away. In addition to the destruction of more than 65,000 Mississippi homes, the hurricane had destroyed dozens of public buildings and large portions of municipal water and sewer systems. Decades of public investment had been lost. The property tax base was laid low, leaving no local financial foundation for cleanup and reconstruction. The costs of clearing the 46 million cubic yards of destruction—let alone public infrastructure replacement—would have bankrupted Mississippi coastal towns and counties but for the federal aid promised in the Robert T. Stafford Disaster Relief and Emergency Assistance Act. The law reflected the generosity of the American people. Yet municipal and county officials also found themselves navigating complex federal regulations to avail their communities of the promised assistance. In the matter of disaster cleanup, harried local officials could either turn the whole problem over to FEMA and the Army Corps of Engineers, or they could bid the debris contracts themselves and seek FEMA reimbursements. The FEMA process demanded formal requests and specific state and federal project approvals.[15] In addition, the Stafford Act required state or local governments to "indemnify the Federal Government against any claim" of harm arising from removal of debris or wreckage on public and private property.[16]

From the start of the local response and recovery effort, the indemnity requirement created a nagging fear that far-off federal officials slavishly devoted to rules scripted for lesser disasters might at some later date withhold payment for local decisions taken in good faith at the height of the emergency. In the matter of debris contracts, the uncertainty about audits and reimbursements led the Jackson County Board of Supervisors and smaller Harrison County towns like Pass Christian to shy away from bidding out the work themselves.[17] They, along with every local entity in Hancock County, chose the Army Corps of Engineers and its "no-bid" contract with AshBritt Corporation of Pompano Beach, Florida. However, Harrison County and the larger cities of Gulfport and Biloxi decided to bid the debris removal jobs themselves. The larger local jurisdictions were confident in their abilities to handle the federal paperwork.

Privately, FEMA field officers urged the Harrison County Board of Supervisors to give the debris job to the Army Corps of Engineers. They pointed out that work done through the corps would free the county of any worries about audits and possible "de-obligation" and payback of federal funds if some deficiency in the contracting or documentation were later discovered. However, the desire to put local people to work plus the county's extensive experience with federal paperwork processes pulled the Harrison County board to a decision to bid their own debris contracts locally. The main Harrison County debris contract came in at $11 per cubic yard. The city of Biloxi, with a greater percentage of demolition debris, cut a deal for $15.89 per cubic yard.[18] Mississippi officials believed that they had gotten better rates by bidding out the work on their own.

In fact, these locally negotiated prices turned out to be a real bargain for taxpayers. Citing contractor objections to potential "competitive harm," the corps kept the details of its half-billion dollar contract with AshBritt shrouded in secrecy.[19] It took nine months of mounting political pressure before AshBritt officials revealed to Congress that the Army Corps of Engineers was paying the Florida company $23 per cubic yard for work done in Mississippi.[20] At the same time, the Mississippi Emergency Management Agency calculated that where cities and counties had bid out their own contracts they averaged $17 per cubic yard.[21] Those who believed local governments negotiating their own contracts could save the taxpayers money were indeed proven to be correct.

Congressional inquiries also confirmed that locally bid contracts were the best vehicles to put local people to work. When the corps awarded the AshBritt contract, company spokesman Randall Perkins had announced a plan to "hire 3,000 to 4,000 workers" through use of in-region subcontractors as part of a "good faith effort to include small and minority businesses."[22] Much press and congressional attention focused on the relationship between big prime contractors such as AshBritt and the multiple layers of low-paid subcontractors and laborers they employed. For the mass of small truckers and backhoe operators at the bottom of as many as five tiers of subcontractors, the pickings were slim. Tracy House, a 33-year-old trucker from Laurel, Mississippi, told the story of hiring on in mid-September at $3 per cubic yard working for an AshBritt subcontractor from North Carolina. Normally, House made his living hauling frozen chicken to East Coast outlets or transporting logs to the mills around Laurel. House had never done debris work, and even though the $3 per cubic yard he was offered looked like "just another guy's leftovers," he took the job thinking it might "open some doors" and give him an opportunity to expand his business. After working for a short time at $3 per cubic yard, House found another out-of-state AshBritt subcontractor who offered him $6 per cubic yard. House took the work. House and other local truckers were far down the line from the main contractor and earned only one-fourth the money the corps paid to AshBritt. However, the decals affixed to their trucks still carried the AshBritt name. Post-Katrina diesel prices of $3.29 per gallon meant that by Tracy House's own calculation he was barely breaking even at $6 per cubic yard—work for which AshBritt was collecting $23 per cubic yard.[23]

In mid-October, in an environment where neither AshBritt nor the corps would break the code of silence on the big Mississippi debris deal, the Associated Press unearthed a pattern of individual haulers being paid $6 to $8 per cubic yard and midlevel contractors earning $15 per cubic yard. This investigation showed that in arranging its Mississippi debris work, AshBritt had contracted with a North Carolina company named Byrd Brothers. Byrd Brothers in turn subcontracted with Natco Corporation of Bristol, Tennessee. Natco then hired the consultants who worked in the field to recruit low-paid haulers like Tracy House and others who lived in the Laurel area. Sometimes these local contractors then subcontracted with still smaller operators.[24]

These and similar reports led Congressman Bennie Thompson of Mississippi, the ranking Democrat on the House Homeland Security Committee, to describe the fate of small subcontractors like Tracy House as "sharecropping." "I am from Mississippi," Thompson said, and "I know sharecropping when I see it." The corps and the prime contractors themselves argued that the oversight they provided from checking skid tickets to inspecting trucks and sorting the refuse for recycle justified their arrangements with the poorly paid subcontractors at the bottom.[25] For Congressman Thompson, it appeared that the only way to keep small and minority businesses from being edged out was to "be aggressive about oversight."[26]

In a November hearing, Mississippi Congressman Chip Pickering echoed this concern when he complained about the tiny percentage of corps prime contracts that had gone to Mississippi companies.[27] Despite the often reaffirmed goal of putting local people to work, of the $3.7 billion in FEMA and Army Corps of Engineers contracts awarded through December of 2005, only $129 million (or 3.45 percent) had been awarded to companies headquartered Mississippi.[28] Through mid-October, Indiana businesses, for example, had garnered $587 million in contracts, or twice the combined value of all contracts won by companies in Alabama, Mississippi, and Louisiana—the storm-impacted states.[29]

Intense congressional criticism of the corps contracts had already resulted in a strong auditing regime for all Katrina-related work. Under renewed pressure, AshBritt promised the Army Corps of Engineers that it would work to eliminate some of its Mississippi contracting layers.[30] However, in February of 2006, the Mississippi congressional delegation produced evidence that the big Florida prime contractor was working behind the scenes in Washington to thwart a FEMA plan to reopen corps debris bidding in Mississippi. The FEMA re-bid plan was a response to political heat and part of the agency's newfound desire to give more work to small companies in the state. Various AshBritt appeals and delays indeed succeeded in stripping Gulfport's Necaise Brothers Construction of an April 2006 corps prime contract deal.[31] AshBritt's success in blocking the move to divide the corps contract attracted still more congressional scrutiny.

The various locally bid debris deals in Harrison County had sent prime contracts to such companies as Neel-Shaffer, Inc., of Jackson, Mississippi; W.G. Yates of Philadelphia, Mississippi; TCB Construction of Poplarville, Mississippi; Crowder-Gulf Joint Venture headquartered in the neighboring coastal town of Theodore, Alabama; as well as Necaise Brothers in Gulfport. The Mississippi counties and municipalities that worked through these locally bid contracts eliminated at least two layers of subcontractor tiering and came in at prices far below the corps deal with AshBritt.[32]

Locally hired cleanup crews also seemed to work with greater speed. In December of 2005, Harrison County had completed 57 percent of a job first estimated at more than 10 million cubic yards. On the other hand, in Jackson County, where the county and all of its municipalities had chosen to work through the corps and AshBritt, only 39 percent of the estimated debris work had been completed.[33] The constant threat that time would run out on 100 percent federal funding made the speed of the work a matter of unending local concern. Disaster-stricken communities knew that they were unable to pay their part of the 25 percent match that could be required whenever that federal clock should stop ticking. In late October, FEMA estimated that 13 million cubic yards of debris had been cleared away in Mississippi. However, 33 million cubic yards remained to be picked up. The threatened loss of federal support occasioned Governor Haley Barbour's first appeal to Washington for more time.[34] Thus, in late October, President Bush approved the first in what became a series of presidential deadline extensions granted over the next two years. Still, without knowing the disposition of any particular time-extension appeal, local officials felt constantly pressured to get things done quickly lest they lose federal support for their efforts.

Differences in approach and decision making sped up the work on locally bid contracts. In Biloxi, for example, working with their own contractor, the city condemned entire neighborhoods. Unless a property owner filed a protest, debris crews moved onto private property and demolished condemned structures and removed storm refuse. By December, Biloxi had removed 740 homes in three condemned neighborhoods. Some Biloxi residents objected to the abbreviated process, but to Mayor Holloway, the speedy clearance of condemned properties was justified as a public health and safety measure and because it meant a faster return to normalcy.[35] In contrast, only 25 condemned residences had been cleared in Pascagoula under an Army Corps of Engineers contract. The corps required a house-by-house approach, rather than the neighborhood-by-neighborhood basis that Biloxi had implemented. It took the federal agency weeks to decide on the wording of the release it required individual home owners to sign before a structure could be torn down. Once the form got to its proper wording, new demands for measurements and GPS locations for each house arose to clog the wheels of the agency. Then, the EPA convinced the corps to require demolition contractors to open, sanitize, and remove Freon from refrigerators before each demolition.[36]

Manly Barton, the president of the Jackson County Board of Supervisors, complained that there were "so many levels of approvals" in the corps approach "that nobody seemed to be able to make a decision and get things done." Local government could do nothing to change the process or the priorities behind it. As corps approval processes grew more cumbersome, the speed of cleanup in Jackson County slowed from 75,000 cubic yards per day to a mere 12,000 cubic yards a day. Contemplating the threatened ending of 100 percent federal reimbursement, county board member Frank Leach could not help but believe that "something [was] very wrong here." As Leach saw it, "Our federal government is paying an extraordinary amount of money for services that are not being performed adequately." Nevertheless, there were those who defended the corps house-by-house approach. Some valued the extra time in their dealings with insurance agents and adjusters. However, in December of 2005, uncertainty over exactly when 100 percent federal reimbursement might end, together with the apparent speed of the Harrison County cleanup, prompted the Jackson County Board of Supervisors to terminate their deal with the corps and AshBritt.[37]

It took four months for Jackson County to declare that it wanted no more debris dealings with the Army Corps of Engineers. However, on the national level, controversy had enveloped the big corps' no-bid contract almost as soon as the first dump trucks rolled down Mississippi streets. On September 15, after an abbreviated three-day competition, the Army Corps of Engineers had hired four politically well-connected companies to remove debris in Mississippi and Louisiana. Each contract was worth up to $500 million with an option for another $500 million deal. With only three days' notice, instead of the usual 30-day period, 22 companies had managed to submit proposals.[38] Two of the companies selected were headquartered in Florida, one in Minnesota, and one in California. In awarding the big Mississippi contract to AshBritt, the corps had passed over the lone Mississippi company to place a bid. The day the AshBritt contract was announced, *USA Today* carried a troubling article questioning all of the abbreviated-competition or no-bid contracts. Noting that it was "routine for government agencies to award non-competitive contracts for emergency work" to speed recovery operations, the article focused on an emergency housing contract which had been awarded to a California company previously fined for padding its bills on federal work.[39] Danielle Brian, executive director of the watchdog Project on Government Oversight, characterized this and other so-called no-bid contracts as "an invitation to major defense and homeland security contractors to loot the federal treasury." Criticism of the corps' AshBritt deal in Mississippi soon followed. Rep. Henry Waxman, the ranking Democrat on the U.S. House Government Reform Committee, raised immediate complaints that under the Bush administration, the value of no-bid contracts had "skyrocketed." Waxman also expressed alarm about the administration's outsourcing of the oversight of many federal contracts to private companies "with blatant conflicts of interest" such that when federal auditors identified abuses "their recommendations [were] often ignored."[40] The next day, Senator Joe Lieberman and Senator Susan Collins, the ranking Democratic and Republican members of the U.S. Senate Homeland Security and Governmental Affairs Committee, announced a bill to "expand the role" of the Special Inspector General for Iraq Reconstruction to include oversight of Katrina recovery. They aimed to get strict accounting procedures applied as quickly as possible to the looming federal Katrina spending.[41] Simultaneously, legislation authorizing the hiring of more FEMA inspectors general moved forward in the Republican-controlled House of Representatives.[42] Anger over the administration's early mishandling of Iraq War spending was now transferred to Katrina. Distrust and rancor charged the Washington political atmosphere. Inevitably all of this was translated into more checks and balances, more appeals, and more paperwork for crisis-weary local officials. Thus, over the next several years, counties and municipalities that had chosen to bid their own debris contracts came to respect and dread the phrase "FEMA Inspector General."

The corps' AshBritt contract for Mississippi drew particular scrutiny. Early on, experienced hurricane recovery experts joined various Washington watchdog groups in denouncing the AshBritt deal as unreasonably expensive. Troubling questions arose from the fact that AshBritt was a client of Barbour, Griffith, and Rogers, the Washington lobbying firm founded by Mississippi Governor Haley Barbour. Congressional sources noted that in early 2005, AshBritt paid Barbour, Griffith, and Rogers $40,000 specifically to help the Florida company secure Army Corps of Engineers contracts.[43] Barbour himself maintained that when he took office as Mississippi's governor in 2004, he had put his assets into a "blind trust" and cut his ties with his former lobbying firm.[44] The blind trust kept the sources of Barbour's $25,000 per month in private income secret. Thus, it could not be determined whether the Mississippi governor was on a fixed pension or actually profiting from shares in the Barbour, Griffith, and Rogers firm or its parent company, the Interpublic Group. Though the Mississippi Ethics Commission had accepted Barbour's financial arrangements, the Barbour trust device was assailed because it did not meet the more exacting disclosure standards required of federal officeholders who use such instruments. As a result, no less a conservative columnist than Mississippi's Charlie Mitchell of the *Vicksburg Post* wondered publically, "Is Barbour Profiting from Katrina?" Mitchell asserted that he was posing a question "that has a simple verifiable answer." Nonetheless, because the terms of the trust were held confidential, no answer had appeared. Thus, using a southern colloquialism, Mitchell quipped that in the matter of whether the governor profited from Katrina, "it's a secret, son, it's a secret."[45] Impervious to the pressure, Barbour refused to make public the specific sources of his private income, and he refused to appease critics through release of his income tax returns. He did not change his stance during his 2007 reelection campaign.[46] The secrecy surrounding AshBritt's Army Corps of Engineers contract acted in tandem with the governor's refusal to disclose his own finances to further gin up suspicions.

The controversy impacted Barbour's former business associates, and it brought increased federal attention to all Mississippi contracts and contractors. In its October 24, 2005, issue, *Roll Call*, the influential Capitol Hill publication, noted that "the sensitivity of Barbour's position" had led his old lobbying firm to stop accepting new business from companies seeking Katrina-related contracts. The governor's old firm did, however, continue its work for The Southern Company, the parent company of Mississippi Power. The AshBritt contract in Mississippi attracted more attention when it became known that the company had hired former Mississippi Republican Congressman Mike Parker to beef up its lobbying effort just two days after Katrina struck. Still more doubt arose from the fact that Parker himself was a former Army Corps of Engineers official.[47]

Barbour's supporters claimed that this was all a case of smoke without fire. Passage of time supported their assertions. Through five years of tight audits under two federal administrations, no investigator filed any formal charges of wrongdoing in these matters. Nonetheless, the smoke plumes of suspicion surrounding the AshBritt deal brought additional heat to bear on all Mississippi contracts and contractors. Congressional irritation at AshBritt's early refusals to disclose the details of its Mississippi contract prompted Jean Todd, the federal contracting officer who oversaw the deal, to assert her determination to ensure fair pricing. Moreover, Todd felt compelled to promise publicly that "we have auditors that will be looking at all of this."[48] Media critics were not appeased. On September 28, the *St. Louis Post-Dispatch* published an editorial associating the Mississippi AshBritt deal with the corrupt image of the Huey Long era in Louisiana. The editorialist warned that America was now being threatened with a "Category 5 hurricane of peculation" in the gulf.[49] Cries of "crony capitalism"[50] and revelations that AshBritt CEO Randall Perkins and his wife, Sally, had given tens of thousands of dollars to the Republican National Committee further clouded the issue.[51] It was little wonder that at the end of the first week in October, Michael Jackson, the deputy secretary of Homeland Security, told House members that he now favored rebidding the no-bid contracts.[52] At the same time, Homeland Security Inspector General Richard Skinner told a House subcommittee that reviewing the Mississippi debris contracts was now "high on our priority list."[53] The heat was now on, and the pledge of rigorous audits was indeed one pledge that federal agencies kept.

Across the Mississippi Gulf Coast, debris contract decisions had to be made long before the federal furor erupted. Even so, there were early signs that suggested caution. For Harrison County board member Marlin Ladner, the thing that was "most curious" about FEMA in its relationship with local officials was the refusal of FEMA field representatives to take a public position on the appropriateness of any locally bid contract. Ladner recalled a board meeting in which he attempted to get the FEMA debris specialist to give prior approval for a county contract proposal. Ladner asked point-blank, "Is this okay; are these prices right?" The FEMA representative's response typified much that frustrated local officials. "I'm here to advise you that the ultimate decision is yours," he said. In Ladner's view it was a polite way of telling the Harrison County board, "I'm not going to tell you if your decision is right or wrong, and we're *definitely* not going to give you anything in writing telling you that this is okay." Thus, the Harrison County Board of Supervisors and other local governments had to make huge financial decisions with no prior assurance that they would pass muster in the FEMA inspector general's final accounting. Moreover, they were informed that FEMA might initially pay the bill and then later "de-obligate," or force disaster-ravaged communities to pay it all back. Thirty-two percent (14.5 million cubic yards)[54] of Mississippi's 46 million cubic yards of debris lay on the ground in Harrison County. In this one county various debris contracts would eventually total almost $260 million—a figure well beyond anything the local tax base could pay.[55]

Even so, Harrison County and many other local governments had decided to bypass the Army Corps of Engineers and hire their own contractors. Monies were borrowed. Invoices were paid. Reimbursement requests were then sent forward to FEMA through the Mississippi Emergency Management Agency. Without knowing the intensity of the Washington political debate over the Mississippi and Louisiana Katrina contracting, local officials operating in good faith had every reason to believe that the federal government would pay for this essential part of the disaster recovery work.[56]

The city of Biloxi was one of the first jurisdictions to feel the heat from the Washington contract furor. In Biloxi, Mayor A. J. Holloway had actually taken pre–storm season bids on a so-called "push contract." The push contract was limited to clearing the main streets in the first 72 hours after a storm so that emergency vehicles could get in for search and rescue. The intent was to lock in a predisaster price-per-cubic-yard agreement and thus avoid crisis-driven decision making. By the time Katrina struck, Biloxi had taken bids and selected a company, but a formal contract had not been signed. In the immediate aftermath of the storm, when faced with the destruction of 6,000 of Biloxi's 25,000 homes and businesses, the mayor believed that critical search and rescue issues made it imperative that he move immediately on the push contract.[57] However, when the two prestorm low bidders attempted to add fuel surcharges to their original proposals, the mayor sent them packing and quickly found a third company willing to do the work at the prestorm low-bid price. The mayor thought he had done due diligence and driven a hard bargain. Biloxi's 72-hour push contract went to W. G. Yates Construction Company of Philadelphia, Mississippi.[58] City officials were confident that their previous experience with FEMA's recordkeeping requirements would mean that they could withstand any audits.[59]

Months later, to the veteran mayor's surprise, FEMA rejected Biloxi's reimbursement request. There was no question that push contracts were eligible under the Stafford Act, and the prices were not in dispute. However, in the crisis rush to get things moving in East Biloxi, there was apparently a procedural misunderstanding. Not one to bite the hand that feeds, Mayor Holloway was reluctant to criticize FEMA and MEMA. After all, the federal funding which these agencies oversaw played an essential role in the overall recovery effort. Still, the Biloxi mayor could not understand why state and federal authorities ruled that Biloxi's first push contract was "not eligible" for federal reimbursement. There had been a dire need. At the time, there was only one FEMA representative for the entire county, and Biloxi had done its best to negotiate a fair deal even as the city operated under extreme duress. Biloxi entered an appeal, and the mayor known for his "economy of words" went personally to lay out the case. In a meeting with FEMA and MEMA representatives Holloway explained how the contractor was employed and again presented copies of the city's proof of payment. Biloxi's appeal was eventually successful, and FEMA paid the cost of that initial push contract. However, this defense of the city in what amounted to a procedural dispute had cost the mayor and his staff time and effort that was much needed for other pressing recovery issues.[60]

A year and a half after the storm, 24 other Mississippi cities and counties found the FEMA inspector general's office questioning their locally bid contracts and threatening to force return of portions of reimbursements already paid. One of these entities was Jones County, located 100 miles inland from Biloxi. In the immediate aftermath of Katrina, the Jones County Board of Supervisors had exercised the option to bid their own debris work. At $27 per cubic yard, the bid seemed high, but according to County Administrator Charles Miller, Jones County officials had consulted a FEMA representative before accepting the contract. According to Miller, the FEMA representative had stated that under the circumstances the price was reasonable. At the time, the terms of the Army Corps of Engineers' $500 million agreement with AshBritt were being kept secret. Months later, after averaging all of the locally bid contracts in the state, federal auditors agreed that up to $19.95 per cubic yard was now to be considered "the reasonable" rate. Good faith local decisions made in a time of crisis were now second-guessed. Federal agencies showed their diligence, at least where smaller, locally bid contracts were concerned. Ex post facto standards now applied. As a result, FEMA served Jones County with notice that $2 million of $9 million in its federal debris-removal reimbursements might have to be repaid. County officials were shocked. As Miller put it, "Had we known at the time that the price was too high, we would, of course, have rebid it." By May of 2007, some 20 percent of the locally bid debris contracts in Mississippi were called into question. Citing consultations with FEMA at the time of the contract, Jones County board member Andy Dial felt betrayed. "It's ridiculous," he said. "When you make a promise to help, I think you ought to keep your end of the bargain." The Mississippi Emergency Management Agency supported Jones County in an appeal. Unfortunately, the state could not buy back the time and effort the county was forced to spend on the appeal.[61]

A much larger dispute loomed for the Harrison County Board of Supervisors. With almost one-third of the state's Katrina debris load, Harrison County had the largest debris problem. When the Harrison County Board of Supervisors elected to bid its debris contracts locally, they well understood that in the matter of debris and all other federal "public assistance" projects, vast documentation was required. In Harrison County, the job of maintaining that paper trail fell on the shoulders of County Administrator

Pam Ulrich. Well schooled in FEMA's "project worksheet" culture, Ulrich was in the county courthouse keeping the paperwork current "from the time the winds died down," and she did not leave the office for two weeks after the storm. She ate at work. She slept at work, and her family kept her in clean clothes. Her bosses thought Pam Ulrich was extraordinarily meticulous. There was no hope of FEMA reimbursement without the kind of devotion to documentation that people like Pam Ulrich brought to the job. Board president Connie Rockco recalled seeing assembled in the county administrator's office a stack of paperwork three feet deep that related to tree removal on a single road.[62] All of this care meant that there were no problems with the main parts of the huge Harrison County debris contract. However, the county wound up in a $12 million, four-year dispute with FEMA over reimbursement for work done clearing away some 38,000 unsafe trees—so-called "leaners and hangers"—which the storm left dangling or slanting precariously over some 780 miles of county roadways.[63]

For the hazardous tree contract, Harrison County hired TCB Construction of Poplarville and also engaged an experienced monitoring company, Florida-based R. W. Beck Disaster Recovery, to handle documentation. Only trees with a 45-degree or greater lean or limbs actually dangling over the right-of-way could be removed. Each of the 38,000 trees or limbs removed was photographed, and its exact GPS location recorded for later verification.[64] Months later, in the summer of 2006, when FEMA's audit process turned to Harrison County, a tangled knot presented itself. In the initial federal auditing sample, FEMA inspectors claimed that they were unable to locate two-thirds of the stumps and trees which the county had paid to have removed. Under these circumstances, $17 million in federal reimbursements were withheld while the discrepancies were probed. Nearly a year later, in May of 2007, federal officials publically announced that they would not reimburse the county for $12 million worth of the work done on the tree contract. Federal documents cited high costs, insufficient quality control, and inadequate documentation for the work.[65] These charges called into question the integrity of both the tree contractor and the monitoring company. With millions of dollars riding on the outcome, the accusations set up an immediate adversarial atmosphere. The lapse of time between tree removals and audits could have accounted for the disappearance of some stumps due to overgrowth, fire, rot, or property owner stump grinding. However, such actions were unlikely to account for the FEMA claim that in its samples taken on a dozen county roads, two-thirds of the stumps could not be found.[66]

Connie Rockco, the county board president at the time, recalled that the basis for one FEMA complaint arose from work done on a county route called Allen Road. The auditors had randomly pulled Allen Road without realizing that there were actually three different thoroughfares called Allen Road under county jurisdiction and two additional streets of the same name within the municipalities of Long Beach and Biloxi. In questioning, it became apparent that the federal inspectors did not visit each Allen Road. They had been unaware that there were three such routes, and did not know which route they had actually examined.[67] On closer review, it was also demonstrated that federal auditors had not understood TCB's practice of ticketing major thoroughfares with work also done on off-shooting side streets as well as the route actually named on the document. Fortunately, the monitoring company had photographed and taken GPS locations for each of the more than 30,000 trees that were cut. Thus, repeat audits showed that 98 percent of the trees removed could actually be identified.[68]

However, as multiple audits supported the county view that its tree counts were accurate, "reasonable costs" became the larger area of dispute. In the county board meeting in which the tree contract was approved, Supervisor Marlin Ladner remembered personally questioning the FEMA debris advisor on the cost formula. FEMA's man-on-the-spot had been evasive in his answer, but according to Ladner, he had given the board absolutely no indication of any problem. Nonetheless, months later after money had been borrowed and the work completed, FEMA auditors called into question the contract's provision of a single price per tree regardless of the size of the tree. Harrison County's price per tree included the cost of hauling the trees off. FEMA's auditors missed this point in their initial dispute with the county, as they inexplicably assumed that they would find an additional charge for hauling. There was no such additional charge. Still, the dispute continued over whether the overall cost of the contract was "reasonable." FEMA alleged that on average the TCB charge of $390 per tree was "excessive." This round of questioning put reimbursement for $11.8 million of a $19 million contract into jeopardy. The potential requirement that the county "pay back" nearly $12 million in federal funds would be a heavy hit for a locality in which a major portion of the ad valorem tax base had been destroyed.[69]

The county engaged local attorney Tim Holleman to appeal its case. When Holleman sought to compare the Harrison County tree removal charges to the price paid to AshBritt under the Army Corps of Engineers contract, he found that even two years after the fact, the corps still claimed that the contracts were privileged and that release of the information would constitute a breach of confidentiality. In congressional testimony, AshBritt had only released its price per cubic yard for ordinary debris removal. It did not release details of its tree contract. If it did not quite take an act of Congress to get the county the information needed to defend itself, it did take the employment of a statistical research firm, CRA International of Washington, D.C. The CRA statistical study demonstrated that TCB Construction's charges actually fell below the prevailing regional tree removal rate. Working through Congressman Gene Taylor's office, county officials gathered information indicating that the TCB price was also below AshBritt's charges to the corps for similar work.[70]

The appeals process involved multiple audits and multiple submissions of voluminous paperwork that was sometimes lost and had to be resubmitted, and the process involved multiple trips to Washington. Meanwhile, the county held up $6 million in payments to TCB. All that company president Jennifer Fagan could do was "hope that it [would] all work out." Four years after Katrina, the Harrison County Board of Supervisors still did not know whether, or how much, the county might have to repay the federal government for work done in good faith in a time of crisis. County officials were confident that in bidding debris contracts locally they had saved the federal taxpayers significant sums of money. However, the time and effort consumed in audits and appeals made them wonder if saving federal taxpayers money really served the best interests of the disaster victims themselves, who were federal taxpayers but also taxpayers in Harrison County.[71]

In the spring of 2008, on her eighth trip to Washington, Connie Rockco pointed out to FEMA auditors that county governments "run on taxpayers' money just like FEMA does." Rockco asked a simple question: "If a contractor submitted claims illegally, why not just indict *them*, rather than make the citizens of Harrison County, after all we have gone through, take another hit" from the federal government because of something a contractor did wrong? In Rockco's view, going back on county decisions taken in good faith at the height of a federal emergency amounted to punishing the victims rather than going after the perpetrators of fraud.[72] In their press for accountability, federal auditors were somehow unable to take account of the extreme circumstances in which local cleanup contracts had been executed. Whether intended or not, the combination created a Catch-22 for exhausted local officials.

For the tens of thousands of storm victims who had lost everything, the struggle over contracts seemed only a distant drum beat. After all, it was the actual clearing of the massive wreckage that gave victims their first tangible indicator that recovery was under way. For individuals it meant saying final good-byes to the ruined reminders of life prior to Katrina. Like many other Katrina victims, Yvette Gonzales, a 76-year-old widow in Bay St. Louis, wanted to be present when the remains of her home were hauled away. Her hopes that the demolition crews would find an heirloom handmade quilt were disappointed. Still, even in this final moment of disappointment, Mrs. Gonzales was surprised by joy. Working under contracts that had drawn such heated debate in Washington, crewmen employed by an unknown contractor found the miniature bride and groom statue from her 1949 wedding cake. Political furor could not detract from the moment in which a kind-hearted stranger handed a widow such a memento. A *New York Times* reporter recorded the encounter. "It brings it all back," the widow said. "It makes you remember those good times."[73]

On the individual level, there was much to be grateful for and much to celebrate. Early predictions that removal of the storm wreckage might take from 18 months to five years were proven wrong. In September of 2006, six months ahead of its own initial time estimates, the Army Corps of Engineers announced the completion of land-based debris removal in Mississippi. In the perverse dealings of Mother Nature, the leveling of so many Mississippi Gulf Coast structures in the 30-foot Katrina tidal surge had opened the way for unexpected speed in the cleanup. A year after Katrina, much heartbreaking work still remained in New Orleans, where the structural soundness and demolition of tens of thousands of homes that had for weeks stood in floodwater had yet to be determined. In Mississippi, however, pride could be taken in the fact that the 46-million-cubic-yard volume of storm wreckage had been reduced such that only 10 percent of the state's prestorm landfill capacity had to be devoted to Katrina debris. Lesser but more difficult work in Mississippi's wetlands, marshes, and navigable waterways was finished by the end of 2008.[74] All of this meant that an important corner had been turned in the recovery. Storm victims could rebuild and get on with their lives. But for those local officials who had stepped up to the plate in the chaos of the Katrina aftermath to make the hard decisions about debris contracts, the celebrations of success were muted. The Washington hullabaloo over the well-connected businesses and lobbying firms behind Army Corps of Engineers contracting had produced a federal bureaucratic backlash of intensified audits. In a curious twist, the energies arising from heated questions about the actions of powerful men in the nation's capitol had been deflected onto the small actors and ordinary citizens at the periphery where atonement was exacted for the suspected sins of the mighty. For many of the jurisdictions that opted to bid the debris contracts on their own, the time and energy later taken up in audits and appeals to unsympathetic functionaries far removed from the destruction called into question the wisdom of trying to save public money through normal local competitive bidding processes. The nation, through the generosity of the Stafford Act, had provided essential recovery funding. However, there was no free grace in the bureaucratic scheme of redemption. Where grace abounded, it was more likely to be seen in sympathetic neighbors or in the hearts of those who came from afar to work as volunteers.

Chapter Six

The Grace of Volunteers

Aside from the respect, even fear, that Katrina taught us, there were positive lessons. Perhaps the chief of these was a new sense of perspective and gratefulness. . . . [which] has led us to profoundly understand our dependence on others.

—STAN TINER

Editor, *Sun Herald*[1]

The bedrock of recovery lies in the passion and compassion of citizens helping each other and their communities.

—DAVID EISNER

Corporation for National and Community Service[2]

Hurricane Katrina drove Biloxi City Councilman Bill Stallworth and many other more hardened souls to prayer. It was not easy for an elected official to face thousands of threadbare, suddenly homeless constituents when there were no real answers about how their survival needs were going to be met. Almost every home in Stallworth's East Biloxi city council ward had flooded, and in this one section of town 3,000 houses were totally destroyed. FEMA's logistics failure meant that storm survivors in this impoverished, mainly African American and Vietnamese neighborhood were thrown onto their own resources for days on end. The improvised soup kitchen at Main Street Baptist Church cooked whatever could be scavenged from stores and seafood processors. The burden of not knowing how, when, or if relief would find its way to this impoverished area weighed heavily on Biloxi's only black elected official. There was no doubt in Bill Stallworth's mind that the thousands of volunteers who soon stepped into the breach were an answer to prayer.[3]

Bill Stallworth was 51 years old when Katrina struck. As he grew up, his father had been a pastor in the African Methodist Episcopal Church. Stallworth finished college, and before being elected to the city council, he had worked several public service jobs including a stint as a grant writer at the Joint Center for Political and Economic Studies in Washington, D.C., following which he had served as a Biloxi business relocation officer. Later he worked as the city's personnel director. Along the way, he started several small businesses, including a computer company, and he did small business consulting as well. However, tough personal experiences with divorce and a failed bid to become mayor of Biloxi had given Bill Stallworth a taste of life's disappointments. Somewhere along the way, as Stallworth put it, "God and I had a falling out," and "looking at the human condition . . . I [had become] absolutely cynical about people."[4]

Yet, in the midst of the human tragedies that surrounded him in the days immediately after Katrina, Bill Stallworth found himself praying hard—"I mean constant prayer," he said. In their desperation, people brought life-and-death requests to him—a generator for an oxygen machine, critical medicine, or some special piece of equipment—needs that a city councilman had no way of supplying. Faced with such urgent and seemingly hopeless solicitations he had often thought, "Lord, what am I going to do?" as he breathed a prayer for some vulnerable person in dire straits. Time and again he heard a knock at the door or was approached in parking lots by volunteers offering the very items he had despaired of being able to find. A hardened city councilman was certain that he saw prayers answered from the hands of volunteers from all across the nation. He had seen volunteers with willing hearts provide life-saving medical services and deliver food and water before FEMA or the Red Cross could get their acts together. Unbidden, they had pushed putrid mud out of houses, carried mold-covered, foul-smelling furniture to the street, and ripped out ruined Sheetrock by the ton. When asked why they had come, their answers were invariably simple. Stallworth recalled that most often "they just said, 'we had to come,' or '[our] spirit couldn't be still.'" In other words, "they just literally had to come." Looking back, Bill Stallworth was convinced that the volunteers who came by the hundreds of thousands had "provided an opportunity for God not only to show up, but to show out." In that desperate situation, he avowed that "the God in them came through."[5]

Before the last battering waves of Hurricane Katrina crashed onto the Mississippi Gulf Coast on August 29, 2005, out of the goodness of their hearts, ordinary people across the United States mobilized. Sometimes one by one, sometimes two by two, sometimes working through established charities and faith-based organizations, volunteers began organizing the first of thousands of aid missions to Katrina's ground zero on the Mississippi Gulf Coast. Over the next four years, FEMA and the Mississippi Commission for Volunteer Service estimated that as many as 1,000 different organizations and church groups with more than 800,000 volunteers came to the aid of Mississippi's storm victims and provided an estimated 18.2 million hours of free labor in the relief and recovery efforts.[6]

Far away in Ohio, marriage and family therapist Alise Bartley of Akron and emergency room nurse Wendy Frost from Findlay had separately followed national news reports of Katrina's march through the Gulf of Mexico, little thinking that the storm would impact their lives. Storms on the Gulf Coast were commonplace, they thought, and people there knew how to handle them. As a married mental health professional with four children, Bartley couldn't imagine being needed in the aftermath of a hurricane. For nurse Wendy Frost, with a husband and four children from ages six to seventeen, volunteer work far from home was not even a thought in her mind. Neither Frost nor Bartley had ever done disaster volunteer work. Yet, within weeks of the storm both Wendy Frost and Alise Bartley found themselves bunking at the U.S. Naval Construction Battalion Base in Gulfport in a large warehouse that had been equipped with over 1,200 cots closely packed to accommodate Red Cross volunteers from throughout the nation.[7]

For Alise Bartley, the sojourn to volunteer relief work in Mississippi began when she saw and heard stories of "the deplorable conditions" with which storm victims contended. As Bartley described it, "I felt a pain in my gut that I knew I could not ignore." The pain went away when she registered with the American Association of Marriage and Family Therapists as an available volunteer. Many days went by with no news about whether she would be needed, but as she saw it, she had done what she had to do, and the matter was beyond her control. When finally the Red Cross called to ask for her services on the Mississippi Gulf Coast, Alise Bartley was filled with anxiety and doubt about leaving her family and professional responsibilities. It would have been easy to say no, but for "that familiar pain" in her gut that returned "stronger than ever." So, she kept her commitment and prepared to deploy to the Gulf Coast on a Sunday afternoon flight. Bartley decided to attend church that morning and "cried almost the entire service without knowing why." In her words, "I believed I was being 'called' to help." She put aside her trepidations and let compassion put her on that plane headed south into the disaster zone.[8]

For Wendy Frost, "the call" that brought her to Mississippi came audibly and directly—from the mouths of her children. They had seen their mom finish nursing school and gain various advanced R.N. certifications. The children were proud of her emergency room work, and as they sat at home in Findlay, Ohio, watching television reports of the disaster, they said, "You know, Mom, you're a nurse, and you really do have to go. Those people need you."[9] The outpouring of the kind of compassion that sent Frost and Bartley to Mississippi moved Councilman Stallworth to start calling his encounters with volunteers "divine appointments."[10]

Stallworth had his first "divine appointment" at the Main Street Baptist Church soup kitchen where a day or two after the storm he ran across two men clad in jeans who said they were from a relief group called Oxfam America. One was a Scot, Kenny Ray, who spoke with a thick Scottish accent. With him was a young Hispanic man named Alejandro. They were clearly out of place, but they announced that they were looking for a way to help. They said they could get money for food and supplies, but they needed a point of contact, an organization to plug into. The councilman had never heard of Oxfam, and part of his mind wondered if they were just wasting his time. But he had prayed for help, and something within him said, "Don't blow them off. Just listen." From this encounter came an immediate $10,000 donation to Main Street Baptist Church to keep the soup kitchen going and an additional $10,000 Oxfam donation to purchase the generators, computers, folding tables, and chairs that got the East Biloxi Coordination, Relief, and Redevelopment Agency (popularly known as Hope Coordination Center) off the ground. Stallworth soon became the full-time director of the Hope Coordination Center. Over the next several years this agency worked to prioritize and coordinate the work done by the thousands of volunteers who gave their time in hard-hit East Biloxi. In the selfless work of these volunteers, a tough elected official thought he had come to a new and very personal understanding of "the real meaning of what God is about." For Bill Stallworth, when a desperate neighborhood seemed to have no resources and no way of getting any, "God stepped in, and He provided."[11]

Stallworth's East Biloxi colleague, Councilman George Lawrence, whose own home on First Street had been scoured from its foundations, found himself running constituent services from his FEMA trailer at all hours of the day and night. In normal times city councilmen do not arrange housecleaning or make medical appointments for the people they represent. However, Katrina changed that. Thus when a group of freelance Kentucky volunteers showed up at his trailer, George Lawrence found himself arranging cleanup help for his constituents, and he worked with Sarah Hamilton, a nurse with Hands-On Gulf Coast, to coordinate volunteer nursing visits in his neighborhood. Lawrence believed that the volunteers had often provided the "glimmer of hope" that allowed people to face their losses and come back home to salvage or rebuild.[12]

Sometimes the volunteers who came had a local connection, but far more often the Mississippi Gulf Coast benefited from the kindness of strangers. Moreover, that kindness knew no national boundaries. Johan Jaffry of Pontlevoy, France, was visiting a friend in Indiana when Hurricane Katrina struck. Pontlevoy is a small village in the Loire Valley south of Paris. Hurricanes were unknown to him in Europe. With some English language skills and a little money, Jaffry decided to travel to Mississippi and help in any way possible. David Romero, a friend who had been stationed in Biloxi when he was in the United States Air Force, accompanied Jaffry. Unbidden, the two men headed south with two trucks and a trailer filled with donations collected from various businesses in Indiana. Jaffry and Romero had no idea what to expect. Upon their arrival in the ravaged Mississippi disaster zone, the men could not find words in either language, French or English, that were adequate to describe the devastation. They only knew that they had two good hands and a desire to help people in need. After making their aid delivery, Jaffry and Romero worked at a relief center located at the old Biloxi Community Center. Here they distributed food, clothing, and medicine and gave storm victims assistance in completing paperwork for various relief agencies. On average, the center helped approximately 800 people a day in the first few critical weeks after August 29. Jaffry was deeply touched by the many individuals he encountered who had lost everything. He left the area certain that he would never forget his weeks in Mississippi.[13]

Many volunteers like Romero and Jaffry came on their own. Others were connected with colleges or church groups who relied on local organizers like Bill Stallworth to direct and help prioritize their efforts. Others came through the efforts of well-known national organizations. By whatever means that brought them, as David Eisner, the chief executive officer for the Corporation for National and Community Service stated, their "passion and compassion" provided "the bedrock of recovery."[14]

The contributions of the volunteers were multifaceted. Some sent provisions and supplies. Hundreds of thousands came personally to give helping hands; still others provided monetary resources. In the latter category, the heartfelt giving of the tiny 15-member congregation of Enon Methodist Church in Carroll County, Mississippi, illustrates the spirit of many small organizations and churches across the country. Located in northwest Mississippi some 225 miles from the coast, Carroll County is one of Mississippi's economically poorer counties. Nonetheless, immediately after Katrina struck, the members at Enon church dug into their limited resources and voted to donate $1,000 to a Hurricane Katrina relief fund.[15] That a 15-member congregation in such an impoverished corner of the state would make such a large donation might have seemed surprising but for the fact that prior to Katrina, the IRS had ranked Mississippians highest in the nation in the percentage of income given in charitable contributions.[16]

Still, the means available within the poorest state in the union by themselves would have been woefully inadequate to meet the challenge of Katrina. Fortunately, all across the country countless groups collected and sent donations. In so doing, little Enon Methodist Church and thousands of others took part in what became a massive relief effort that mobilized whole armies of compassion. The U.S. Government Accountability Office reported that in the first three months after Katrina, charities across the nation had raised more than $2.5 billion for aid to storm survivors in the four states impacted by Hurricane Katrina and Hurricane Rita. In that 90-day period, the Red Cross had raised more than half of that total ($1.5 billion), and the Salvation Army raised the second highest amount, $270 million. The Bush-Clinton Katrina Fund and Catholic Charities, with the third and fourth highest totals, had each raised $100 million.[17] Moreover, in a gratifying display of international generosity, the Emir of Qatar, Sheikh Hamad bin Khalifa Al-Thani, donated $100 million for various Mississippi Gulf Coast recovery projects including Habitat for Humanity, the Boys and Girls Clubs, and medical services for uninsured storm victims.[18]

Two years after the storm a local survey of nonprofit and corporate giving found that at least $1.5 billion of the massive outpouring of private charitable giving had made its way into Mississippi.[19] This figure was thought to be a conservative estimate because Red Cross spending was not tracked state by state, and many church-to-church donations could not be tracked. During the same two-year period, the federal government had disbursed more than $5.8 billion in Mississippi for housing, personal assistance, debris removal, and repair to various public facilities, roads, and utilities in the state. Of this latter figure, $2.4 billion had come to Mississippians through FEMA's National Flood Insurance Program.[20]

As shown by the leading role of the Red Cross in disaster fund-raising, and as seen in the cases of Wendy Frost and Alise Bartley, once the American Red Cross found its legs and got ramped up, it was a tremendous conduit of dedicated and idealistic volunteers for the Mississippi Gulf Coast. A Red Cross contingency of 20,447 staff and trained volunteers brought their special brand of aid and comfort to Mississippians.[21] Red Cross volunteers working in Mississippi represented all 50 states, Puerto Rico, and the Virgin Islands.[22] The grit and determination of these Red Cross volunteers cannot be doubted. Judith Lowe, a resident of Long Beach, Mississippi, and a reserve Red Cross disaster administrator, lost her own home in Katrina. Nonetheless, just days after the storm, she accepted responsibility for working the in-processing and out-processing office for Mississippi Gulf Coast Red Cross volunteers. As Lowe described the agency's process, while the Red Cross does not put temporary disaster workers on salary, the agency typically provides its volunteers with plane tickets and a modest daily expense allowance for food, laundry, and personal incidentals connected with their deployment away from home.[23]

The Red Cross Mississippi Katrina response worked under the concept of "centralization with outreach." It created and manned a center of operations and then fanned out in all directions from that main complex. Smaller units of volunteers and staffers drove out daily from the central headquarters in order to reach as many people as possible in the disaster area. Volunteers quickly discovered that some people in dire need were too proud to present themselves at relief centers to ask for help, and others lacked transportation. Once the Red Cross storm shelters closed, the outreach aspect of Red Cross work was a vital part of the recovery. Each individual sortie carried supplies to meet storm victims' needs. In personal encounters with those being served, medical and health problems were noted, and medicines and medical personnel were sent to follow up. As summer gave way to fall and winter, hundreds of vulnerable people found themselves still living in tents and in need of blankets. Red Cross volunteers delivered the warmth of blankets and winter clothing until FEMA and its many contractors could finish distribution of camper trailers to fully meet the overwhelming need for emergency housing.[24]

Though sometimes hampered by rules which prohibited establishing official Red Cross centers in floodplains, where it was possible, Red Cross volunteers outfitted satellite centers for relief distribution in the worst impacted locations. With that strategy in place, and as the available volunteer pool expanded, small Red Cross outposts sprang up in many locations across the Mississippi coast. Under tents in the blazing Mississippi sun or in damaged but stable buildings, Red Cross stations served storm victims who needed financial or medical help, or both. Sometimes the emergency sites were established in the midst of debris-strewn parking lots such as the Red Cross center near the ruins of Biloxi's Edgewater Theater. The locations chosen were near residential areas and easily accessible for people. While citizens waited in line for financial aid or other help, volunteers would pass out bottles of water and offer reassuring words of comfort. Some centers remained in a particular location for only a few days so that the volunteers could relocate to other areas that had not been served with opportunities for financial or medical assistance. During a move, tents were struck, laptops closed, and tables folded as the itinerant Red Cross aid station went mobile. When a new Red Cross center set up housekeeping, word somehow spread in nearby neighborhoods, and even without working telephone service or televisions, lines of thankful people formed.[25]

Wendy Frost, the emergency room nurse from Findlay, Ohio, whose children had pressed her to volunteer, described the outreach work that many Red Cross volunteers did following Katrina. Frost arrived in Mississippi on October 3, 2005. She and up to 1,250 other volunteers slept in a converted warehouse provided with port-o-lets and communal showers and eating facilities on the U.S. Navy Base in Gulfport. Each morning she and her colleagues loaded small vans which they dubbed "Nurses' Emergency Response Vehicles" or NERVs for short. Once loaded, they headed out on specific assigned routes for aid distribution. On one of these morning forays, the last stop on Frost's assigned route was Pearlington, Mississippi. Pearlington was a small unincorporated community of less than 1,000 people situated on the Pearl River in Hancock County, about a 45-minute drive west of Gulfport. As Frost stated, "It's about as far as you can go [in Mississippi] without being in Louisiana." In Pearlington, the Charles B. Murphy Elementary School had become the local center for Red Cross assistance. The school also functioned as a shelter for some homeless storm victims until alternative emergency housing became available. After Wendy Frost's first visit to Pearlington, she requested permanent assignment to that route because she felt that she had formed a bond and established a basis of trust with the people. She believed that because of its isolation, the community had not gotten the attention that the larger towns had gotten. Moreover, the spirit of the people impressed her. They were reluctant to take handouts from strangers, but they clearly needed and would accept a hand up. Frost enjoyed building the network of friendships that came with her repeated missions to Pearlington. On the foundation of trust built up through her many visits, she believed that she had been able to accomplish much in one-on-one health education with older diabetics who needed accurate dietary and other health education. She came to understand that they would listen to her if she took the time to first hear their stories. Storm victims had lost a lot, as Frost saw it, and they greatly valued simple human contact and interaction. "To let them know that somebody cares what they think and what they feel and what they are interested in" seemed a key element of her mission. "It made them happy," Frost said, and "it was a wonderful experience for me."[26]

Frost knew that her colleagues doing mission support work in the base warehouse were missing the satisfaction of dealing one-on-one with people in need. She took photographs of her field work. Each evening back at the base, she made an effort to share with logistics staffers the stories of the people who had been helped that day. Frost wanted the warehouse volunteers to have some sense of what the supplies they assembled meant to the people in the field who ultimately received them. Like so many other volunteers, Frost came away believing that she personally had gained something from the experience. "Somebody asked what I was going to take from this experience," she recalled, "and even though these people [Pearlington citizens] have nothing to give, you know they've given me a lot. And the one thing I'm going to take from here is their stories, and I'm going to tell their stories."[27]

Whatever might be said about national-level Red Cross organizational shortcomings, Red Cross volunteers like Wendy Frost did vital work that was absolutely essential to the disaster response and recovery in Mississippi. In the lead-up to Katrina and in the storm's immediate aftermath, the Red Cross opened shelters throughout Louisiana, Mississippi, Alabama, and beyond. The agency committed to supply food to refugees hunkered down in its own shelters and also delivered supplies and meals to scores of churches and schools that had opened outside the official Red Cross network. At one point, there were as many as 229 shelters operating in Mississippi. An estimated 42,768 storm victims passed through them.[28]

In the shelters and in the stricken neighborhoods beyond, by September 9, Red Cross volunteers working in coordination with the Southern Baptist Convention Disaster Services had served more than 5.4 million hot meals to storm victims across Mississippi and Louisiana. By the end of

November, regionwide this Red Cross Katrina feeding outreach had served 27.4 million hot meals and 25.2 million snacks to hurricane survivors.[29] On the Mississippi Gulf Coast the meals distributed through the Red Cross and the Salvation Army were usually prepared and assembled at one of 12 larger feeding kitchens operated by the Southern Baptist Convention disaster teams. Smaller mobile Red Cross and Salvation Army vans were then used to bring hot meals with plastic utensils into distant neighborhoods or to refugees housed in Red Cross and other public shelters. Often, the delivery would also include cases of water or juice and sometimes infant formula, disposable diapers, and baby wipes.[30] Just as importantly, the Red Cross vans brought news and information from the outside world to people who had no access to electricity, phones, and radio or television reports.[31]

The Salvation Army won praise from Mississippi Gulf Coast officials for its willingness to step in and plug the holes in the Red Cross feeding van coverage. Major Dalton Cunningham, the Salvation Army's division commander for the gulf states, stated that he had "never seen devastation so bad. . . . I've been through [hurricanes] Andrew, Hugo, Charley, Ivan, [and] this is by far the worst." By September 1, the Salvation Army had 72 "canteens" plus 54 smaller mobile kitchens on the way to the disaster zone with a capacity for feeding 420,000 people per day. The day before this announcement, at the site of the destroyed Salvation Army building on Point Cadet in East Biloxi, volunteers in a mobile cantina began distributing food even before they had a kitchen available. A *Sun Herald* reporter witnessed "mudcaked residents" carrying away "armfuls of bananas and cornflakes—the first meal some had eaten in two days."[32] By September 3, the local newspaper carried a notice that Salvation Army mobile cantinas were up and running in a variety of locations beyond hard-hit East Biloxi. Under the headline "Important Information From Emergency Management Officials," the Salvation Army announced the availability of "hot meals from mobile canteens" in Bay St. Louis, Pass Christian, downtown Long Beach, two locations in Gulfport, plus locations at Edgewater Mall in Biloxi and in D'Iberville, Ocean Springs, and Gautier. Together, these facilities were already serving 20,000 meals twice daily, and the Salvation Army predicted that working in tandem with the large Southern Baptist disaster kitchens it would have a capacity for 30,000 meals twice daily by the afternoon of September 3. At the same time, the Salvation Army's Team Radio Network joined several other organizations to help survivors locate missing family members through an Internet-based inquiry and registration system.[33]

After the need for mass feeding had passed, the Salvation Army created a number of long-term recovery programs which worked out of four long-term recovery centers situated in Pascagoula, East Biloxi, Gulfport, and Waveland. One program tutored people in filling out paperwork for available disaster relief services. The Salvation Army also partnered with the National Business Services Alliance to provide job training and skill certification to persons thrown out of work as a result of the storm and provided money to survivors for the purchase of building tools and cleanup supplies. It also devised special children's programs to help youngsters cope with life in the disaster area. In partnership with Habitat for Humanity the Salvation Army administered a home ownership grant program to help qualified applicants purchase Habitat-built houses.[34]

AmeriCorps also sent volunteers to Mississippi. One of the pet projects of President Bill Clinton, this organization was created in 1993 under the auspices of the federally chartered Corporation for National and Community Service. On July 3, 2004, President George W. Bush signed legislation which strengthened this agency and doubled the number of available AmeriCorps volunteers. As a result, more than 70,000 graduated annually from AmeriCorps training centers to provide direct service to address unmet community needs in education, public safety, health, and the environment. In addition, federal legislation gathered such volunteer programs as AmeriCorps, VISTA, NCCC, Senior Corps, and Learn and Serve America under the umbrella of the Corporation for National and Community Service. On the Mississippi Gulf Coast these groups dug in for long-term recovery assistance, beginning with such tasks as food and water distribution and the erection of temporary shelters for refugees and tent facilities for the tens of thousands of volunteers. By August 2006, the multiple service units under the Corporation for National and Community Service had contributed more than 1.6 million hours to the relief and recovery efforts in Mississippi in projects that cleared tons of debris, installed thousands of tarps on damaged roofs, and mucked out and sanitized thousands of homes.[35]

Two years after the storm, the Corporation for National and Community Service rolled out a program to educate nonprofit organizations about available grant opportunities and how to best improve and use recovery mechanisms. The importance of this investment in grant-writing strategy cannot be overstated. While Mississippians were per capita the most generous people in the nation in charitable giving according to itemized donations reported to the Internal Revenue Service, the state had the "fewest number of grant-making foundations in the Southeast." Moreover, as of June 2006, foundations and corporations nationally had made available over $577 million for hurricane relief and recovery projects, but groups headquartered in Mississippi had received only $21.3 million or 3.7 percent of these corporate and foundation grants.[36] This training effort bore fruit in June of 2007, when the Corporation for National and Community Service announced that three of the groups it had trained had successfully secured grant awards worth a combined total of $900,000. Local Habitat for Humanity groups were the largest immediate beneficiaries of the effort.[37]

Beyond AmeriCorps, the Salvation Army, and the Red Cross, hundreds of faith-based organizations also rallied to provide assistance to Mississippi and other storm-impacted areas. Virtually every Protestant and Catholic group in the nation sent a steady steam of volunteers from day one. Jewish, Muslim, and Buddhist groups joined the great outpouring of compassion in Mississippi. Hundreds of college service organizations and countless individual religious congregations sent teams of volunteers who amazed and awed survivors with their willingness to reach out to total strangers to help with hot, nasty, and physically difficult tasks. In the hundreds of Katrina survivor interviews collected by the University of Southern Mississippi's Center for Oral History, when questioned about their "best or most positive" memories of the Katrina experience, interviewees almost invariably stated their profound feelings of appreciation for the thousands of volunteers who turned up so unexpectedly and kept coming for so long to do whatever work was needed.

In the early days of disaster recovery, no denominational or faith-based volunteer group was more prominent on the Mississippi Gulf Coast than the North Carolina Baptist Men. This organization consisted of approximately 6,000 core volunteers—both men and women—who were all North Carolinians. However, for its Mississippi mission, workers from 42 states joined the North Carolina Baptist Men. Many returned for repeated tours of duty.[38] The core group's origins date back to 1978, when founder James Bullard overhauled a large semi–tractor trailer rig to serve as a disaster feeding station. The group is now an internationally recognized disaster recovery organization that has undertaken relief efforts in diverse places from Armenia to Cuba as well as in the U.S.[39]

Eddie and Martha Williams led the North Carolina Baptist Men's effort in Mississippi. Hailing from Spruce Pine, North Carolina, this couple arrived on September 5, just six days after the storm. In coming south, the Williamses left their families behind, resigned from their jobs, and committed themselves to a two-year stint of service in Mississippi. The organization planned to rebuild 500 homes in the hurricane-devastated region but wound up completing work on 700. Eddie Williams had worked in Sri Lanka after the 2004 Asian tsunami. When Williams first arrived in Gulfport, he encountered what he described as devastation "as far as the eye could see." In Williams's view, what he saw on the Mississippi Gulf Coast was "identical to what I saw in Sri Lanka—there wasn't any difference." Using materials purchased by the group and supplemented with donated supplies, the North Carolina Baptist Men made a long-term commitment to help house the people that Katrina had left homeless.[40]

The North Carolina Baptist Men initially set up a feeding station in the parking lot of Pass Road Baptist Church. This unit had the capacity to prepare 3,000 to 5,000 hot meals three times per day. Meals could be eaten under large white open tents, or people could get food to go. Very often, however, every seat under the tents was occupied because so many of those being served valued the opporunity to share their experiences with empathetic listeners as they ate.[41] In the early days of crisis response, three couples lived and worked in Gulfport and slept each night in the church parking lot in recreational vehicles or travel trailers. The full-time on-site staff eventually grew to 16.[42] By early 2006, this North Carolina–based group had served over 818,472 meals, made available 44,560 showers, washed more than 6,000 laundry loads, and provided child care for 560 children.[43]

The Gulfport City Council agreed to provide the North Carolina Baptist Men better quarters in an abandoned former National Guard Armory when the group's long-term housing program got under way. The old armory made feeding and sleeping volunteers for one or two weeks of service much more manageable.[44] During the summer of 2006, more than 1,000 North Carolina volunteers worked in the Gulfport area each week. In the peak week of operations the group deployed more than 1,200 volunteers on the Mississippi coast.[45]

With the city of Gulfport as a facilities partner, by January of 2008, Eddie and Martha Williams had organized and directed an overall total of 30,000 volunteers in Harrison County.[46] Throughout the Mississippi, Louisiana, and Alabama storm impact region it was estimated that 120,000 Southern Baptists responded as volunteers. For the North Carolinians the overriding goal was "to get people back into their homes as quickly and as efficiently as possible." The North Carolina Baptist Men, like virtually all of the faith-based groups working in Mississippi, undertook home restoration work regardless of the religion or race of the homeowner. Thus, the predominantly white volunteers of the North Carolina Baptist Men had a major impact in rehabilitating homes in the Forrest Heights subdivision, a predominantly African American neighborhood in North Gulfport.[47]

Urban Life Ministries (ULM), a faith-based group headquartered in New York, did similar work in East Biloxi. Supported by a network of churches and civic organizations, the first cadre of 60 Urban Life Ministries volunteers headed south three days after Katrina. Upon arrival on the Mississippi Gulf Coast, they set up a base camp and started serving meals from seven mobile kitchens. Their largest site in D'Iberville served 5,000 breakfasts and 5,000 dinners each day. During the first six months ULM served over 250,000 meals. Like the North Carolina Baptist Men, ULM had decades of experience with overseas projects. Their main efforts had been in Africa and the Philippines. However, the 9/11 attack on New York City was the group's first work in an American disaster. In Mississippi, after the initial emergency relief stage passed, ULM also made a transition to a housing reconstruction focus and consolidated its volunteers to one site in East Biloxi. Here three bunk houses and several army tents gave them the capacity to sleep up to 180 volunteers. Mark Jones, a seasoned ULM volunteer, eventually became the on-site Biloxi group leader.[48]

For Jones, an experience working with the victims of a catastrophic mudslide in the Philippines in 1990 had changed his life and prompted him to "look for opportunities to continue to help people." When Katrina hit in 2005, Jones was running an Internet-based business in New York. Jones recalled that after the tragic 9/11 attack on New York City "so many people from the South had come up to help, . . . that we couldn't sit by when this disaster hit here without coming in to help." He made his first visit to Biloxi about a month after the storm and decided to stay. The ULM center on Howard Avenue in East Biloxi stood on the site of a devastated VFW building in an area where entire blocks of older wood-frame shotgun houses, bungalows, and duplexes had been scoured away. The site was well suited to ULM's commitment to long-term housing reconstruction. Councilman George Lawrence secured the needed VFW approvals.[49]

Working through contacts in churches and various large companies, ULM made a concerted effort to recruit volunteers from the ranks of contractors, builders, and building trades specialists. Urban Life Ministries aimed for a ratio of at least four skilled builders in each group of ten volunteers. When church groups contacted Urban Life they were asked to shoot for this mix in the teams they sent. Jones believed that this approach may have reduced the overall numbers of ULM volunteers, but the higher percentage of skilled tradespeople made each group more effective than it would have been if the crew had been totally inexperienced with construction work. Occasional exceptions were made, as in the case of three groups from a Michigan radio station, WJQ, FM 99. Each time the station led a group to Biloxi they did live broadcasts back to Michigan from Urban Life's Biloxi construction sites. The radio outreach produced a huge volunteer response from the station's Michigan listening area. With volunteers committed to service stints of one to three weeks, during the peak of its reconstruction work, ULM deployed an average of 100 volunteers per week in East Biloxi. By June of 2007, Urban Life Ministries volunteers had mucked out, gutted, and rehabilitated 1,250 homes for persons who lacked sufficient insurance or grant monies to get the rebuilds done themselves. Jones and his ULM team committed to keep working the East Biloxi housing problem as long as funding and volunteer support allowed.[50]

As a result of Katrina, many local churches and pastors found themselves transforming their own sense of mission and stewardship. At First Baptist Church of Gulfport, a church whose facilities were totally destroyed in the storm, Pastor Charles "Chuck" Register believed that Katrina had taught a powerful lesson about "improper value structures in life." One "can work all [one's] life for material possessions," he observed, "and all of that can be gone in a twelve-hour period." As a result of the hurt that came with Katrina, Register's personal understanding of the mission of the church in the world changed toward a "more community-oriented focus" with more outreach "in alleviating the suffering of people." Three years after the storm, Register, a former seminary professor with an earned doctorate, went to work full-time with a faith-based disaster relief organization.[51]

In devastated Bay St. Louis, the seemingly unlikely congregation at St. Rose de Lima Catholic Church undertook the kind of community ministry that Register spoke of, and did so on a scale that the little congregation itself could have never before contemplated. Its young immigrant pastor, Father Sebastian Myladiyil, told one of his parishioners that in working to alleviate the suffering after Katrina "I have learned how to be a priest." Father Sebastian was a native of India. He finished his seminary training in India before being ordained to the priesthood in 1999. In June of 2001, he had become the pastor at St. Rose de Lima. His parishioners credited this immigrant priest with providing the real energy and leadership for the tremendous community outreach undertaken by St. Rose in response to the Katrina disaster.[52]

St. Rose de Lima Catholic Church was organized as an African American parish in 1926. Over the 30 years prior to Katrina, the congregation had become a place where increasing numbers of Caucasians and people of all ethnic backgrounds felt welcome and enjoyed St. Rose's distinctive adaptations of Catholic worship, including its spirited gospel choir. The old white church building on Necaise Avenue and its 13-room school building suffered major roof damage and serious leakage but miraculously escaped the briny storm surge that enveloped the rest of Bay St. Louis. On Labor Day, a Catholic youth group from Baton Rouge arrived and began cleaning up broken window panes and debris that had blown into the St. Rose School. The school soon became the St. Rose Relief Center, a facility that gave shelter to homeless storm victims, received and distributed relief supplies, and later housed a free laundromat that served the whole community.[53] When thousands of temporary FEMA camper-trailer units were set up in town, the church organized a delivery service that filled and exchanged butane tanks for the elderly and disabled. Beyond this, the St. Rose Hurricane Task Force created its own volunteer center and housed volunteers in facilities down the street on the grounds of the Divine Word Catholic Seminary and in two large homes donated to the church for this purpose. In the first three years following Katrina, the church hosted over 6,000 volunteers from more than 100 Catholic parishes and a variety of Protestant and Jewish groups. Through its role in rehabilitating hundreds of houses in Hancock County, this historically African American church became a major resource for the whole community. In the process, as one parishioner put it, "Father Sebastian helped us . . . [to overcome] prejudices that we may have had about other religions . . . and [to] realize that there's one God . . . and . . . this is the work of God."[54] Beyond the efforts of St. Rose, Sister Rebecca Rutkowski, director of Catholic Social and Community Services for the Catholic Diocese of Biloxi, estimated that volunteers working through her agency had rebuilt more than 500 houses across the Mississippi coast in the two years following Katrina.[55]

St. Rose was one among the scores of coast churches to open centers to feed and house volunteers. Two years after Katrina, Lagniappe Presbyterian Church in Bay St. Louis had hosted 5,188 volunteers, and at the end of five years, First Baptist Church of Bay St. Louis had opened the upper floor of its education annex to some 14,000 volunteers.[56] In Gulfport, over a three-year period, Westminster Presbyterian Church put up another 14,000 volunteers on its grounds.[57] Moreover, it seemed that almost every United Methodist Church on the Mississippi Gulf Coast provided shelter in their education and fellowship halls for a portion of the 125,000 volunteers from the United Methodist Committee on Relief (UMCOR) that flowed into Louisiana and Mississippi. Over that entire region, UMCOR volunteers had provided long-term recovery assistance that touched almost 69,000 households by August of 2008.[58] For example, little St. Mark United Methodist Church, an African American congregation in North Gulfport, hosted roughly 4,000 persons in 182 teams of UMCOR volunteers from all across America over the three years following Katrina.[59] During the same time period, the congregation of Little Rock Baptist Church in West Gulfport put up almost 6,000 volunteers, most of whom came from churches in the Midwest through an organization called World Hope.[60] Thousands of Hands On Gulf Coast and AmeriCorps volunteers passed through the tent city at Beauvoir Methodist Church in Biloxi and worked a variety of tasks from cleanup and reconstruction to tutoring in schools and in local Boys and Girls Clubs.[61] Skilled Mennonite construction volunteers had an important impact on Long Beach and Pass Christian.[62] Up to 100 volunteers per week worked from Camp Coast Care to rebuild homes in the Pass Christian area with interdenominational support from Episcopalian, Lutheran, Catholic, and Baptist groups.[63] Lutheran Episcopal Services in Mississippi set up three case management and construction team sites on the Mississippi Gulf Coast, including Camp Victor in Ocean Springs. Lutheran Episcopal Services volunteers provided cleanup or housing rehabilitation for more than 2,000 storm victims.[64]

So many volunteers came forward that any attempt to catalog and thank all of the different groups from across the nation who offered help or to list all of the local churches who supported them in their work would fall short. In January of 2007, a newspaper story on a major Habitat for Humanity building blitz found Amish from Pennsylvania, Catholics from Massachusetts, Methodists from Illinois, Baptists from Mississippi, and a nondenominational Florida church group working at various Habitat sites just in the little town of Pearlington. Many of these volunteers had slept the night before at a camp run by Presbyterians.[65] On the second anniversary of Katrina, Marsha Meeks Kelly, executive director of the Mississippi Commission for Volunteer Services, documented dozens of local churches and nonprofit organizations from Pascagoula to Pearlington that were housing and feeding volunteers[66] in the ranks of a relief army that eventually swelled to include 800,000 volunteers from perhaps 1,000 organizations that offered a hand up to the victims of Katrina.[67]

Students from high schools, colleges, and universities performed a large share of the cleanup drudge work across the coast through groups like Habitat for Humanity College Challenge, Campus Crusade for Christ, the

Foundation for Jewish Campus Life, the Hands On Network, Break Away, Community Collaborations International, and many others.[68] Hundreds of law students found that their legal training could also be put to good use helping the elderly, disabled, or disadvantaged cope with the bureaucratic obstacles associated with FEMA's emergency housing program or the Mississippi Development Authority's homeowner grant operation. Most of the volunteer law students in Mississippi worked for the Mississippi Center for Justice, a privately funded, nonprofit, social justice advocacy organization. In the aftermath of Katrina, Martha Bergmark, the center's founder, had recruited attorneys Reilly Morse and John Jopling to open an office on the coast to provide legal aid to Gulf Coast disaster victims.[69]

Reilly Morse, a third-generation Gulfport lawyer, had started his career as a defense attorney in a law firm doing work for insurance companies. However, at the time of Katrina he had gone into practice on his own as a trial lawyer and had taken on an increasing amount of environmental advocacy work. Now, at age 47, Morse himself was a storm victim. His own house had survived Katrina with comparatively minor damage. However, his law office was wiped off the map in the storm surge. All of his legal research, all of his clients' evidence files, and all business-related correspondence was gone. Unable to service billable clients, Morse was forced to take bankruptcy. Thus, in the wake of Katrina, Reilly Morse accepted the offer from the Mississippi Center for Justice and became a full-time public interest attorney.[70]

When Morse and Jopling set up shop in October of 2005, they had no office, so they worked out of their personal automobiles with cell phones and legal pads. They routinely visited different disaster recovery centers to provide legal advice. Housing, more particularly affordable housing, emerged as the key focus for their efforts. The Lawyers' Committee for Civil Rights Under Law engaged early on with the Mississippi Center for Justice and helped Morse and Jopling develop a model for regular community outreach workshops. Volunteers from prestigious law firms across the country made themselves available for pro bono work. Within a short time students from law schools began offering their help during academic breaks. The law student volunteers conducted systematic interviews and carried out the on-the-ground execution of block-by-block surveys to collect accurate housing data. That data was destined to have important impacts on public policy debates during the recovery. The center eventually settled into offices on Division Street in East Biloxi.[71]

Morse described the post-Katrina bureaucratic processes that many refugees endured in seeking housing assistance at the hands of various federal and state agencies as a "financial strip search." He observed that when volunteer lawyers from other locales "would come to our clinics and see the aftermath [of paperwork failures]," they were in effect conducting "the autopsy of that person's encounter with FEMA." Morse found that his visiting attorneys "would be very careful, some of them taking notes about all of this, and you could just see these lawyers' heads seize up with the absurdity of the illogic of it all." To Morse it seemed that in the wake of Katrina "all kinds of legal norms" were relaxed "to allow society to regenerate itself." However, when it came down to low-income households "things got pulled as taut as a violin string."[72]

Clients who had lost everything in Katrina were faced with seemingly impossible demands when they approached federal and state housing administrators or insurance companies for the assistance due them. Clear property titles, insurance records, or copies of rental agreements simply did not exist anymore for many people whose homes had been destroyed. Moreover, it was difficult to secure copies or find working copying machines in post-Katrina conditions. Many applicants found that one or more of the agencies with which they dealt had lost the only available copy of a key document. They needed help locating suitable replacements to avoid being denied benefits. Sometimes the legal volunteers were successful and sometimes they were not.[73]

In the three years after Katrina, over 500 law students from almost every state in the union worked on the Coast for the Mississippi Center for Justice. In addition, over 200 practicing lawyers rendered assistance. Moreover, DLA Piper and O'Melveny and Myers, large firms with thousands of attorneys and offices in major cities worldwide, took on long-term projects on real estate titles and contractor fraud—two thorny problems which beset disproportionate numbers of low-income, elderly, and disabled storm victims.[74]

Almost any need that touched human lives, living conditions, health, or emotional well-being attracted selfless volunteers. Many of Mississippi's 5,000 Vietnamese immigrants who lived on the Gulf Coast had special needs. Because so many made their living in the fishing and seafood industries they were often among the most severely impacted by the disaster. Burning Man, an organization with members all across the United States, rallied volunteers to gut out and rebuild the Vietnamese Buddhist temple on Oak Street in Biloxi.[75] Boat People SOS, a California-based Vietnamese service organization, sent dozens of volunteer translators to Mississippi to help older Vietnamese immigrants understand and navigate the complicated paperwork requirements of various relief programs.[76]

The special needs of children also attracted focused volunteer effort. The Bucks-Mont Katrina Relief Project, a volunteer group from Bucks and Montgomery counties in Pennsylvania, sent money, supplies, and expertise to help with constructing a new building for the Hancock County Child Development Center that had been destroyed in the storm.[77] Moreover, when children whose families lived in cramped FEMA emergency housing or who attended storm-damaged schools found that Katrina had robbed them of many of their former playground facilities, their loss attracted an organization called KaBoom. KaBoom volunteers built or rebuilt and equipped 100 playgrounds in areas hit by Hurricane Rita and Hurricane Katrina.[78]

Pets are just as closely associated with children as playgrounds. The fate of the animals belonging to the 65,000 Mississippi families who lost homes offers another example. When pre-Katrina evacuation orders came down, families were specifically warned to leave their pets at home. At the time, the Red Cross storm shelters could not accommodate animals. The result was a large-scale post-Katrina animal control problem. Three days after the storm Mayor Brent Warr issued a plea to the Gulfport citizens, asking for volunteers to help rescue stranded and injured animals. "Some people left their dogs chained up during the storm," the mayor said, "and we need help rescuing these animals. They don't have any food and water."[79] Volunteers quickly mustered at local animal shelters. Contact was made with various animal welfare organizations including the Humane Society of the United States, and the animal rescue volunteers went straight to work.[80] At the Humane Society's Gulfport animal shelter flooding had drowned 23 dogs. Tara High, the local Humane Society board president, worked with Harrison County Chancery Clerk John McAdams to transport the remaining 120 animals to safety. Seven national Humane Society disaster teams worked in Mississippi including 35 trained responders with eight to ten vehicles.[81] In the end, approximately 1,000 animals were rescued, and many of them were returned to their families. For Bob Gentry, the North Carolinian who coordinated animal rescue in Mississippi, it was "very rewarding to see people reunited with their animals." As Gentry saw it, "There's an immediate return on the work that you're doing that is often unique in disaster situations."[82] Jane Garrison, another national Humane Society volunteer, spoke of the disaster animal rescue work in very human terms. "Every animal I rescue," she said, "helps a whole family.

A lot of people have lost everything. When they have their animal back, they are so happy."[83]

Volunteers brought an unexpected wealth of blessings to the communities on which Katrina had delivered such grievous blows. For some coast residents, the work of volunteers made the difference between having a home and becoming permanently homeless or being forced to leave the area. For others, the outpouring of compassion from the hands and hearts of strangers renewed their faith in the goodness of God. For people who had come to see their nation as hopelessly bound up in selfish pursuits and bitter political gamesmanship, the massive presence of volunteers became a powerful sign of the enduring strength of American idealism and of the continuing capacity of American citizens for serious and selfless civic engagements and long-term commitments. No one who saw the volunteers at work could walk away without being inspired with a spirit of thankfulness. As one eloquent *Sun Herald* letter to the editor put it, "The whole world came and we were thankful. They came and lived in tents and slept on the ground. . . . They clothed us and fed us. They sheltered us . . . [and] lifted our spirits. . . . And we were thankful. . . . Still they come."[84] Grateful they were, but still, many coast residents were left in wonder about the powerful inspirations that brought so many people to their aid.

Young Mary Ashlyn Alderman, a high school student from Radford, Virginia, who came to Mississippi with her church's volunteer group said simply, "I came to Bay St. Louis because I wanted to help people who needed a lift. They would do the same for me."[85] Martha Williams, the office manager for the North Carolina Baptist Men, offered some insights. Volunteers became "family" to the people they helped, she said. "The volunteers that [went] to these homes ended up coming back with more than they gave."[86] This theme of reciprocal goodwill between volunteers and beneficiaries was a phenomenon that many volunteers echoed. Rev. Rod Dickson-Rishel, a long time UMCOR volunteer whose own Gulfport church was destroyed in Katrina, observed that something "dynamic" happens to people who come face to face with "a real need" in which their personal efforts can "make a difference." Those "injunctions of scripture—to feed the hungry and serve the needy—become real in ways that . . . people have never experienced" in the day-to-day routines of ordinary life.[87] Tim Anderson, an officer in the Knights of Columbus from Flint, Michigan, reflected that "the Knights of Columbus believe in charity work and helping others, but I don't think I had a true understanding of what charity is until my trip to Mississippi." There was "such a spiritual aspect to it," Anderson said. For

Anderson, the realization of the impact he could have on people "was a life-changing experience."[88] The relationship that developed between those who helped others in need and the recipients of that help was a physically transitory occurrence, but a psychologically and spiritually lasting experience. As Mark Jones of the Urban Life Ministries team in Biloxi stated, "From what I've seen in the thousands of volunteers that I've come in contact with, they're not looking for credit. They get their credit when they go home and they can think back and remember the faces of homeowners that they helped move in."[89] In casting their bread upon the water, many of those who brought grace also received it.

Chapter Seven

The Long Wait for Housing

Build ye houses, and dwell in them; . . . and seek the welfare of the city . . . and pray unto the Lord for it: for in the peace thereof shall ye have peace.

—JEREMIAH 29: 5–7

In the wake of Katrina . . . no issue is more important to our region than affordable housing.

—BRIAN SANDERSON
Gulf Coast Business Council
Congressional Testimony
February 22, 2007[1]

Only by enhancing housing opportunities for all coastal residents, including low and moderate income homeowners and renters, will the workforce and economic engines of the Gulf Coast reach their full potential.

—GOVERNOR HALEY BARBOUR
U.S. Senate Testimony
May 20, 2009[2]

Hurricane Katrina destroyed or rendered uninhabitable some 65,000 homes in Mississippi alone. These numbers represent an average of the high and low estimates of FEMA and the American Red Cross. In addition, the storm inflicted some degree of lesser damage onto at least another 155,384

Mississippi abodes.[3] Behind the numbers are the stories of individual people who suffered great loss and often struggled for years to get back on their feet psychologically and spiritually as well as financially. By FEMA's count, Katrina's devastation in Mississippi left 216,558 individuals and families qualified for FEMA housing assistance,[4] and as many as 129,600 of the dehoused storm victims lived for a period of time in one of the 48,000 FEMA campers or trailers that were set up in Mississippi for emergency housing.[5] For those who lost homes in Katrina, much of the next three to four years and beyond would be a waiting game involving unprecedented numbers of citizens caught in entanglements with insurance adjusters, labor-short construction contractors, and a variety of state, local, and federal agencies from FEMA and the Small Business Administration to local building inspectors and the Mississippi Development Authority.

The waiting further tested the mettle of a people who had shown resourcefulness and neighborly concern in the chaotic days immediately following the storm. The results were not always heartening. The misery of FEMA campers and trailers took an inevitable toll on the very young, the very old, and on family life in general. The phasing of the Mississippi Development Authority housing grant program forced renters and homeowners without insurance to endure the longest waits of all. Beyond this, persistent and sometimes bitter objections to the placement of affordable apartment developments pointed to a community retreating from its pervasive post-Katrina spirit of benevolence. All of this prolonged the recovery and inflicted great suffering on those left behind.

The housing loss was overwhelmingly centered in the three urban counties of the Mississippi Gulf Coast where 70 percent of all homes received some type of damage, including 90 percent of the housing units at ground zero in Hancock County.[6] However, anyone who attempts to gain an exact numerical accounting of Katrina's destructive impact will be struck by the imprecision of the early damage estimates and the incompleteness of the later studies. The lack of precision and detail in the estimates available before 2009 played a role in delaying the recovery of rental units and provided fuel for protracted and often bitter public debates over who should be helped first and whether Governor Haley Barbour's administration was committed to a recovery strategy that was sufficient to deliver adequate supplies of affordable housing for the Gulf Coast's low-wage service-sector workforce.[7] Yet, even the most precise numbers could never provide an adequate description of the storm's impact upon the lives of the hundreds of thousands of individual people who suffered losses and persevered through the frustrations and despair that became a part of the long recovery and rebuilding process.

Behind the numbers stood the realities of people like Laura Creel of Long Beach, an 84-year-old widow who lost her long-time family home to Hurricane Katrina. Mrs. Creel was a storm-wise native of Biloxi who liked to remind people that the Hurricane of 1947 "was a dress rehearsal for [Hurricane] Camille," and "Camille was a dress rehearsal for Katrina." Creel remembered staying with her husband and two young daughters in her father's house in East Biloxi near the old Buena Vista Hotel during the '47 hurricane. Her father had assured her that the house was safe, "because the neighbors had all come there" over 30 years earlier during the 1916 hurricane, and the old home had not flooded. Indeed, the Biloxi house did not flood in 1947, but Mrs. Creel remembered that the sight of "the debris . . . [which] formed a barricade along the beachfront" had shocked her the morning after the storm. She recalled that after the '47 storm she had seen a number of destroyed highway patrol cars belonging to officers caught off guard while attending a convention at the Buena Vista Hotel. By the time Hurricane Camille hit in 1969, the family had moved to a modest wood-frame house a block and a half from the beach in Long Beach. Better storm warnings with better estimates of storm intensity convinced the family to evacuate in 1969. A few shingles were lost and a tree went down on the carport, but the Camille storm surge had not touched the Long Beach house. Because the house had never flooded, neither mortgage holders nor insurance agents ever suggested the need for flood insurance.[8]

In August of 2005, Katrina's unprecedented 30-foot tidal surge wrote a new chapter in Laura Creel's long family history with hurricanes. A widow now, she heeded warnings and evacuated to Mobile to stay with one of her daughters. After the storm passed, a phone call from her son Cecil, a nurse working at an Ocean Springs storm shelter, brought the first report of the condition of her house. The Katrina storm surge had wrecked the house where she had raised five children. Though her home was damaged beyond repair, she took the news stoically. Tears did not come until the next day when her youngest daughter pulled her aside to say, "I have to tell you something; Anthony's house is gone." At this news, 84-year-old Laura Creel wept. Anthony was her grandson, a longshoreman with a young wife and a new baby. The little family had recently moved into a new home in the Delisle community on a plot of ground that had not flooded in Camille. They had found safety at a relative's house, but they no longer had a home of their own.[9]

In her grief over news of the destruction of her grandson's house, some time passed before Mrs. Creel thought to ask about the fate of her oldest daughter's house also located in Delisle. A sturdy brick structure, her eldest daughter and son-in-law's house had often been used as a family storm refuge because it, too, had not flooded in Hurricane Camille. By some strange twist of fate, the couple was traveling when Katrina struck, so there had been no family gathering at their house. "Well," the family matriarch finally asked, "what about Diane and John?" That answer was also shocking. "Mamma, their house is gone too." In this one family, three homes were lost to the 30-foot Katrina storm surge. Laura Creel cried for her children, grandchildren, and her little great-grandchild. She did not cry for herself.[10]

For two weeks, in the storm's aftermath, Mrs. Creel remained in Mobile before relocating to her son's house in Ocean Springs. Here she stayed for two additional months until she could get into a FEMA camper. During this time her daughter-in-law "almost had the telephone glued to her ear" trying to get registrations and paperwork problems solved so that her mother-in-law could get lined up for emergency housing. The octogenarian widow observed that "it was a matter . . . of communicating through these agencies with perseverance." The destruction of the sewerage system around her home in Long Beach meant that Mrs. Creel's camper had to be placed on her daughter's property in Delisle where there was a functioning well and septic tank.[11]

Laura Creel had no flood insurance, and her wind insurance had only provided enough funds for the roof—a sum that was nowhere near what was needed to replace the house. Her age and fixed income status argued against new mortgages or SBA loans. However, in 2006, the state's federally funded homeowner grant program seemed to offer a way forward. Unfortunately, new elevation requirements and rising construction costs meant that through two rounds of state grants meted out over a three-year period, this courteous and dignified senior citizen only had enough money to purchase materials. She, like thousands of others, could not pay for the labor needed to rebuild her home. Meanwhile, during three years of patient waiting, life in a FEMA camper unit gave way to life in a stronger temporary unit called a Mississippi cottage. In the third year of her sojourn in these little quarters, volunteers from Christian Aid Ministries, an Ohio-based Mennonite and Amish disaster relief organization, became available to rebuild the wood-frame house in Long Beach. When the rebuild was finally finished, Laura Creel, a Catholic lady of deep faith, asked to attend the volunteer group's weekly prayer service. In offering her thanks to these Mennonite and Amish workers, she said, "I know you are doing this for me, but I know ultimately you are doing it for the Lord."[12]

For thousands who had lost their homes, the long days of waiting began in close quarters doubled up with friends or family members. For some, the waiting began in storm shelters or in hotel rooms provided through the Red Cross or FEMA. For still others, there were weeks or even months of sleeping on the ground in small tents near their destroyed homes or on cots in large military-style tent cities. There was insurance paperwork and the wait for adjustors. To the burden of personal loss, Katrina added long lines and often confusing registration processes for FEMA emergency housing and Small Business Administration loan applications. The phasing and slowness of the state grant program further tested the will and endurance of homeowners and renters alike.

For local government officials caught with a sudden housing crisis, the first step in recovery was to move people out of school-based shelters. Schools needed to reopen quickly for working families to be able to remain available in the community to rebuild the economy. However, because life in a public shelter afforded no privacy, simple compassion combined with the logistical strain of holding large numbers of people in gymnasiums and recreational facilities provided ample motivation to find alternatives.[13] Places for people were needed immediately. Unfortunately, in the aftermath of Katrina, "immediately" had no meaning. Everyone hurried up in order to wait.

There could be no disputing that in Gulf Coast counties, Katrina's devastation of housing units had struck at the core capacity of communities to sustain and revive themselves. Whether the victims were renters or homeowners, whether they had insurance or had none, if working families could not be housed, they could not be available to the community for the hard recovery work that lay ahead. Even under the best of circumstances, it would take months for the nation's production capacity for campers and trailers to meet the needs that just twelve hours of wind and water had created in Mississippi and Louisiana. Interim steps had to be taken. FEMA took over a Red Cross hotel program that paid for extended stays for homeless families in hotel rooms, and a FEMA rental voucher program soon filled all vacant apartments. Recovery workers quickly took undamaged hotel rooms, so by mid-September, there was literally no room left in the inn for displaced storm victims. At Pascagoula, on the eastern side of the Mississippi Gulf Coast, almost every residence within the city limits appeared to have taken some water.[14] Here, FEMA contracted for the mooring of a cruise ship, the Carnival *Holiday*, which could accommodate up to 1,800 refugees. Though the cost of this move was much criticized later,[15] stabilizing the work force for a critical oil refinery and a major shipyard appeared to justify the effort. In fact, within days of the storm, the Chevron oil refinery at Pascagoula opened a tent city to house 1,500 of its employees and their families.[16] In due time, some 7,000 FEMA trailers would house an estimated 18,000 of Pascagoula's 26,000 citizens.[17]

Given the thousands of people put up in storm shelters and the apparent speed with which tent cities could be constructed, officials in Harrison County decided to establish public tent cities. Indeed, units stationed at the U.S. Naval Construction Battalion (Seabee) Base in Gulfport specialized in building tent cities for forward deployed Marine Corps groups. The logic of matching dire need with readily available know-how led to meetings in which the local Navy commander expressed personal enthusiasm for the mission. Sites were identified in D'Iberville, Long Beach, and Pass Christian, and the Navy commander pledged to get started immediately. However, weeks passed with no evidence of Seabee activity on the tent city sites. The mystifying inaction prompted County Supervisor Marlin Ladner to start making phone calls. Finally, someone in the FEMA hierarchy shed some light. "Well, I'll be honest with you," he said, "[private] contractors want to put up those tent cities, and that's the delay." In response, military commanders had pulled the Seabees off the project. In a public meeting, Ladner exposed the issue. People had "no place to stay," he reported, "because we [are] dealing with somebody's contractors." The media spotlight triggered wider protests, and the contractor issue went away. The Seabees constructed the three tent cities,[18] but the delays and indecision meant that it was November before these facilities could be occupied.[19] The waiting for housing had only begun.

Between them, the three officially sanctioned Harrison County tent cities could shelter 700 people. Each tent city was composed of a series of windowless 18-by-32-foot structures draped in green canvas with interior floors and walls made of plywood. The Seabees called the units "strongbacks." In Pass Christian the residents dubbed their encampment "The Village." Each of the tents was subdivided to accommodate cots for at least four adults, along with whatever clothing and personal items they owned. Though strangers sometimes had to bunk together, efforts were made to place families under one roof or to put people with friends or previous acquaintances. At the Pass Christian site, FEMA supplied food for meals that were served in a giant white tent. Another pavilion contained a makeshift communal living room with couches and television sets. A row of outdoor portable toilets was lined up beside a tractor-trailer shower house to take care of basic personal hygiene.[20]

Boredom often stalked camp residents. After a few weeks in residence at the Pass Christian camp, David Frisby thought that the whole thing felt "a bit like a tomb." In the Long Beach camp where there was no electricity to charge cell phones, residents spoke of being unable to stay in touch with friends and family. Delores King, a 76-year-old asthmatic with a portable oxygen tank, told a *Dallas Morning News* reporter that she wished for a window in her tent and some privacy at the shower house. While keeping her vigil for a FEMA trailer, she occupied herself with crossword puzzles and watched soap operas with her pet cockatiel named Tweety Bird. Some people felt insecure in the tent cities, and fear of crime influenced some to set up tents on their own property rather than go to the camps. A spate of drug arrests at the D'Iberville site in December of 2005 led city manager Richard Rose to express publicly his regret that the city had ever requested a camp. Nonetheless, many tent city residents bore up remarkably well. In the Pass Christian "Village," 47-year-old Mary Magee, who shared a tent with her 28-year-old daughter, three grandchildren, and an adopted 10-year-old son, still managed to have patience with the system. When frustration with her plight caused her to lash out about little things, she reminded herself that a lot of people on the coast were in need, and at least her family was warm and well fed.[21]

The tent cities were designed to bridge the gap between shelters and more secure and stable FEMA trailers and campers, and it was hoped that the canvas neighorhoods would close by January 31. However, despite setting a new record for volume and speed of delivery of emergency camper units, FEMA's speed could not satisfy the record housing needs begging for solution in the wake of the storm. In mid-April, there were still 133 households living in the three officially sanctioned tent cities and at least another three dozen families in unofficial camps that sprang up elsewhere.[22] Nationally, trailer and camper manufacturing had to ramp up, and at ground zero in Mississippi and Louisiana, utility construction, together with zoning and wetlands concerns, slowed the development of large FEMA trailer parks.[23] According to Steve Loughrey, the FEMA division supervisor for Jackson County, the biggest holdup in trailer installation was the storm's destruction of sewerage systems over the region.[24] Moreover, FEMA required applicants to fill out SBA loan applications, and FEMA's antifraud regulations required victims to prove that they had lived in the area at the time of the storm. If paperwork had been lost when houses or apartments washed away, or if a rental lease had been taken out in someone else's name, meeting FEMA's standards required legal assistance.[25] Then, too, the constant shuffling of FEMA registration clerks in and out of the disaster zone led to lost paperwork and for many people necessitated multiple reregistrations for aid.[26]

For local officials, the effort to move people out of tent cities and shelters and into emergency trailer units also involved additional education in the frustrating bureaucratic complexities of FEMA disaster recovery programs. Connie Rockco of the Harrison County Board of Supervisors "started having a bad feeling" about housing four days after the storm when FEMA officials started finding reasons why the most obvious locations for emergency trailer parks were unacceptable.[27] The county board had quickly identified open land at the Long Beach Industrial Park as good for a FEMA trailer park, and the city of Long Beach wanted to establish a trailer park on a plot near its school administrative offices. Both sites were publically owned and had easy access to existing sewerage and water lines. Thus, both locations could be developed quickly and without legal complications. They offered hope that police officers, teachers, and firemen could quickly get into stable living situations with their families and thus be more likely to stay in the community to aid the recovery. However, on the Friday after the storm, FEMA's on-the-scene representative curtly rejected the notion. "You've got a wetlands problem here," he said. Developing sites on wetlands without environmental studies and appropriate mitigation was unacceptable to FEMA. Thousands of people across the coast were doubled up with relatives, living in gymnasiums or tents, or sleeping in their offices at work, but FEMA had a wetlands problem. Unfortunately the people who set this rule were not on the scene to see the implications. Thus, the waiting would go on still longer.[28]

This so distressed board member Marlin Ladner that he telephoned FEMA headquarters in Jackson to plead the case without even knowing the name of the person in charge of the emergency housing operation. When he connected, Ladner just kept asking, "Who's in charge? Let me talk to them," until he got to a person who was able to talk about housing. At first, the Jackson headquarters staff dismissed the inquiry with the same explanation—"Well, you've got a wetlands problem." In frustration, Ladner replied, "My gosh, man, what are you talking about, 'a wetlands problem.'" In Ladner's mind, this was a housing crisis, not a wetlands problem. "We need to get our people back," he pleaded. "We need places for people to stay." Wetlands problems could be dealt with later. After some give and take, the administrator on the other end of the line pledged to come to the coast to get a firsthand look at the whole situation. As a result of this personal visit, FEMA eventually gave emergency approval to the proposed sites. For Ladner this episode illustrated the difficulty that authorities distant from the scene had in grasping "that . . . what was normal could not be applied to this abnormalcy that we were dealing with."[29]

In late October, the delivery pace for FEMA trailers in Mississippi climbed to 400 to 450 units per day and set a new record in speed of delivery of disaster housing.[30] In November, the *Sun Herald* reported that FEMA had approved 55,000 applications for temporary housing in Mississippi. Even at its new record speed, it took five to six months to manufacture and distribute the 48,000 FEMA campers and trailers ultimately installed in Mississippi. Thus at Christmastime, notwithstanding the record speed of placements, Bechtel and its subcontractors had managed to put only 29,181 trailers into service. With the onset of winter, the cup seemed half empty for the 19,000 families still on the waiting list.[31]

Initially, the trailer park near the Long Beach School Board office housed teachers and other public employees, including Elizabeth Doolittle, a bespectacled and witty 63-year-old librarian from the University of Southern Mississippi's Long Beach Campus. Doolittle, a native of New Orleans, was no stranger to storms. Two years before Katrina when she accepted the job at USM, she had rented a house on Henderson Point, just outside the Pass Christian city limits. Elizabeth Doolittle's rental home had taken water in Camille, so it had been easy for her to decide to evacuate and accept the invitation of lifelong friend Mary Judice to stay in her home in the Oak Grove community near Hattiesburg during the storm. On Monday morning as Katrina's winds bore down on the Hattiesburg area 75 miles inland from the coast, the two ladies moved to an interior hallway. In the darkened hallway, they heard repeated loud cracking noises followed by big thuds as Katrina felled more than two dozen trees in Mary Judice's yard.[32]

On the coast, little remained of Elizabeth Doolittle's home. When she returned home, she found a refrigerator and a couch lying beside the roof which had been bulldozed out of the street and sat "crunched up" in the yard. Elizabeth Doolittle cried over the loss of her family photographs and over the destruction of the scrapbooks she had kept for each child and grandchild to detail their accomplishments. She was left with nothing but the three changes of clothes she had packed as she evacuated. Doolittle spent a month doubled up with her friends in Hattiesburg and then accepted the invitation of Laura and Orv Andre to move into the spare room of their Diamondhead home so that she could be nearer to work.[33]

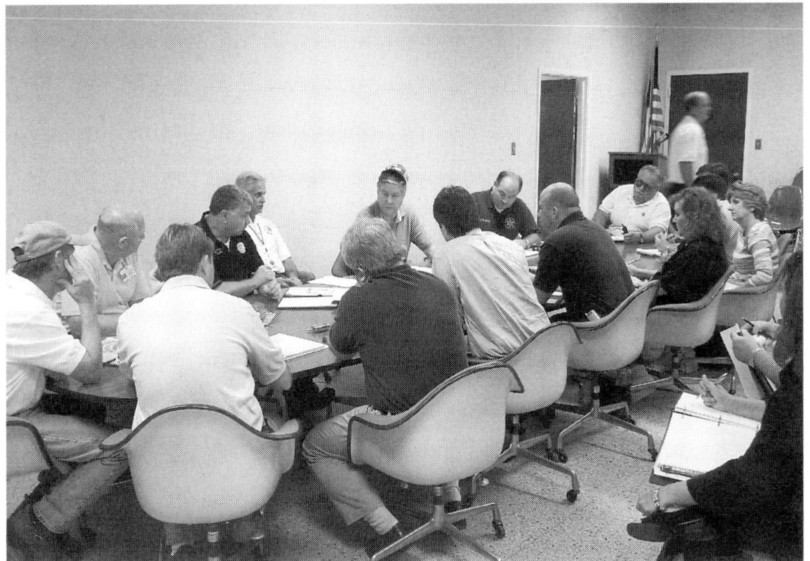

Planning meeting involving city and county officials and first responders. Back row facing the camera from left to right: Harrison County Emergency Operations Director, General Joe Spraggins; Gulfport Fire Chief, Pat Sullivan; Rupert Lacy of the Harrison County Sheriff's Department; Superintendent Henry Arledge of Harrison County Schools; Wayne Payne of the Harrison County Sheriff's Department; and unidentified. Photo by Brian Sullivan.

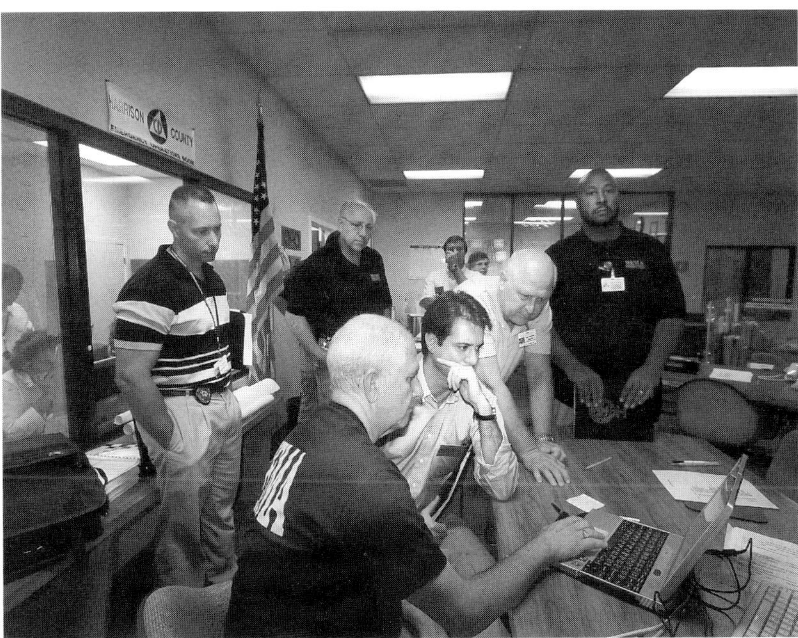

Inside the Harrison County Emergency Operations Center in Gulfport, Mayor Brent Warr of Gulfport (seated center) studies a computer screen as Harrison County Emergency Operations Director Joe Spraggins (light shirt) and Mississippi Emergency Management Agency Director Robert Latham (dark shirt) look over his shoulder. Photo by Pat Sullivan.

Bumper-to-bumper traffic near Gulfport as Mississippi and Louisiana residents in the predicted storm path head east toward Florida and Alabama. Photo by Pat Sullivan.

Search and rescue teams work into the night trying to find trapped or injured disaster victims in damaged buildings in Gulfport, Mississippi. Photo by Pat Sullivan.

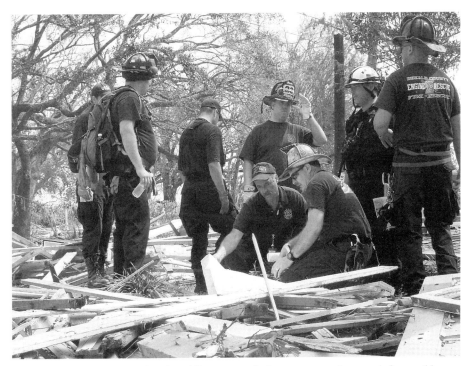

Members of a FEMA Urban Search and Rescue team look over maps as they search for possible survivors in this residential neighborhood on Second Street in Gulfport. The professionalism of FEMA's USAR teams drew much praise from local first responders in the aftermath of Katrina. Photo by Pat Sullivan.

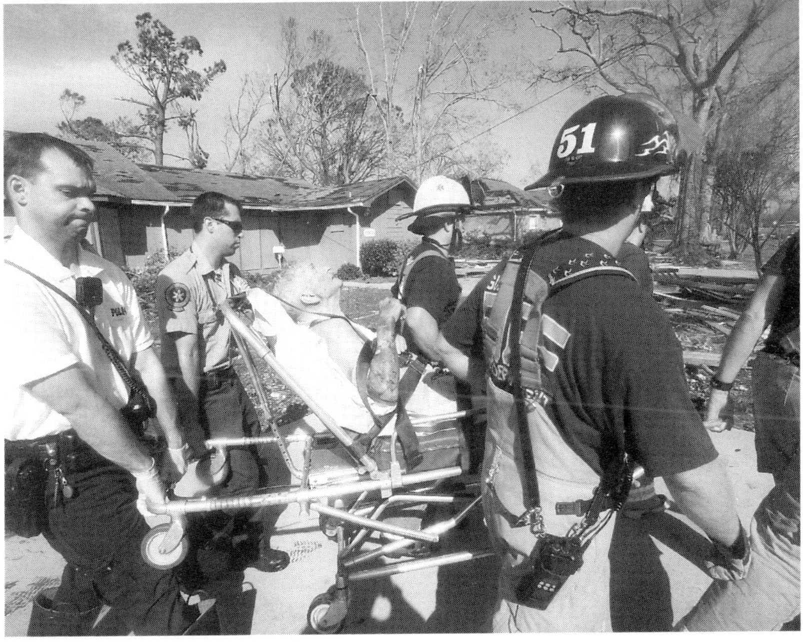

Gulfport firemen and police officers carry an elderly man found alive in the wreckage of his home several days after the storm. Photo by Pat Sullivan.

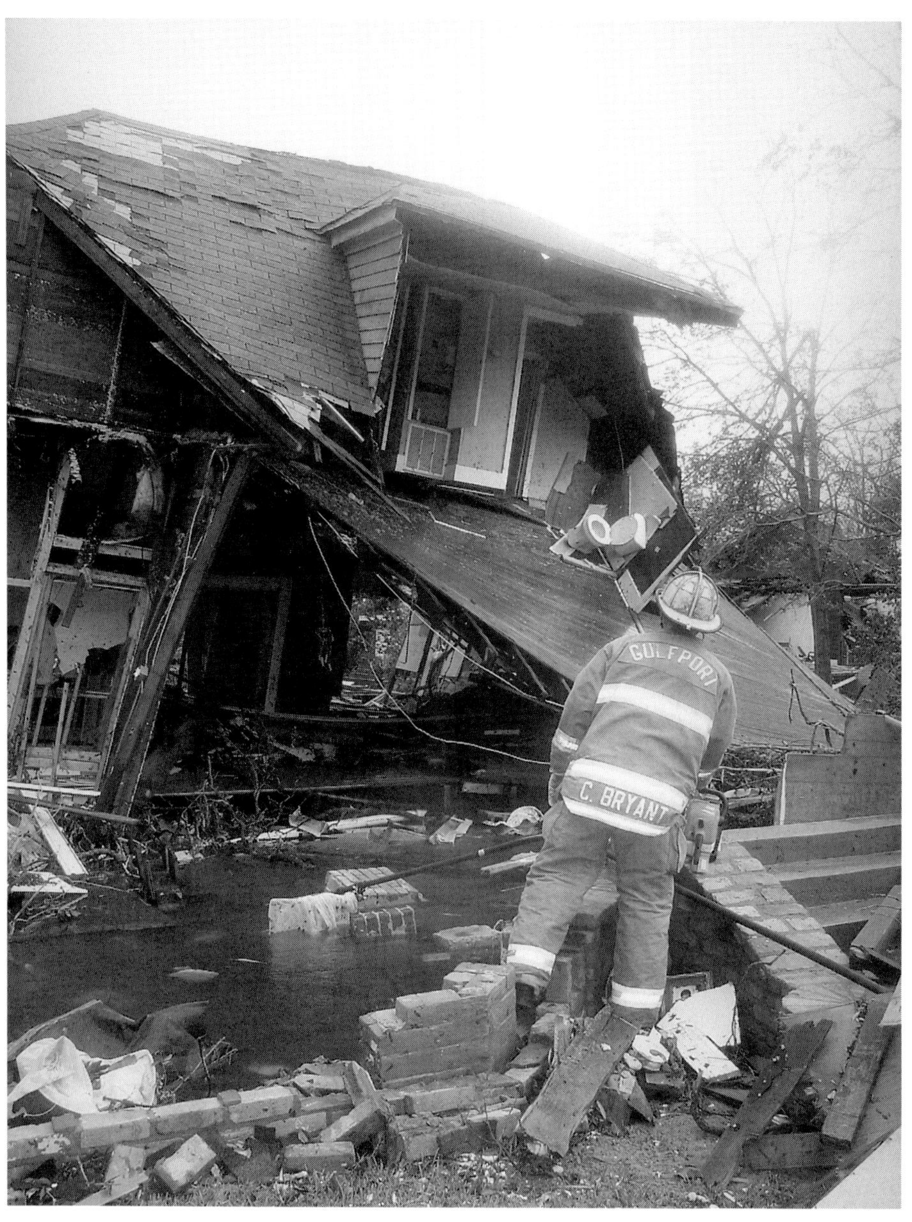

Gulfport firefighter Chad Bryant checks for injured survivors or dead victims in a destroyed home. Photo by Pat Sullivan.

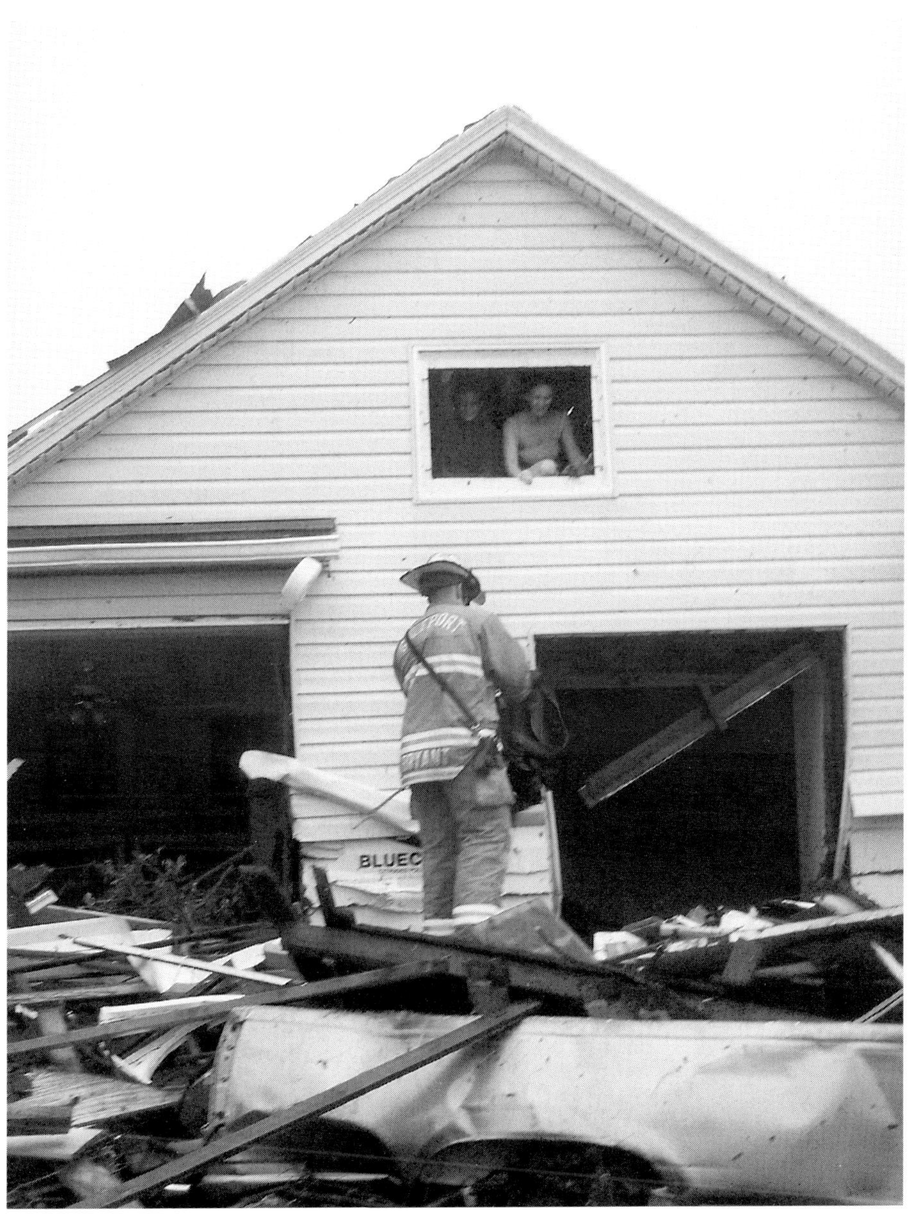

Gulfport firefighter Chad Bryant helps two people found alive but trapped in the attic of a home destroyed by Katrina. Photo by Pat Sullivan.

In one of the more heartrending duties undertaken in the aftermath of Hurricane Katrina, a coroner watches as heavy equipment digs into the wreckage of an apartment complex in a search for suspected human remains. Photo by Pat Sullivan.

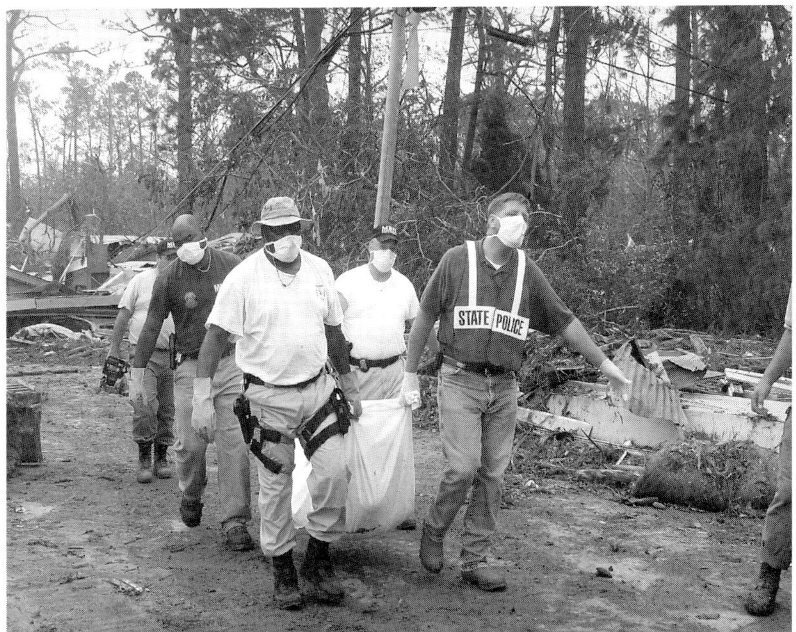

State police and officers from the Mississippi Bureau of Narcotics remove the dead body of a storm victim from the wreckage of a home in Bay St. Louis. Hundreds of Mississippians died in the unexpected 30-foot Katrina storm surge. Photo by Brian Sullivan.

Thousands of leaks in water systems and gas lines ripped apart in the wreckage of homes and buildings created an enormous fire danger in the aftermath of Katrina. Here a house goes up in flames as Gulfport firefighters discover that they have insufficient water pressure to fight the blaze. Photo by Pat Sullivan.

Aerial photo showing complete destruction of a business and residential area west of the harbor in Gulfport where hundreds of cargo containers from the port washed ashore and collided with buildings to complete Katrina's demolition of the area. Photo by Pat Sullivan.

At the intersection of 30th Avenue and Highway 90 in Gulfport the mountain of cargo trailers washed inland from the port terminal brings a complete halt to commerce. Photo by Brian Sullivan.

A resident of west Gulfport stands dwarfed by the enormous scale of the destruction on a newly cleared street. Photo by Brian Sullivan.

This commercial building south of the CSX railroad tracks in Gulfport was collapsed by winds, storm surge, and possible tornados spawned by Katrina. Photo by Pat Sullivan.

Mayor Tommy Longo estimated that over 90 percent of the buildings in Waveland were destroyed in the storm. Photo by Brian Sullivan.

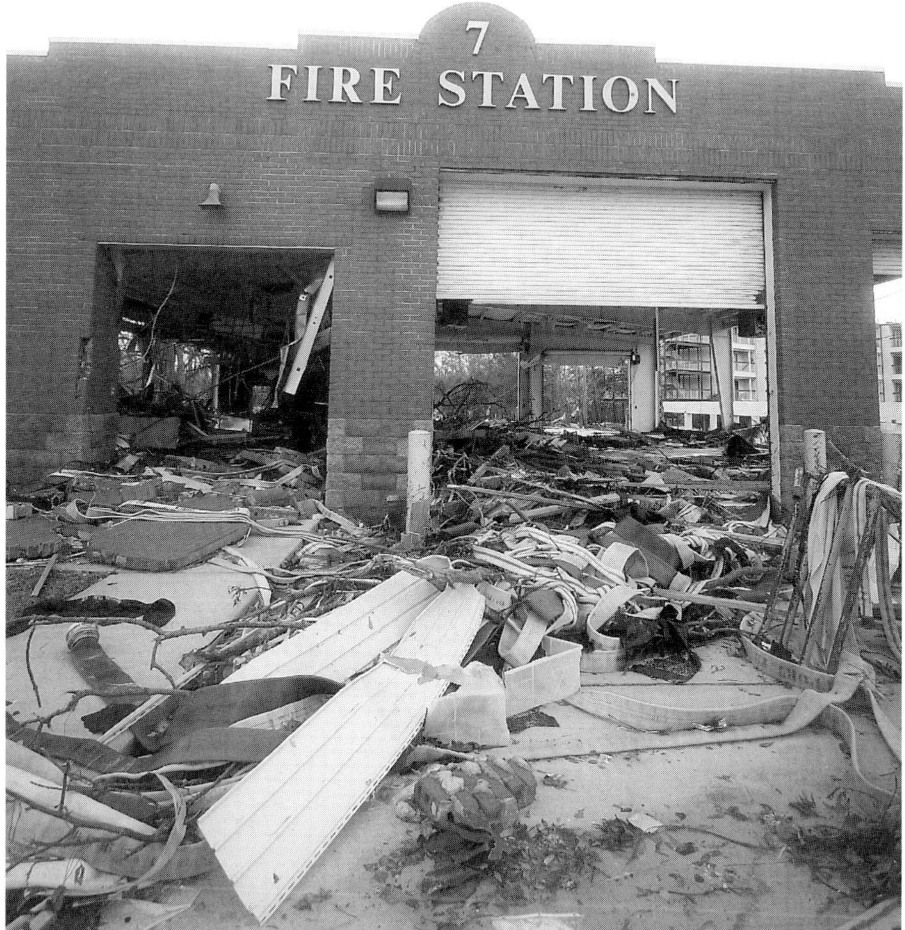

The gutted remains of Gulfport Fire Station 7 on Cowan Road symbolized the hundreds of public buildings and emergency vehicles lost in Katrina's winds and storm surge in the three Mississippi Gulf Coast counties. Various red tape battles hindered the rebuilding of this station for more than five years after the storm. Photo by Pat Sullivan.

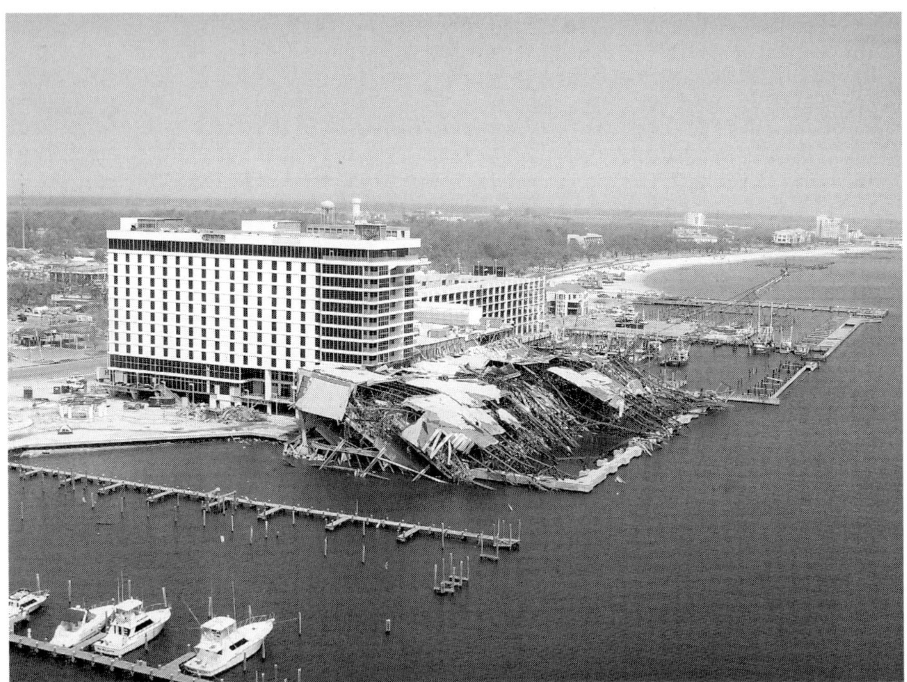

The new Hard Rock Casino and Hotel in Biloxi was scheduled to open on the weekend Hurricane Katrina struck. Its addition to the coast's casino inventory pushed pre-Katrina Gulf Coast casino employment totals above 17,000. This photo shows the Hard Rock destroyed at its moorings. Photo by Pat Sullivan.

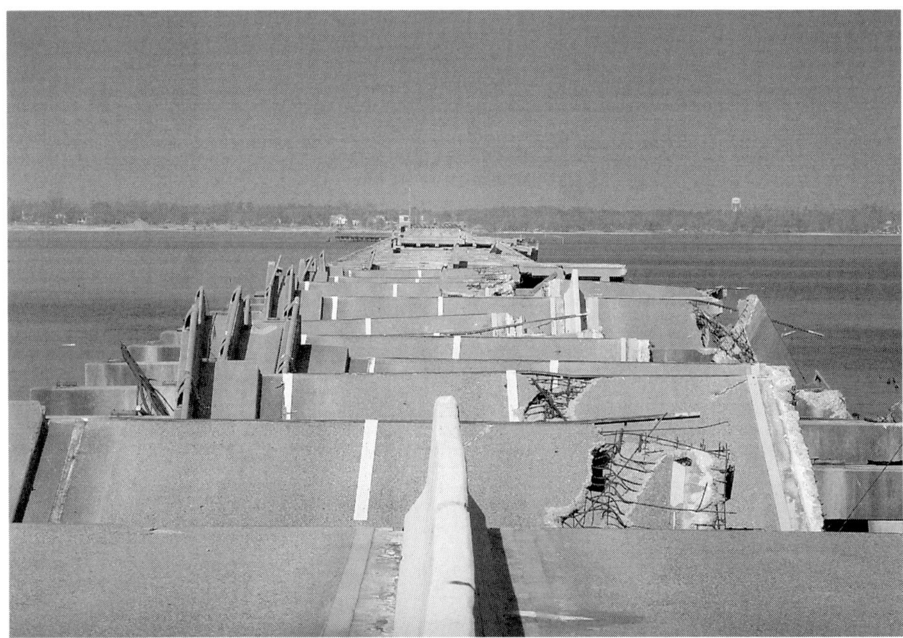

Winds and storm surge floated and collapsed the massive concrete sections of the Highway 90 Bay St. Louis Bridge, leaving Hancock County virtually isolated for many days after the storm. Photo by Brian Sullivan.

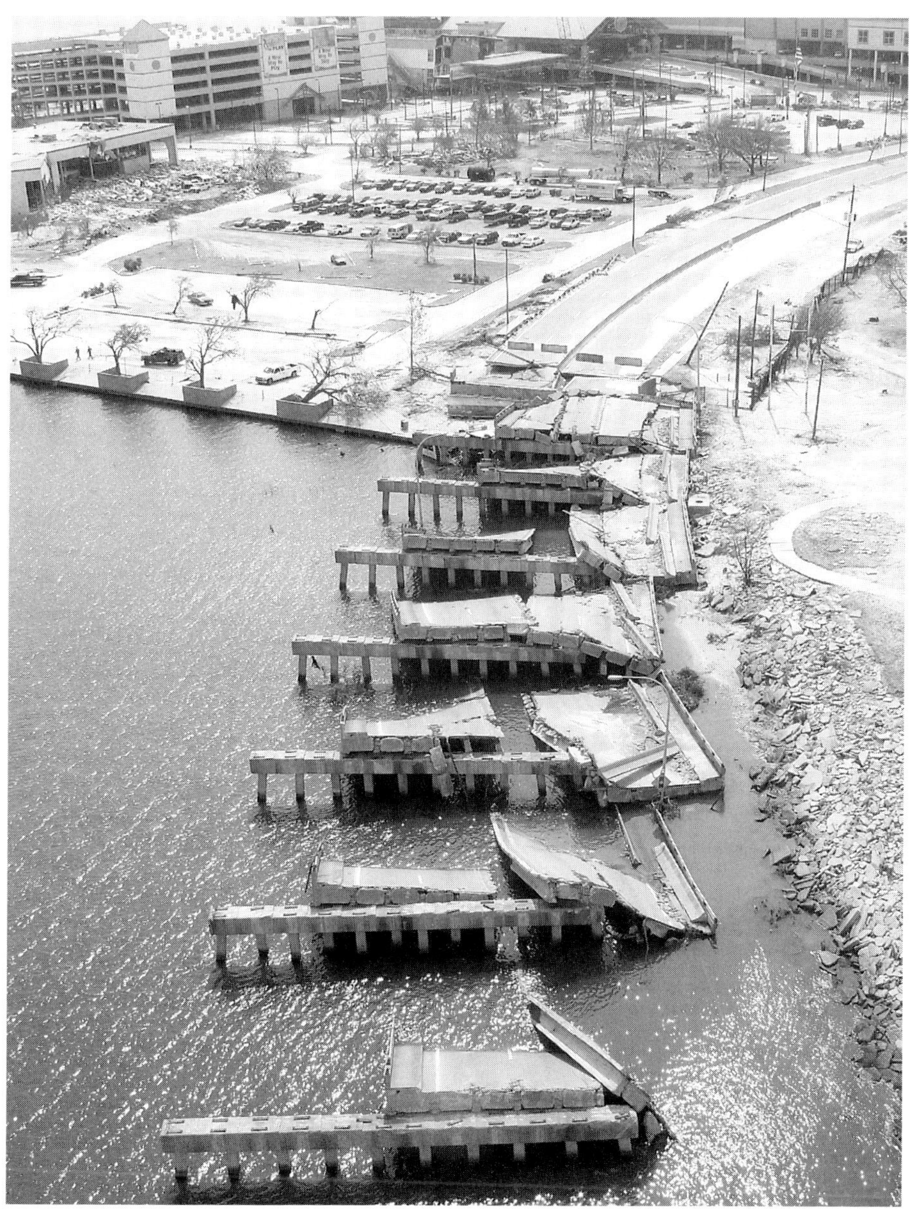

The destruction of the Biloxi–Ocean Springs Bridge left what remained of Biloxi's Highway 90 Casino Row isolated and detached from museums and restaurants in Ocean Springs for two years. Photo by Pat Sullivan.

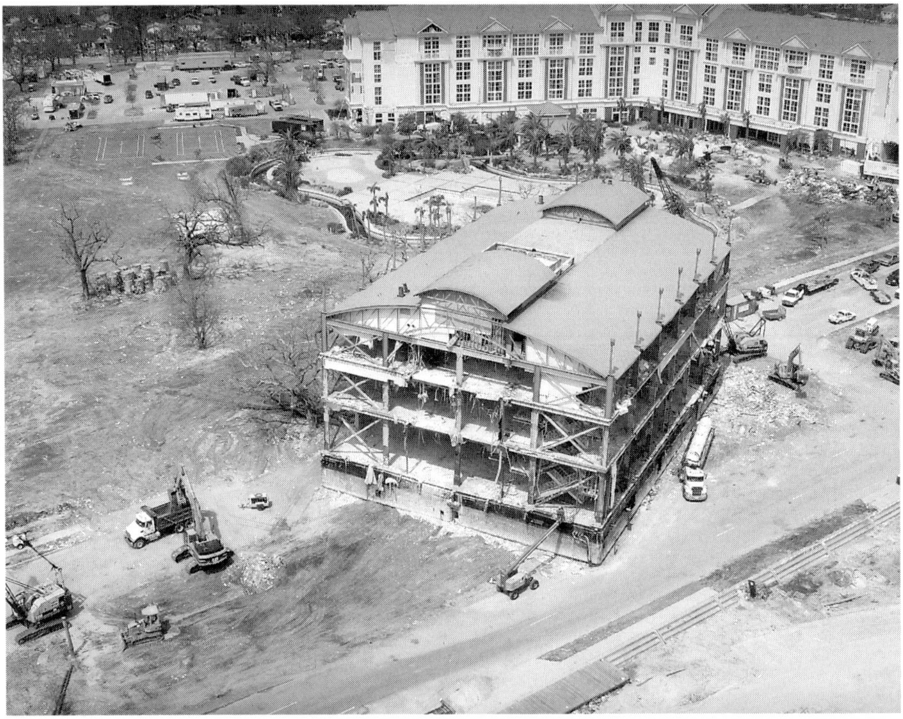

The sight of this casino barge astraddle Highway 90 in Gulfport made banker John Hairston realize that Katrina had put tens of thousands of Mississippi jobs in jeopardy. Photo by Pat Sullivan.

The huge gaming barge from the Grand Casino Biloxi broke its moorings and wound up beached on the north side of Highway 90. Ten of the Mississippi Gulf Coast's thirteen casinos suffered similar catastrophes. Photo by Brian Sullivan.

An American flag planted in the rubble at the Port of Gulfport keeps a lonely vigil over washed-out warehouses. Photo by Pat Sullivan.

The massive scale of the destruction south of the CSX railroad line in Harrison County led officials to cordon off the entire 26-mile-long zone with barbed wire in order to force those who entered to do so through military checkpoints. Photo by Pat Sullivan.

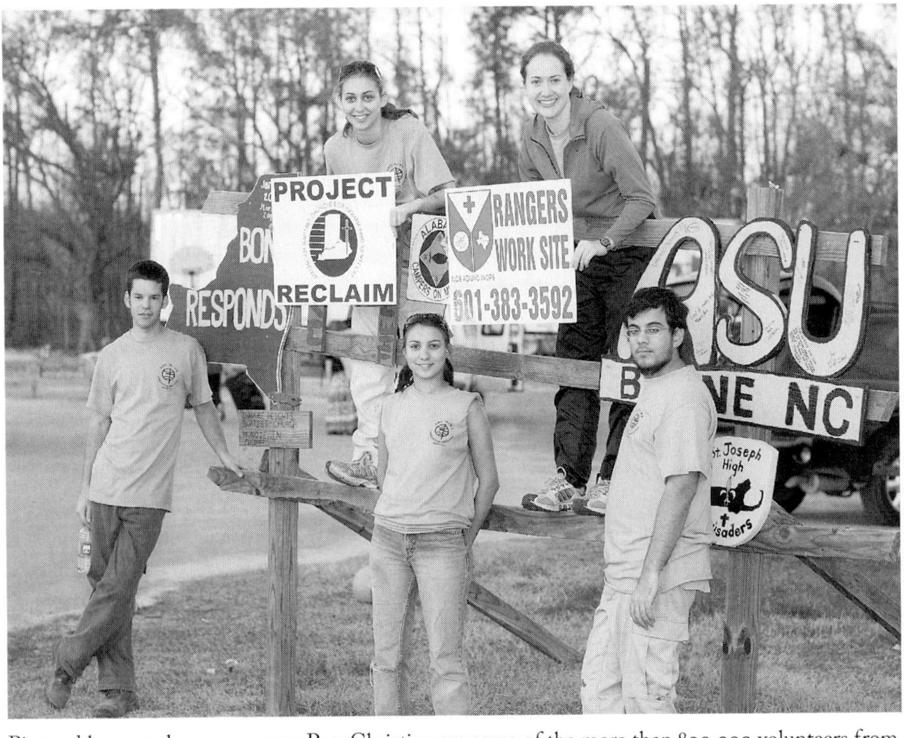

Pictured here at a base camp near Pass Christian are some of the more than 800,000 volunteers from all across the U.S., Canada, and many parts of the world who came to the assistance of the tens of thousands of Mississippians who lost their homes in the disaster. Photo by Pat Sullivan.

Navigating the FEMA processes to get into a camper unit was at least an adventure and often a trial by ordeal. For Elizabeth Doolittle, a series of close encounters with FEMA began in Hattiesburg some time during the week after the storm. The media reminded victims and evacuees to call FEMA or go online to register for assistance. On the coast, where all phone lines and computer services were nonexistent for months, this seemed a ridiculous instruction. However, in Hattiesburg, Doolittle managed to find a working computer to fill out the online forms. Then she entered the brave new world of FEMA trials and traumas. When she went online to verify her registration, the prompt told her that her file did not exist. Naturally, she resubmitted her registration and was assigned a FEMA case number. Soon media stories of fraudulent multiple registrations caught Elizabeth Doolittle's attention and made her wonder if she was considered fraudulent because of the second registration. Her anxiety drove her to call the well-advertised FEMA 800 number to make sure everything was all right. She and thousands of others discovered that the number was always busy. Rumor had it that people who called in the middle of the night actually got through, so the librarian got up in the middle of the night, and after repeated attempts, she got through to a FEMA representative.[34]

The midnight call made things worse. When Doolittle explained her anxiety about the computer mix-up and possible double registration, an abrupt response came back: "Oh no, you can't do that . . . you could go to jail for that." After repeated and emphatic statements about possible jail time, the telephone voice stated that this could not be fixed without a personal visit to a FEMA office. When asked where the nearest office might be found, the voice informed the worried librarian that as a telephone rep, she did not know anything about locations, as her only assignment was to take registrations from people who had no computers. Daily perusals of the newspaper turned up no location for a local FEMA office. After several weeks, it was the Hattiesburg rumor mill that brought word of a FEMA office opening in Purvis, Mississippi, a few miles to the south. Ms. Doolittle took off to Purvis, and after a considerable wait in a long line, she finally got to talk to "a real live FEMA person." His cross-checking found that indeed the system had accepted two registrations, but if it had not been straightened out her file would have been pulled and referred to a committee. This would have meant more waiting, but likely no jail time. Over the next several months, Elizabeth Doolittle had occasion to visit other FEMA offices in Gulfport and Waveland to straighten out various paperwork errors. The lines were long, and the armies of newly hired temporary

FEMA workers showed varying degrees of fitness for the job of working with frazzled storm victims. In the FEMA offices people sometimes found patience and kindness, but all too often for a disaster-stressed population there was rudeness and incompetence. One could not fail to recognize that the training of FEMA's new disaster field force was minimal and that most of the workers had little knowledge of the agency beyond the forms they specialized in distributing or filling out. As a result, frustration often negatively afflicted all parties to an encounter.[35]

For prestorm renters like Elizabeth Doolittle who owned no property, FEMA placed trailers in 130 existing mobile home parks, and when these filled, the agency built an additional 43 group sites in Mississippi.[36] In early November of 2005, Elizabeth Doolittle moved into the FEMA park near the Long Beach school system's administrative offices. Here, the trailers were lined up side by side with 10-foot spaces between. The compound had a communal laundry room with washers and dryers for residents. Like many others, Elizabeth Doolittle occupied a 240-square-foot FEMA camper, and though it was small, she was glad to have a little place of her own in a trailer park located near her work. Families with children got larger units or even full-length trailers. Still, no matter what the model, the quarters were always cramped. Tiny steps at the door had to be navigated with care to avoid slips and falls, and the narrow doorways themselves produced many bruised elbows.[37]

Ms. Doolittle found that the people who set up her unit knew nothing about its operation. A separate maintenance contractor was responsible for repair and upkeep, but after the reporting of problems to an out-of-state FEMA call center, it could take days to get someone out to take care of leaks or faulty appliances. Elizabeth Doolittle believed that her trailer park went through four different maintenance contractors over the year that she stayed there.[38] In the Pascagoula area, after Fanett Landry got her trailer, it took two more weeks to get the keys. Once she moved in, a propane leak emptied the tanks within three days. When she first called the maintenance help line, Landry encountered "a large number of prompts calling for different types of information." These steps finally gave way to a recorded message that said "all representatives are busy." A sudden hang-up followed, necessitating repeated calls and repeated data inputs.[39]

People who coped best "learned to let a lot of little things go," or looked for the humor in the situation. Paul and Tracie Sones of Pascagoula built a deck outside their trailer and cooked and ate outside as much as possible to gain a sense of space. They took to spreading a tablecloth outside on a card table to pick up their spirits at mealtime.[40] When asked about life in her little trailer, 84-year-old Laura Creel would smile and tell people, "Well, I always wanted to go camping—just not for two years." One camper occupant described the glory of "living like a pack of gypsies." Then, there was the cooking. For two years, Laura Creel warmed things with a microwave because she could not bring herself to use the butane stove.[41] Others discovered that the quarters were so close that vapor from cooking on the gas burners would sometimes set off the fire alarm. Elizabeth Doolittle, a determined cook, bragged that she always disconnected the fire alarm before cooking. She proudly reported that after two maintenance calls had produced repairmen with two different and unsatisfactory theories of how she should light the oven, she discovered on her own that the stove top would lift to allow easy ignition. Ms. Doolittle enjoyed telling people that in her camper she could sit at "the kitchen table, . . . reach into the refrigerator for dinner, put it on the stove, turn on a burner, stir what's in the pot, put it on the table to eat, and when finished put the dishes in the sink, . . . all without moving off the kitchen bench." Other camper residents variously observed that it was possible to make up the bed while using the restroom, or "touch the ceiling and both side walls without stretching." Tubs were so small that adult use seemed unimaginable. The occupant of one unit claimed that the best approach to the small shower stall was to step in and get wet, step out to lather up with soap, then get back in and turn round and round to let the walls scrub you while you rinsed.[42] For those who had lost everything, finding the humor in the situation was an uplifting alternative to crying.

However, life in the FEMA trailer parks also had a grim side, and the longer people had to wait for apartments or other permanent housing solutions, the greater their suffering. Unfamiliar surroundings coupled with living among strangers could generate feelings of isolation, especially for the thousands who lost jobs and their attendant social outlets as a result of the storm. Families sharing cramped quarters got on each other's nerves with increasing frequency as time wore on. Jeff Bennett, the director of the Gulf Coast Mental Health Center, observed that for many of the people who turned up in his office, living in close quarters created highly stressful "boundary issues." Moreover, living in proximity to total strangers of a different socioeconomic or ethic background added to the stress. Loud music in a unit went "right through the walls" to disturb people on all sides. If the neighbors fought, families next door heard it and worried about how the violent-sounding adult rows would affect the children who inevitably heard them. Inside the trailers, the lack of space and privacy for even changing clothes produced friction. Some residents would sit up talking outside at all hours of the night, oblivious to the fact that they were disturbing their neighbors' sleep. Disabled cars sitting on blocks could sometimes be seen here and there cluttering the lots. As Bennett put it, "you are into a place that you don't know," and that was a major source of psychological distress.[43]

Beyond the anecdotal evidence, a 2007 International Medical Corps study of Mississippi and Louisiana FEMA trailer park residents showed that on average they had suffered a 25 percent decline in household income after the storms. Moreover, half of all trailer park residents did not feel safe walking around the area at night. Suicides and general mortality rates rose, and fully half of the victims still housed in FEMA campers and trailers "met the criteria for suffering from some kind of depression." Similarly, the Columbia University Mailman School of Public Health's 2007 Mississippi Child and Family Health Study produced evidence that children living in Katrina trailers or parks in the most devasted zones showed markedly higher than normal rates of depression, anxiety, and psychological vulnerability accompanied by much higher than normal rates of absenteeism from school. Gulfport therapist Jeff Bennett saw many kids who may have experimented with illegal drugs or alcohol before Katrina, but all too often after Katrina they had started using drugs as a form of habitual "self-medication" for anxieties and malaise. Over time, increasing numbers of adults also turned to substance abuse in their struggle to cope with prolonged stress, depression, and lingering uncertainty about how they would manage to get back on their feet.[44] Reports of domestic violence, child abuse, and suicide spiked upward as the housing crisis lingered and months in trailers turned into years.[45] Waiting for a permanent place to live took its toll.

Under normal circumstances, FEMA regulations called for an end to emergency housing within 18 months of a disaster. However, the size of the Mississippi catastrophe and the slow pace of the housing recovery delayed the official end of the trailer program until May 1, 2009.[46] Meanwhile, in the summer of 2007, concerns over formaldehyde in the trailers generated a congressional hearing, and early in 2008, the Centers for Disease Control and Prevention confirmed that the gaseous formaldehyde levels in the trailers made them unsafe. This confirmed Bay St. Louis physician Scott Needle's suspicions about the cause of the high incidence of respiratory problems among trailer inhabitants.[47] For those who as yet had no housing alternatives, health fears now added to the burdens of waiting.

Beyond numbers on paper, Katrina's destruction of over 65,000 Mississippi homes had far-reaching implications. The economic as well as the psychological and social recovery of the community demanded focused attention to long-term housing solutions beyond FEMA campers and trailers. It was clear that Katrina had inflicted a gaping wound that available private resources, insurance, and charity could not heal. Both Mississippi and Louisiana were near the bottom of national per capita income statistics. There could be no state resources to address a housing crisis of this magnitude. Neither personal savings nor available charitable support could be expected to make people or their communities whole.

On the national level, the Stafford Act made the repair of damaged public infrastructure and debris removal largely a federal financial obligation, and federal law made available to victims the temporary emergency camper and trailer program. The Small Business Administration routinely made low interest loans available for those who could qualify, but Katrina left tens of thousands of uninsured homeowners for whom payments on even a low-interest mortgage would be impossible. Large-scale foreclosures and bankruptcies became a very real and troubling possibility. In the fall of 2005, a banking survey revealed that 123,000 Louisiana and Mississippi borrowers had fallen behind on their mortgages. This was double the number from the previous year.[48] Most lenders offered a 90-day foreclosure forbearance program, but if there was to be a real solution to the Katrina housing crisis, if tens of thousands of mortgage holders were to avoid defaults on slabs or unliveable properties, the solution would have to come from the financial resources of the nation made available through the taxing authority and borrowing power of the federal government.

The stark post-Katrina housing reality pushed Mississippi Governor Haley Barbour, one of the staunchest of Republican fiscal conservatives, to deploy his considerable leverage on the reluctant leadership of a Republican-controlled Congress to break the logjams that blocked or slowed efforts to channel federal housing money to the coast. In the years ahead, Barbour's ultimate allocation of Mississippi's share of the resulting federal recovery funds came to be disputed. In truth, however, his critics and supporters alike would all concede that without Governor Barbour's influence with the Bush administration and with the leaders of the U.S. House of Representatives, there almost certainly would have been much less federal money available for investment in the housing recovery. One might legitimately disagree with Barbour's priorities and the timing and urgency with which he addressed them. Still, all of the state's competing recovery priorities were better funded as a result of his efforts. Likewise, if Senator Thad Cochran of Mississippi had not been serving as chairman of the U.S. Senate Appropriations Committee,

Barbour's leverage with House leaders and President Bush would have been missing one of its most important tools.

In September of 2005, the Republican-controlled U.S. House and Senate quickly passed a $62 billion emergency appropriation to cover the cost of FEMA relief operations and the recovery of public infrastructure, but the administration had not yet confronted the long-term housing recovery problem which was outside the FEMA emergency mission mandate. By the end of the month, proposals to deal with the long-term recovery had split the GOP and stalled in Congress. Rising estimates of the tremendous cost of recovery upset many Republican lawmakers and prompted the Republican Study Committee, an alliance of 100 conservative House members, to propose a round of federal spending cuts to offset the anticipated Katrina outlays. Notwithstanding the fact that there had been no requirement for offsetting budget reductions to finance previous disaster efforts, after four years of tax cuts and mounting deficits, the Republican caucus now pressed hard for Katrina offsets. Cuts were proposed in Medicaid, the manned space program, and Medicare. Already disturbed over the speed with which September's FEMA emergency appropriation had passed the house, Republican budget hawks focused anger on House Majority Leader Tom Delay for his statement of support for borrowing for disaster relief without requiring offsetting cuts.[49] A late September Louisiana request for $250 billion for Louisiana recovery projects alone so intensified the conservative deficit rebellion that the Republican House and Senate leaders felt compelled to move forward a new budget plan featuring $35 billion in reductions over five years. Even these cuts failed to satisfy hard-core Republican budget hawks who wanted to see cuts of $50 billion. The ensuing debate over how to move forward with offsetting budget cuts while jousting over whose ox would be gored split Republican ranks in Congress and stalled all long-term recovery proposals until mid-December.[50]

In late October, with congressional purse strings tightening,[51] the Bush White House forwarded a request to Congress that $17 billion of the $62 billion in FEMA's emergency appropriations be reallocated to cover disaster-related costs for the repair of federal highways, levees, military bases, and veterans hospitals. Included in this reallocation request was a White House proposal that $1.5 billion be redirected to the Community Development Block Grant program operated through the U.S. Department of Housing and Urban Development. There was ample precedent for using CDBG funds for long-term disaster recovery projects, and the White House hoped that an offer to rescind $2.3 billion in unspent funds elsewhere in the current budget might enable the proposed reallocation to get around the troublesome question of offsetting cuts.[52] Senator Cochran immediately embraced the idea, and in his role as chairman of the powerful Senate Appropriations Committee, Cochran went to work to push the Senate to expand the Bush CDBG proposal upwards to an eventual $11.5 billion package.[53]

However, House Republicans still adamantly resisted reallocations for Katrina recovery unless there were offsetting cuts. To Blue Dog Democratic conservatives like Congressman Gene Taylor from the Mississippi Gulf Coast, the stance smacked of hypocrisy. Taylor took to the floor of the House to remind the Republican leadership that when major tax cuts were enacted "for the wealthiest 1% of Americans," there was no talk of budget offsets, nor were there any offsets enacted to help fund the Iraq war. "Suddenly, after taking care of those who had the most" with tax cuts, House Republicans were saying to "the poor folks in Mississippi who lost their homes, [and the] poor folks in New Orleans whose houses were flooded, 'we can't do this unless we . . . hurt some other Americans.'" Taylor contended that after considering four years of freewheeling spending without offsets, "it was the cruelest lie of all," to say "that the only way you can help people who have lost everything is by hurting someone else."[54] Taylor's protest came to naught. By the end of November, no long-term recovery proposals, Republican or Democratic, seemed to be going anywhere.[55]

In early December, in testimony before the House Select Committee investigating the federal response to Katrina, Governor Barbour made an eloquent public plea for action. After praising the spirit of Mississippians who "hitched up their britches, . . . [and] did what had to be done" in the storm's aftermath, Barbour pointed out to the committee that "more than 100 days after Katrina made landfall, our people face a problem they can't overcome" on their own. "For us to continue moving forward," he said, "Congress must act." The governor then listed a litany of recovery projects delayed because the money had been "stalled in Congress." Road and bridge repair had ground to a halt; school districts and local governments that had borrowed money to reopen or to continue to pay their employees faced bankruptcy; and tens of thousands of owners of destroyed homes who had mistakenly relied on federal floodplain guidelines were left wondering how they could pay mortgages on concrete slabs. Barbour ended with a warning that "we're at a point where our recovery and renewal efforts are stalled because of inaction in Washington, D.C., and the delay has created uncertainty that is having very negative effects on our recovery. . . . It is taking the starch out of people who've worked so hard to help themselves and their neighbors."[56]

Still, in mid-December as Congress headed toward a Christmas recess, negotiations reportedly stalled and "tempers flared" when House conservatives "dug in against the cost" of Senator Cochran's Community Development Block Grant proposal. Behind the scenes, Governor Barbour now brought his influence into play. Over the previous 15 years, first as chairman of the Republican National Committee and later as a lobbyist, Barbour had raised huge sums of money for Speaker Dennis Hastert and other House Republicans, as well as President George W. Bush. According to a report from the *New York Times*, at a critical juncture on December 16, Governor Barbour attended a private meeting to discuss the Cochran proposal with Speaker Hastert and the Republican whip, Representative Roy Blunt of Missouri. Barbour argued that the federal government had a duty to help people outside the floodplain who had relied on inaccurate federal flood maps when they had decided not to buy flood insurance. Whether by the strength of Barbour's pleadings and political connections, or through the resolve of Senator Cochran as chairman of the Senate Appropriations Committee, "the logjam broke," and the reluctant House Republican leadership agreed to Senator Cochran's numbers. A similar Barbour-Cochran magic worked to overcome White House and the Office of Management and the Budget resistance to Cochran's numbers. The centerpiece of the funding package was $11.5 billion in Community Development Block Grant funding. Over $5 billion of this was allocated to support housing and other recovery programs in Mississippi.[57] Louisiana clearly got the short end of the stick in the Republicans' Christmastime deal, but additional appropriations early in 2006 balanced the scales.

Almost from the very beginning, the development and phasing of the Mississippi program provoked controversy. Under the CDBG guidelines, the governor had the discretion to either invite the state legislature to help shape the program or develop a plan on his own. In a characteristic move, Barbour chose the latter approach—an approach which may have saved time, but one that also invited suspicion and constant second-guessing from critics as Mississippi's own homegrown bureaucratic delays slowed implementation of the program. Thus, in March of 2006, when Barbour announced that the first leg of his CDBG "Partial Action Plan" would make housing grants of up to $150,000 available only to homeowners outside the federal floodplain who had purchased wind insurance but not flood insurance, there was an immediate outcry from advocacy groups representing low-to-moderate-income homeowners and renters whose needs appeared to be shortchanged or at least sent to the back of the line to wait. Representatives of 24 civic groups, nonprofits, and church organizations that were deeply involved with volunteer efforts on the coast lodged a 19-page protest. After constructing the program without formal legislative input, the Barbour administration's limitation of the comment period to "a mere week" drew fire. Making use of law student volunteers, the Mississippi Center for Justice quickly gathered over 2,000 signatures protesting the inadequacy of the Phase I plan.[58] In the Mississippi House of Representatives, two bills passed in the spring of 2006 attempting to create some form of legislative oversight, only to face death at the hands of Barbour supporters in the state senate. In the heat of the struggle, House Speaker Billy McCoy lamented that it seemed that in Mississippi "everything had to come from the mighty paw of Haley Barbour."[59]

Moreover, the governor's simultaneous request for a waiver of HUD's rule that 50 percent of the CDBG funds be spent on low-to-moderate-income storm victims raised persistent questions about whether the governor's plan was being deliberately designed to "disproportionately benefit higher-income homeowners to the detriment of renters and low-income homeowners who were unable to afford insurance."[60] In essence the protest asked why "out of the whole universe of disaster-stricken people" were people outside the flood zone sent to the front of the line, ahead of people in some of the worst devastated low-income neighborhoods nearest the waterfront in East Biloxi, Pass Christian, Bay St. Louis, or Waveland?[61] While many outside the governor's inner circle found cause to doubt his ultimate intentions, to Democratic Congressman Gene Taylor it was clear that the argument that had won the day in Congress had centered around the fate of the homeowners that Barbour had singled out for Phase I benefits. Taylor and his staff remained confident that the needs of renters and uninsured low-income homeowners would eventually be addressed.[62]

Unfortunately, Barbour's March and April Phase I announcements provided only short statements of a general intention to provide funding at an unspecified later date for uninsured homeowners and rental owners who did "not meet the initial grant criteria."[63] The vagueness of the official statements and the lack of detailed plans for dealing with the needs of those left out of Phase I left ample room for doubt and suspicions about insensitivity, political calculation, or malice on the part of those who were developing the plans inside the governor's office.[64]

In moving ahead with a multibillion-dollar housing plan without organized public input and scrutiny, the governor's team failed to take heed of a key finding from the final 2005 report of the Governor's Commission on Recovery, Rebuilding, and Renewal that "rebuilding will be most successful if citizens are actively engaged in the process . . . [including] meaningful involvement from a broad social spectrum."[65] As a direct result of the decision not to vet plans with representative groups even six months after Barbour's Phase I announcement, the Jackson *Clarion-Ledger* was still noting that the continuing political "wrangling over the pace of getting federal housing grant checks into the hands of storm victims . . . [had]focused the heat of withering criticism from legislators" on Governor Barbour. The paper quoted Representative Diane Peranich, a coast Democrat, who contended that the conflict over the governor's housing plans was "not about politics or power," but rather "about helping people who are suffering on a daily basis." For Peranich, the nightmarish slowness of the grant process was less significant than the reality that "too many storm victims simply won't qualify for help under this program, and they have no place left to go." Peranich and other legislators called repeatedly for legislative oversight or at least a strong legislative advisory role in developing and prioritizing the various phases of the grant program.[66]

In choosing not to respond to such calls, Barbour owned personal responsibility for all of the program's sins and shortcomings as well as its blessings. Barbour well understood his position, and given congressional irritation over FEMA's no-bid contracts and the consequent insistence on strong accountability for Katrina spending, it is not surprising that the governor told a reporter that he had asked HUD to preaudit the program to "make sure the money was spent right." The governor conceded that this move had slowed implementation and delayed the grant checks' getting into homeowners' hands.[67] However, given his decision to develop everything behind closed doors in the governor's office, if things were not right, the blame would rest squarely on his shoulders and his alone.

Beyond issues of inclusion, the governor's office had proceeded in developing the housing program without accurate and detailed data about the nature of the housing loss and the demographics of the various affected population groups on the coast. This, too, was a pitfall that the Rand report to the Governor's Commission had warned against.[68] In defense of the governor's office, it must be said that no such demographic study existed five months after Katrina, but neither had the governor's office taken the lead in commissioning one. The gross numbers that did exist were collected by different methods, and because they did not use a common terminology in describing damage, they were confusing and subject to conflicting interpretations when compared to each other. More importantly, they lacked the detailed analysis of the types of units destroyed and the socioeconomic status of the persons who occupied them—data critical to any serious effort at effective planning.

Lack of congruity and lack of detail in the various existing damage reports both confused the public and fueled needless controversy. For example, in Mississippi the Red Cross showed 68,729 "dwellings destroyed" plus another 65,237 with "major damage,"[69] while the FEMA estimates five months later showed a combined total of only 61,386 Mississippi homes destroyed or suffering major damage. While the FEMA data was broken into counts of rental units versus owner-occupied units, wind versus water destruction, and insured versus uninsured damage county by county, it included no socioeconomic data about storm victims or the type of dwellings they could afford, and thus it provided incomplete guidance for targeting the housing effort.[70] Beyond this, a 2007 report from the University of Southern Mississippi's Bureau of Business and Economic Research contended that the FEMA numbers did not adequately account for the dislocated population which could be identified in census reports in 2007. The USM team concluded that these numbers supported their much higher estimate that 68,000 to 70,000 residential units had been "destroyed or rendered uninhabitable." The USM report lamented the fact that there was no satisfactory data for estimating the numbers and types of housing units being built or rehabilitated.[71] In the absence of a more detailed study, the FEMA report of February 2006 became the default data base for the governor's staff despite its inability to answer serious socioeconomic questions about those who had lost everything.

Without a detailed study, the governor's staff defended the questionable phasing of its CDBG housing plans in language that cast insured homeowners as "acting responsibly" in contrast to uninsured low-income homeowners who were presumed to be "irresponsible" as well as poor.[72] This rhetorical tone tended to reinforce advocacy groups in their belief that the governor's staff remained grossly insensitive to the day-to-day financial dilemmas of low-income households. One local attorney characterized it as "the height of cruelty and callousness" to blame storm victims or characterize as irresponsible those who were surviving on minimum Social Security retirement checks or working in the coast's low-wage service economy in circumstances that forced them to choose between paying the light bill and buying groceries or buying insurance.[73] Had the governor's office followed the Rand recommendation and commissioned an immediate in-depth study early on, credible data would have gone far to reassure critics that the need for appropriate targeting of housing funds was being taken seriously.

In a December 2007 editorial, the *Sun Herald* (Biloxi-Gulfport), a newspaper that twice endorsed Governor Barbour, complained about its inability to properly "size up the housing situation" and pointed to three of its own recent stories which presented seemingly conflicting numbers—"numbers that mystify more than clarify"—derived from FEMA and the U.S. Government Accountability Office. Were 80,000 affordable housing units needed on the Mississippi Gulf Coast, as the local Steps Coalition contended based on their reading of FEMA reports? Had 13,800 rental units in Mississippi been destroyed in the storm as FEMA said, or merely the 10,000 counted in a GAO report? Was a serious housing shortfall for low-wage service workers looming? If only 25 percent of Mississippi's $5.4 billion in CDBG funds was being spent on low-income residents, as the nonprofit Mississippi Protection and Advocacy Program contended, would that be sufficient to cover the need? Beneath a headline that asserted "We Need Numbers About Housing That We Can Crunch With Confidence," the editorial concluded that "We don't know if any of these numbers are accurate. We don't know how much [low-income residents] can afford to pay and how much should be provided. . . . We need a census. We need an inventory. We need an accounting. Obviously, the housing needs of many pre-Katrina residents of South Mississippi have not been satisfied. And just as obviously, no one really knows just how many people we are talking about."[74]

In the absence of solid housing and demographic assessments, Governor Barbour's fall 2007 decision to divert $600 million in CDBG money to a futuristic expansion plan for the Port of Gulfport drew vigorous protests from local housing advocacy groups, produced a round of congressional hearings and negative national press stories, and eventually drew a federal lawsuit.[75] As fate would have it, no really adequate Gulf Coast housing study was available until early 2009 when the Mississippi Housing Recovery Data Project issued its first report.[76]

That the initial allocation decisions were made without solid housing numbers in hand did not instill confidence in the governor's plan or in the assumptions which guided its evolution over the next two years. Housing advocates pointed to the 2006 Rand report's caution that marked declines in available low-income housing typically follow disasters. The Rand report had warned that in the aftermath of disasters, private markets find it less profitable to replace affordable rental housing than to build units for middle- and upper-income groups. Moreover, the report pointed out that the pattern of disbursement of federal recovery monies in past disasters had often been inadequate to "address the more difficult financial challenges faced by lower-income households in the rebuilding process."[77] There could be little doubt that such postdisaster developments had tended to slow overall recovery of workforce numbers and population counts. Given the slow pace of the unfolding of Mississippi's programs for addressing affordable housing needs, it should have come as no surprise that a January 2010 U.S. Government Accountability Office report found that in both Louisiana and Mississippi federal assistance had funded an estimated 56 percent of the damaged homeowner units, but only 26 percent of the damaged rental units. The GAO concluded that, just as in previous disasters, federal assistance for permanent housing following Katrina had primarily benefitted homeowners to the detriment of renters. Thus, GAO suggested the need for more restrictions on state uses of CDBG funds in future disasters.[78]

Phase I of Governor Barbour's program was announced in March of 2006. However, it was the end of August 2006, a year after Katrina, before all the red tape could be cleared to get checks to the first 40 grantees from the pool of 17,000 who had applied. These Phase I awards were limited to homeowners who lived outside the federal floodplain, but lost their homes to the Katrina storm surge. They provided grants of up to $150,000 and required homeowners to enter a covenant to obtain and maintain flood insurance on their property in perpetuity.[79] Only storm surge losses were eligible. By FEMA's count this meant 5,393 uninsured owner-occupied Mississippi homes that were destroyed or subjected to major damage from wind acting alone were excluded from this and all other phases of the governor's housing grant program with no consideration as to whether the victims were rich or poor.[80]

Even for the grant recipients eligible for Phase I benefits, the waiting seemed like an eternity. Chandretta Lewis from Gautier told an Associated Press reporter that she had applied for the state grant in April, but it had taken until October to finalize it with her mortgage company. In January, a missing signature from her long-gone ex-husband was still holding up the funds. State officials applied a more stringent standard than had FEMA in granting her funds. Officials with the Mississippi Development Authority, which administered the state grants, ruled that her husband's signature on a divorce decree was insufficient to establish her clear title to the property, even though both FEMA and her insurance company had accepted it, and an attorney had advised her that this would be sufficient legal proof. In the interim, she had started repairs using her small FEMA emergency home repair assistance check and the wind insurance money she had received to cover roof damage.[81]

Ms. Lewis's plight demonstrated the web of state-level red tape with which storm victims contended on their way to actual payouts of the housing recovery grants. Of course, the fact that closing on the grant was scheduled to take place at a mortgage company office indicated that MDA spent time checking for liens on the property. In addition, the MDA routine involved searching insurance records to verify the exact amounts of any insurance proceeds.[82] FEMA records were checked, SBA loans had to be repaid, insurance had to be settled—all so that the Mississippi Development Authority could be assured that there was absolutely no fraud and no duplication of benefits—a defect which could have brought the program into collision with the Stafford Act. To attorneys working to aid storm victims with the state grant process, it appeared that MDA employees were so afraid that HUD auditors would come back to criticize the state that they asked "total perfection" in the paperwork from stressed and depressed storm victims, but offered no assistance. Minor defects in the way a notary public signed or executed a document, defects that had no legal implications, could trigger MDA to kick the paperwork back to the applicant.[83]

Some of MDA's over-abundant caution arose in response to stinging criticism leveled at Mississippi from a national coalition of bankers. In an April 2006 article in the *Wall Street Journal* the bankers' group complained that the Mississippi grant processes then under development were too lax and open to abuse. The bankers pressed hard for stronger restrictions and antifraud measures in the Mississippi program.[84] Coming at a time when ongoing hearings in Washington were probing FEMA's no-bid contracts and auditing practices, such private sector criticisms could not help but impact the development of Mississippi grant procedures. In June of 2006, Governor Barbour told the legislature that objections from the National Mortgage Bankers Association and other finance industry groups had caused the issuance of the first grant checks to be "delayed until this issue is resolved."[85] Despite the governor's desire not to make national headlines for the wrong reasons, both Senator Trent Lott and Representative Gene Taylor urged the Mississippi Development Authority to find a middle ground between fraud prevention and quicker distribution of the grants. In a statement to the U.S. House Committee on Financial Services, Taylor criticized the resulting overly cumbersome state process as "treating every disaster victim with suspicion." Despite the long waits and despite the criticisms from Lott and Taylor, both Governor Barbour and State Auditor Phil Bryant continued to uphold the stringent MDA approach.[86]

On December 19, 2006, Phase II of the Mississippi housing grant program won HUD approval. At this time, some 16 months after Katrina, FEMA reported that 31,211 Mississippi families were still housed in emergency campers and trailers.[87] For Phase II, the governor's office reallocated $700 million in CDBG money for an initiative focused on low-to-moderate-income homeowners either in or out of the known flood zone who had suffered storm surge damage for which they were not insured. While the maximum Phase I benefit had been $150,000, the maximum Phase II benefit was only $100,000, and eligibility was limited to families whose income was at or below 120 percent of the area median.[88] This represented the first effort to target housing assistance to groups the Rand report had identified as especially at risk in disaster recoveries.

Recipients of assistance in both phases of the homeowner grant program were eligible for elevation grants of up to $30,000 to meet FEMA's post-Katrina revised floodplain elevation standards. In addition to the normal MDA processes which slowed grant payouts, elevation grant recipients faced additional waits because of federally required multistep environmental reviews. Thus, in May of 2008, of the 2,915 elevation grant applications in process, only 100 applications had been approved.[89] The governor's office established March 15, 2008, as the closing date for applications for both phases of the Homeowners Assistance Program. Jack Norris, executive director of the Governor's Office of Recovery and Renewal, testified that between the two phases of the homeowner program, 23,698 grants had been approved. The average award had paid out just over $71,000.[90]

Prior to Katrina there were 2,316 public housing units on the Mississippi Gulf Coast. Virtually all of these suffered damage and 800 units were totally destroyed. On August 31, 2006, one year and two days after the storm, HUD announced that it had accepted Governor Barbour's May 18, 2006, proposed amendment to his CDBG spending plan to send $105 million to the five regional housing authorities with Katrina-damaged or destroyed units. The funds were expected to result in a significant increase above the pre- Katrina levels of available public housing resources in the coastal counties.[91] With no HUD funds available to rebuild public housing, this step was vital. Coming a full year after the storm, it represented the governor's first measurable commitment of Mississippi's CDBG funds toward restoration of rental units lost to the most vulnerable segment of the population.

Eight months later in 2007, the governor's office announced "the opening of a public comment period" for a $262.5 million Small Rental Assistance Program directed at the recovery of private rental property. The plan was submitted to HUD on June 12, 2007, almost 22 months after Katrina, and gained HUD approval the next month. The Small Rental Assistance Program was designed to restore as many as 5,000 privately owned affordable rental units whose owners could receive forgivable loans of up to $30,000 per unit if they were willing to enter an agreement guaranteeing "low-to-moderate rental rates" targeting tenants at 80 to 120 percent of the area median income level.[92] Given the FEMA numbers which showed that 19,113 rental units in the three coast counties had suffered major damage or destruction,[93] grants for 5,000 units could not restore opportunity for most of the de-housed renters.

As statewide election season got under way in the summer of 2007, the slow pace of the unfolding of the governor's plan drew fire from Mississippi Democratic Party Chairman Wayne Dowdy. In an opening volley, Dowdy charged Barbour and the MDA with dragging their feet while countless numbers still lived in temporary housing.[94] Meanwhile, rents in the bottom three counties had spiked upward by 40 percent above pre-Katrina levels, and the average price of a home had surged from $149,000 before the storm to $181,000 in August of 2007.[95] The Democrats obviously believed that the lagging housing recovery might provide fertile fields for the fall campaign.

On the coast, even groups usually allied with the governor seemed to sense a lack of urgency at the state capitol about the housing crisis. In February of 2007, Brian Sanderson, president of the Gulf Coast Business Council, told a congressional committee that "to date, the [housing recovery] efforts have been well-intentioned but piecemeal." Sanderson testified that "a large portion of the workforce is in desperate need of affordable housing," a need which Sanderson said was "not being effectively met by existing state and federal programs." He revealed that the need for a "more comprehensive and collaborative initiative" executed "at a much more rapid pace" had driven the Gulf Coast Business Council to raise money and hire staff to create the private nonprofit Gulf Coast Renaissance Corporation in an effort to jump-start coast initiatives for affordable workforce housing.[96] The Renaissance Corporation Board represented a cross section of coast business and community leaders, including Anthony Topazi of Mississippi Power, former mayor Gerald Blessey of Biloxi, and one of the most persistent critics of the governor's housing program, attorney Reilly Morse, who served as the group's secretary.[97]

In August of 2007, Tish Williams of the Hancock County Chamber of Commerce told a town hall meeting that both small businesses and major employers were facing a serious labor shortage. "When you trace back the cause for the shortage," Williams said, "all roads lead back to affordable housing and the lack of affordable insurance."[98] In the same month, the shortage of affordable housing and the resulting loss of workers after Katrina led the coast's largest private employer, Northrop Grumman Ship Systems in Pascagoula, to team with the Renaissance Corporation in the creation of a system of forgivable housing loans of up to $10,000 for shipyard employees. A few weeks later in September of 2007, a second Rand report highlighted the slow recovery of rental housing which was putting low-income renters into a "recovery squeeze." The report made a strong case for a more focused effort on the affordable housing front and pled for "broad dissemination of accurate information." Moreover, Rand observed that "inclusion of the various parties involved in decisions about the process may be very important to promoting cooperation in the recovery effort."[99] The governor's small rental program was a small step in the right direction, but obviously not a sufficient commitment to the larger problem of affordable housing.

Statewide elections were slated for the fall of 2007, two years after Katrina. Thus, against a background of more than 18,000 families representing upwards of 48,000 individuals cooped up in FEMA trailers,[100] the governor's September 7, 2007, proposal to divert $600 million in CDBG funds to an ambitious plan to expand the Port of Gulfport was bound to produce a storm of controversy. On the coast, ministerial groups, church groups, the Steps Coalition, and other advocacy groups called the governor to task.[101] The sight of protesters on the sidewalks of Biloxi led the *Sun Herald*, a newspaper that was normally in the governor's corner, to venture the observation that as regarded the diversion of CDBG money to the Port of Gulfport, "housing advocates" had "raised a $600 million question that deserves an answer."[102] Thrown on the defensive, the governor stated that the port project had always been on his agenda, and he objected to calling the redirection of the money "a diversion." It was, he said, a reallocation of unused funds from the homeowners housing grant program.[103] With thousands of families still in FEMA trailers, the point rang hollow to housing advocates. Still, Barbour cruised to an easy reelection victory over political novice John Arthur Eaves in November.

Nonetheless, in January of 2008, HUD Secretary Alphonso Jackson informed Barbour of his continuing concern that the proposed expansion of the Port of Gulfport did "indeed divert emergency federal funding from other more pressing recovery needs, most notably affordable housing." However, the secretary conceded that the legislation creating the Katrina CDBG funds allowed the secretary of HUD little choice but to release to the port project the money originally allocated to the homeowners assistance program.[104] Barbour had won an important round, but he had not satisfied his critics that sufficient effort had yet been undertaken on housing.

In February of 2008, the governor defended his programs including the port initiative and housing plans before the *Sun Herald* editorial board. His defense did not produce the praise the governor normally expected from the the *Sun Herald*. After the session, the paper editorialized that "housing advocates . . . need to be heard by Barbour and others setting the direction of the state's recovery." The paper chided the governor for being "inexcusably passive" in his approach to solving the insurance crisis which was troubling both the housing and business recovery on the coast.[105] Though Barbour remained inalterably committed to the port project through a round of congressional hearings, coast housing advocates believed that the vigor of their protests, including a federal court challenge, now began to have more influence in the shaping of housing programs in the governor's office.[106]

In March of 2008, with the state's own figures reportedly showing that up to 40,000 disaster-damaged housing units were still not liveable,[107] Barbour announced that he would add $100 million in CDBG money to a Long Term Workforce Housing proposal then under development, thereby bringing the allocation up to $350 million, a figure that was twice the amount he had originally planned. Moreover, as credit markets tightened at the onset of severe economic recession in 2008, the Barbour administration reallocated $30 million in CDBG money to create an affordable housing loan fund to provide additional incentives for investors to undertake Low Income Housing Income Tax Credit projects under the Gulf Opportunity Zone (GO Zone) Act of 2005.[108] Of equal significance, whether as a result of pressure from housing advocates or some logic of its own, in May of 2008 the Mississippi Development Authority commissioned the kind of major detailed housing study called for by the Rand policy group in the aftermath of Katrina. Though the detailed report would not become available for many months, the resulting Mississippi Housing Data Project would provide information critical to the shaping of the later stages of the governor's housing program.[109]

Still, in August of 2008, as the third anniversary of Katrina approached, frustration with the slow pace of the housing recovery emboldened the

Housing Working Group of the Gulf Coast Business Council to ask the governor to appoint a "coast housing and redevelopment czar." At the time, there were still 7,203 Mississippi families including roughly 19,000 individuals housed in either FEMA trailers or compact Mississippi cottages.[110] Driven by a nagging awareness of FEMA's March 2009 deadline for ending both programs, the Business Council wanted the governor to empower a coast housing czar to cut through red tape and reduce the bureaucratic drag on redevelopment. More pointedly, they wanted someone "with a sense of urgency" who "wakes up on the Coast each day" and is "suffering here with us" and able to inspire imaginative solutions.[111] Business Council President Anthony Topazi, the CEO of Mississippi Power, told the *Sun Herald* that though there had been progress, "we need a kind of mid-course correction." The newspaper, the business community, and Gulf Coast housing advocates united behind the proposal. Perhaps as a measure of his own frustration, Barbour told the *Sun Herald* on August 15 that he was "very interested" in the concept of a czar "as long as we find someone from the Coast." The governor so often accused of holding his cards too close to the vest now affirmed that "the people of the Gulf Coast have to decide how to rebuild." On August 28, 2008, the eve of the third anniversary of Hurricane Katrina, Governor Barbour appointed former Biloxi mayor Gerald Blessey, a Democrat, to the newly created post of "Mississippi Coast Housing Director."[112]

Blessey quickly assumed his duties. Whether due to Blessey's newfound influence or by coincidence, a week later the Mississippi Development Authority announced that it would reduce the governor's allocation to the controversial Port of Gulfport expansion plan by $30 million in order to add $181 million to the homeowners assistance program.[113] In February of 2009, the Mississippi Development Authority announced more than 26,900 grants had been awarded and projected that all awards would be distributed by the end of April, or one year ahead of previous projections.[114] Blessey soon made rounds through 11 community meetings where he took input on workforce housing and sought to educate the public on the relationship between adequate supplies of affordable housing and the ability of employers to attract employees and grow the economy.[115] Two years after the creation of this new post, some of the most vocal critics of the governor's programs believed that Gerald Blessey's actions and influence as housing czar had measurably "changed the curve" of the Mississippi recovery for the better.[116]

The lack of a sense of urgency in the state capitol was not the only problem which the Housing Working Group laid before Governor Barbour in August of 2008. In comments to the press, Anthony Topazi stated that "there are opportunities for everyone to do better," and Gerald Blessey noted that "leaders at all levels as well as members of the public should not be let off the hook."[117] In a special *Sun Herald* Housing Editorial Board meeting the previous month, members of the Gulf Coast Business Council had decried rising local resistance to proposed workforce housing initiatives. Fear of decreased property values or simply fear of the poor in general had driven crowds to pack several local zoning board hearings to denounce new apartment developments near their homes or schools. As the Business Council saw it, weak local leadership responded to the cries of "not in my neighborhood" by delaying or disapproving projects that were a key to the housing recovery and the future health of the local economy. The *Sun Herald* had noted that coast cities differed in the "size of their welcome mats," but Biloxi seemed most welcoming. General Clark Griffith, who chaired Biloxi's post-Katrina Renewing the Renaissance Commission, believed that in Biloxi most citizens carried a deep pride in the city's heritage of ethnic diversity, and this he thought had helped to ease the acceptance of affordable housing developments in that city.[118]

On the other hand, in Gulfport the resistance to housing units built with low-income housing tax credits was so intense and uniform that Roy Necaise of the Region 8 Housing Authority accused the city of "blatant discrimination toward hardworking families." In June of 2007, the Area Housing Authority had filed suit against the city of Gulfport for denial of permits for two affordable housing developments. All of this had transpired while thousands waited for the opportunity to escape the close and increasingly miserable world of life in a FEMA trailer.[119] Given the massive loss of housing and the mathematical certainty that most of the households in any Mississippi Gulf Coast community would fall below the median income level, the local resistance to housing developments targeting this segment of the workforce seemed incredibly ill-informed and devoid of any compassion for those whose needs were visible to all. In short, Jackson and Washington bureaucracies were not the only entities which could be accused of lacking an appropriate sense of urgency.

The lack of local sensitivity was a special tragedy given the mountains of federal red tape that had to be navigated to get any rental project, large or small, off the ground. In May of 2009, Governor Barbour testified that "more than 1,000 applications for the Small Rental Program were tied up in the CDBG environmental review process for over 10 months." Barbour counted eight state and federal agencies whose efforts had to be coordinated to gain approvals in nine areas of environmental concern to get any rental developments out of the ground. Local resistance simply added to an already difficult and time-consuming approval process. Given these complications, part of the coast housing czar's job had to include educating local citizens about the larger moral and economic implications of the community's own failure to deal squarely with its own affordable housing needs.[120]

The story of the post-Katrina housing recovery in Mississippi is a story of waiting. The waiting began in long lines at local FEMA emergency offices or with repeat telephone calls to understaffed FEMA call centers to establish or verify registration for emergency housing. The waiting continued as FEMA and Bechtel, its major housing contractor in Mississippi, delivered campers, set them up, and inspected them. From life in FEMA trailers to housing grant applications or the long quest to rebuild or find new apartments for the 65,000 Mississippi families who lost homes in Hurricane Katrina, at every step impersonal bureaucratic processes tried the patience of disaster survivors and tested their ability to endure and persevere through the complicated hurdles thrown into their pathway by state and federal agencies. By 2008, the impersonal economic forces that led to the collapse of credit markets and the astronomical rise in coastal insurance rates joined to further slow the housing recovery. However, on a more personal level nearer to home in the disaster zone itself, neighbor often looked on neighbor through the all-too-personal lenses of fear and misguided self-interest and sometimes coldly acted to block or delay affordable housing for those most in need or for those whose labors were essential to the economy.

In the salvos of numbers thrown back and forth in the political controversies that surrounded the housing recovery, numerical abstractions camouflaged the real-world plight of thousands of ordinary people who languished in FEMA trailers. Elderly fixed-income retirees and disabled victims were lost in the war of numbers. Also lost from view over much of the three-and-a-half-year housing debate was the inevitable plight of thousands of hardworking families whose labors were needed to power the recovery, but who could not remain in the community if affordable solutions to their housing needs were not addressed with all possible speed.

Still, in looking back over these many struggles, coast housing advocate Reilly Morse was gratified by attitudinal changes he perceived in important segments of the coast business community. As Morse saw it, one of the more encouraging things that emerged from the Katrina housing struggle was that "some great leaders in the business community . . . stepped up significantly" their commitments to "dealing with the societal ills and economic ills of the Mississippi Gulf Coast." Morse especially praised the emergence of "an increased civic dialogue about the reality of poverty and . . . substandard housing, . . . and the harm done" to the community in "not having a living wage." Informed local leaders who faced a community in disaster had stepped up to challenge a popular governor and push a community toward a nobler vision of itself. For the best of the local leadership on the Mississippi Gulf Coast in the wake of Katrina, the seeking of the welfare and peace of the city had begun with the building of houses for all who dwelt there.

In defending his uses of Mississippi's $5.4 billion in Katrina Community Development Block Grant money, Governor Barbour consistently stated that his goal was "a comprehensive recovery" that focused on "all aspects that make a community" and "not focusing on any single area of recovery; . . . not just those areas with a high proportion of low and moderate incomes." In the governor's mind these broad goals justified his requests for waivers of the HUD 50 percent low-to-moderate-income CDBG benefit rule and made room for ambitious projects such as the major expansion of the Port of Gulfport, regional wastewater programs, or utility ratepayer and wind insurance mitigation. However, he also consistently avowed an "unwavering commitment to housing." In May of 2009, after over three years of what seemed a tortuously slow unfolding of his overall housing program, Barbour told a U.S. Senate panel that "only by enhancing housing opportunities for all coastal residents, including low-and-moderate-income homeowners and renters, will the workforce and economic engines of the Gulf Coast reach their full potential." In his oral comments at the same 2009 hearing, Governor Barbour stated that "We have learned in the last several months that the biggest issue for housing on the Mississippi Gulf Coast today is . . . that people that are left in FEMA housing and in Mississippi cottages cannot afford to pay market rent. They are people who must have deep subsidy HUD vouchers."[121]

The data that drove this point home for Haley Barbour and his staff came from the long-delayed detailed study of coast housing that was released in January of 2009. Hard numbers now led Governor Barbour to make an eloquent plea for 5,000 additional HUD housing vouchers, a move which the new data suggested could close the housing gap for the coast's low-wage service workers and fixed-income elderly and disabled citizens by 2011. Gone was the talk of responsible versus irresponsible disaster victims. The stark reality that rents had increased by 40 percent and threatened to drive thousands of previously self-sufficient working people out of the housing market had to be addressed. To his credit, and to the lasting benefit of Mississippi, Haley Barbour had been instrumental in shaking loose billions of dollars in CDBG disaster recovery funding that the political rigidities of his own partisan allies in Washington might have otherwise denied to the state. Had detailed data-driven housing and socioeconomic analyses been made available earlier to inform policy at the beginning of the recovery, much heated criticism would have been averted. Had the vision articulated in 2009 been more fully articulated and included in the plans for Phase I of the Mississippi housing program three years earlier, much painful worry and doubt would have been laid to rest in the hearts of the long-suffering low-income storm victims.

It was difficult for those on the outside of the disaster looking in to appreciate the full meaning of the massive loss of housing and infrastructure. People who visited the Mississippi Gulf Coast two and three and four years after the event were often shocked at scars still visible in the community landscape. The psychological and social scars that were an inevitable part of personal loss and the perpetual struggle to return to normal family life were not so easily seen. Many factors beyond the state's control conspired to delay recovery. FEMA's housing programs did not adjust paperwork processes to fit the size of the disaster. Federal environmental regulations rolled on, blindly impeding the recovery of rental properties as if there had been no emergency at all. Closer to home, the Mississippi Development Authority created complicated grant processes that showed more fear of federal audits than understanding of the meaning of the resulting delays to those who endured them. Had the governor and his staff somehow acted with more urgency across all aspects of the housing problem, or had more of the neighbors who shared a community found the compassion to support a full housing recovery for all, or had the recession not collapsed credit markets, the misery of life in FEMA trailers would not have gone away, but a clearer and less impeded path to recovery would have gone far to lift the psychological burdens of those left struggling and waiting to find someplace decent to live.

For over 4,400 of the poorest of Katrina's victims the final act in Mississippi's long housing recovery did not open until November of 2010. At this time, Governor Barbour, under pressure from the Obama administration and a federal lawsuit, agreed to a $132 million means-tested program to provide up to $75,000 each to uninsured low-income homeowners in nine southeast Mississippi counties whose houses were damaged or destroyed by wind, rather than floodwaters. Notwithstanding the fact that early on,

HUD had approved such a means-tested wind-only program in Louisiana, for four and a half years Governor Barbour steadfastly contended that in its 2005 CDBG housing-recovery appropriation, Congress had only intended to assist people with flood damage and had specifically intended to deny aid to persons who had failed to insure their homes against wind hazards. Thus, wind-damaged homes had been long excluded from Barbour's state-crafted grant program. The Steps Coalition, the Mississippi Center for Justice, the Gulf Coast Fair Housing Center, the Mississippi N.A.A.C.P., and the Lawyers' Committee for Civil Rights Under Law argued that wind insurance had been beyond the means of thousands of Mississippi homeowners who lived on meager Social Security checks or subsisted on low-wage service-sector jobs. On this basis, advocacy groups had filed a lawsuit in federal court aiming to block the use of $570 million in CDBG funds for the Port of Gulfport until all of Mississippi's Katrina-related housing needs had been met.[122] Once again, Coast Housing Director Gerald Blessey played a major role bridging the gap between the Barbour administration and housing advocates. The solution which emerged from months of negotiation offered a hand up for victims who had been shut out of previous Mississippi housing programs while simultaneously bringing an end to the lawsuit. This in turn smoothed the way for the huge CDBG-financed expansion project for the Port of Gulfport.[123]

In a November 15, 2010, statement announcing the new program, Governor Barbour reiterated his understanding of his original agreement with Congress and the Bush administration to the effect that "people who didn't have homeowners insurance, who were outside the flood plain would not be eligible for the homeowners assistance program." In the governor's mind, over the previous five years he had upheld his end of that bargain. However, he noted that the new Obama administration "felt like people who were damaged by wind, . . . should be covered if they were poor, if they had tried to help themselves over the last five years. . . ." Though it was Barbour's contention that this was "contrary to our initial agreement with Congress," he pronounced himself ready to cooperate with the administration "because it will help some Mississippi families."[124]

In working toward the agreement, both Barbour and HUD Secretary Shaun Donovan had insisted on first documenting the need. As part of the process the Mississippi Development Authority conducted door-to-door surveys showing that 42 percent of those with unmet housing needs were disabled, while 53 percent were elderly and most were well below the median income for the area. Reilly Morse, of the Mississippi Center for

Justice and one of Barbour's most consistent critics, praised the governor for his willingness to "take a look under the hood," and respond to hard data. In the same spirit, HUD Secretary Shaun Donovan praised Barbour for his willingness to rise above party and work with the Obama administration "to make things right."[125]

In this the final episode in Mississippi's housing recovery sojourn, Governor Haley Barbour once again proved his essential pragmatism. When presented with reliable data, albeit after lengthy delay, he had made a good decision. Still, a distant echo of the prophetic voice of Jeremiah could be heard in the *New York Times* complaint that the Republican governor had for "five long years . . ." delayed ". . . in serving these needy families." The news giant further chastised the Bush administration for erring in the first place in granting Mississippi waivers of the requirement that states spend half their CBDG money on low-to-moderate-income families. However, in the disaster zone on the Mississippi Gulf Coast, the editorialists at the *Sun Herald* ventured a less judgmental and more practical assessment. In the local reckoning, the final agreement for wind-damaged low-income homeowners appeared to be "one of the best solutions to one of the worst problems left by Katrina." Thus, rather than casting blame for the lateness of the solution, south Mississippi's newspaper offered commendation to "all who arrived at it."[126]

Chapter Eight

Disaster and Recovery in the Schools

This is a business of people and not bricks and mortar. We are going to take care of our people and we are going to look out for our students. . . . This is how [we] are going to be remembered for the rest of [our] lives.

—RUCKS ROBINSON
Superintendent, Jackson County Schools[1]

[FEMA] works at a lot slower pace than we do, and that's been an issue. I think they thought we would just take our time getting back in school. . . . But no, we wanted school open, . . . because for schools to be open meant [that]the community [could] rebuild. . . . So, we were on a little bit different mission.

—GLEN EAST
Superintendent, Gulfport Schools[2]

In normal times teaching is a challenging profession, the success of which at any level depends in good measure on the strength of the hopeful commitments to children and the future which animate school faculties and staffs. In the aftermath of Katrina, a strong sense of mission at the local level became the driving force in the recovery of the schools and an essential counterweight to the doubts that inevitably arose from the clouded horizons of wrecked local tax bases and long delays in the FEMA funding process for the recovery of destroyed buildings. In devastated communities where 65,000 families had lost their homes, the fate of children and their families depended on the restoration of islands of stability and normalcy at school. The massive destruction of school buildings and the loss of faculty and staff housing presented unprecedented challenges. In the three Mississippi Gulf Coast counties 16 entire public school campuses and 5 parochial school campuses were destroyed in the storm, and another 24 schools suffered "severe damage." More than half of the destroyed school campuses in the state were located in the Bay-Waveland and Hancock County districts or in neighboring Pass Christian.[3] South Mississippi also temporarily lost 76 child care centers with capacity to care for over 6,000 preschool children. Moreover, in the realm of higher education, the regional branch campuses of the University of Southern Mississippi and William Carey University were both devastated beyond use, leaving over 3,000 place-bound university students without services.[4]

It did not take long for school and college administrators to discover that FEMA's slow-moving bureaucratic processes could not take into account the urgency they felt about the need to reopen schools. It would be years before the destroyed brick and mortar school buildings could be replaced. However, FEMA authorized the Army Corps of Engineers to enter into a no-bid contract with a private company to supply 425 portable classrooms to replace lost school buildings in Mississippi. Five weeks after the storm, the Army Corps of Engineers had managed to deliver only 140 of the promised units. It was now clear that on the changing FEMA and corps timetables, it would take months for the full complement of portable buildings to be manufactured, delivered, and installed. Still, in district after district, decisions were made to bring the schools back on line with or without replacements for the lost buildings. In early October, Henry Arledge, superintendent of the 13,000-student Harrison County District, told a reporter that he would find portables himself if the 36 units he needed did not show up soon. Nonetheless, by October 3, with only one-third of the needed portable classrooms on site, 9 of the 11 public school districts on the Mississippi Gulf Coast were back in operation with many running double sessions in surviving facilities.[5] In the words of Gulfport Superintendent Glen East, "[FEMA] works at a lot slower pace than we do. . . . I think they thought we would just take our time getting back in school. . . . But no, we wanted school open, . . . because for schools to be open meant [that] the community [could] rebuild."[6]

In retrospect at least, it became clear that decisions taken in individual districts to get the schools up and running as quickly as possible in fact met a critical need for Katrina's youngest victims. The release in 2007 of two important studies of children who lived with their families in the cramped confines of FEMA campers and trailers raised serious questions about the impact of the disaster on the mental health of children and their long-term prospects for resiliency.[7] These studies confirmed that school life, with its regularity, safety, and sense of caring, was a vital part of the recovery for children. The well-being of children justified the sense of urgency that animated local school staffs who worked day and night to make damaged facilities operational as soon as possible. Beyond what was right for children, the enormity of the physical damage to the schools together with the massive faculty and staff dislocations posed a threat to the community at large. If the needs of children could not be met, their parents would have no choice but to leave the area, and in their leaving, the core of the workforce needed to sustain the broader recovery would be gone.

In the end, the financial support of the American people which flowed through FEMA made possible the material reconstruction of destroyed schools. However, in the moment of crisis when decisions had to be made amidst uncertainties about promised equipment and FEMA funding, it was the local leadership, faculty, and staff that pulled the schools back together in sometimes makeshift facilities to begin meeting the needs of students. The sense of mission was paramount. As Superintendent East put it, "Being committed to kids really [came] to the forefront within the tragedy. . . . Folks were not going to let this thing beat us. . . . They stepped up and did what they had to do."[8]

In Mississippi, Hurricane Katrina's damages to the public schools alone totaled more than $1.2 billion, a sum which approached 30 percent of the total annual state budget at the time. Across the state of Mississippi, 266 schools in 79 districts suffered some degree of damage. In the three counties of the Mississippi Gulf Coast, all 11 districts lost buildings in the storm, and 10 of the 11 lost entire campuses. The replacement of these lost buildings and campuses brought the schools into the nexus of FEMA's multilayered Project Worksheet approval processes.[9] On the ground, the team of school building planners and engineers which FEMA sent to help school districts understand federal requirements met with mixed reviews. In Mississippi, conflicting information and unmet delivery dates for portable buildings suggested things to come for the schools in their dealings with FEMA. Nearly all of FEMA's financial help would arrive in the form of reimbursements of approved expenses. This alone put a strain on cash-strapped districts and further obscured an already cloudy recovery horizon.

The Mississippi Department of Education brought in Dr. Harold Dodge, the superintendent of schools in Mobile County, Alabama, to give advice on dealing with FEMA. At every turn, the bottom line was simple: FEMA money would take a long time to come.[10] Down the line, after successfully restarting schools in alternate facilities and portable classrooms, school administrative capacities for years to come would be stretched to their very limits coping with the paperwork burdens associated with accessing FEMA funding for the reconstruction of lost buildings.[11] On the other hand, looking beyond the trials of the moment FEMA eventually committed over $252 million to the rebuilding of schools in the lower six counties,[12] and in the overall scheme of things, by January of 2010, FEMA was in line to provide over $3 billion for recovery or replacement of Mississippi schools, public buildings, public utilities, and the removal of debris.[13] However, in September and October of 2005, the immediate challenge was to get the schools up and running, and the two coast school systems facing the greatest difficulties were the Bay-Waveland and Pass Christian districts.

In the schools, as in other local government operations, storm preparation for Katrina had followed a familiar routine. In the Bay St. Louis and Waveland area, in what would be the hardest-hit communities in Mississippi, Superintendent Kim Stasny and her administrative and maintenance staff had worked through the morning and into the afternoon on the Saturday before the storm securing school buildings and grounds in the six-campus Bay-Waveland School District before heading home to get their own property ready for the onslaught of hurricane-force winds predicted for Monday, August 29. There had already been discussions with school superintendents in neighboring districts about whether to try to reopen schools on the Tuesday after the storm or wait until Wednesday. Unknown to Kim Stasny, Hancock County was about to become the epicenter of Hurricane Katrina, and it would be 70 days before any school in the Bay-Waveland District could venture to open again for instruction.[14]

On Saturday night before the storm, while they were still blissfully ignorant of the shocking dimensions of the disaster that loomed ahead, Superintendent Kim Stasny and her husband, Chris, debated whether to evacuate from their home on high ground in the Diamondhead community just north of town. On Sunday morning, the superintendent managed to get a call through to Circuit Clerk Tim Keller at the Hancock County Emergency Operations Center and asked his advice. “Pack up and go,” Keller said. “I am telling you this is going to be a bad storm.” With this, the family debate ended. Stasny and her husband quickly readied themselves, picked up an elderly couple in the neighborhood, and drove a hundred miles inland through heavy traffic to Laurel, Mississippi, where Stasny's mother, Mrs. Juanita Myrick, put them all up for the next three days.[15]

On Monday, August 29, Katrina roared through Laurel still packing hurricane-force winds. Trees swayed violently back and forth, snapped, and crashed down in the yard. The power failed early in the day when a transformer unit exploded, fell from its pole, and hit the street. The sounding of tornado warning sirens repeatedly drove the group to the interior hallway to wait out the danger. Despite what she had seen in her mother's Laurel neighborhood and what she had heard on the radio, the enormity of the destruction did not sink in until Wednesday morning when Stasny and her husband began their trek back to the coast. When they found the interstate highways and Highway 49 closed to southbound traffic, they switched to back roads where they constantly encountered downed trees and crews with chainsaws working to clear the route. Tree and roof damage became more severe the further south they went.[16]

It took the Stasnys five hours to cover the one hundred miles of secondary routes from Laurel back to their Diamondhead home. Their neighborhood was located on the north side of Interstate 10 in Hancock County. Still, even here, large numbers of houses had been flooded and destroyed. The Stasnys felt blessed to discover that while there was some minor roof damage and 13 or 14 large pines had blown down in the yard, their home had not flooded. Though for a time they would share their residence with friends who were more seriously damaged, the intact home would become a welcome refuge for this soon-to-be-overwhelmed school superintendent.[17]

After clearing their driveway on Wednesday afternoon, Kim and Chris Stasny made their way down Highway 603 past scenes of unbelievable destruction and on into Bay St. Louis to check on the schools. Stasny's first stop was at Second Street Elementary School, where she was surprised to find that six inches of water had penetrated the main building that was built up some four feet off the ground. This building had survived Hurricane Camille in 1969 and had never before flooded. The Second Street gym, built on a slab at ground level, had taken four to five feet of water. Dazed and forlorn people who had lost their houses and cars had already found their way into the building and begun to use it as an impromptu unofficial shelter. Continuing her sojourn, the superintendent found that the central office had taken two feet of water which deposited a slick, nasty coating of mud on the floor such that "getting in there was like ice skating." Here, Stasny searched for master keys for the other campuses and found them lying in the mud on the office floor.[18]

With keys in hand, she set out for the campus of the Bay-Waveland Alternative School. The destruction of homes and street signs in Bay St. Louis left the superintendent completely disoriented. A familiar three-story brick home at the end of Nicholson Avenue was completely gone. On the beachfront, at Christ Episcopal Church, only a bare steeple was left on the lot marking the sanctuary's former location. Stasny and her husband wound up abandoning their vehicle to hike to the grounds of the alternative school. Here they found that the buildings had been reduced to a pile of rubble with exposed steel girders bent as if they were made of rubber. Only an overturned piano laying on its back suggested that the ruins had recently served some social purpose. Chairs and desks were gone, rags and rugs hung draped in the trees, and some distance away office machines were found scattered in a gully. As Wednesday afternoon turned into evening, Chris and Kim Stasny made their way toward the beach road, where an eerie calm spread over the water. She reflected that it was as if the sea were pleading its innocence in the case of the monstrous destruction inflicted only 48 hours earlier.[19]

On Thursday morning, Stasny resumed her effort to reach all of her district's campuses to finish an initial assessment. At North Bay Elementary she found walls knocked down and knew that the campus would be condemned. Both the high school and the middle school had been flooded. At the high school, she encountered a crowd that she estimated to be 500 people seeking shelter, food, and water. With officially designated shelters located far north of town, the schools were not prepared for such an onslaught. A police officer and a social worker began registering people on a roster, but there was a palpable sense of desperation in the air. Everywhere she went as she made her rounds to the school buildings, people would flock to the car asking, "Where do we go? What do we do? Who is coming to help us?" Heartbroken, and without working cell phone service, Stasny dropped what she was doing to drive around looking for officials who might be able to provide resources or answers to urgent questions.[20]

At some point, Superintendent Stasny connected with the school district's business manager, Garland Cuevas. Their initial assessments showed that four of the Bay St. Louis-Waveland district's six school campuses had been destroyed, and the two remaining sites had suffered "heavy, heavy damage." Stasny found herself feeling exhausted and overwhelmed by the task that lay before them. Over the next several days, she discovered that 10 of the Bay-Waveland district's 16 principals and central office administrators had lost their homes. The destruction was so wide-ranging in Hancock County that when schools finally reopened, 61 percent of the students and 33 percent of the faculty and staff of the Bay-Waveland system were unable to return.[21] Moreover, beyond the Bay-Waveland district, the damage to the educational infrastructure in Hancock County extended into the neighboring Hancock County system where both the Gulfview and Charles B. Murphy elementary schools were in ruins. In the town's parochial school system, St. Clare Elementary and Our Lady Academy were destroyed, and St. Stanislaus High School for boys was severely damaged.[22]

Across the Bay of St. Louis in the Pass Christian School District, Katrina had destroyed or rendered uninhabitable the houses of 90 percent of the district's faculty and staff, including the residence of Superintendent Sue Matheson. Matheson, like Stasny, had spent the Saturday before the storm with her administrators, technical support, and maintenance staff trying to ready the campuses for the bad weather predicted for Monday. Matheson remembered meticulously placing computers on high shelves to save them from flooding, a measure that proved to be of no avail in the 30-foot Katrina storm surge. The belief that she should be available to check on the fate of the schools as soon as possible after the storm passed led Matheson and her husband, local dentist Dr. D. F. Matheson, to decide to ride out the bad weather in their home located in the same Diamondhead community where her colleague Kim Stasney resided. Unfortunately, several feet of storm water invaded the Matheson home, backed up the sewerage lines, and drove the family to an upstairs bedroom. Superintendent Matheson and her husband were fated to live for almost a year in a trailer while the house was being repaired.[23]

Matheson's personal search for alternate shelter meant that it was several days before she was able to survey the damage that Katrina had wrought on the Pass Christian School District. The destruction was so complete that the basic assessment could be done quickly. It appeared that 15 feet of water had swept over the central office on Davis Avenue and destroyed all personnel records. Both Pass Christian Elementary School and Pass Christian Middle School were totally destroyed. All student records going back to the 1920s were lost. Five of the district's 20-vehicle bus fleet were ruined in the salty inundation that swept over the parking area near the middle school. One bus washed out to sea and was later reported to have been spotted 10 miles offshore on Cat Island. The new Pass Christian High School campus, completed in 1999, had taken 13 feet of water. Windows had blown out, the gymnasium floor had been floated into the bleachers, and the ground floor of the beautiful two-story main classroom building was left mangled, muddied, and scoured beyond recognition and beyond all use. The destruction of three of the district's four school campuses posed a serious challenge, but the devastation of the Pass Christian city water and sewer system ruled out the placement of portable classroom units on these or any available properties inside the city limits. Moreover, the city tax base was virtually wiped out. The local budget supplements that had helped propel the district to top level academic ratings would not be there for the foreseeable future. After years of effort that had produced real results for students from a diverse and challenging demographic base, a painful thought shot through Matheson's mind. "This is the end of our school district," she thought.[24]

Somehow in that long moment of despair, Maintenance Supervisor Monroe Necaise stepped up and reminded Sue Matheson that the district actually owned several acres of wooded ground beside the campus of Delisle Elementary School. Located north of town, the Delisle campus had its own water well and septic system and was not dependent on the destroyed city systems. At the Delisle property, the main building had taken three inches of water. Carpets would have to be pulled out, but there was no structural damage. Wooded areas surrounding the playgrounds would have to be cleared, and fill dirt would have to be brought in. However, if the Delisle building could be cleaned up and fully used, there was enough space on the site to lay out 55 portable classrooms which, with some creative adaptations in the elementary school's main building, just might produce the capacity to serve all of the district's 2,000 kindergarten through 12th grade students, or at least the portion that remained in the area and would return to school. Against all odds, all grades of the Pass Christian School District reopened at Delisle on October 11, six weeks after the storm. However, 35 percent of the students and 25 percent of the district's pre-Katrina faculty were gone.[25]

Across the Mississippi Gulf Coast, the roll call of destroyed school campuses included Harper McCaughan Elementary in Long Beach and 28th Street and East Ward Elementary in Gulfport. In Biloxi both Gorenflo and Nichols elementary schools were washed through, and in D'Iberville, the D'Iberville Middle School campus was lost. Nearby in Jackson County, the walls in both the St. Martin Lower Elementary and Upper Elementary campuses were washed over and knocked down, and the storm surge laid waste to Magnolia Middle School in Moss Point and to Gautier Elementary and Beach Elementary in the Pascagoula system. In addition to this, tornados destroyed gymnasiums at Ocean Springs and Gautier high schools, along with six individual classrooms at Ocean Springs's Oak Park Elementary.[26]

Beyond the K-12 school infrastructure, Katrina struck a devastating blow to the four-year institutions of higher education on the Mississippi Gulf Coast and disrupted the higher education progress of thousands of coast junior college and university students. Storm surge knocked down buildings and flooded every structure on the Long Beach and Ocean Springs satellite campuses of the University of Southern Mississippi, and in Hattiesburg Katrina inflicted major roof damage on seven more USM buildings. Among the 30 structures severely damaged at USM's Gulf Park Campus in Long Beach, three of the World War I–era buildings which the university inherited from Gulf Park College for Women experienced ruinous ground-floor washouts. These grand old buildings remained unrepaired or had not been replaced for over five years after the storm had passed. A fourth building, the Cox building, collapsed, and the old Gulf Park president's home washed away. The newer buildings constructed on the north end of the Gulf Park Campus in the late 1990s experienced ground-floor flooding and extensive roof damage which put them out of service for two or more years.[27]

The devastation of USM facilities on the coast went well beyond the destruction of the Long Beach teaching site. At Point Cadet in Biloxi, the university's J. L. Scott Marine Education Center with its complement of public aquariums and labs was totally destroyed. In Ocean Springs, Katrina unleashed an equally devastating storm surge on USM's flagship research facility, the Gulf Coast Research Lab, where wind and wave destroyed five buildings and decades of accumulated research data, scientific specimens, and equipment.[28]

William Carey University on the Coast, a branch campus of a Southern Baptist liberal arts college headquartered in Hattiesburg, lost its Highway 90 campus located on the site of the former Gulf Coast Military Academy in Gulfport. Several hundred students from William Carey attended night classes in the facilities of Gulfport High School and in the Sunday School Annex of First Missionary Baptist Church in Gulfport until 16 portable classrooms could be assembled on the storm-ravaged beachfront site. Enrollment at William Carey dropped from 800 pre-Katrina to 500 in the term immediately following, but the private college quickly charted a new course for its future at an alternative location 12 miles inland at the Tradition development in Harrison County, which opened in the fall of 2009.[29] In comparison to William Carey and USM Gulf Coast, the vast majority of the buildings in Mississippi Gulf Coast Community College's multicampus system suffered only light damage. However, the disaster left some 200 MGCCC employees homeless, and the community college's enrollment, which stood at 10,055 in August of 2005, took a post-Katrina plunge of more than 3,000 students.[30]

The loss of all of the classrooms on the USM Gulf Park campus presented a stark challenge. Despite a commitment from President Shelby Thames that no one would lose his or her job, if a tuition revenue stream could not be restored, large-scale layoffs would only be a matter of time. Notwithstanding the fact that 128 members of the USM Gulf Coast faculty and staff had lost their homes, on October 10, USM Gulf Coast managed to reopen its teaching operations in an abandoned hospital facility located in Gulfport two miles to the east of the university's devastated Long Beach site. Through pure determination and creative schedule juggling, faculty and staff at USM Gulf Coast managed to recover 80 percent of the pre-Katrina course offerings in a facility that allowed only 20 percent of the pre-Katrina teaching space. [31] For months before an adequate supply of portable buildings arrived, faculty worked without offices, and office staffers worked at desks set up wall-to-wall in nooks and crannies that invited claustrophobia. Yet, when classes resumed on October 10 for a compressed 10-week fall term, 1,677 of the 2,500 commuter students who had originally registered resumed their studies at USM Gulf Coast in classrooms carved out of former labs, conference rooms, intensive care wards, and surgical suites. Over the next few weeks and months portable classrooms arrived to augment these oddly shaped make-do lecture halls, and a line of outdoor port-o-lets provided the necessary complement of restrooms. The teamwork which stood behind this accomplishment was all the more impressive given the fact that the campus's chief executive, Dr. Pat Joachim, had only been on the job for one week before Katrina struck. By the spring semester following Katrina, USM Gulf Coast enrollment had recovered to 1,850 students, and by the fall semester of 2006, 2,446 students returned to classes despite the crowding, inconvenience, and poor curb appeal of the cobbled-together alternate teaching site.[32]

For both school and college administrations, housing hundreds of faculty and staff posed another unprecedented challenge. Katrina had destroyed or rendered uninhabitable one-third of the available housing across a three-county area. However, the loss of housing to school faculty and staff was far more severe in several coast districts. In the Bay-Waveland and Biloxi school systems, over 60 percent of the faculty and staff lost their homes. However, in the Pass Christian District there was a startlingly high 90 percent loss of faculty and staff housing. Even on the eastern and somewhat weaker edge of the storm in Jackson County, Superintendent Rucks Robinson reported that 27 percent of his faculty and staff had lost everything, including homes, cars, and all else but the clothes on their backs. Moreover, Robinson found that another 24 percent of his faculty and staff had lost half of their belongings. Significantly, Robinson's Jackson County District served areas north of Pascagoula on the eastern side of the storm where City Manager Kay Kell thought that almost every residence within the city limits had taken water. The Harrison County District serving areas north of Biloxi and Gulfport reported a 13 percent destruction of faculty and staff housing, the lowest figure reported by any coast school district.[33]

Getting these wounded school systems to resurrect themselves demanded a high sense of professional commitment to children and a willingness to work 15 and 16 hours per day six and seven days per week to get school buildings and equipment in shape. By October 3, in an amazing tribute to their faculty, staff, and administration, 9 of the 11 coast public school systems had opened to children, and as sufficient portable classrooms became available, the hard-hit Pass Christian and Bay-Waveland districts followed over the next month.[34]

At the superintendents' level, a preexisting interdistrict superintendents' support network also played an important role in helping schools across the entire region get back into service. Superintendent Carolyn Hamilton of Long Beach remembered that by the Thursday following the storm, Henry Arledge, superintendent of the Harrison County School District, had managed to get in touch with the chief administrators of the five districts operating in Harrison County to invite them to meet at his office to discuss a common "game plan" and how the different districts could help each other "do what we needed to do." Both Sue Matheson of Pass Christian and Carolyn Hamilton of Long Beach expressed appreciation for Arledge's leadership. Henry Arledge was the longest serving superintendent in the storm-ravaged region. Arledge had been through the rituals with FEMA after numerous lesser storms stretching back to the 1980s and was thoroughly familiar with the law. He considered physical plant issues to be one of his strong points. The superintendents' meetings became regularly scheduled weekly occurrences, and by the second Thursday after the storm, they had expanded to include the Southeast Mississippi Regional Consortium of Superintendents led by Dr. Tom Clark. State Superintendent Hank Bounds and representatives of his office also attended and offered information, advice, and support.[35]

The superintendents were able to put together global estimates of their needs, establish goals for common reopening dates, and share ideas on split shifts, busing, and other means to make maximum use of surviving buildings until the full complement of 425 portable classrooms could be delivered and installed. A need would be mentioned in one district, and the superintendent in another sometimes found a way to share an asset to help meet that need. Thus, since the Pass Christian Central Office was in ruins, the Harrison County superintendent made his offices available to them for regular Pass Christian administrative meetings. Arledge also found a way to get sets of handheld mobile radios donated to Bay-Waveland school administrators who had no other means of communicating with each other. When Superintendent Rucks Robinson of the Jackson County district reported that the loss of 29 buses meant that he could not restart his schools, within 24 hours he had received enough backup vehicles from three neighboring districts to allow him to patch together the bus routes that made reopening possible. These meetings allowed superintendents to compare notes on their dealings with FEMA and various state agencies. The gatherings also served as a psychological support system for overburdened administrators. As Henry Arledge put it, "We . . . talked and cussed and fussed . . . [and got] some of that frustration off."[36]

Within individual districts, principals and administrative staff established daily tasks and goals. Some met twice per day to assess progress and set new goals. As the school-based Red Cross storm shelters gradually closed, and as campus cleanups and roof repairs got under way, plans were made for assembling teachers and for the return of thousands of disaster-stricken and potentially traumatized students. Staff reunions were sometimes emotional. In Jackson County, Superintendent Rucks Robinson assembled his administrators a week after the storm and set the tone for recovery with these words: "This is a business of people and not bricks and mortar. We are going to take care of our people, and we are going to look out for our students. . . . This is how [we] are going to be remembered for the rest of [our] lives."[37] Robinson's views reflected the kind of compassion mixed with determination that was common in local leaders in the midst of the crisis. This people-first attitude often seemed to be missing from the impersonal mandates of FEMA and state auditors who looked over the shoulder of every administrator dealing with the region's massive loss of school buildings.

Alongside the public schools, the parochial school system of the Catholic Diocese of Biloxi suffered the destruction of 5 of its 18 campuses in a system serving 4,600 students. Beyond St. Clare Elementary and Our Lady Academy in Hancock County, St. Paul's Elementary in Pass Christian and St. Thomas Elementary in Long Beach lay in ruins. In Biloxi, Mercy Cross High School was destroyed and St. Peter's Elementary in Pascagoula was too heavily damaged to be used. As Superintendent Mike Ladner recalled it, the initial meeting of the Catholic principals in the wake of Katrina was very emotional. "We prayed and cried and prayed and cried," Ladner said, "... and reminded each other that God answers prayers in His time." With this faith in mind, Ladner reported that he and his team simply began executing plans one step at a time.[38] Rucks Robinson of the Jackson County School District, whose own home was left in a shambles with $60,000 in damages, indicated that the praying was not limited to Catholic school administrators.[39] Commenting on how his system could cope with 267 homeless employees and two destroyed school campuses, Robinson avowed that in the Jackson County School District, "we pray, I mean we pray hard." Public school administrators, like their parochial school counterparts, also had to just start putting one foot in front of the other. Whether in public schools or in parochial, roofs of remaining buildings had to be patched, cleanup work had to be undertaken, and faculty and staff had to be contacted and often assisted in finding housing. In Jackson County, Gulfport, and Long Beach, school grounds themselves became trailer park sites for homeless faculty and staff who did not own lots on which a FEMA camper could be placed. Plans were made to provide extra counseling services for both students and staff. Training sessions were scheduled to equip principals and faculty with techniques to help children cope with residual emotional baggage arising from the disaster or from crowded postdisaster living conditions.[40]

October 3, 2005, became the target date for reopening coast schools. Some districts were able to beat the target date by a few days. Of course, the timing of the manufacture, delivery, and installation of 425 portable classrooms was in the hands of FEMA, the Army Corps of Engineers, and their contractors. As FEMA and corps delivery dates began to slide, the ability to make that October reopening depended on whether the remaining brick and mortar buildings and campuses in a given district could be reconfigured or rescheduled in some way that would allow classes to be taught with or without the portable units. All hinged on creative thinking about the use of surviving facilities and the willingness of storm-stressed faculty and staff to adapt and make less-than-ideal arrangements work. In the Harrison County system, the lack of portable classrooms forced D'Iberville Middle School and D'Iberville Elementary to share the same buildings on a split-shift schedule. Elementary students and teachers worked a long morning schedule and then relinquished their classrooms to the displaced middle school teachers and students for a long afternoon session ending at 5:30 p.m. Similar temporary split-shift sharing of classrooms worked in other districts awaiting delivery of portable classrooms sufficient to replace destroyed facilities.[41]

The massive destruction in the Pass Christian and Bay-Waveland districts left no capacity for double-shifting. In both districts, official school opening dates had to be delayed until the promised portable classrooms arrived. Even so, in Pass Christian the creative adaptations undertaken at the Delisle Elementary campus went beyond clearing grounds for the 55 portable classrooms that would accommodate the relocation of high school and middle school students. Here, local administrators and teachers in the elementary grades agreed to double the normal 20-student class enrollments to an upper limit of 40 so that the youngest children could all be placed in the cleaned-up permanent buildings at Delisle. Each 40-student elementary classroom was then staffed with two teachers and an aide working in a team-teaching arrangement. Thus, the smaller kids could be placed in a room with their own previous teacher. The younger children were placed in the brick and mortar building, where they would have less exposure to the elements and less vulnerability to the fears that were expected to arise during stormy weather in the trailer-type portable classrooms that served the older students.[42]

Because the water well at Delisle Elementary lacked the capacity to support the 1,500 K-12 students who ultimately occupied the site, cases of bottled water were kept stacked in every classroom on site, and outdoor port-o-lets were rented to augment the limited number of available indoor restroom facilities.[43] The need for a new well at the Delisle site became a matter of a two-year-long negotiation with FEMA which resolved itself only after U.S. House Speaker Nancy Pelosi drew national attention to the issue when she toured the school in August of 2007.[44] The makeshift water supplies and toilet facilities at Delisle offer an excellent example of the determination of local school staffs to get back into service regardless of the confused priorities of the federal bureaucracies with which they dealt.

As the start of school approached, principals brought their faculties together for planning sessions. Peggy Sullivan, an English teacher at D'Iberville Middle School, recalled that her principal, Mrs. Annette Luther, began contacting faculty and staff shortly after the storm. Since the campus was in ruins, the principal held informal weekly meetings at her home.

Information about FEMA housing assistance was distributed, and faculty who had lost homes were paired in support groups with faculty whose homes were intact. Roughly a quarter of the faculty and staff at D'Iberville Middle School had lost everything. The school principal personally gave shelter to an assistant teacher whose home had been destroyed.[45]

While a quarter of the faculty of D'Iberville Middle School had lost their homes, Katrina left between 60 and 70 percent of the D'Iberville student body without housing. The fate of the students weighed heavily on teachers like Peggy Sullivan. In the weeks before school reopened, on several occasions Sullivan had driven from her Gulfport home over to D'Iberville. She had seen the ruins of the school and the devastation of homes in the areas surrounding the school. "Anytime I went to D'Iberville," she said, "I would just bawl on the way home." For Sullivan, the opening of school relieved her worst fears. "Once I found out [that] all of my students were safe," she said, "I was okay." One of her students lost his father, some had to swim to safety in the midst of the storm, others had ridden it out in attics, and some had the experience of evacuating with family only to return to the total ruin of their houses and the loss of all of their possessions. However, none of Peggy Sullivan's students had died in Katrina.[46]

Federal grants made extra counselors available to the schools, and teachers were coached on how to provide opportunities for the children to talk about their experiences. When the day arrived for students to report back to school, Robert Hirsch, principal of Ocean Springs High School, was disappointed that only about half of his previous enrollees showed up. He found things to be "extremely quiet." Hirsch recalled that "the kids were excited to get back and see their friends. . . , but it was just a bizarre kind of calm." The comparatively small numbers of students meant that there was plenty of opportunity for discussion, but teachers moved toward conducting "business as usual" in an effort to provide a sense of normalcy and structure in a safe haven with running water, air conditioning, and hot meals.[47]

Peggy Sullivan was somewhat surprised that at first, her seventh and eighth grade students at D'Iberville Middle School did not want to talk about the storm. In planning for the opening of school, the English teacher had purchased several game sets including chess, checkers, and various card games. The idea was to give students time to interact with each other over games while the teacher made rounds to talk to each one individually. There was no pressure to share their experiences, but the opportunity was provided. Still, as Sullivan saw it, most middle school students did not want to talk about Katrina when they first came back to school. "They were really glad to see that their friends were all right," but as Sullivan recalled, at first very few of them talked about the disaster. Over a few days the classroom routines returned to something as close to normal as split-shift schooling would allow, and after several weeks the delivery of portable classrooms allowed the return to a normal schedule. Still, considering the fact that 60 to 70 percent of the D'Iberville students were living in tents or FEMA trailers with no place to stow books or school supplies, most teachers suspended the assignment of homework.[48]

However, toward the end of the year the storm experience began to come up spontaneously in the students' written work. So many groups had sent school supplies, clothing, and other aid to the students at D'Iberville that the English teachers decided to require each student to draft at least one thank-you letter. The letters sometimes presented touching personal revelations from kids who had spent the storm in attics as water filled their houses. Some of the students reported swimming to safety. Someone with a boat rescued one child's family from the top of their roof. Another told of sitting on a bunk bed until the water rose high enough to soak the top mattress. For the young teens and preteens who had lost everything, simple things like a change of clothing were deeply appreciated.[49]

A year later when Sullivan required students to try their hand at writing a poem as part of a unit on poetry, the veteran teacher was again surprised when a number of students asked if they could write about Katrina. More than a year after the storm, there were still notes of grief like the lines from a young girl who said, "Since Katrina has passed by we have all had our share of cries. . . . We cry and cry until our tear ducts are dry." By this time, there were also poetic teenage expressions of frustration or humor associated with packed living conditions. "I once lived in a FEMA trailer," one student wrote, "and it was as small as a pea." Another found that life in a FEMA camper meant that "Everywhere you go it's wall to wall, no space at all. . . . Space, Space, Space there is never enough. Trying to store stuff is just too tough."[50] The poems and letters revealed much. One of Sullivan's students lived for a time in a three-bedroom house with twenty-one people. Once again, it appeared to teachers that for students living in such conditions, or for students whose families were in crowded FEMA trailers or in the D'Iberville tent city, just being at school was a relief. At school there was more room than in a tent, a FEMA camper, or piled up with relatives in a single-family house. At school students could exercise and play without stumbling over debris, and they could reconnect with friends. Moreover, donations of clothing, books, and supplies from charitable groups all across the nation meant that without arousing embarrassment, the school could provide supplies or changes of clothes to sensitive teenagers who had lost everything.[51]

If school was a safe haven to students, it was also a safe haven for faculty and staff members who were experiencing the grief and the struggles associated with the recovery of their own families. At Pass Christian, where 90 percent of the faculty and staff had lost housing, Superintendent Sue Matheson believed that "it was helpful for all of us to come back to work." At work faculty and staff could talk to each other, provide comfort, and compare notes on dealings with insurance companies, FEMA, or the Small Business Administration's home loan program. The superintendent concluded that focusing on getting kids back in classes "kept our minds off of what we were facing personally." In Matheson's words, being back at school was "very, very helpful. . . . It was therapy for everyone."[52]

Several days after D'Iberville Middle School opened on split shifts, site clearing and the installation of 55 portable classrooms allowed all Pass Christian schools to open on the grounds of Delisle Elementary. Here, Al Roughton, a veteran Pass Christian High School history and government teacher, was surprised at the number of seniors who managed to return even though their families had left the area or still awaited FEMA trailers. What Roughton observed provides a glimpse into the importance of the recovery of the schools for disaster-displaced families. Several of his students returned to the coast from Atlanta and Birmingham when they heard that the Pass Christian schools were reopening. One returned from as far away as Seattle, Washington. For students whose families had found housing in neighboring towns and counties, the district waived the normal out-of-district fees if the child wanted to go back to school with friends or return to the comfort of a familiar teacher.[53]

For the high school students, at an age when social interests and friendships were increasingly important, understanding the reality of the tragedy seemed to amplify the joy of the return to classes. As Roughton put it, "Everybody was happy because nobody was dead." Despite the utter devastation of Pass Christian, no students had lost their lives. However, the pace of delivery of FEMA campers meant that many of Roughton's students also lived doubled up with family or friends, or came to school from individual pup tents on family property or from the Pass Christian tent city. A few determined souls seemed to "just live in their cars." Roughton reported that through the year after Katrina, it was not unusual for him to arrive on campus and find students in the parking lot asleep in their cars.

He would "just wake them up" and tell them to "go get your shower." Some of these students reported that they had awakened in a tent or FEMA trailer in the wee hours of the morning unable to sleep and just got up and drove to school to sleep, so as to be there as soon as the buildings opened. School officials allowed such students to shower on school grounds, and for an extended period of time, federal funding provided a free breakfast and lunch, although the limitations of the on-site kitchen and cafeteria meant that it was usually cereal for breakfast and sandwiches for lunch.[54]

Scenes such as these inevitably raise questions about whether anger or depression arising from the disaster or its aftermath produced behavior problems in the schools. Despite the negative conditions in which so many students lived, the eight Gulf Coast school superintendents interviewed for the USM Katrina Oral History Project each avowed that in the year after Katrina there were fewer behavior problems and fewer school expulsions than in normal years. Three factors might account for such a trend. First, in many schools, start-up was accompanied by an abundance of available counseling services. Secondly, the teacher-student ratios actually improved during the year after the storm due to initial losses in enrollment averaging 20 percent or more. Finally, the regularity of school life may have reduced tensions and provided welcome relief to the stresses of life outside of the school grounds.[55]

However, these same superintendents believed that they saw a spike in behavior difficulties at school during the second year after Katrina, and many superintendents believed they were seeing rising divorce rates among parents of school-aged children as months in crowded living conditions dragged on to become years.[56] The school superintendents' observations about rising behavior problems in the years after the Katrina year dovetailed with the findings of the 2007 Columbia University Mailman School of Public Health study of Mississippi child and family health, which showed markedly higher rates of depression, anxiety, and psychological vulnerability accompanied by much higher than normal rates of absenteeism from school in children living in FEMA trailers in the most devastated neighborhoods. Moreover, as many as 40 percent of the displaced children suffered from chronic health problems.[57] This data suggested that the longer families stayed in crowded living conditions, the greater the negative impact on children.

However, even during the first year following the storm, Al Roughton reported that at Pass Christian "we did have a big attendance problem." According to Roughton, attendance was so bad that the district stopped punishing students who ran up excessive absences because if normal rules had been enforced "nobody would have graduated in 2006." Roughton attributed much of this to personal and family problems. However, he also noted that at Pass Christian High, teachers observed greater than the normal rate of sickness-related absence among students. As time went on, the school nurse discovered that almost all of the students with chronic illnesses were living in FEMA trailers. Still, Roughton believed that the majority of his students at Pass Christian High that year kept up with their school work, "even though everything that was going on . . . with their families meant that they just didn't come every day."[58]

Disrupted school attendance naturally raises questions about academic performance in the wake of the disaster. Despite contemporary obsessions with testing in the public schools, standardized testing undoubtedly falls short as a measure of ideal educational outcomes. However, Mississippi's state-mandated testing regime did produce a body of data that allows at least some estimate of the impact of the disaster on student performance. In the use of this data, it must be noted that changes in Mississippi's statewide test standards in the years after Katrina make comparisons of "pass rates" from year to year impossible. Still, it is possible to compare annual rankings of schools. For example, in the years prior to Katrina, the Pass Christian schools consistently ranked near the top in statewide measures of annual student progress. Out of 242 high schools rated on the basis of state test data gathered during the spring before Katrina, Pass Christian High School ranked number 12 in Mississippi. In that same year, 14 of the 15 public high schools in the three Mississippi Gulf Coast counties ranked in the top third of all high schools in the state. However, after Katrina, the number of coast high schools ranked in the top third dropped from 14 to 10 during the period from 2007 through 2010. Significantly, Bay High, the school serving students from the Waveland and Bay St. Louis high impact zone, dropped out of the top third listing in 2005–2006 and in the succeeding years through 2010 never returned to the top tier ranking.[59] The drop from 14 to 10 coast high schools ranked in the top third in the state suggests an important impact of the Katrina-inflicted housing disruptions on students and teaching staffs. Of course, differing demographic characteristics of districts and different impacts of the out-migration of storm victims almost certainly had a bearing on school performance. In the Bay-Waveland district during the year after Katrina, there was a precipitous decline in state math scores among all students, but the declines were more severe for low-income and minority students.[60]

Still, even if some high schools did maintain their absolute statewide rankings, most Mississippi Gulf Coast districts including the hard-hit Bay-Waveland and Pass Christian districts saw their students' raw test scores recover to their prestorm levels over the next two years. Even the simplest perusal of the data suggests that the correlations between measures of devastation or homelessness among students and their test performances are imperfect. For example, in badly devastated Pass Christian, a district with a 26 percent minority student population in 2006,[61] the high school dropped from number 12 in the state rankings to number 36 in the Katrina-year testing. However, in testing done in the spring of 2007, as attendance returned to more normal patterns, Pass Christian High rebounded to claim ranking as number three in the state. Furthermore, despite severe ongoing problems associated with the reconstruction of the community, Pass Christian High claimed the number two ranking in the state in 2009, and the Pass Christian district as a whole was ranked number one in state test results in both 2009 and 2010.[62]

In a similar vein, one of the most heartwarming stories of recovery and resilience in the schools came from the devastated low-income area of East Biloxi. Here, against all socioeconomic predictors, in 2010 Nichols Elementary School won honors as the highest performing elementary school in the Biloxi School District and was the only school in south Mississippi to be named a U.S. Department of Education Blue Ribbon School. However, the celebrations of these honors for the predominantly African American student body at Nichols were bittersweet. Declines in post-Katrina enrollments in the Biloxi schools combined with the recession to bring the Biloxi School Board to the reluctant decision to close this banner school. The Blue Ribbon Nichols Elementary School team fell victim to the lagging recovery of housing in the surrounding neighborhoods. A beautifully refurbished school facility carrying the names of educators long revered in the African American community was closed.[63] Still, in their ability to achieve against the odds, the Nichols student body and faculty demonstrated that the roots of resilience were not always to be found in the material or social circumstances of the families being served. As in so many other instances in the post-Katrina world of the Mississippi Gulf Coast, it was the strength of commitments to the mission at hand that had enabled children to transcend the devastation and seeming hopelessness that surrounded them.

In the immediate aftermath of Katrina, the condition of school buildings and the suffering of their faculties and staffs mirrored the hard circumstances of the larger community. Yet, on the Mississippi Gulf Coast, neither the spirit of the schools nor the spirits of the children were broken by this storm. Within six weeks of the greatest natural disaster in American history, all but one of the devastated school districts of the Mississippi Gulf Coast were back in operation. Though it would be years before the reconstruction of lost buildings could move thousands of children out of portable classrooms, the speed of the recovery of Gulf Coast school performance rankings strongly suggested that in sustaining predictable schedules of instruction with continuing high expectations and supportive extracurricular activities, the schools had found the way to carry on the most important fundamentals of their work. The surprising rebound of the most severely devastated districts bears witness to the dedication of faculty and staff, but it also perhaps serves as a reminder that children and young people and those who work with them are by their nature oriented toward the future. What children needed were stable classroom experiences that continued to point them in the direction of healthy growth and achievement.

It would take years of wrangling with FEMA to restore destroyed buildings, but the success of the schools in the hard months and years following Katrina in great measure confirmed Superintendent Rucks Robinson's assertion that schools are primarily "a business of people and not bricks and mortar."[64] Through the difficult days of bringing the schools back into operation, teachers and school staffs created the conditions that allowed tens of thousands of working families to remain in the area who might otherwise have been forced to leave. In looking out for their students, teachers and school staffs were really looking out for the entire community. Rising test scores in cobbled-together schools where children came from FEMA campers to study in portable classrooms carried an important message about the essential psychological, social, and spiritual support systems needed for long-term recovery of the community at large. In demonstrating and sustaining a spirit of caring, personal engagement, and hope for the future, the schools joined families and churches in providing something basic that children, their parents, and entire disaster-stricken communities needed in order to thrive even in the midst of devastation and poor living conditions. In reality, no distant bureaucracies, however well-motivated, could be expected to provide the scale of individual outreach required to meet such needs.

Chapter Nine

The Great Red-Tape Battle for Public Buildings

The citizens of Waveland have been through hell in the past three years. Nothing would raise their spirits like seeing their government buildings going up. . . . I have been promised at all levels of government that everything was being expedited to begin rebuilding in Waveland. Yet we stand here almost three years post-Katrina's landfall, still trying to build the first structure.

—WAVELAND MAYOR TOMMY LONGO
Congressional Testimony
June 19, 2008[1]

It was the most frustrating thing in my whole life that I couldn't make anything happen. . . . At one point my husband sat me down. He put a hand on both shoulders, and he said, "Kay, if the president, if Trent Lott, if the governor can't fix FEMA, why do you think you can?"

—KAY KELL
City Manager
Pascagoula, Mississippi[2]

No part of the early response phase of the Katrina disaster had been easy for anyone at any level. However, two years into the long-term recovery, the *Sun Herald* observed that "the recovery and rebuilding effort in the aftermath of the worst natural disaster in American history" had been "even more challenging." The brunt of the battle to rebuild school facilities, public buildings, and infrastructure fell squarely on the shoulders of local officials and their already-overburdened cadres of county and municipal employees. Every aspect of the long-term recovery tested their endurance, their physical stamina, and the depth of their commitment to the communities they served. In an editorial that alluded to the fighting qualities of the mythical movie hero, boxer Rocky Balboa, the local newspaper expressed the hope that despite mounting frustrations with the slow progress in long-term rebuilding, "passion, . . . and knowledge of the challenges that lay ahead" would "keep all levels of government engaged in South Mississippi for the long haul." Like the 15 rounds of the movie title fight, in the red-tape battles that appeared likely to stretch out for years to come, the *Sun Herald* could foresee "no knock-out punch in achieving recovery." Perseverance through round after frustrating round was essential. The editorialist surmised that "like Rocky, we must never lose sight of the goal," because "every round . . . must be won for recovery to be a success."[3]

The editorialist's play on the movie theme arose from a candid real-life exchange between Rocky Pullman, the president of the Hancock County Board of Supervisors, and President George W. Bush as Bush visited Bay St. Louis on a fact-finding trip two years after the storm. When the president asked Pullman how things were going, he got an unexpected earful reflecting two years of struggle and the frustrations of large numbers of citizens and local officials alike. According to news accounts, Rocky Pullman reeled off a list of nagging problems from the lack of progress in replacing the local jail and the county Emergency Operations Center to crumbling Katrina-damaged roads and a lack of FEMA presence in the county. In effect, he told Bush that things were "not going well and the feds just don't get it." At the same time, Councilman Jim Thriffiley of Bay St. Louis told reporters that "the federal government from the President on down" needed to understand that they had "never seen anything like this," and added his view that "those guys" at FEMA in particular "don't have a clue about this type of disaster." Pullman told reporters that the main point he had attempted to make with the president was that Hancock County had been "ground zero in the hurricane," and the sluggishness of federal agencies was ensuring that the county remained "ground zero in the restoration."[4]

Pullman's blunt candor struck a chord with a general public which had come to expect that presidential visits would produce overly rosy reports and rounds of cheerleading that seemed disconnected from the harsh realities of the long-term recovery. That Rocky Pullman had dropped the mask in the presence of President Bush and revealed the truth about rising public frustrations was somehow refreshing. The mood led the *Sun Herald* to imagine chants rising from Hancock County—"'Rocky! Rocky!' Then a little louder and clearer, 'Go, Rocky, Go!'"[5] On the local level there was a wide and deep consensus that Mississippi needed a more energetic response from a strong federal government. No one in Mississippi advocated for reduced or limited federal involvement in the Katrina recovery. The need was just too great, and state and private resources were just too limited.

Mississippi's leaders and Mississippi's citizens were, in the end, pragmatists and not small-government ideologues. The complaints heard in Mississippi were pleas for greater federal efficiency, greater federal presence, and greater federal effectiveness. The intention of federal recovery programs was everywhere applauded. Thanks to the vision and generosity of the Stafford Act, in addition to funding emergency response operations and emergency housing, federal dollars administered through FEMA would eventually cover the lion's share of more than $3 billion in costs associated with debris removal and rebuilding schools, public buildings, parks, and other infrastructure lost in the storm.[6]

However, delay and uncertainty dogged the federal programs. Delay and uncertainty constituted the main enemy confronting the local leaders who bore responsibility for getting these long-term recovery projects moving. From the grassroots perspective, delay most often appeared to arise from federal indecision and from tedious multilayered federal and state approval processes that generated mountains of paperwork, conflicting interpretations, and distress. Years of delay in highly visible public projects had taken a toll on grassroots morale and threatened to slow the momentum of the broader recovery effort.[7]

Congressman Gene Taylor and his staff encountered local concerns about delays on almost a daily basis. For Congressman Taylor, at the end of 2007, the most frustrating thing about the recovery was the fact that not one public school building and not one city or county building that Katrina had destroyed in Mississippi had even started reconstruction. For Brian Martin, Congressman Taylor's Washington-based policy director, this fact provided clear proof that FEMA was tripping over its own red tape in the long-term recovery effort just as it had stumbled over itself in the emergency response phase of the disaster. Despite the heroic efforts of beleaguered school staffs and city and county administrators, Martin predicted that because FEMA was "so nitpicking about every detail of every one of those projects," schools and public buildings are going to be "the last things to be rebuilt in Mississippi."[8]

A Princeton-educated native of the Pascagoula area who had worked for Congressman Taylor in various capacities since 1989, Brian Martin related an early incident to illustrate the way federal processes and procedures impeded common-sense solutions to problems. Four days after Katrina struck in 2005, Congressman Taylor brought Martin back home from Washington to the Mississippi Gulf Coast to work on disaster issues in the district. On the weekend following Katrina, a member of the Jackson County Board of Supervisors approached Martin in the Jackson County Emergency Operations Center with a request that he get the congressman to call the Army Corps of Engineers about the disabled Pascagoula–Moss Point Sewerage Treatment Plant. This request started a sequence of communications which revealed to Martin the nature of the enervating bureaucratic battles which local officials would soon face in their quest to restore public infrastructure.[9]

Martin immediately drove to the damaged sewerage plant, where he discovered that pumps were not working, and raw sewage was flowing into the Pascagoula River. Workers had confiscated a supply of swimming-pool chlorine from a local store and were busily pouring it into the muck in an effort to disinfect it. There was an obvious need for engineering assistance to plan the repairs needed to bring the plant back online. The Army Corps of Engineers Office in nearby Mobile, Alabama, had done work on the plant years before. Thus, Martin placed a call to the corps' Mobile office. This started a long-distance telephone chase that led through four federal offices and two state agencies with each referring the request to another level in the bureaucracy.[10]

The Mobile corps office referred Martin to Army Corps of Engineers Regional Headquarters in Vicksburg. The Vicksburg headquarters had orders not to act unless ordered to do so through the military's Joint Task Force Katrina, operating from Camp Shelby near Hattiesburg. Joint Task Force Katrina officers were under orders to wait for authorization from FEMA, which in turn would not act without an official request from the Mississippi Emergency Management Agency (MEMA). MEMA demanded an official request from local Jackson County authorities, rather than a congressional aid, and described a process that would send the request to the Mississippi Department of Environmental Quality for on-site verification before MEMA would request FEMA to officially task the corps or some other entity to do the engineering assessment. If the county deviated from this procedure it risked incurring expenses that FEMA would not reimburse.[11]

It took a full week to finally get engineers on site, in this case Navy Seabees from Gulfport, to do the engineering assessments needed before the repair project could be put out for bids. Meanwhile, raw sewage and all of the health and environmental hazards that went with it continued to flow into the river past the city of Pascagoula and on into the shallow-water fisheries of the Mississippi Sound and the Gulf of Mexico. Thus, in the midst of an emergency, Brian Martin got his introduction to what he labeled "the insane bureaucracy" with which local school officials and city and county leaders would have to deal on a project-by-project basis in order to gain access to the federal disaster assistance funds to which their communities were by law entitled.[12]

The FEMA Project Worksheet was the starting point for these and each of Mississippi's 23,275 individual disaster recovery projects.[13] At its peak of staffing in the first few months after Katrina, there were 325 FEMA employees assigned to Mississippi to assist in the early phases of project formulation. On the local level, each of the 23,275 projects generated its own thick file of documentation. Congressional hearings in 2007 revealed that individual project files sometimes contained 2,000 pages of documentation.[14] For city and county employees who were themselves often storm victims, the deadlines associated with the initial formulation of projects dictated seven-day work weeks for weeks on end in the aftermath of the disaster. To make matters worse, by June of 2007 when upper level FEMA project reviews were in full swing, the FEMA staff in Mississippi had dwindled to only 34 employees.[15] Thus, the full burden of responding to questions or disputes arising from later FEMA reviews fell squarely on local officials and their employees. City and county employees were called upon repeatedly to copy or rework the files for a succession of FEMA functionaries. For hard-hit towns like Bay St. Louis, the audit and record-keeping needs arising from federal projects were overwhelming, and there were no federal grants to hire additional city workers. Bay St. Louis City Clerk David Kolf, an accountant by training, observed that the Katrina recovery had exacted high costs to the personal lives of city employees which would never be seen on any ledger book. Even five years after the storm, Kolf asserted that the disaster-related paperwork load was still driving stressed and exhausted local government employees to the breaking point.[16]

As the recovery unfolded, local officials discovered that even the most scrupulous following of the rules with detailed input from local FEMA representatives during the Project Worksheet formulation stage carried no guarantees of reimbursement for work done. Projects could be, and often were, repudiated months or even years later at higher levels in the FEMA bureaucracy in Atlanta or Washington. In testimony before Congress in June of 2008, Waveland Mayor Tommy Longo described his frustration with one of the many paper battles he was waging with FEMA. Two years after the required FEMA Project Worksheet to rebuild the municipal pier had been written and repeatedly "combed through checking for accuracy," and after FEMA had taken months to review engineering plans, in March of 2008, the city put the project out for bids. Two weeks into the bid process, FEMA representatives visited the city bearing news that FEMA now had "problems with the project." A project winnowed through two years of approvals and engineering work was suddenly halted in its tracks with no clues as to when it might proceed.[17]

The prospect that FEMA could have reclaimed or clawed back monies after they were actually spent was especially disturbing for Mayor Longo. In the same round of testimony, the Waveland mayor gave an account of the replacement of a critical piece of city equipment for which a proper Project Worksheet was "written and gone over numerous times." With a string of authorizations in hand "supporting the step-by-step action FEMA needed us to take," Longo said, a bid had been awarded, the equipment was purchased, and the FEMA reimbursement was deposited into the city account. Months later, FEMA officials notified the city that "they had made a mistake" and promptly removed 50 percent of the allocated funds from the municipal account. According to the mayor, this triggered a "devastating" cash-flow crisis for Waveland, a town whose tax base had been virtually annihilated.[18]

In the same June 2008 hearing, MEMA Director Mike Womack urged that the FEMA Office of Inspector General refrain from deobligation of funds that had already been paid to local governments, unless there was a demonstrable attempt to defraud. Womack pointed out that the FEMA Office of Inspector General's staff operated under protocols that allowed them to provide only the most "general and non-definitive guidance" to state and local officials "until months or years after projects are completed." Such delayed adverse rulings meant that federal monies spent in good faith had to be repaid. The MEMA director urged that "if local governments made mistakes, either based on guidance from FEMA staff or [based on] their inability to get any guidance," they should not face demands for repayment of FEMA funds already spent.[19]

Congressman Gene Taylor was particularly angered with the FEMA auditors who, long after the fact, challenged the necessity of Bay-Waveland

School Superintendent Kim Stasny's removal of certain trees and stumps from school campuses to prepare the sites for portable classrooms. With no FEMA guidance available to her at the time, the school superintendent followed the state bid laws, obtained three bids, and awarded a contract for removal of dangerous limbs, leaning trees, and stumps. Two years after the work was done, FEMA notified one of the hardest-hit school districts in Mississippi that stump removal was a luxury, the expense of which FEMA would not pay. Furthermore, unless it could be documented that any tree that was cut down on school property was leaning more than 30 degrees, FEMA, once again, would decline to pay. The only recourse for such after-the-fact rulings was a time-consuming appeal to a higher level within FEMA. Congressman Taylor was appalled at the implication that school authorities acting in emergency circumstances to get the schools back in operation as quickly as possible were somehow out to defraud FEMA. The fact that FEMA had "handed out billions in no-bid, cost-plus contracts to Bechtel" and other big contractors, but then "sent people out measuring stumps and limbs to deny reimbursement to the local school" seemed particularly outrageous to Taylor.[20]

These were not isolated cases. In testimony before a U.S. House committee in May of 2007, Congressman Taylor described a juggernaut in which hundreds of FEMA Project Worksheets from Mississippi were "indefinitely delayed by a never-ending process of objections, revisions, and disputes." By law, upon orders of the president, FEMA was obligated to fund 90 percent of the expense for such disaster-related projects, but as Congressman Taylor saw it, distant FEMA functionaries routinely worked to narrow the scope "to exclude many costs" that were "necessary to comply with building codes and standards."[21]

Additional rounds in the boxing match between FEMA and the Bay-Waveland School Distict reinforced the congressman's point. When planning got under way for the reconstruction of the destroyed North Bay Elementary School campus, FEMA dug in its heels and refused to pay for the relocation of portable classrooms—a step necessary to clear the site for construction. In fact, FEMA resisted any plan that might for any reason give the new school more square footage under roof than contained in the destroyed structures.[22]

The latter stance posed a special difficulty. The North Bay Elementary School had been built decades earlier on a plan that had featured three classroom buildings in which all rooms had opened directly to the outside with no interior hallways. The realities of twenty-first-century school-security concerns about the dangers of such multiple-entry layouts, together with rising energy costs and modern accreditation standards, dictated that new school construction avoid such multiple-access open-campus layouts. The district proposed to rebuild using a modern design with everything placed under one roof so that all classrooms opened onto central hallways with controlled access to the outside. However, because hallways under roof added square footage, FEMA rejected the plan and insisted that the campus be built back on the footprint of the old structures regardless of other considerations. In FEMA's view, if the district proceeded with their proposal it would become an "improved project" that would be eligible for only 75 percent federal funding, rather than the 90 percent the district had been led to expect.[23]

Across town at Waveland Elementary where the campus consisted of a central building with two wings connected by covered walkways, FEMA ruled that the central building was damaged beyond repair and would have to be rebuilt, but at a higher elevation. However, the two wings were less than 50 percent destroyed and would have to be repaired on the low-lying spot where they stood. Again, any other approach would reduce federal funding from 90 percent to 75 percent, a burden which the small district could not bear. At Second Street Elementary, FEMA agreed to cover new flooring, but would not cover the cost of replacing the wiring in the old building to bring the building up to modern code standards.[24]

Finding the best solutions for children involved months and even years of appeals and negotiations and delayed the day when Bay-Waveland elementary students could move out of portable classrooms until the fall of 2010.[25] Meanwhile, an ongoing dispute over whether the leaking roofs and windows at Bay-Waveland High School and Bay-Waveland Middle School should be replaced dragged on until 2010, when a new third-party arbitration process upheld the district in a $7 million claim against FEMA.[26]

Similar experiences with FEMA drew fire from across the Mississippi Gulf Coast. Superintendent Sue Matheson of Pass Christian pointed reporters to her two-year quest for FEMA approval for a new water well to serve 55 portable classrooms on the grounds of Delisle Elementary School as an example of the difficulty her district had in "getting anyone to make a decision."[27] In July of 2007, Superintendent David Kopf of the Hancock County schools described "the bombshell" FEMA had dropped on his district when, after 22 weeks of planning, including the awarding of a $33 million contract to Roy Anderson Corporation for the replacement and relocation of the destroyed Gulfview and Charles B. Murphey elementary schools, FEMA officials issued new regulations which called the entire project into doubt.[28] In Long Beach, Superintendent Carolyn Hamilton faced a similar "throw-down with FEMA" over the relocation and reconstruction of the destroyed Harper McCaughan Elementary School campus. Once again, FEMA wanted to unload the $ 2.5 million cost of road work and an extension of water and sewer lines for the school onto the cash-strapped Long Beach School District.[29]

However, it was not just the cost of relocation or building to modern standards that could throw a monkey wrench into the works. Thirty miles inland at Picayune, Katrina's winds had blown over wooden light poles around a city ball field. When City Manager Ed Pinero discovered that the city could upgrade to stronger concrete poles with more efficient lighting at no extra cost, he pursued this as a good investment for everyone. To his surprise, even though the upgrade involved no additional cost, FEMA ruled that such a change would create an "improved project" that would then only be eligible for 75 percent reimbursement. The time required to appeal these kinds of penny-wise but pound-foolish interpretations was particularly maddening to local officials who were trying to rebuild in ways that would reduce taxpayer losses in future storms.[30]

Quite apart from FEMA's tendency to look for ways to shift costs onto local entities, Mayor Billie Skellie of Long Beach found that many of FEMA's initial estimates of project costs were "way too low." For example, FEMA's field representative originally estimated that the new Long Beach Police Station should cost $500,000. When the bids came in, all of them far exceeded this estimate, and at the time the city moved into the new building the actual cost turned out to be $1.5 million, or three times the original FEMA estimate. Poor initial estimates produced many arguments, and as Skellie observed, "lots of explaining" took time and energy.[31]

Part of the problem stemmed from escalating post-Katrina construction costs, but Skellie also pointed to the inexperience of the staffers FEMA put in the field to do the first project estimates. Often the people FEMA hired had never been involved in public works construction. Some were young engineers just out of college with no real background in preparing estimates for the varied projects they were assigned. Experienced city engineers sometimes had to take time to teach novices about the effect of salt water on electrical devices, or make the case for the replacement of individual water control mechanisms when a better qualified person would have understood without explanation or argument. Moreover, inexperienced people had a natural tendency to fall back on "FEMA guidelines for what prices should be in every area of the country" for everything from sewerage line replacements to cost per square foot for building or paving. However, the guidelines just did not match the bids that came back on jobs. Skellie conceded the need for some broad guidelines, but he thought that too much time was lost in arguing over the initial FEMA template which "just was not adequate here."[32]

Skellie credited many individual FEMA employees with good will and thought some had gained real understanding of local needs and recovery challenges. However, almost three years after Katrina, the Long Beach mayor observed that "much of what we're doing right now . . . is going over and redoing numbers and plans" that the first wave of FEMA field representatives prepared but which distant functionaries in the FEMA hierarchy later declared to be unacceptable or faulty in some respect. Skellie pointed to the constant rotation of FEMA personnel as the source of many problems. Every time a new FEMA person arrived on the scene, Skellie said, "it [was] almost like you never, ever visited on the subject before." According to Skellie, "You went over the same information [and] supplied the same documents" to the new person, "just like they never had a copying machine at their office." Constantly starting over with a new person meant lost time and more borrowing of money to stay afloat while awaiting FEMA reimbursements. In Skellie's view, this was "just not the way to do business."[33]

FEMA processes and procedures drew rounds of congressional testimony from witnesses who echoed these frustrations. In these settings, Mississippi's state-level officials tended to offer carefully crafted statements of gratitude for progress made and diplomatic summations of problems or "challenges" with the process which were often delivered behind statements to the effect that Mississippians "are not whiners and they're not into victimhood." A few months before Rocky Pullman's blunt unloading of local frustrations to President Bush, Brian McDonald, director of the Governor's Office of Recovery and Renewal, ventured a more delicate observation before the U.S. House Homeland Security Committee. "Mississippi is committed to working to maintain the positive momentum and cooperative spirit" that he avowed to exist between FEMA, the state, and its local entities. McDonald then added this gloved criticism: "In recognition of the cooperative spirit that exists, we also seek to ensure that FEMA headquarters continues to honor critical decisions made by local FEMA leadership and field personnel in the weeks and months immediately following the disaster." Always staying positive, McDonald held that it was critical that state and local officials be able to "act . . . in good faith" based on rulings from FEMA local representatives. McDonald then assured the committee that governments in Mississippi "have provided great leadership" in building back "better than ever."[34]

Louisiana officials were often more blunt in stating their difficulties to Congress. In July of 2007, Mayor Ray Nagin of New Orleans testified that "the cumbersome and often lengthy process of funding recovery projects through . . . [FEMA's] Project Worksheets" had been a "significant impediment" to his city's recovery. Nagin faulted "the broad discretionary powers" which the Stafford Act reserved to FEMA administrators who in turn did not apply it "consistently." According to Nagin, even if projects went unchallenged, the FEMA reimbursement system created serious cash flow difficulties for local communities. Given the unprecedented levels of infrastructure destruction and damage to the local tax base, Mayor Nagin declared that the requirement that municipalities pay contractors up front before seeking reimbursement from FEMA had greatly slowed recovery. The disaster, according to Nagin, had negatively impacted city bond ratings and made borrowing for these purposes more difficult. As a result, the city of New Orleans found itself "locked in a cycle of needing money to undertake projects so that we can seek reimbursements for work undertaken."[35]

Early in the recovery, Mississippi took a bold and creative step which took some of the sting out of the problem of up-front money. In Mississippi, the state legislature authorized a $200 million state bond issue to provide the up-front money in the form of low-interest loans for the three coast counties. Of course, those who accessed the money would have to repay it when they received their FEMA reimbursements, but the state arrangement won praise from the U.S. Government Accountability Office. In praising the Mississippi initiative, the GAO's Director of Strategic Issues, Stanley Czerwinski, told the House Homeland Security Committee that the front money requirement had "a choking effect." In the GAO view, where local infrastructure had been "torn apart" and local "finances decimated," there was in fact often an insufficient revenue flow to create the needed pool of up-front money. Czerwinski further observed that the lack of up-front money limited the pool of available contractors to those few who were well-heeled enough to wait months or years for payment. As a result, competition was dampened and costs were driven up as contractors exacted a premium in exchange for their willingness to wait for their money. In creating a state pool for the up-front money, the GAO official pointed out that Mississippi made it possible to avoid these costs. Nonetheless, if higher levels of the FEMA bureaucracy decided to deobligate or claw back a previously approved expenditure, the Mississippi county, municipality, or school board still faced repayment of the state loan out of its own limited local revenues.[36]

Despite the possibility of low-cost state loans, in April of 2007, Jackson County officials contemplated delaying their annual budgeting process because of the uncertainty of when they would be paid the $3.2 million reimbursement which FEMA owed the county at the end of 2006 and the additional $200,000 which was due them from MEMA. Delays involving misplaced paperwork and changing auditors were blamed for a two-year delay in payment to Lamar County for FEMA-qualified road repairs completed in 2007. In fact, as late as July of 2010, the city of D'Iberville faced the possibility of laying off city employees because the Mississippi Emergency Management Agency had delayed the release of $800,000 in federal funds owed to the city.[37]

An additional source of difficulty hovered around what one mayor called FEMA's "deadline culture." FEMA's practice of setting deadlines and threatening decreased or lost funding if the deadlines were not met interacted with the enormity of the destruction to force many Project Worksheets to be written in haste with the intention of revising and more fully investigating damages at a later date. However, when the project's realistic cost was better understood, these revised Project Worksheets faced a hard line of FEMA resistance to increased cost estimates.[38]

Still, on the Mississippi Gulf Coast there was at least one dramatic example of the unexpected rewards that were possible for those who approached the recovery with clear goals and a determination to stay doggedly engaged through various levels of appeal up the FEMA hierarchy. In one of the more impressive cases, Harrison County School Superintendent Henry Arledge told the crowd assembled for the dedication of a the new D'Iberville High School that "on five separate occasions FEMA ruled that we would not be allowed to build this high school." In fact, the Harrison County School District had suffered the destruction of the D'Iberville Middle School Campus and designed a plan that entailed moving the middle school faculty and students to the old high school campus, which had not flooded, and building a brand new facility for D'Iberville High School on high ground north of town. However, the school board's plan involved the added cost of high school versus middle school science labs and athletic facilities plus construction of a self-contained 150,000-gallon water system to serve structures built to withstand 200-mile-per-hour winds. In the board's vision of the future, the new school would double as a storm shelter. Additionally, on the west side of the county, the Harrison County School Board proposed to build a totally new high school to serve a post-Katrina population that was expected to migrate inland in large numbers. West Harrison High School would be built to the same standards as the new D'Iberville High and also serve as a reinforced public storm shelter.[39]

Persevering through five FEMA rejections of the $91 million proposal, the Harrison County school system wound up with two new high schools that more than replaced the lost middle school campus. However, the final go-ahead for the two new and improved campuses required the county to put up $18 million in local money, notwithstanding the fact that they were designed as community hurricane shelters. In the spring of 2009, almost four years after Katrina, the new D'Iberville High School became the first totally new replacement school building to open on the coast, and West Harrison High School followed in the fall of the same year.[40]

Beyond FEMA, state government also played a role in creating red-tape tangles for local government. In Mississippi, a new system of zealous state-level Katrina project auditing practices drew special attention in the press. An article appearing in the *Wall Street Journal* in 2007 focused on the "constipated spending sytem" which had produced a "deep stall" in 57 individual FEMA-financed recovery projects in Bay St. Louis. Chief City Administrator Buz Olsen and Recovery Director Les Fillingame showed the visiting reporter a four-inch-thick file on one of the simplest of those stalled projects—a $3.2 million proposal to clear Katrina-deposited sand, silt, and debris from the city's network of drainage ditches. Fillingame led the reporter through the steps in the months-long FEMA and MEMA approval process required before the project could be put out for bids. Once the work started, the state of Mississippi applied an audit regime that sent every load ticket for every truckload of muck through four layers of state examiners before payment could be made to the contractor. In addition, both the state and FEMA conducted on-the-spot surprise inspections to further validate the paperwork. As a result, it had taken a year of paperwork to complete a project that involved only one month of actual shoveling and hauling. Waiting in the wings, in Bay St. Louis alone there were 56 other Katrina-related reconstruction projects of far greater complexity than simple ditch digging.[41]

To explain the origins of the additional and time-consuming state-imposed audit program, the *Wall Street Journal* pointed to "the region's reputation for corruption."[42] Specifically, the article asserted that the additional state audits grew out of accusations from the Washington, D.C.–based

Corporate Crime Reporter to the effect that Mississippi and Louisiana led the nation in public corruption convictions per 100,000 citizens. The advocacy group's negative rating had produced a front-section story in the *Washington Times* and other major newspapers early in 2004, the year before Katrina.[43] The stories were well known in Washington. Indeed, General Russel Honoré, the former commander of Military Joint Task Force Katrina, recalled that in many of the federal meetings he had attended after the storm, there had been a tendency to toss around bitter accusations that southerners in general were especially prone to public corruption.[44] Furthermore, the *Wall Street Journal* contended that the Mississippi/Louisiana image of corruption lay behind the Bush administration's insistence on requiring that there be a 10 percent state and local match for Katrina-related FEMA public assistance projects, despite the fact that there was a history of waiving the matching requirement entirely for states involved in far less destructive disasters.[45]

A few days after the *Wall Street Journal* article appeared, the *New York Times*, in an editorial sympathetic to the plight of Mississippi, chided President Bush for his lack of generosity in the matter of continuing to require the local match in the face of Katrina's unprecedented infrastructure destruction. The New York–based editorialists pointed out that since 1985, the local match requirement had been waived entirely for 32 separate disasters with damages that, on a per-capita basis, were far less destructive for the states involved than Katrina had been for Mississippi and Louisiana. The paper pointed to New York's 9/11 terror attacks as an example. Thus, in the context of the history of such presidential waivers, what most Mississippians looked on as a magnanimous gesture on Bush's part may not have been magnanimous at all.[46] Still, either because they dared not bite the hand that fed them,[47] or because they were unaware that the president's hand bore less than they should have expected, Mississippians accepted the 10 percent local match requirement without complaint. Moreover, this potentially stifling requirement did not go away until much later in 2007, after Nancy Pelosi and the Democrats took control of Congress and mandated the waiver of the 10 percent Katrina local match requirement in amendments that President Bush allowed to pass into law in Title IV of the 2007 U.S. Troop Readiness, Veterans' Care, Katrina Recovery, and Iraq Accountability Act.[48]

When the *Wall Street Journal* confronted Mike Womack, the executive director of the Mississippi Emergency Management Agency, with the accusation that it had been doubts about Mississippi's integrity among national

Republican leaders in Congress and the White House that had prompted Governor Barbour to create extra state-level Katrina audits and red-tape burdens, Womack defended the Mississippi approach as a necessary evil. "The governor knows what the perception is outside the state of Mississippi," Womack said. He went on to add, "It's a perception that there is a huge amount of corruption in local government." Furthermore, the MEMA director declared, "There are lots of contractors that are trying to rip the government off." When asked if he thought the $100 million the state was investing in the rigorous state-level Katrina audits was preventing $100 million in fraud, Womack replied, "Unfortunately, I think that's the case."[49] In testimony before Congress, Womack credited "Governor Haley Barbour's guidance" for the creation of the state-level audits. Furthermore, Womack noted that the state's system had led to the hiring of "an engineering firm to make sure the scope of the work was properly determined and an accounting firm to confirm that finances" were properly documented. Womack believed that compared to systems used in "any other state," Mississippi was managing FEMA funds "at the highest level."[50] The state was allowed to use federal recovery dollars to pay for these huge auditing contracts. However, no such federal dollars were made available to the storm-ravaged local governments to add employees to cover the resulting paperwork overloads.[51]

For anyone who questioned the wisdom or need for spending tens of millions of dollars on the state-level audits, an element of poetic justice might have been seen to be at work when, in March of 2010, the FEMA Office of Inspector General brought forward allegations that the Mississippi Emergency Management Agency itself had misspent millions in its own audit contract—dollars that the state would have to repay. MEMA allegedly had paid a Jackson-based accounting firm prices ranging from $87 to $109 per hour "to scan and code" paperwork which added up to $7.7 million in what FEMA ruled were inappropriate uses of federal recovery funds. On this occasion, in defense of his agency, MEMA Director Mike Womack bitterly accused the FEMA IG's office of having "the same mind set as an IRS auditor. They are going to see how much money they can take back from state and local government," Womack said, and "I'm just opposed to that kind of mentality."[52]

Mississippi Lieutenant Governor Phil Bryant, who once held office as the state auditor, told the Joint Legislative Budget Committee that at the time of the disaster, federal authorities had predicted that in Mississippi "5 percent of Katrina dollars would be lost to fraud." However, for the record, in September of 2010, Lieutenant Governor Bryant noted that in

Mississippi there had in fact been less than a 1 percent rate of loss.[53] Despite the reality of lower-than-expected rates of fraud, worries about the image and perception of corruption meant that spools of state-level red tape were added to the mix of complex federal regulations and appeals processes to further slow the recovery of public infrastructure.

The most challenging local projects were those involving more than one local, state, or federal agency or authority. The Bay St. Louis city government believed that the recovery of the old downtown area required a $50 million reconstruction of Beach Drive, a roadway severely damaged in the Katrina storm surge. This project involved coordination between the state highway department, the federal highway commission, and FEMA. However, because it entailed the reconstruction of the seawall running parallel to the street, the project also involved the Army Corps of Engineers. Despite the completion of the appropriate FEMA assessments and Project Worksheets in the immediate aftermath of the storm, the Army Corps of Engineers did not put forward the request for a congressional appropriation until November of 2006, more than a year after the storm. Thus, Bay St. Louis Recovery Director Les Fillingame told a *Wall Street Journal* reporter in January of 2007, "The whole rebuilding of downtown Bay St. Louis is contingent on this seawall, and we don't even know if it'll be funded." Bay St. Louis Mayor Eddie Favre, whose own home was destroyed in the storm, had famously pledged that he would wear shorts every day—cold or hot, rain or shine—until the city was rebuilt. On the cold morning in January of 2007, when the reporter visited him, Favre conceded that "at this rate, it looks like I'll be buried in my shorts."[54]

Most of the trouble with the road and seawall project arose from the need to coordinate several federal agencies. However, in 2007, Donald Powell, FEMA's Gulf Coast federal coordinator, turned the tables on critics of the slowness of FEMA processes and asserted that inaction at the local level caused many, if not most, delays. Decisions involving multiple state and local agencies or jurisdictions, Powell observed, were "often difficult and contentious" because they could "affect the character of the communities being rebuilt."[55] In Mississippi two high visibility projects lent credence to Powell's contention. In the first instance, local disagreements over the size and design of the new Biloxi Bay Bridge threatened to delay the rebuilding of a vital transportation artery. In the second case, state and local difficulty in deciding on the future mission for the Katrina-ravaged University of Southern Mississippi Gulf Park Campus in Long Beach interacted with conflicts with the Mississippi Department of Archives and History and FEMA to delay the start of major recovery efforts for more than five years.

Katrina's winds and storm surge lifted the massive four-lane concrete plates off the pilings of both the Biloxi Bay Bridge and the Bay St. Louis Bridge, leaving them looking like a line of collapsed dominoes in the water. Assured of federal funding, the Mississippi Department of Transportation (MDOT) proposed to replace the destroyed four-lane drawbridge over Biloxi Bay with a massive six-lane high rise to accommodate projected future traffic counts. These grand ideas became points of contention on the local level. Biloxi Mayor A. J. Holloway wanted the six-lane design, and in his view the high rise feature was a desirable way to eliminate the traffic tie-ups that had occurred whenever shrimp trawlers entered or exited the bay using the draw spans of the old bridge. However, to Ocean Springs officials, MDOT's proposed massive concrete ribbon thrown high into the air seemed likely to detract from the panoramic views that had been a part of the ambiance of the coast for generations. Furthermore, on the Ocean Springs side, residents worried that a six-lane expressway-style structure would dump traffic into the heart of the town's tree-lined business district. Thus, Ocean Springs Mayor Connie Moran fought for a smaller, less intrusive design. The wrangling between Biloxi and Ocean Springs went on for months. Meanwhile, a 40-minute detour impeded the flow of tourist traffic between the shops and restaurants in Ocean Springs and Casino Row in Biloxi.[56]

With things at a seeming impasse, Hancock Bank President George Schloegel took the lead in convening a meeting between the two mayors, MDOT officials, and former Netscape CEO Jim Barksdale. Mayor Moran insisted that she would only agree to the more massive design if MDOT added a pedestrian walkway and improved landscaping designs with displays of local artwork to adorn the naked concrete so as to make the massive bridge a better fit with the traditional small-town atmosphere that her administration was dedicated to preserving on the Ocean Springs side of the structure. The pedestrian pathway was essential to this, as Moran saw it, but such a structure paralleling the planned six lanes would necessitate additional pilings and run the price up by millions of dollars. The added cost threatened to be a deal breaker. MDOT did not have the money. At this strategic moment, Jim Barksdale stepped in and said, "Stop this. I'll give you the $9 million." The logjam broke, and the project quickly got back on track. Before construction ended, MDOT found additional grant money that allowed the placement of walking paths alongside the new bridges that spanned both Biloxi Bay and the Bay of St. Louis, and Barksdale was let off the hook. Amidst much fanfare, both of the bridge projects were finished in 2008. As Barksdale saw it, "We could have spent months debating how many lanes the bridge was going to have, but we killed the snake and kept moving forward."[57] If local disputes had slowed the project, local initiative resolved the conflict in ways that led to valuable improvements.

In the case of the University of Southern Mississippi's Gulf Park Campus, there were no private pockets deep enough to produce such results and break a more complicated logjam. Two years after the two new bridges had opened, and five years after Katrina, the ragged remains of the stately old Spanish mission–style buildings on the south side of the Long Beach campus still stood in ruins, bearing silent witness to the difficulties of bringing the university administration, its board, FEMA, the Mississippi Department of Archives and History, the city of Long Beach, and the state legislature to firm and sustainable decisions as to the appropriate mission for the Gulf Park site. The future mission for this old campus hinged on whether funds could be found to build a new campus in a less vulnerable location to serve the instructional program needs of the 2,500 university students studying there at the time of Katrina. As home of the 500-year-old Friendship Oak, the Gulf Park Campus stood on a 20-foot bluff on the north side of U.S. Highway 90 overlooking the Gulf of Mexico and had for over 80 years been hailed as one of the scenic jewels of the Mississippi Gulf Coast. The city of Long Beach had framed its future community development plans around the continuing vibrance of the campus,[58] but Katrina had torn it asunder.

To the consternation of Long Beach officials, serious talk arose about permanently closing the University of Southern Mississippi's Gulf Park Campus. Within days of the storm, USM President Shelby Thames had himself initiated discussions about abandoning the Gulf Park site for a new location further inland. Going forward, Commissioner Tom Meredith of the Board of Trustees of State Institutions of Higher Learning (IHL) favored a plan to meet the higher education needs of the coast through a new university center that would contract for classes from several institutions on another site.[59] However, the university center concept was anathema to Dr. Thames, who was adamant that any new campus be clearly attached to USM. Long Beach officials viewed any proposal to abandon the Gulf Park Campus as a serious threat to the future of the town.[60] Consultants were hired to study the problem and advise the board. In June of 2006, ten months after the storm, the Board of Trustees of State Institutions of Higher Learning came to a compromise with the community calling for both the rehabilitation of the Gulf Park Campus and the construction of a major new campus with USM academic programs retaining their leading role. It was hoped that insurance and FEMA funds would be sufficient to rehabilitate the Gulf Park Campus, which was to be assigned a limited mission as a university fine arts center and conference facility.[61] The decision to restore Gulf Park meant that there would be no FEMA funds to help defray the estimated $100 million cost of a new campus. However, in 2007, the Hancock Bank and local businessman W. C. Fore stepped forward to donate 200 acres of land for the proposed new campus in the Cross Creek development just north of Long Beach. In quick order, Hancock Bank officers pledged to help round up private donors to supplement whatever state bonds might be available to get the new campus off the ground.[62]

From her position on the Legislative Budget Oversight Committee, and in concert with her colleagues from the coast, Representative Diane Peranich supported the Cross Creek project and managed to deliver a significant state bond issue for architectural work. Peranich had played a key role in obtaining bond money for the new buildings at the Gulf Park Campus itself from 1996 to 2004. However, while she took up legislative work for the Cross Creek project, she was always candid in her assessment of the difficulty of building a new university campus without major federal dollars. Though the Mississippi IHL Board had gone on record in favor of the Cross Creek campus, Peranich was skeptical that a majority of the board would commit to actually pursue $100 million in new state bonds for this project unless the killing weight of other major university construction projects were part of the proposal. "I would have to see stigmata," Peranich said, "before I could believe" that board members would actually back a bond bill that didn't have an equal share for each of the eight state universities. Moreover, if such a bond bill came to the floor of the Mississippi House and Senate, Peranich pointed out that under Mississippi law, it would take a super majority to pass it. Again, this would be politically very difficult unless there were clear benefits to all eight universities.[63]

Meanwhile, the university's proposed demolitions on the old campus brought the proposed fine arts facility and conference center project under the intense scrutiny of the Mississippi Department of Archives and History. The old washed-out structures at Gulf Park were, after all, the only recognizable historic landmarks left along Highway 90 between Gulfport and Pass Christian. The old administration building was at the center of the controversy. FEMA further muddied the waters with a ruling that, despite initial assessments to the contrary, the building had not sustained greater than 50 percent damage—the key threshold that determined whether FEMA would pay for a totally new building or merely for the rehabilitation of the old one on the site where it stood.[64]

At a critical moment in 2008, the major stock market crash that confirmed the onset of a deep recession totally disrupted the plan. In this environment, the proponents of the Cross Creek development could not identify any funding stream, public or private, that could accommodate a $100 million investment in a new university campus. The Gulf Coast business leadership cadre that had united so effectively in Coast 21 and the Gulf Coast Council of Governments to force improvements in USM's Gulf Coast programs and facilities in the 1990s was itself overwhelmed with an array of other disaster recovery problems from housing to insurance. When last-ditch efforts failed to get the new campus included as one of the Mississippi Development Authority's choices for funding in President Barack Obama's 2009 recession stimulus package, it became clear that the university would have to focus its whole efforts on the recovery of the Gulf Park Campus, and that this campus would remain as the main teaching site for USM degree programs on the coast. In 2008, as the recession slowed economic activity, Diane Peranich noted that Governor Barbour had committed himself to vetoing any new bond bills unless they were for job creation projects. In the best-case scenario, Peranich concluded that the Gulf Park Campus would need to serve the teaching mission of USM Gulf Coast for at least another ten to fifteen years.[65] Thus, the emergence of stark new economic realities forced USM and the Board of Trustees of State Institutions of Higher Learning to once again redefine the mission for which the Gulf Park Campus would be restored.

In 2009, as the fourth anniversary of Katrina came and went, the university was still bogged down in a historic preservation dispute with the Mississippi Department of Archives and History and a million-dollar battle with FEMA over Gulf Park renovation costs. That year, as part of the Obama administration's economic stimulus bill, Congress authorized the reference of lingering high-value disputes between local entities and FEMA to binding arbitration at the hands of neutral third-party expert panels drawn from the ranks of senior administrative law judges outside the FEMA bureaucracy.[66] The new arbitration process led to a satisfactory resolution of the longstanding USM claims, and the new avenue of appeal also produced additional funds for the Bay-Waveland school system, the

Moss Point school system, Pearl River Community College, and the Port of Gulfport. In August of 2010, FEMA reported that as a result of the arbitration process, six of nine disputed projects in Mississippi had received new awards totaling more than $24 million.[67]

The resolution of USM's dispute with FEMA in 2010 resulted in an additional $837,000 in federal funds for its Gulf Park recovery project. However, the historic preservation dispute still swirled over the university's plan to demolish the old administration building and use the FEMA monies designated for its repair to improve the renovation projects for three other heavily damaged buildings.[68] In the summer of 2010, more than five years after Katrina had ripped through the campus, the university and the Mississippi Department of Archives and History finally agreed to a compromise plan allowing the demolition of the building while providing for the reconstruction of remaining structures on the Gulf Park Campus with strict adherence to protocols of historic preservation. Competing local interests had combined with changing economic realities to dictate repeated redefinition of the mission of the old campus, while historic preservation authorities held the ultimate fate of any mission-driven plan for restoration of buildings in their hands. With these issues settled, the university hoped that recovery of the remaining storm-battered buildings on the Gulf Park Campus would be completed by the fall of 2012, on the seventh anniversary of Hurricane Katrina.[69] In FEMA's defense, Donald Powell had pointed to local issues as a source of delays in key recovery projects,[70] and at first blush the fate of the Gulf Park Campus would seem to offer support for his point. However, in the case of this high-visibility project on the scenic front door of the Mississippi Gulf Coast, it had taken five years to complete the appeal of an unfair funding decision through the various levels of the FEMA bureaucracy. Thus, among storm-damaged city halls, fire and police stations, courthouses, and public school buildings, the stately old buildings of the Gulf Park Campus seemed likely to earn the distinction of being the last publicly owned structures to be recovered from the massive wave of destruction that Hurricane Katrina swept over the Mississippi Gulf Coast on August 29, 2005.

For local officials and their employees who stayed in the ring and went the distance with FEMA, the new federal arbitration process represented the sounding of the last bell at the end of many long rounds in the red-tape battle for recovery. In 2009 and 2010, after long delays, dirt was beginning to be turned up for a host of public works projects that symbolized hope for the long-term return to normalcy. Moreover, for cities, school boards, and hospitals across the region that had borrowed FEMA money to pay their employees in the aftermath of Katrina, the Obama administration announced a loan-forgiveness program. Towns such as Waveland, Bay St. Louis, and Pass Christian, whose tax yields had been insufficient to cover normal operations in the three years following the disaster, could breathe an additional sigh of relief as they looked forward to the complete cancellation of these debts.[71]

On a personal level, the costs of the struggle for recovery had been high. Five years after the storm, local officials continued to see signs of burnout and stress among their employees. Bay St. Louis Public Works Director Buddy Zimmerman reported that of the 39 employees in his department when Katrina struck, only 15 remained with the city in 2010.[72] In Mississippi, the employees of three counties and their 11 municipalities had carried an unbelievable burden for their fellow citizens, and so had local elected officials. Just a few days after Congressman Taylor's statement before Congress detailing the problems of the Bay-Waveland District, Superintendent Kim Stasny told an interviewer that she had gone through many moments of "being so overwhelmed" that she did not know how she could face another day in a process that seemed "to have no end."[73] In March of 2009, after serving ten years as superintendent of the Bay-Waveland district, Kim Stasny announced her resignation. "This recovery has worn me down," she explained. "I have not been focused on academic leadership, and I want to get back to that."[74] Despite the fact that construction was finally getting under way for the two new elementary schools for which she had fought long and hard, the strain of years of protracted engagement in bureaucratic battles with FEMA had taken its toll.

Across town at Bay St. Louis City Hall, citing burnout with the recovery process, the longtime mayor Eddie Favre became one of the six sitting Mississippi Gulf Coast mayors who decided not to seek reelection in 2009. Stress-related health problems had already forced Mayor Billy McDonald of Pass Christian to resign in the middle of his term. The casualties included four of the five newcomers who had been voted into Gulf Coast mayoral offices in the summer before Katrina struck. Instead of pursuing the agendas on which they were elected, within six weeks Katrina had taken them to the school of hard knocks with the seemingly endless tasks of disaster response, recovery, and rebuilding. Thus, Brent Warr of Gulfport, Xavier Bishop of Moss Point, Pete Pope of Gautier, and Mathew Avara of Pascagoula joined Mayor Favre in choosing not to seek reelection. Mayor Bishop likely spoke for the group when he told a reporter he was fatigued. "The demands have been great since the hurricane," he said. "There's just been constant motion since I took office." Bishop intended to "take time off" to decide where his career would take him once the burden of office was lifted from his shoulders.[75]

Nonetheless, however tedious the process had been, it is certain that recovery from a disaster of Katrina's magnitude would have been impossible for states like Mississippi or Louisiana without the deep pockets of the federal government. Mississippi communities simply could not have rebuilt without the massive infusions of billions of federal dollars that came to them through FEMA public assistance grants for schools, public buildings, and sewer and water systems or through the Community Development Block Grants for housing. Local initiative in the form of individual heroism, true grit, and perseverance was certainly there in abundance. However, it was the generosity of the American people working through these federal assistance programs which gave the disaster-ravaged communities of the Mississippi Gulf Coast the essential financial underpinning which enabled them to recover their public services and make themselves liveable again.

Chapter Ten

Faith, Hope, and Jobs

Progress and Frustration for the Business Recovery

Private capital, entrepreneurs, small business people are going to have more to do with how the coast comes back and how Southeast Mississippi comes back than all the governments in the world.

—GOVERNOR HALEY BARBOUR

September 12, 2005[1]

In 30 years, when I'm dead and gone, people will look at the south coast and look at what it has become. If it has become just another version of what it had been, we will have failed.

—GOVERNOR HALEY BARBOUR

Address to the State Legislature

September 27, 2005[2]

We thought Katrina was the storm of the century, but we didn't know then we'd also have to face the deluge of insurance struggles and now the economy. And who could have dreamed nearly four years after the storm we'd have so far to go?

—MARY PEREZ

Sun Herald Business Reporter

June 12, 2009[3]

In the horrible topsy-turvy of the disaster aftermath, retired Air Force General Clark Griffith received a strange phone call from an employee of BancorpSouth, a call which vividly demonstrated the fragility of so many coast business enterprises after Hurricane Katrina. In 1998, Clark Griffith, a former Keesler Air Force Base commander, had settled in Biloxi and taken up consulting work for several international businesses. Griffith's service on the boards of three local nonprofit organizations had led to his election as president of the Biloxi Bay Chamber of Commerce and to his being named one of the coast's top ten community leaders. In the months before Katrina struck, the retired general had given long hours of voluntary service to the state of Mississippi in its efforts to stave off threats that the Defense Base Realignment and Closure Commission would reduce Keesler Air Force Medical Center from a major 2,200-person teaching hospital to the status of a mere outpatient clinic. He had flown to Washington, D.C., during the last week of August for the final push that saved the base hospital. He was keeping an eye on the developing storm in the gulf on the morning of Saturday, August 27, 2005, when the commission finally announced that Keesler Medical Center would not be downgraded or closed. Thus, Griffith caught an evening flight back home to Biloxi, where he and his wife spent the next day boarding up their house in preparation for Hurricane Katrina. Now, in the storm's aftermath, as he made temporary repairs to his house, the strange call from BancorpSouth requested a different type of service.

Since Griffith was well known in the business community, in normal times a call from a bank officer might not have been unusual. However, it was not the call itself, but rather the caller's unique request that amazed the retired general. "We need to get $2.8 million out of the Palace Casino and put it into our branch at Keesler," the caller said. "Can you help get us on the base?"[4] Like everything else in East Biloxi, Katrina had torn asunder both Keesler Air Force Base and the Palace Casino complex.[5] Many airmen and their families from Keesler Field had been evacuated ahead of the storm. Still, flooding had destroyed 60 percent of the base housing[6] and left 4,000 airmen and their families in military shelters. As a result, Keesler Air Force Base was on lock-down under martial law. At BancorpSouth's request, Griffith contacted General William Lord, the base commander, who quickly agreed to help secure the casino's hoard of cash. Driving a big SUV and "armed to the hilt, . . . two of the roughest looking deputies [he] had ever seen" picked Griffith up at his house and drove him to the casino, where they loaded the money. With the money on board, this odd crew then made their way through the East Biloxi debris fields to the air base. At the gate, the Keesler commander met Griffith and his party with a detachment of military police, who then escorted the unsecured $2.8 million to a proper vault on the base.[7] The necessity of such cobbled-together arrangements for millions of dollars in unsecured cash spoke volumes about the vulnerable condition of the region's economic backbone in the wake of Katrina.

In the midst of this uncertainty, General Clark Griffith emerged as key leader in the long-term recovery effort as a member of the Governor's Recovery Commission and as chairman of the Steering Committee for the city of Biloxi's post-Katrina Reviving the Renaissance planning effort. A fighter pilot by training with 280 combat missions in Vietnam, Clark Griffith had risen through the officer corps to become commander of the U.S. Second Air Force. Air combat had shaped in him enduring habits of leadership and problem solving. When invited to speak, he often asked audiences young and old, whether civilian or military, a simple question: "What do you do if you've got a MiG on your tail, and he's just about to shoot at you?" People ventured all sorts of answers, but Clark Griffith's response was always the same: "What you have to do is turn into the threat as hard as you can turn. . . . Face it, and fix it."[8] Griffith applied the metaphor to every type of challenge. In speaking engagements to young and old alike he urged that only when faced squarely could any problem be solved. He exuded confidence that if the enormous difficulties that appeared in the wake of Katrina were faced head-on, these too would yield to the kind of teamwork that kept high performance fighter planes and their pilots fit enough to make those high-*g* 180-degree turns to face down an enemy threat.[9] Indeed, in the enormous destruction left by Katrina, tens of thousands of people in south Mississippi and tens of thousands of volunteers from across the nation almost instinctively turned to face the challenge as they reached out to neighbors in need and started the hard work of rebuilding homes, businesses, and community institutions.

Before electric power had been restored, the flickering image of George Schloegel, the president of Hancock Bank, had radiated from battery-powered televisions with bold assurances that despite the unprecedented destruction, the Mississippi Gulf Coast would "come back bigger and better" than ever before.[10] Governor Haley Barbour's many assertions of his own utter confidence "that we'll come back," both mirrored and encouraged the early hopefulness he saw in the people he served. "In six months," the governor predicted, "we will see that single great surge," and "in two or three years the coast will be better than we've ever known it." Within two weeks of the greatest natural disaster in American history, with overwhelming ruin covering the region, Barbour told a reporter that "30 years from now people will look back and say, 'That terrible, dreadful storm that was so bad in so many ways actually was an opportunity for us to make Mississippi what it could have been but had never been before.'"[11]

At the grassroots level, for many who had lost everything, the spirit of resolve often swelled to a level of defiant determination to rise from the ruin as if will power and faith alone could move the mountains of wreckage before them. A few days after the storm, Jackie Robinson, a Pascagoula shipbuilder drafted to operate a front loader on cleanup duty at Ingalls Shipbuilding, told an Associated Press reporter, "This ain't fun, but you watch me. I'll get it done."[12] Those who visited the Mississippi Gulf Coast following the storm almost invariably expressed amazement at the apparent resilience of ordinary Mississippi disaster victims as they returned to work. One wire service reporter commented, "These people ain't right." It "would be understandable," he said, if people felt sorry for themselves after losing all they had, and "yet there is very little 'woe is me' in the outlook of . . . survivors along Mississippi's Gulf Coast." Rather, he said, "One finds a what-do-we-need-to-do-now?-and-let's-get-it-done attitude."[13] The pervasiveness of such reports gave credence to Governor Barbour's oft-repeated mantra that Mississippians would "hitch up [their] britches and . . . get this done."[14] The Mississippi legislature took note of the fortitude, resilience, and neighborly concern that ordinary people had shown in the wake of the disaster when, early in its 2007 session, the lawmakers passed a bill designating August 29 of each year as a "Katrina Day of Remembrance" to honor victims of the storm and "as a statewide expression of faith and hope."[15] In 2007, few in the Bible Belt would have argued with this echoed refrain from the writings of St. Paul, and few would have challenged the proposition that faith and hope had been an essential element in the progress that had been made after the horrible cyclone.

An objective person surveying the damage the day after the storm might have reasonably concluded that some or all of the coast's most critical enterprises might never come back into production. Businesses large and small seemed to hang by slim and fraying tethers. From Keesler Air Force Base to the coast casinos, from Northrop Grumman's Ingalls Shipbuilding and the Chevron Oil Refinery in Pascagoula to the Port of Gulfport, Katrina left every major employer and almost every mom-and-pop motel, restaurant, or small business on the Mississippi Gulf Coast with serious damage—much of it rising to the level of catastrophic loss. The massive destruction of wharfs and processing plants knocked out 4,300 jobs in the seafood industry. Storm surge had swept the wreckage of thousands of buildings into the waters of the Mississippi Sound, where it created an all-but-impossible minefield of navigation and trawling hazards for the coast's 500 shrimp boats.[16] Beyond the urban centers, the Mississippi Forestry Commission estimated that almost half of the longleaf pine trees in the timber-rich inland areas of south Mississippi lay on the ground.[17] Overnight, one out of every four jobs had disappeared from Hancock and Harrison counties, and by the end of the year unemployment rates had soared past 20 percent.[18] Ten days after the storm, with tens of thousands of jobs obliterated, the Stennis Institute of Government at Mississippi State University estimated that Katrina had taken away fully one-quarter of the state revenue stream.[19] An economic catastrophe of the first magnitude had struck the Mississippi coast.

By the end of the first week after the storm, Governor Barbour took the first step to put into action the optimism that he claimed. In the midst of destruction, he conducted his first meetings with coast business and political leaders to begin engaging them in talks about the future and the kind of long-term recovery the region needed and deserved. In this, Barbour was a step ahead of the governors of neighboring states in the Katrina impact area.[20] It was clear that federal dollars would eventually repair and rebuild destroyed public buildings and infrastructure, but the process would be slow. Thus, early on, Governor Barbour expressed his conviction that "private capital, entrepreneurs, small business people" were "going to have more to do with how the coast comes back and how Southeast Mississippi comes back than all the governments in the world."[21] The common faith held that the business community and the magic of the marketplace would be as impressive in their creativity as Katrina had been in her reign of destruction. Still, the massive damage to the waterfront hotels and their floating casinos raised troubling questions about the viability of the tourism industry. Everywhere it was assumed that Katrina had created "a clean slate," but for the tourism corner of the slate to be re-created, sensible revisions in the state's gaming laws would be required. If the casinos could be granted the right to move off of the storm-vulnerable barges and reconstitute on shore, it was widely assumed that new private investment would flood the area and grand new casinos would lead the way in a great recovery and renaissance on the Mississippi Gulf Coast. Given the "can do" spirit and almost defiant hopefulness that seemed to fill so many souls from the highest power brokers to the lowliest laborers, at least for a while, it seemed that truly all things were possible.

Despite the dominance of the casino issue in the headlines, the truth was that military spending on the Mississippi Gulf Coast created more jobs, and in this sector, too, there was also cause for concern. The fact that the Defense Base Closure and Realignment Commission had finished its work only hours before Katrina struck left many influential coast leaders concerned that issues related to Keesler might be reopened. A thousand base housing units had been destroyed. Early assessments showed that it would take at least $915 million to recover lost housing and repair damage to training facilities. With such an expensive price tag, it was feared that raw politics might incline the commission to "pick on a cripple." The initial anguish over the fate of Keesler Air Force Base came to an end three weeks after the storm when Air Force Secretary Pete Geren visited the base and pledged that the Department of Defense would spend more than $1 billion to rebuild and restore the base—including Keesler Medical Center—to its full pre-Katrina mission.[22] This action secured the future of 11,223 on-base military and civilian jobs and another 3,500 local and contract jobs that were dependent on the base. Beyond Keesler, the federal commitment to retain another 4,500 positions at the U.S. Navy Seabee Base in Gulfport added up to a total defense employment cornerstone of over 19,200 jobs in Harrison County with a combined estimated impact of nearly $1.7 billion in the local economy.[23]

In the larger scheme of things the military bases could access federal funds for restoration, but, having survived the recent round of cuts, they were unlikely to be bringing in any large number of additional jobs. Similarly, the shipyards and oil refinery in Jackson County could be expected to restore operations to pre-Katrina levels, but no dramatic growth was on the horizon for these enterprises. The casinos were the one sector where there was both real anguish about the future and a serious hope for much "bigger and better" post-Katrina development.

The coast's twelve operating casinos provided the second largest source of jobs in the region. These highly regulated waterfront enterprises were concentrated in Hancock and Harrison counties, where in calendar year 2004 they took in almost $1.3 billion, produced approximately $47.3 million in local taxes, and paid $100 million to the state.[24] State regulation made gaming legal only when conducted on barges moored beside hotels. Just before Katrina struck, up to 60,000 people per day visited coast casinos. In Harrison and Hancock counties, the casinos and their associated hotels and golf courses employed 16,490 people and accounted for more than half of the two-county total of 29,290 hospitality and leisure jobs. Moreover, the day Katrina struck, the new Hard Rock Casino in Biloxi was poised to add a thirteenth casino and another 1,000 positions to this total. In one fell swoop, Katrina wiped out 98 percent of the casino jobs on the Mississippi Gulf Coast. On Highway 90 in Biloxi, the beached wreckage of the 134,000-square-foot Grand Casino and the ragged hulks of all the other slot machine palaces came to symbolize the region's economic devastation. The destruction of the casinos along with hundreds of beachside motels and cafes meant that by January of 2006, two out of every three hospitality and restaurant jobs had disappeared from Hancock and Harrison counties.[25]

Yet, within 48 hours of the storm, the *New York Times* published an article reporting that corporate casino sources at Harrah's, Pinnicale, and Isle of Capri were already thinking about building "bigger and better" gambling complexes on the Mississippi coast. However, after years of chafing under state laws that required casinos to float, it was clear that they would now be "pressing the state to let them rebuild on land." At the same time, economist Steve Cochrane at Economy.com pointed out the "perverse positive aspect to natural disasters." Before the casinos could reopen, Cochrane was sure that the region would be "feeling flush" with insurance checks and cash flow from the inevitable building boom that would follow.[26] In remarks to a Las Vegas paper, Deutsche Bank analyst Marc Falcone made plain the real issue for Mississippi gaming proponents when he stated that he did not "know how they will get these companies to invest millions into these projects unless they are allowed to build them on land." However, Falcone held out hope that more expansive Las Vegas–style casinos would be built in Mississippi if the law did change.[27]

On the coast the following day, the *Sun Herald* carried an article quoting local banker Chevis Swetman's conclusion that on the Mississippi Gulf Coast, barges anchored by concrete pilings would no longer "stand the test." In Swetman's view it was plain that the time had come for the Mississippi legislature to permit land-based casino operations on the coast. Before the end of the week in which Katrina struck, the local paper editorially called for an immediate special session of the state legislature "to consider any measures that would make casinos a more secure investment," including legal permission to rebuild them on land.[28]

However, in Mississippi's Bible-Belt politics, land-based casinos would be easier to talk about than to realize. The casino industry had always had a tense relationship with upstate legislators whose constituents viewed gambling as sin rather than recreation. In their hands the decision would rest. However, Harrah's spokesman Lance Ewing pointedly stated that his corporation would withhold any decision about rebuilding its Grand Casino Biloxi and Gulfport properties, with combined payrolls of 4,300 persons, until the legislature determined whether they would be forced to remain on barges to stay in business. House Gaming Chairman Bobby Moak from rural southwest Mississippi expressed concern that the loss of the casinos "could paralyze the state." Beverly Martin of the Mississippi Casino Operators told the local press that officials from "both large and small establishments" had told her they "will not rebuild without the change." On the other hand, Harrah's CEO Gary Loveman pledged to "build something spectacular" if land-based casinos were legalized. After two weeks of mulling things over, Moak, who was initially noncommittal, voiced reluctant support for legislation to "allow the casinos to crawl out of the water." Most legislative leaders conceded that things were serious enough for at least a careful reconsideration of the issue. Nonetheless, House Speaker Billy McCoy, a devout Baptist from rural northeast Mississippi; Lieutenant Governor Amy Tuck, the presiding officer in the state senate; and Governor Barbour all refrained from making any commitments on the still taboo idea of land-based gaming.[29]

On Monday, September 19, Governor Barbour issued a call for a special session of the legislature to deal with Katrina-related issues. Under the pretext that he was awaiting recommendations from the state gaming commission and legislative leaders, Barbour made no specific proposals related to the casinos. Still, he speculated that the legislative body would likely deal with the future of gaming.[30] In fact, during the previous week, Mississippi Gaming Commission chairman Jerry St. Pé and executive director Larry Gregory had flown to Las Vegas for talks with top gaming-industry officials who had made clear their desire to move the coastal establishments onshore. The day the governor issued his call for the special session, St. Pé told *USA Today* that with the prospect of onshore arrangements in mind, casino executives had made commitments to stay in Mississippi and "in the future have an even larger presence on the Mississippi Gulf Coast."[31] The stick and the carrot were on the table for all to see.

For weeks, hints that a land-based proposal would be brought forward had generated protests from religious groups. The Christian Action Committee of the Mississippi Baptist Convention announced its opposition "to all measures that would benefit the gaming industry" and maintained that if land-based casinos were allowed on the coast, "attempts to move inward to other locations" were sure to follow. In the minds of many religious leaders and upstate politicians, if given an inch, the gaming industry would take a mile. Therefore, any vote that benefitted the casinos was a vote to expand gaming. As Senator Alan Nunnelee of Tupelo put it, if allowing the casinos to go ashore would lower their insurance rates and make them more profitable, "Why should I vote to increase their profit margins with the stroke of a pen?" The Baptists launched a church-based telephone campaign in opposition to measures which they believed would "expand gambling in the state."[32]

Under the state constitution, the governor controlled the agenda of legislative special sessions. When it became clear that Barbour would allow the casino issue to be considered, some in the religious right expressed a bitter sense of betrayal. Methodist minister Donald Wildmon of the Tupelo-based American Family Association protested that as a candidate for governor, Haley Barbour had pledged not to expand gaming. According to Wildmon, Barbour's constituency was "the money people and the moral people, but he's chosen to . . . side with the money people." Thus, Wildmon promised a fight. "They may have the money," the preacher said, "but we have the people, we have the votes, and he [Barbour] is going to pay."[33] Thus, the stage was set for a tough statewide political fight over the future of gaming on the Mississippi Gulf Coast.

When he opened the special legislative session on Tuesday, September 27, Governor Barbour finally laid all of his cards on the table. In a speech in which he was twice moved to tears, the governor called on lawmakers to help "lead a renaissance for Mississippi." Barbour held that the lawmakers had the opportunity before them to help create on the coast a true world-class destination resort rather than simply settling for bringing back what had been there before Katrina. This vision, the governor said, required safer casino locations, and he for the first time proposed publically that the casinos be allowed to move inland up to 1,500 feet from the water. "In 30 years when I am dead and gone," Barbour conjectured, "people will look back at the south coast and look at what it has become. If it has become just another version of what it had been," the governor declared, "we will have failed." In his mind land-based casinos and the enlarged entertainment complexes they promised had become a key element in bringing the coast back "bigger and better" than ever before.[34]

The heat from religious groups was such that the state Senate declined to introduce a gaming bill of its own, preferring to await a verdict from the lower chamber before asking members to stick out their necks. In the House of Representatives Speaker Billy McCoy, who personally opposed gaming on moral grounds, agreed to at least allow a bill to move forward for consideration in his chamber. In the lower house an onshore casino proposal cleared committee and went to the floor for debate. All week, coast lawmakers and business leaders "lobbied, pleaded, cajoled, called in favors, and at times wept tears of frustration" in their efforts to persuade legislators to allow the coast's destroyed gaming halls to move onto land. Many upstate lawmakers were being asked to cast votes against the personal recommendations of their own pastors. In the climactic Friday evening session, the land-based casino bill allowing coast gaming establishments to move their operations up to 800 feet inland passed the 122-member Mississippi House of Representatives by a vote of 60 to 53. The closeness of the margin of victory indicated that some lawmakers had been persuaded to "take a walk" or abstain. Across the capitol in the Senate, the bill was expected to pass, but in the Senate, an amendment threatened to delay action or force a conference committee and a second vote in both the House and the Senate. Proponents of the bill feared that the longer it was rehashed, the greater its chances of being killed altogether in multiple rounds of voting. The following Monday, these worries were laid to rest when the 53-member Senate stripped out the troublesome amendment and passed the House version by a vote of 29 to 21. A few days later Governor Barbour signed the bill into law.[35]

In affixing his signature Barbour characterized the onshore gaming bill as "taking the first few steps" toward "rebuilding South Mississippi and the Gulf Coast bigger and better than ever." While he noted that safer casinos would secure thousands of existing jobs, there was a clear hope that much better prospects were in the offing. The previous restriction of gaming to floating barges had created practical limits to the size of the enterprises. Press reports of the signing ceremony fed hopes that, with permission to go onshore, coast gambling operators would build mega-resorts with enough gaming floor space and other amenities to compete with the casino giants in Las Vegas and Atlantic City. Larry Gregory of the Mississippi Gaming Commission asserted that, with the new legislation, Mississippi could rival Atlantic City in total gaming revenues. There were a few skeptics such as gaming analyst John Mulkey of Wachovia Securities, who pointed out that Atlantic City had generated $4.8 billion in casino business in the previous year compared with $1.2 billion for the Mississippi coast and $1.6 billion for Mississippi's river counties. To catch Atlantic City, the Mississippi coast would have to recover and then practically quadruple its best pre-Katrina performance—something Mulkey believed the regional population base could not deliver.[36] However, in the heart-wrenching struggle to find a silver lining in the Katrina tragedy, skeptical voices got little attention in Mississippi. The mayor of Biloxi soon predicted that in three to five years, his city alone would have 15 to 20 casinos in operation, in comparison to the nine operating there before Katrina.[37] It would be more than three years before the realities of the Great Recession poured cold water on the exuberant hopes that filled the air when the legislative special session adjourned.

Weeks earlier, on the Sunday following the storm, Governor Barbour had met for two hours with a number of coast mayors and other community leaders and "literally on the back of an envelope" sketched out what became the Governor's Commission on Recovery, Rebuilding and Renewal. With further advice from Governor Jeb Bush of Florida, less than 10 days after the storm Barbour began naming commissioners. In shaping this 35-member body the governor appointed blacks and whites, men and women, Democrats and Republicans. Former Netscape CEO Jim Barksdale accepted the chairmanship. In the 2003 governor's race, Barksdale had been one of former Democratic Governor Ronnie Musgrove's strongest financial backers. However, in the Katrina crisis Barksdale not only accepted appointment to the commission, but also personally donated $1 million to help cover the commission's expenses. With a matching grant from the Knight Foundation the Commission got off the ground in grand style. Vice presidents of the commission included Derrick Johnson, the Mississippi NAACP president, as well as Ricky Mathews of the *Sun Herald*, Anthony Topazi of Mississippi Power, Joe Sanderson of Sanderson Farms, and retired shipyard president-turned-gaming commissioner Jerry St. Pé. Former Democratic governor William Winter served as legal counsel. The 35-member group was charged with sketching the way forward for the region, and Barbour asked the commission to have a report on his desk by December 31.[38]

Within days of the passage of the casino legislation, the commission met in a storm-damaged hotel in Biloxi to undertake an intensive six-day brainstorming process which brought together 200 city and county leaders in sessions with 150 designers and community-planning experts from across the nation.[39] Internationally renowned architect Andres Duany of Miami led this first intensive six-day meeting. Using input from local officials, teams of experts working in community-based charrettes or design groups produced architectural renderings of idealized redevelopment concepts tailored to the unique geographic and historical features of each of the 11 Mississippi Gulf Coast municipalities.[40] Over the weeks that followed, the governor's commission and its offspring, the Mississippi Renewal Forum, used citizen feedback gathered in dozens of town meetings to refine the proposals.[41]

As the intensive six-day effort unfolded, Gavin Smith, a FEMA long-term recovery consultant who went to work for the commission, sensed that in their forward-looking focus, the sessions became "very therapeutic" for local officials still grappling with monumental public works, debris, and housing problems.[42] In fact, a kind of shock therapy was intended.

According to Andres Duany, the governor's challenge to "bring it back better" arose from a sense that if the communities were "ever going to be spiritually whole," they could not be continually "pining about their past," and saying that "it was better before Katrina." The only way to get past it was to come back better than before.[43] To this end the governor's commission produced visionary cityscape designs, augmented by a wealth of 238 specific policy recommendations for everything from new building codes and zoning laws to such mundane issues as sewerage, land use, ecosystems, housing, education, transportation, and small business. All were aimed at mitigating potential damage from future storms and rebuilding the three-county public infrastructure to accommodate long-range development that would be fitted to the designs that emerged from the planning process. In this unprecedented postdisaster undertaking, 500 volunteers serving on 18 committees took Mississippi to the front of the line in recovery planning.[44]

At the end of the intensive charrette process, veteran political reporter Geoff Pender remarked that "beatific smiles" had replaced "Katrina grimaces" on the faces of leaders he had observed for years as if "they had seen the Big Rock Candy Mountains." D'Iberville Mayor Rusty Quave thought the planning process had been "one of the greatest things to ever happen in the history of the Gulf Coast."[45] Local resident Joe Floyd told another reporter that the process had "instilled hope in the hopeless." The designers "drew lots of pretty pictures," Floyd said, "but those pictures had an impact. A lot of local people . . . have now drunk the Kool-Aid."[46] Given the challenge expected from new FEMA elevation requirements for flood insurance, the question of whether these exciting and forward-looking designs would be acted upon remained to be answered.[47]

By the time the commission's report was released in January of 2006, it was manufacturing that was leading the recovery. Manufacturing employment in the region had risen to 93 percent of its pre-Katrina level. Three out of every four coast manufacturing jobs were located in Jackson County, where various industries employed over 16,000 people.[48] Twelve thousand of those jobs were centered at Pascagoula at Northrop Grumman's Ingalls Shipbuilding, making it the largest single private employer in the state. Across town the Chevron oil refinery employed another 1,500 in the city.[49] In the offshore oil business the 2005 hurricanes destroyed 115 of the 4,000 Gulf of Mexico production platforms. Onshore at Pascagoula, the hurricane's giant tidal surge breached the levee surrounding the Chevron refinery, sending ruinous salt water to foul thousands of switches, gauges, and valves. It took 40 days to get the refinery back into production.[50]

At Northrop Grumman's big Pascagoula shipyard, Katrina had pushed 8 to 12 feet of water across the 800-acre production site and destroyed electrical networks, various components of the manufacturing infrastructure, and construction equipment valued at close to $1 billion.[51] Doubts about the future of the facility were removed when the company announced the resumption of ship production work on September 12 and guaranteed all employees two weeks' back pay.[52] However, as a result of lost machinery and lingering Katrina-related labor shortages, production deadlines for the 13 Navy ships had to be adjusted. Still, by January of 2006 the yard delivered two new ships to the Navy and was reportedly back near pre-Katrina levels of employment. More importantly, from the standpoint of recovery, the shipyard was actively searching for another 375 workers to add to the force.[53] For the region as a whole, it was taken as a good sign that there were more jobs available at Ingalls and other Jackson County manufacturing concerns than there were workers available to fill them.

In a June 2006 report prepared for Capital One, noted LSU economist Loren C. Scott referenced the rapid return of Pascagoula's shipyard employment to pre-Katrina levels as a sign of a more "aggressive recovery pattern," than was being seen in Harrison and Hancock counties or New Orleans.[54] The point was driven home in 2007 and 2008 when Chevron announced expansions totaling $700 million to its Pascagoula refinery which, when finished, would make it the fifth largest refinery in the U.S.[55] From early 2006 onward, the only limits on industrial employment growth in Jackson County seemed to be set by housing shortages and wage competition from the booming post-Katrina construction business. The fate of the casinos had stolen the headlines and come to symbolize much of the hope for the economic future, but industrial expansion was proving to be the most reliable business mainstay.

On the Mississippi Gulf Coast, Katrina was often called an equal opportunity destroyer in that she had visited her afflictions on rich and poor alike. However, in postdisaster recovery a different principle applied. With a few exceptions, large manufacturers with vast corporate resources at their disposal recovered faster than small businesses.[56] Three days after the storm, Biloxi banker Chevis Swetman predicted as much. Swetman told a reporter that rebuilding the coast economy would not be as simple as getting the casinos back in business. Big gaming companies could assemble the resources to rise from the wreckage, but the mom-and-pop hotels, restaurants, and grocery stores that made up a large part of the tourism infrastructure would be out of business. In Swetman's view, this was "the real negative."[57]

Small business owners, whether confronting the physical destruction of their buildings or the disappearance of their customer base, faced an immediate decision as to whether to collect any insurance, sell out and leave, or to somehow try to get back into business. For 34 out of the 36 hardest-hit Mississippi car dealerships, the answer was comparatively easy. The tens of thousands of cars destroyed in the storm had to be replaced.[58] According to Gulfport auto dealer Bert Allen, a quarter of his 60-person workforce left because of housing problems or higher pay in construction work. Thus, his biggest challenge was finding and keeping labor.[59] Others faced even harder realities. For dairyman Dwayne Peterson of Poplarville, the cold fact that had to be faced was that even one missed milking for his 76 Holstein cows could irreparably damage engorged milk sacks and force him to send the high-value milk producers to slaughter. With the electrical grid down and fuel for emergency generators nowhere to be found, Peterson and many other farmers were forced to scramble to find buyers outside the region and quick-sell prized herds for half their value.[60] On the waterfront, Mississippi shrimpers and oystermen faced destroyed docks and ice plants and damaged boats. Between August of 2005 and August of 2007, two-thirds of Mississippi's licensed commercial fishing trawlers disappeared from coastal waters.[61]

One-third of Mississippi's shrimping licenses were held by Vietnamese immigrants, most of whom lived in the East Biloxi Vietnamese community. Here, family-centered small-business entrepreneurship was legendary. Outside the fishing community Vietnamese proprietors owned nineteen motels and an impressive sprinkling of small shops. The destruction in East Biloxi made it difficult to know whether a business could sustain itself there.[62] When Sue Nguyen-Brown returned to East Biloxi she found her house destroyed, but the building on Oak Street where she and her family operated Le Bakery Café remained intact. Seven feet of water had penetrated the bakery and destroyed all of the equipment. For Nguyen-Brown, family and community became key considerations in the decision to try to rebuild the business. It was clear to the whole family that they loved baking, and they loved their interactions with the walk-in customers that had been a pre-Katrina mainstay. They also loved the immigrant traditions in East Biloxi where French, Slavic, Anglos, African Americans, and Vietnamese interacted daily, and they were confident that despite the wreckage that surrounded them, Biloxi would somehow revive itself. Thus, the family set out to gut the building, clean up, and get back in business. Late in 2005, when the nearby Palace Casino reopened, the family's gamble on a future in Biloxi was rewarded by a steady stream of buyers for baked goods and po-boys, and Le Bakery quickly gained notoriety as one of the recovery's triumphs of the spirit.[63]

Despite these successes, there were hundreds of pre-Katrina small businesses that never reopened. CPA Chuck Benvenutti of Bay St. Louis was a member of the governor's commission and one of the small-business success stories. As Benvenutti saw it, small business people "have got to be optimists" to have any chance of success. Chuck Benvenutti was an optimist. In looking over the scenes of massive destruction, Benvenutti asserted that even on that first day, he "never questioned whether he would be back." He just knew that he was going to have more clients than ever. Like so many others, he had returned to town the day after the storm to find that both his home and his office had flooded and stood in horrible disarray. Moreover, four of the eight people working for Benvenutti's small accounting firm had lost their homes, and two of his CPAs soon left the area. Because the ground on which his office building sat had never flooded, he had no flood insurance on the building. Thus, Chuck Benvenutti's eight-employee small business faced uninsured losses of $300,000, and to make matters worse, most of his local clients were in the same boat—washed out with no flood insurance to cover it.[64] The towns of Bay St. Louis and Waveland were all but destroyed. Their futures hung by threads of prayer and the vaguest of hopes.

At first glance, a more dismal scenario for a small business would be hard to imagine. Nonetheless, as a CPA, Chuck Benvenutti reasoned that those who had survived the storm were going to have more complicated tax returns and need his services more than ever in accounting for casualty losses from damaged or destroyed homes and businesses. That belief got him moving quickly to gut his office and set up client services under a tarp on a folding table in his parking lot. Here, in the late summer heat, he gave free advice to a steady steam of clients for the better part of a month. He told his wife, Beth, "It's going to take a year . . . ," but "give it a year, sweetheart, and we'll be back." No doubt, this kind of confidence played an important role in moving people through the overwhelming difficulties of the early disaster response. Years later, with his community still struggling, Benvenutti wondered at the incredible simplicity of that early faith. "God," he declared, "if we had all realized it was going to be two, three, four, five years, it would have been a lot rougher."[65]

Nonetheless, behind Chuck Benvenutti's early optimism stood sensible preparation, a willingness to borrow money to cover payroll and uninsured losses, and a support system that kept spirits buoyed in regular church, civic club, and chamber of commerce gatherings. The weekend before the storm he and his staff had worked to create electronic copies of all of the files on the computer system. New equipment had to be bought and the old files loaded in, but in due course the saved information enabled his business to take up where it had left off the day before the storm. Still, he had no flood insurance to cover the loss of his building, and he faced more than a month with no income. Many of the small businessmen he knew feared taking on the kind of debt necessary to start over from scratch. However, he knew that he had to do to it in order to keep skilled employees and replace lost equipment. Benvenutti turned first to a line of credit at his bank, and immediately after the Mississippi Legislature passed a no-interest loan program for small business, he signed up for the full $25,000 limit without a second thought. When federal SBA loans became available he borrowed more at the low 4 percent SBA rate. This optimistic risk taking paid off when his client base doubled. On the other hand, Chuck Benvenutti saw many small-business pessimists decline such loans and go under, pulled down by worry about when and how they would be able to pay it all back.[66]

The path forward was not a bed of roses. Many obstacles pressed upon small businesses—most commonly labor shortages and skyrocketing insurance costs. Moreover, these two problems interacted with each other. Wind insurance rates for businesses quadrupled, while homeowners' insurance rates doubled. Tish Williams of the Hancock County Chamber of Commerce told a congressional delegation that, by itself, the post-Katrina explosion of wind insurance costs drove apartment rent up by $250 per unit per month and pushed mortgage payments beyond the reach of the workforce. With affordable housing already in short supply, increased rents forced many working families to leave the area. The lack of affordable housing meant staff shortages. Lack of staff meant that when Chuck Benvenutti's workload doubled, as he had believed it would, he was forced to put in 10 and 12 hours a day seven days a week for more than a year. This took a toll.[67]

At the same time, wind and fire insurance costs on his building rose from $450 to $1,700 per month, and to this he added a new federal flood policy for an additional $166 per month. Insurers who stayed in the market justified the rate hikes based on their payment of $8.36 billion in Katrina-related claims on 235,849 properties in the three coast counties.[68] In a 2007 survey, Tish Williams of the Hancock County Chamber of Commerce found that every business in her sample had seen its insurance rates triple or quadruple in the year after Katrina. On top of huge rate hikes, insurers demanded high wind deductables, and some refused to renew wind and fire coverage unless all other insurance was taken out through the same company.[69] Worse still, many of the national big-name providers cancelled policies and stopped writing wind altogether on the Mississippi Gulf Coast. This forced over 45,000 businesses and homeowners alike into the state-sponsored Mississippi Wind Pool, a last-resort, high-cost self-insurance system that could not spread risks beyond the coast.[70]

Many businesses large and small were caught up in protracted legal battles with their insurers over the wind-versus-water issues that arose from concurrent causation clauses in wind policies. Through these clauses insurers often sought to limit or avoid responsibility for wind damage to a building if, later in the storm sequence, surging water also damaged or destroyed the structure. No less a corporate giant than Northrop Grumman filed a $500 million lawsuit against FM Global, a leading commercial insurer, when the underwriter refused payment. A huge entity like Northrop Grumman could easily cope with the extra legal costs and years of potential delay in payment involved in pressing such matters in court.[71] More than 1,000 lawsuits were filed in federal court, but few small businessmen or homeowners could endure lengthy legal proceedings.[72] As a result many settled for amounts less than what was needed to make them whole.

With major insurance providers withdrawing their wind coverage for the region, and in an effort to preempt debilitating wind-versus-water legal disputes in future disasters, Congressman Gene Taylor introduced an insurance reform proposal in the U.S. House of Representatives. Taylor's so-called Multi-Peril Bill sought to provide a wind insurance option through FEMA's National Flood Insurance Program. The National Flood Insurance Program had come into existence decades earlier when private insurers began declining to provide flood coverage. With the support of new House Speaker Nancy Pelosi, who visited his district twice in the wake of Katrina,[73] Taylor's insurance measure passed the House in 2007, but failed in the Senate. When the bill came forward once again in the House in 2010, an election year, it was defeated under withering fire from the insurance industry and the U.S. Chamber of Commerce.[74] Thus, years after the storm, editorial writers at the *Sun Herald* were asking readers to "imagine where the Coast would be if insurance were not a problem."[75] Beyond the reach of federal and state regulators, the insurance industry used its political clout to block reform while simultaneously refusing to craft alternative solutions. Thus, small business continued to lag in recovery and affordable housing remained a troubling problem for the region.

To the woes of wind insurance, FEMA added additional challenges for small business. FEMA's new flood maps expanded the defined floodplain, and under threat of loss of coverage from the federal flood insurance program, FEMA's post-Katrina mitigation standards created expensive new building elevation requirements. Any mom-and-pop motel, gift shop, or restaurant contemplating rebuilding near the waterfront had to consider whether the business could absorb major additional construction costs or whether doing business on stilts above street level was even feasible.[76] To cope, small businesses could either raise prices, cut other costs, or go out of business. Hundreds went out of business.[77]

The fate of small business got few headlines. For many of the community's optimists, the casinos were the stars of the recovery. When the Governor's Commission on Recovery, Rebuilding, and Renewal finished its work in December of 2005, Chairman Jim Barksdale had expressed the belief that the casinos would stand out as "the great starting engine" for the recovery.[78] Certainly the new land-based gaming law had an immediate and demonstrably positive effect on the Mississippi Gulf Coast. Existing casinos moved quickly to open operations in their onshore hotel lobbies and convention spaces. The cannibalizing of convention halls made for a quick jobs recovery, but it robbed the gambling establishments of the meeting spaces that formerly made them attractive for large national and regional conferences. However, by January of 2006, three of the 13 destroyed casinos were back in business on land employing 4,245 people. An additional 1,500 casino jobs came back before the first anniversary of the storm—jobs that would have been far slower returning if the operators had been required to construct new barges. During the first six months of 2006, on a monthly basis, the three restored gaming halls took in revenues amounting to more than half the yields produced by all 12 coast operators before Katrina. Seven more casinos were scheduled to reopen by the end of 2006.[79]

Throughout 2007 and into the summer of 2008, as more of the pre-Katrina operators got back into business, casino employment and revenues continued to grow. Simultaneously, a stream of reports of new developers with plans for the coast market continued to buoy hopes.[80] In March of 2007, with 10 casinos back in operation, coast casinos equaled their pre-Katrina high performance of just under $118 million in gross gaming revenues. The long-delayed opening of the Hard Rock Casino in Biloxi in July 2007 added an eleventh property to the mix and boosted coast gaming totals to an all-time monthly high of nearly $125 million. Through August of 2008, with 11 of the 13 pre-Katrina gaming facilities in operation, the take continued to exceed monthly records set in 2004 and 2005, and total casino employment climbed to 14,920 in July of 2007. Within two years of the introduction of land-based gaming, 90 percent of the coast's gaming jobs were back, and in all three coast counties overall unemployment rates had dropped below 5 percent.[81] It all suggested that the high hopes for the tourism sector had not been misplaced.[82]

With the jobs recovery on track and casino revenues at best-ever levels, Harrah's Entertainment, in partnership with singer Jimmy Buffett, broke ground on the $700 million first phase of the Margaritaville Casino and Resort, a project which expected to carry a final price tag of $1 billion. Across Highway 90 from Harrah's Biloxi Grand, the Margaritaville development expected to add 800 rooms, 100,000 square feet of gaming space, and an additional 66,000 square feet of convention space.[83] The enormous scale of this, the first post-Katrina development on casino row, pointed to the kind of mega-projects hoped for when land-based gaming passed in the legislature. In the fall of 2007, construction workers prepared the site, and the concrete foundations began to rise out of the ground underneath tall construction cranes. A full-blown optimism appeared to be merited. Beyond the Margaritaville, a half-dozen other new casino projects seemed ready to go, with proposed names like Baracan Bay, Bay View, Royal D'Iberville, South Beach, and Pine Hills. In addition, plans announced for the old Tivoli and Broadwater Hotel properties added excitement to the mix.[84] Moreover, the way seemed open to bring to fruition the 21 condominium projects that were in the permitting pipeline when Katrina hit.[85] All of this reinforced the impression that the casinos and tourism would be driving a truly spectacular recovery for the Mississippi Gulf Coast.

However, there were signs of trouble in the small business segment of the tourism business. Even at the height of the post-Katrina casino boom, membership in the Gulf Coast Chapter of the Mississippi Hospitality and Restaurant Association stood at only 70 percent of its pre-Katrina strength. Few of the mom-and-pop motels and eateries that once dotted Highway 90 had rebuilt. As a result, the Mississippi Gulf Coast stood 5,151 rooms short of its pre-Katrina hotel-motel room count.[86] Despite such omens, the booming Mississippi Gulf Coast casino business continued to buoy high hopes for the long-term business recovery.

Two years after Katrina, in a summer of great optimism, *USA Today* reported Gulf Coast Business Council President Brian Sanderson's prediction that gaming in Mississippi would "one day overtake Atlantic City." In the same article, Rick Carter of the Island View Casino in Gulfport stated his hope that the Mississippi coast would soon become "the Las Vegas of the South."[87] Within a few months of the utterance of these words, the Great Recession took its toll on the nation's investment banks. In the wake of the financial calamity, condominium plans were suddenly shelved, and the coast's nascent casino boom was reduced to a fizzle.

In the spring of 2008 at the Southern Gaming Summit in Biloxi, analyst Alex Picou of KeyBanc Capital markets pronounced the casino boom dead. "The bubble has been burst," Picou asserted. The data was in. Gaming was "not recession proof."[88] While coast casino revenues did not show dramatic declines until September of that year, the lavish Margaritaville mega-project—with all the dreams and symbolism that went with it—became the first casualty of the Great Recession. On July 22, 2008, Harrah's Entertainment announced that "over the next few weeks, residents of Biloxi will notice less activity and fewer workers at the Margaritaville work site. Rest assured," the statement continued, "Harrah's is not canceling the project." The company explained the halt in construction as a necessary step "to better align" the development with the "economic environment on the Gulf Coast and the current financing environment." With an estimated $20 million already spent on months of foundation work, the construction cranes went silent.[89]

Soon thereafter coast gaming revenues plunged. The coast's September 2008 revenues dropped to levels not seen (except for the Katrina hiatus) since 2003 and remained stuck at these low levels throughout 2010. At the same time, coast casino employment dived from 13,468 in July of 2008 to 11,327 in December of 2009—almost 5,200 fewer jobs than at the pre-Katrina peak.[90] More disturbingly, the construction cranes that remained in suspended animation over the rusting remnants of the Margaritaville site for 18 months were at last totally removed. Meanwhile, two other billion-dollar mega-project proposals—South Beach and The Tivoli—failed to clear regulatory hurdles. In July of 2010, based on a Harrah's executive's report that the company was no longer in negotiations with investors on the Margaritaville development, Mayor A. J. Holloway told the Biloxi Chamber of Commerce that in his view, the much-heralded mega-project was dead.[91] The dream of Margaritaville and the larger hopes it represented stood now as little more than weathered concrete and rusting steel rising from a piece of scarred earth surrounded by a tall chain-link fence on Biloxi's Casino Row. By the end of 2009, the recession reduced overall Mississippi Gulf Coast hospitality employment to 73 percent of its pre-Katrina total, while the highly touted casino sector was left at a mere 69 percent of its prestorm jobs level.[92] The unbounded visions of grandeur that had fed so many hopes in the hard days after Katrina suddenly crashed into a wall of limits.

Beyond the heavily regulated Mississippi gaming halls, Wall Street gamblers in the unregulated derivatives markets robbed the nation and the region of the capital pools needed to move forward. Meanwhile, faraway insurance bigwigs withdrew from the Gulf Coast market and deployed their tremendous nationwide assets into a political battle to block all reasonable alternatives. The reality of a short-circuited disaster recovery hit home as the forces of national recession drove unemployment rates back up to 10 percent and beyond.[93] The mediocre prospects left to the people of the gulf region fell short of the kind of recovery their suffering, their hard work, their spirits, their endurance, and their vision merited. *Sun Herald* business reporter Mary Perez offered this lamentation: "We thought Katrina was the storm of the century, but we didn't know then we'd also have to face the deluge of insurance struggles and now the economy. And who could have dreamed nearly four years after the storm we'd have so far to go?"[94]

Chapter Eleven

Conclusion

A Persevering People

> *. . . We also rejoice in our sufferings, because we know that suffering produces perseverance; perseverance, character; and character, hope.*
>
> —ST. PAUL THE APOSTLE
> Epistle to the Romans
> Chapter 5, Verses 3–4 (NIV)[1]

In the swirling wind of Hurricane Katrina and in the unprecedented 30-foot tidal surge she brought ashore, south Mississippians suffered enormous loss, but they quickly showed real grit in the face of stark scenes of death and destruction. Too many of them—confident and self-reliant survivors of lesser storms—had underestimated the forces that could converge upon them from the sea. Yet, in the aftermath, even when government bureaucracies sometimes faltered, they stood up and faced the unprecedented calamity that had befallen them with fortitude and resourcefulness. Moreover, despite the wreckage of tens of thousands of homes and businesses, they retained surprising inner wellsprings of hope and faith which sustained them on the long road toward recovery. A generous nation through its federal treasury and an army of volunteers met these hardy spirits and provided an essential and much appreciated hand up to get them started on their way. There were after all physical and financial limits to what even the most willing spirits could do on their own to wipe away such mind-boggling community-wide devastation.

Five years after the monster storm, many miles still stretched before them in that journey. The Great Recession, the failure of the insurance markets, and new elevation requirements conspired to leave vacant 44 percent of all the lots in East Biloxi at the end of 2010.[2] Housing officials predicted that new census data would likely show that population in Mississippi's three hardest-hit counties still hovered at 7 percent below its pre-Katrina level.[3] For reasonable people questions remained about whether the cup of recovery should be viewed as half full or half empty. In the spring and summer of 2010, the BP Global Horizon oil spill added anger to frustration and raised serious questions about whether the environmental side effects of this new example of corporate malfeasance would further dim the prospects for tourism and fishing for yet more decades to come.

Yet, for a hopeful people still looking for silver linings in the dark clouds that had descended, the fifth anniversary of the monster storm produced newspapers filled with recitations of accomplishments worthy of celebration. Despite sometimes tortuous wrangling with FEMA, a record amount of debris—46 million cubic yards in Mississippi—had been removed in record time. Moreover, the fruits of federal investments could be seen in the repair and reconstruction of thousands of homes and in the rebuilt fire stations, schools, and other public buildings in every municipality on the Mississippi Gulf Coast, and many more public-sector projects were nearing the starting blocks. Before the storm, Beach Boulevard—the Highway 90 corridor—had given the people of the Mississippi Gulf Coast so much of their sense of place. Here, the completion of the massive new bridges across Biloxi Bay and the Bay of St. Louis had reunited communities in 2007 and brought forth tears of joy and "prayers of thanksgiving uttered with fervent appreciation." Beside both bridges, wide pedestrian walkways rising 95 feet above blue waters stretching toward the horizon added a striking new means to partake of the soul-healing mysteries of the region's majestic and unobstructed seascapes. Five years after Katrina, on the landward side of the highway vast expanses of vacant lots reminded residents that much remained to be done. However, along the south side of the scenic thoroughfare, a 26-mile stretch of beautiful white-sand beaches had been cleansed and replenished.[4] Here, along the Mississippi Gulf Coast, resplendent natural beauty held forth the promise that the storm-tossed region would still have much to recommend it once the clouds of recession parted.[5]

In more mundane matters, a huge expansion for the Port of Gulfport was on the horizon, and strong new building codes and a major new investment in a regional waste-water plan were laying the foundations for future resilience.[6] The generosity of the American people, acting through their federal representatives, provided billions of dollars for all of these forward-looking public-sector projects. Unfortunately, beyond the reach of regulatory accountability, corporate perfidy in high finance and big insurance and in Gulf of Mexico oil developers left the future in doubt and made it clear that, in the words of a *Sun Herald* editorialist, "faith and hope" could go "only so far" in the rebuilding effort.[7]

Beyond concrete and steel measures of progress, those who looked to the inner world of the human psyche and soul claimed gifts of the human spirit as important legacies of the difficult struggle to rebuild. As the recovery stretched on through long months and years, many surveys pointed to an increased incidence of depression, psychological distress, and stress-related physical illnesses among Katrina victims.[8] However, at least one notable study published by the World Health Organization showed that even as they endured great personal hardship and emotional suffering, large numbers of people had found avenues for "post traumatic growth." In overwhelming numbers, respondents indicated that in the disaster experience they had discovered inner strength, developed increased confidence in their own abilities to rebuild their lives, and "drawn closer to their loved ones." Even in the chaos of recovery the vast majority reported finding "deeper meaning and purpose in life" or becoming "more spiritual or religious."[9] This paradox of suffering and hope coexisting in hearts and minds of large numbers of individuals as they struggled to right their circumstances seems counterintuitive. Nonetheless, for many Mississippi survivors and for many of the people who came to their aid, these clinical observations reaffirm an image of a strength and self-reliance that remains fixed in memories of those difficult days.[10]

The experiences of Louise and Richard Perkins of Waveland offer a compelling personal example of the way in which strength and suffering united in so many of the disaster victims. Louise Perkins, a Ph.D. computer scientist, and her husband, Richard, a professional photographer, had moved to Hancock County in 1991 when Louise accepted employment in the Computer Science Department at the University of Southern Mississippi. The Perkinses' marriage represented the union of art and engineering. Before settling in Mississippi, Louise Perkins had worked at the Lawrence Livermore National Laboratory where she did aging simulation test work for nuclear stockpiles, and she had also helped set up the computer science program at Gallaudet University for the Deaf in Washington, D.C. Louise's stint as a postdoctoral research fellow at MIT near Boston made the couple realize that they were warm-weather people at heart, and so they accepted an appointment at USM and moved to Mississippi. They bought a large "fixer-up" house near Waveland, and Louise's engineering mindset quickly led her to an interest in home repair and the technical side of architecture, including such details as the calculation of the load-bearing strengths of walls. She learned enough from the contractors hired for various repairs that on her own she undertook and completed an addition that expanded the floor space by one-third. In Mississippi, construction had become the hobby of the woman of the house. Louise Perkins took special pride in the perfection she had achieved in the leveling and plumbing of the frames in the new section and in the double plywood reinforcement she had built into the walls. The old "fixer-upper" of a house had become a dream home. The Perkinses' only child was born in Hancock County, and at the time of Katrina young Christopher Perkins was a student at Coast Episcopal School.[11]

Though Louise's scientific interests inspired a deep fascination with hurricanes, as Katrina zeroed in on the Coast the family evacuated with a pop-up camper in tow and made for a state park campground south of Vicksburg to wait out the storm. Even at this location far inland, gusty winds made the Perkinses decide to sleep in a van rather than risk the flimsy pop-up. The day after the storm moved through, it was quite apparent that even in this inland refuge the camper would not have held up to the wind blasts that toppled hundred-year-old trees throughout the vicinity. After a day of rest, the family pulled the camper to Oklahoma where relatives sheltered them.[12]

The next week, when Louise Perkins returned to the coast, she was determined to work her way through the debris fields to see what had become of her house. From a distance she could see that part of the house was still standing, but it wasn't standing in the right place. In fact, it had been moved 85 feet from its original location and rotated 120 degrees. Nonetheless, large sections of the house were still recognizable. Parts of the house had been collapsed, but to Perkins's amazement the roof and the section which she had constructed stood tilted over at an angle, but they remained intact. Despite the obvious danger, the engineering instinct in this mother and wife created a tremendous urge to crawl into the wreckage, photograph and investigate the workings of the great natural forces which could move a house 85 feet, and rotate it but still leave large parts standing. In crawling through the wreckage, she found that the three-story structure had been lifted into the air and impaled on a hundred-year-old magnolia that stood in the edge of the debris field which marked the high-water mark of the storm surge. From an engineering standpoint, she concluded that the house had been lifted into the air by the rotational winds of a tornado and set down on the large tree. Off the record, at least one of the several insurance adjusters with whom the Perkinses dealt agreed with that assessment, but declined to put it into writing. Thus, the Perkinses joined U.S. Senator Trent Lott, U.S. Representative Gene Taylor, and hundreds of others in lawsuits against insurance companies that at first refused to pay for wind damage if structures that were alleged to have been destroyed by wind were located in areas affected by storm surge. In the end, between federal flood insurance and the wind policy, the Perkinses won a settlement that was near to the amount they had claimed. However, four years of determined but gut-wrenching and heartbreaking insurance struggles lay ahead for this family as failed arbitration efforts and obstructive insurance company legal maneuvers combined with seemingly purposeful corporate loss of claims documents stretched the day of final resolution further and further into the future.[13]

In the meantime, friends in California sent an RV to replace the rickety pop-up camper, and Robert and Kerryn Liebkemann in Kiln allowed the Perkins family to park it in their driveway and live there for several months. While caught in a web of uncertainty over their home, the Perkinses had waited in lines for "God knows how many things." The lines for FEMA trailers were particularly frustrating because local FEMA operatives repeatedly lost paperwork which then forced repeated submissions of the same applications. For roughly six months the family camped in the borrowed RV and showered in cold water outside under a hose thanking the Lord that at least they had found a way to manage without the frustrations of dealings with FEMA. The Perkinses wound up building a rough-hewn but liveable "barn" on their own property to tide them over until their insurance problems were resolved.[14]

In all of this time, the family continued doing productive work. Richard Perkins continued with his photography business via the Internet, and Louise even undertook unpaid overloads at USM so that her computer science majors could stay on track for graduation. At her son's school Louise had always been an active volunteer, but after Katrina, when the loss of faculty left little Coast Episcopal School without a fifth-grade math teacher, the university professor volunteered to teach elementary mathematics at 8:00 a.m. each morning before reporting to work at USM Gulf Coast. She noticed that her son was happy while school was in session, and "in fact he did better in school that year than he had ever done." However, when they visited the ruins of the house to try to salvage things or "on weekends when he wasn't in school . . . he would cry." Even though they were overloaded with work, the Perkinses took to making trips on the weekend to get young

Christopher's mind off the suffering and loss that surrounded him. "I was fascinated by the destruction," the mother and computer scientist recalled, "whereas my child was devastated by it."[15]

As the school year wore on, Perkins decided that the study of fractions had laid enough groundwork that she could introduce the concept of probability to her fifth-graders. After she had worked with dice and card games to try to communicate basic concepts, a hand shot up, and in the question that came forward she discovered that an awful connection had been made. "I need to know exactly what the probability is that a hurricane like Katrina will hit us again this year," the young questioner stated. "For the rest of the hour" the whole class wanted to talk about nothing but storms "and how often [they] were going to get hit, and how often [their] house [was] going to get destroyed." Louise Perkins did not usually cry about the storm, but that day she could not make herself go on to USM. "I just sat and cried the whole day," because "these poor kids" could not let even an hour pass after they had grasped the probability concept "without wanting to know how often their life would be like this."[16]

Louise Perkins's personal evaluation of her experiences with the storm and its aftermath in many ways paralleled the World Health Organization's observations. There was plenty of suffering for the Perkinses. The four-year struggle with the insurance company sent the family on one emotional roller coaster after another. Legal obstructionism and encounters with self-important or uncaring attorneys and arbitrators could trigger weeks of anger. At the end of what she experienced as a bitter and nasty but reasonably successful four-year insurance struggle Louise Perkins grieved for her lost innocence. She had learned things about people and institutions that she "did not want to know." "I'm left with distrust of . . . FEMA, large companies, lawyers, the Army Corps of Engineers" and others who set out or willfully enabled others to "make money off our misfortune," she said. Moreover, she "did not like knowing" what these aspects of "the world [were] really like." In short, she had become disillusioned and embittered.[17]

On the other hand, for the lady scientist with a steel backbone, there was also pride in accomplishment. She was plainly proud that she had mustered the grit to climb into the wreckage of her house and apply her knowledge of construction and her mathematical competency to correctly diagnose that a tornado, not rising water, had destroyed the building. She was proud that in the midst of her personal woes she had found the energy to teach overloads at the university and reach out to help a fifth grade class keep up in math. "You never know what you'll do until you're tested," she said, "but I think

I did good. I liked who I was during the storm and after." She had never really been a camper before Katrina, but she was proud of adjusting to six months of camper life, cold showers and all. She was proud of finding the way to talk herself into doing difficult tasks. Perkins observed that "if you complain about it, you're going to hate it, but if you say 'it's fun, it's going to be an adventure'" you can do many things that you initially dread. Perkins was particularly grateful for the example and influence of her friend Kerryn Liebkemann, a person of deep compassion "who bled for everyone almost like those healers who are supposed to put their hands on you and take your pain." Louise Perkins described herself as "a true geek" who "didn't pay much attention to people before the storm." She was certainly committed to her family and her students, but caring on a deep level was something she believed she learned from Kerryn Liebkemann. "I watched her for nine months help people recover and sympathize and empathize with them, and I never knew that people could be so important to somebody. . . . Living [there with Kerryn], I learned to really care about people. . . . That was pretty cool."[18] In the aftermath of Hurricane Katrina, Louise Perkins, a woman who came to Mississippi to escape the cold climate of Boston, found an unexpected capacity for new levels of inner warmth, and she had become one with her adopted community.

On a tragic day in August of 2005, when the terrible power of wind and water visited death and unparalleled material destruction on a region, there arose in Mississippi an unexpected chorus of voices vowing their determination to rise again. Here, in an awful time of testing, a people burdened by a tragic history had, without hesitation, stepped forward in countless acts of heroism, sacrificial service, and neighborly kindness—acts which offered proof that what is best in the human spirit can sometimes be found where it is least expected. In the weeks, months, and years of testing which followed, nearly a million volunteers from all across America came to the aid of the stricken region and in so doing made a profound statement about the better angels that still inhabit the character of a nation. The *Sun Herald* declared that through it all, the Mississippi Gulf Coast had proven that it was home to "an enduring people."[19] The Perkins family represented one of the thousands of such enduring individuals and families. In the end, it was the people of the Mississippi Gulf Coast with their battle-tested capacity for perseverance, creativity, and caring that stood as the region's most precious asset as it confronted hard realities not foreseen in the days of grand hopes and great dreams of worldly riches that had emerged in the aftermath of Katrina.

Notes

Preface

1. Stan Tiner, "Mississippi's STILL Invisible Coast," *Sun Herald* (Biloxi-Gulfport), September 6, 2009, C-3.

Chapter One

1. Father Louis Lohan, interview by James Pat Smith, July 11, 2008, University of Southern Mississippi Katrina Oral History Collection (hereafter USM KOH), McCain Archives, Hattiesburg, MS.

2. Commander, Naval Meteorology and Oceanography Command, Stennis Space Center, MS, "Preliminary Model Hindcast of Katrina Storm Surge, 21 November, 2005," http://cbr.tulane.edu/PDFs/NRL-Stennis-Katrina.pdf and http://kerrn.org/pdf/NRL-Stennis-Katrina.pdf (accessed November 10, 2008); and National Weather Service National Hurricane Center, "Hurricane Katrina Intermediate Advisory Number 26A," Miami, FL, 6:00 a.m. Monday, August 29, 2005, http://www.nhc.noaa.gov/archive/2005/pub/al122005.public_a.026.shtml? (accessed October 29, 2008).

3. National Weather Service National Hurricane Center, "Hurricane Katrina Intermediate Advisory Number 26A," Miami, FL, 6:00 a..m. Monday, August 29, 2005, http://www.nhc.noaa.gov/archive/2005/pub/al122005.public_a.026.shtml? (accessed October 29, 2008).

4. Oceanweather Inc., *Hindcast of Winds, Waves, and Currents in the Northern Gulf of Mexico in Hurricanes Katrina and Rita*. Submitted to the U.S. Department of the Interior Minerals Management Service, September 2006, http://mms.gov/tarprojects/580/580AA.pdf (accessed November 10, 2008).

5. The White House, *The Federal Response to Hurricane Katrina: Lessons Learned,* by Frances Fragos Townsend (Washington, D.C.: February, 2006), 5.

6. Governor's Office, State of Mississippi, *Three Years After Katrina: Progress Report on Recovery, Rebuilding and Renewal* (Jackson, MS: 2008), 4. Available at www.governorbarbour.com/recovery.

7. United States Senate, *Hurricane Katrina: A Nation Still Unprepared*, Special Report of the Committee on Homeland Security and Governmental Affairs, 109th Cong., 2nd sess., 2006, S. Rept. 109–322 (Washington, D.C.: Government Printing Office, 2006), 37. The Senate death toll figure includes fatalities among evacuees from stress, heart attack, or loss of access to essential medications in the immediate wake of the storm. See Michelle Hunter, "Deaths of Evacuees Push Toll To 1577, *Times-Picayune* (New Orleans), May 19, 2006, 1.

8. U.S. Department of Commerce National Oceanic and Atmospheric Administration (NOAA) National Weather Service, *Service Assessment: Hurricane Katrina August 23–31, 2005*, by David L. Johnson et al., National Weather Service (Silver Spring, MD, June 2006), 11. This report includes only "direct" Mississippi fatalities the day of the storm and does not estimate deaths among Mississippi evacuees in the storm's immediate aftermath.

9. Mayor Tommy Longo, interview by Kate Doyle and Alanna Tobia, February 21, 2008 (USM KOH); Michael Prendergast, interview by Erwin Townson and Jennifer Kaufman, February 20, 2008 (USM KOH); David Garcia, interview by Amy Roth and Sonia Preisler, February 21, 2008 (USM KOH); and Greg Lacour, "24 Hours of Wind, Water and the Horror of Hurricane Katrina, *Sun Herald* (Biloxi-Gulfport), September 4, 2005, http://www.lexisnexis.com (accessed November 8, 2008).

10. Charles B. (Chuck) Benvenutti, interview by James Pat Smith, February 13, 2008 (USM KOH).

11. Chief John Dubuisson, interview by Claire Gemmil and Jocelyn Wattam, February 19, 2009 (USM KOH); Leo "Chipper" McDermott, interview by James Pat Smith, March 14, 2008 (USM KOH); Kathryn Anne James, interview by Elizabeth Smith, December 6, 2007 (USM KOH); and Tracy Dash and Joshua Norman, "14 U.S. Senators Tour Devastation, Vow to Help," *Sun Herald* (Biloxi-Gulfport), September 17, 2005.

12. John Surratt, "Katrina Punches Pascagoula With Unprecedented Wind and Water," *The Mississippi Press* (Pascagoula), August 30, 2005, 1A and 6A; Greg Lacour, "24 Hours of Wind, Water and the Horror of Hurricane Katrina," *Sun Herald* (Biloxi-Gulfport), September 4, 2005; and Joseph Swaykos, interview by James Pat Smith, June 1, 2007 (USM KOH). Swaykos, a meteorologist by training, is director of the Center for Higher Learning at Stennis Space Center. Swaykos discovered a Pascagoula Airport wind reading of 130 miles per hour as part of a private research contract after Katrina.

13. Marc Caputo, David Ovalle, Erika Bolstad, and Martin Merzer, "Katrina Lashes Gulf Coast; Death Toll Hits 55 and Is Expected to Soar," *Miami Herald* (Florida), August 30, 2005.

14. WLOX-TV Documentary CD, "Katrina: South Mississippi Heroes," Raycom Media, 2007.

15. Kay Kell, interview by Stephen Sloan, January 11, 2007 (USM KOH); John Surratt, "Katrina Punches Pascagoula With Unprecedented Wind and Water," *The Mississippi Press* (Pascagoula), August 30, 2005, 1A, 6A; and Garry Mitchell, "Katrina Floods Downtown Mobile," *The Mississippi Press*, August 30, 2005, 7A.

16. Vincent Creel, interview by James Pat Smith, March 19, 2008 (USM KOH).

17. Melissa M. Scallan, "Firefighters Saved Selves, 20 Civilians," *Sun Herald* (Biloxi-Gulfport), October 2, 2005, A-10.

18. Vincent Creel, interview by James Pat Smith, March 19, 2008 (USM KOH); A. J. Holloway, interview by Stephen Sloan, January 18, 2007 (USM KOH). See also "Biloxi Mayor: Katrina Is Our Tsunami," Associated Press, August 30, 2005; Anita Lee, Don

Hammack, and Scott Dodd, "Coast Begins to Assess Devastation From 'Our Tsunami,'" *Sun Herald* (Biloxi-Gulfport), August 31, 2005, available at http://www.lexisnexis.com (accessed November 8, 2008); and National Hurricane Center, *Tropical Cyclone Report Hurricane Katrina, 23–30 August 2005* by Richard D. Knabb, Jamie R. Rhome, and Daniel P. Brown, December 20, 2005, and updated August 10, 2006, available at http://www.nhc.noaa.gov/pdf/TRC-AL122005-Katrina.pdf (accessed November 10, 2008), 1.

19. Federal Emergency Management Agency (FEMA), News Release May 19, 2006, and "Hurricane Katrina Mississippi Recovery Update," May 7, 2009, http://www.fema.gov/news/newsrelease.fema?id=26400 and 48257 (accessed November 2, 2008); and Mississippi Renewal Forum, *Three Years After Katrina: A Special Report*, http://www.mississippirenewal.com/index.html (accessed November 4, 2008).

20. Jack Norris, executive director of the Governor's Office of Recovery and Renewal, written testimony, Committee on Financial Services, U.S. House of Representatives, May 8, 2008, http://www.house.gov/apps/list/hearing/financialsvcs_dem/hr050808.shtml (accessed May 20, 2008); FEMA, News Releases August 17, 2006, and July 13, 2009, http://www.fema.gov/news/newsrelease.fema?id=29046 (accessed November 2, 2008); and United States Senate, *Hurricane Katrina: A Nation Still Unprepared*, 38. The estimated number of boxcar loads of Katrina's 46,000,000 cubic yards of debris in Mississippi is extrapolated from earlier incomplete FEMA reports based on 45,000,000 cubic yards.

21. A. J. Holloway, interview by Stephen Sloan, January 18, 2007 (USM KOH).

22. Ivor van Heerden and Mike Bryan, *The Storm: What Went Wrong and Why During Hurricane Katrina—The Inside Story From One Louisiana Scientist* (New York: Viking Press, 2006), 13.

23. National Hurricane Center, *Tropical Storm Cyclone Report, Hurricane Katrina*, 1–2; and National Weather Service, *Service Assessment: Hurricane Katrina*, 1n.

24. Chief Pat Sullivan, interview by James Pat Smith, June 4, 2008 (USM KOH).

25. Ibid.; Michael Prendergast, interview by Erin Townson and Jennifer Kaufman, February 20, 2008 (USM KOH); David Garcia, Sr., interview by Amy Roth and Sonia Preisler, February 21, 2008 (USM KOH); see also National Weather Service National Hurricane Center, "Tropical Depression Twelve Forecast/Advisory Number 1," Miami, FL, 9:00 p.m. Tuesday, August 23, 2005, http://www.nhc.noaa.gov/archive/2005/mar/al122005.fstadv.001.shtml? (accessed October 29, 2008).

26. Ibid., and statements by chiefs Alan Weatherford, Wayne Payne, and Pat Sullivan for the Community Politics and Government Panel, Ghosts of Katrina Conference, University of Southern Mississippi Gulf Coast Campus, Long Beach, MS, June 5, 2009.

27. Henry Arledge, interview by Rachel Swaykos, May 31, 2007 (USM KOH); Charlene Favre, interview by Cameron and Bethany Klapwyk, February 20, 2008 (USM KOH); and Susan Stevens, interview by Cameron and Bethany Klapwyk, February 20, 2008 (USM KOH).

28. National Weather Service National Hurricane Center, "Hurricane Katrina Advisory Number 11," 5:00 a.m. Friday, August 26, 2005; "Advisory Number 19," 10:00 p.m. Saturday, August, 27, 2005; "Advisory Number 21," 4:00 a.m. Sunday, August 28; "Advisory Number 23," 10:00 a.m. Sunday, August, 28; "Advisory Number 25," 10:00 p.m. Sunday, August 28, 2005; "Intermediate Advisory Number 26A (Corrected)" 6:00 a.m. Monday, August 29, 2005; National Hurricane Center, *Tropical Storm Cyclone Report, Hurricane Katrina*,1–2; National Weather Service, *Service Assessment: Hurricane Katrina*, 2–3; and National Weather

Service National Hurricane Center, "Hurricane Katrina Discussion Number 23," 11:00 a.m. Sunday, August 28, 2005, http://www.nhc.noaa.gov/archive/2005/dis/al122005.disc.023.shtml? (accessed October 29, 2008).

29. Cheryl Blain, interview by James Pat Smith, July 30, 2007 (USM KOH). Dr. Blain, a civilian employee of the Naval Meteorologic and Oceanographic Command at Stennis Space Center, Mississippi, is a civil engineer specializing in storm surge modeling.

30. National Weather Service National Hurricane Center, "Hurricane Katrina Advisory Number 11," 5:00 a.m. August 26, 2005; "Advisory Number 12,"11:00 a.m. August 26, 2005; "Advisory Number 14," 5:00 p.m. August 26, 2005; "Advisory Number 16," 5:00 a.m. August 27, 2005, http://www.nhc.noaa.gov/archive/2005/KATRINA.shtml? (accessed October 29, 2008).

31. The White House, *The Federal Response to Hurricane Katrina*, 7 and 23–25.

32. Vincent Creel, interview by James Pat Smith, March 19, 2008 (USM KOH).

33. Councilman Bill Stallworth, interview by James Pat Smith, May 22, 2008 (USM KOH); James Crowell, interview by James Pat Smith, May 28, 2008 (USM KOH); and the White House, *The Federal Response to Hurricane Katrina*, 26.

34. National Weather Service National Hurricane Center, "Hurricane Dennis Advisory Number 23," 11:00 p.m. July 9, 2005; and "Advisory 24," 4:00 a.m. July 10, 2005, http://www.nhc.noaa.gov/archive/2005/DENNIS.shtml? (accessed October 29, 2008); and Vincent Creel, interview by James Pat Smith, March 19, 2008 (USM KOH).

35. Benjamin J. Spraggins, "Statement Before the U.S. Senate Commerce Committee, Science and Transportation Subcommittee on Disaster Prevention and Prediction, May 24, 2006," *CQ Congressional Testimony*, http://www.lexisnexis.com. (accessed November 1, 2008); and United States Senate, *Hurricane Katrina: A Nation Still Unprepared*, 57.

36. Anita Lee, "Avoiding Another Katrina, Port Evacuation Will Be Mandatory," *Sun Herald* (Biloxi-Gulfport), July 12, 2008, A1 and A15.

37. The White House, *The Federal Response to Hurricane Katrina*, 24–25, n. 66, and 162; United States Senate, *Hurricane Katrina: A Nation Still Unprepared*, 51–53, 56–58 and 67–68; U.S. House of Representatives Select Bipartisan Committee to Investigate the Preparation for and Response to Hurricane Katrina, *A Failure of Initiative: Final Report of the Select Bipartisan Committee to Investigate the Preparation for and Response to Hurricane Katrina*, 109th Cong., 2nd sess., 2006, 59–61; and Benjamin J. Spraggins, "Statement Before the U.S. Senate Commerce Committee, Science and Transportation Subcommittee on Disaster Prevention and Prediction, May 24, 2006," *CQ Congressional Testimony*, http://www.lexisnexis.com (accessed November 1, 2008).

38. Major General Harold Cross, interview, NPR News, September 3, 2005, http://www.lexisnexis.com (accessed October 20, 2008).

39. United States Senate, *Hurricane Katrina: A Nation Still Unprepared*, 51–53, 56–58, and 67–68.

40. Ibid.; and Benjamin J. Spraggins, "Statement Before the U.S. Senate Commerce Committee, Science and Transportation Subcommittee on Disaster Prevention and Prediction, May 24, 2006," *CQ Congressional Testimony*, http://www.lexisnexis.com (accessed November 1, 2008).

41. Douglas Brinkley, *The Great Deluge: Hurricane Katrina, New Orleans and the Mississippi Gulf Coast* (New York: HarperCollins, 2006), 22–23.

42. Mayor A. J. Holloway, interview by Stephen Sloan, January 18, 2007 (USM KOH).

43. Larry Copeland and Haya El Nasser, "Flattened in '69, Biloxi Again at Risk," *USA Today,* September 14, 2004, 3A, http://www/lexisnexis.com (accessed October 20, 2008); and Mayor A. J. Holloway, interview by Stephen Sloan, January 18, 2007 (USM KOH).

44. National Weather Service National Hurricane Center, "Hurricane Ivan Intermediate Advisory Number 55B," 2 a.m. September 16, 2004, http://www.nhc.noaa.gov/archive/IVAN .shtml? (accessed October 29, 2008).

45. Holbrook Mohr, "September Casino Revenues Are Lowest Monthly Showing This Year," Associated Press State and Local Wire, October 20, 2004, http://www.lexisnexis.com (accessed October 20, 2008).

46. Mayor A. J. Holloway, interview by Stephen Sloan, January 18, 2007 (USM KOH); and Vincent Creel, interview by James Pat Smith, March 19, 2008 (USM KOH).

47. Shelia Hardwell Byrd, "Mississippi Coast Prepares for Possible Ivan Encounter," Associated Press State and Local Wire, September 13, 2004, http://www.lexisnexis.com (accessed October 10, 2008).

48. Vincent Creel, interview by James Pat Smith, March 19, 2008 (USM KOH); and Shelia Hardwell Byrd, "Evacuations Ordered From Mississippi Coast," Associated Press State and Local Wire, September 14, 2004, http://www.lexisnexis.com (accessed October 20, 2008).

49. Constance "Connie" Rocko, interview by James Pat Smith, June 23, 2008 (USM KOH); and Vincent Creel, interview by James Pat Smith, March 19, 2008 (USM KOH).

50. Benjamin J. Spraggins, "Statement Before the U.S. Senate Commerce Committee, Science and Transportation Subcommittee on Disaster Prevention and Prediction, May 24, 2006," *CQ Congressional Testimony*, http://www.lexisnexis.com (accessed November 1, 2008).

51. Vincent Creel, interview by James Pat Smith, March 19, 2008 (USM KOH); and A. J. Holloway statement quoted on UPN Radio News, WLMT Memphis, TN, August 28, 2005, Inews Network Global Broadcast Data Base, http://www.lexisnexis.com (accessed October 19, 2008).

52. Ibid.; and Mayor A. J. Holloway, interview by Stephen Sloan, January 18, 2007 (USM KOH).

53. Vincent Creel, interview by James Pat Smith, March 19, 2008 (USM KOH); and A. J. Holloway, interview by Stephen Sloan, January 18, 2007 (USM KOH).

54. Mayor Gregory "Brent" Warr, interview by James Pat Smith, June 20, 2008 (USM KOH).

55. Ibid.

56. Ibid.

57. Ibid.; and Benjamin J. Spraggins, "Statement Before the U.S. Senate Commerce Committee, Science and Transportation Subcommittee on Disaster Prevention and Prediction, May 24, 2006," *CQ Congressional Testimony*, http://www.lexisnexis.com (accessed November 1, 2008).

58. Mayor Gregory "Brent" Warr, interview by James Pat Smith, June 20, 2008 (USM KOH); Constance "Connie" Rocko, interview by James Pat Smith, June 23, 2008 (USM KOH); and Vincent Creel, interview by James Pat Smith, March 19, 2008 (USM KOH).

59. United States Senate, *Hurricane Katrina: A Nation Still Unprepared*, 51–58 and 67–68.

60. Mayor A. J. Holloway, interview by Stephen Sloan, January 18, 2007 (USM KOH).

61. Mayor Gregory "Brent" Warr, interview by James Pat Smith, June 20, 2008 (USM KOH).

62. Mayor Billie Skellie, interview by James Pat Smith, March 19, 2008 (USM KOH).

63. Robert J. Meyer, "Why We Under-Prepare for Hazards," in *On Risk and Disaster: Lessons from Hurricane Katrina,* ed. Ronald J. Daniels, Donald Kettl, and Howard Kunreuther (Philadelphia: University of Pennsylvania Press, 2006), 154–162.

64. Kenneth P. Wilkinson and Peggy J. Ross, *Citizens' Responses to Warnings of Hurricane Camille* (State College: Mississippi State University Social Science Research Center, 1970), 8, 21, and 30.

65. Frank P. McNeil, interview by Sheena Barnett and Kate Doyle, February 21, 2008 (USM KOH); and Vincent Creel, interview by James Pat Smith, March 19, 2008 (USM KOH).

66. Mayor A. J. Holloway, interview by Stephen Sloan, January 18, 2007 (USM KOH); and Vincent Creel, interview by James Pat Smith, March 19, 2008 (USM KOH).

67. Mayor Leo "Chipper" McDermott, interview by James Pat Smith, March 14, 2008 (USM KOH).

68. Kurt Brautigam, interview by David Tisdale, December 18, 2006 (USM KOH).

69. Sewell Chan, "A Few Mississippians, Unified Only By Death: Details About Katrina Victims Emerge," *International Herald Tribune,* 28 September, 2005, 6, http://www.lexisnexis.com (accessed October 20, 2008).

70. Rev. S. V. Adolph and Virginia H. Adolph, interview by James Pat Smith, June 12, 2008 (USM KOH); and Benjamin J. Spraggins, "Statement Before the U.S. Senate Commerce Committee, Science and Transportation Subcommittee on Disaster Prevention and Prediction, May 24, 2006," *CQ Congressional Testimony*, http://www.lexisnexis.com (accessed November 1, 2008).

71. Rev. S. V. Adolph and Virginia H. Adolph, interview by James Pat Smith, June 12, 2008 (USM KOH).

72. Oxfam America, *Progress Report—Disaster and Recovery Along the U.S. Gulf Coast: Oxfam America's Response to the Hurricanes* (2006), 23.

73. Councilman William "Bill" Stallworth, interview by James Pat Smith, May 22, 2008 (USM KOH).

74. Frank P. McNeil, interview by Sheena Barnett and Kate Doyle, February 21, 2008 (USM KOH).

75. Mayor Gregory "Brent" Warr, interview by James Pat Smith, June 20, 2008 (USM KOH).

76. Rev. S. V. Adolph and Virginia H. Adolph, interview by James Pat Smith, June 12, 2008 (USM KOH); and Rev. Lee J. Adams, interview by James Pat Smith, June 6, 2008 (USM KOH).

77. Rev. S. V. Adolph and Virginia H. Adolph, interview by James Pat Smith, June 12, 2008 (USM KOH).

78. Rev. Lee J. Adams, interview by James Pat Smith, June 6, 2008 (USM KOH).

79. Constance "Connie" Rocko, interview by James Pat Smith, June 23, 2008 (USM KOH); and Greg Lacour, "24 Hours of Wind, Water and the Horror of Hurricane Katrina," *Sun Herald* (Biloxi-Gulfport), September 4, 2005, http://www.lexisnexis.com (accessed November 8, 2008).

80. Marc Caputo, David Ovalle, Erika Bolstad, and Martin Merzer, "Katrina Lashes Gulf Coast: Death Toll Hits 55 and Is Expected to Soar," *Miami Herald* (Florida), August 30, 2005.

81. The White House, "Appendix B—What Went Right" in *The Federal Response to Hurricane Katrina: Lessons Learned*, by Frances Fragos Townsend, 131.

82. Reverend Phan Duc Dong, "Father Dominic," interview by Linda Van Zandt and Von Nguyen, September 26, 2005 (USM KOH).

83. Ronald J. Baker, interview by Linda Van Zandt, Stephen Smith, and Kate Ellis, May 17, 2007 (USM KOH).

84. Greg Lacour, "24 Hours of Wind, Water and the Horror of Hurricane Katrina," *Sun Herald* (Biloxi-Gulfport), September 4, 2005, available at http://www.lexisnexis.com (accessed November 8, 2008); and John Surratt, "Katrina Punches Pascagoula With Unprecedented Water and Wind," *The Mississippi Press*, August 30, 2005, 1A and 6A.

85. National Weather Service National Hurricane Center, "Hurricane Katrina Intermediate Advisory Number 26A," Miami, FL, 6:00 a.m. Monday, August 29, 2005, http://www.nhc.noaa.gov/archive/2005/pub/al122005.public_a.026.shtml? (accessed October 29, 2008); and National Weather Service Forecast Office New Orleans/Baton Rouge, "Hurricane Katrina Post Tropical Cyclone Report," February 17, 2006, http://www.srh.noaa.gov/lix/html/psh_katrina.htm (accessed October 29, 2008).

86. John Pain, "Hurricane Katrina Hit as Category 3, Not 4," Associated Press, December 20, 2006, http://www.breitbart.com/article.php?id=D8EKC9S08&show_article=1. (accessed November 11, 2008).

87. Commander, Naval Meteorology and Oceanography Command at Stennis Space Center, MS, "Preliminary Model Hindcast of Katrina Storm Surge, 21 November, 2005," http://cbr.tulane.edu/PDFs/NRL-Stennis-Katrina.pdf and http://kerrn.org/pdf/NRL-Stennis-Katrina.pdf (accessed November 10, 2008).

88. Rev. Rod Dickson-Rishel, interview by James Pat Smith, June 16, 2008 (USM KOH).

89. Ibid.

90. Betty N. Smith, statements to the author, September 1, 2005, and November 20, 2008.

91. Ibid.

92. Statement by Gulfport Police Chief Alan Weatherford, Ghosts of Katrina Conference, University of Southern Mississippi, June 5, 2009.

93. Constance "Connie" Rockco, interview by James Pat Smith, June 23, 2008 (USM KOH).

94. Vincent Creel, interview by James Pat Smith, March 19, 2008 (USM KOH).

95. Charlene Favre, interview by Cameron and Bethany Klapwyk, February 20, 2008 (USM KOH).

96. Constance "Connie" Rockco, interview by James Pat Smith, June 23, 2008 (USM KOH).

97. William Barry Jones, interview by Deanne Nuwer, November 14, 2005 (USM KOH).

98. Ibid.

99. Ibid.

100. Ibid.

101. Mississippi Adjutant General Harold A. Cross, "Statement Before U.S. House of Representatives Committee on Government Reform, Subcommittee on Select Katrina Response Investigation, October 27, 2005," *CQ Congressional Testimony*, http://www.lexisnexis.com (accessed December 3, 2008); and U.S. House of Representatives, *A Failure of Initiative*, 62.

102. United States Senate, *Hurricane Katrina: A Nation Still Unprepared*, 37. The Senate death toll figure includes fatalities among evacuees from stress, heart attack, or loss of access

to essential medications in the immediate wake of the storm. See Michelle Hunter, "Deaths of Evacuees Push Toll To 1577," *Times- Picayune* (New Orleans), May 19, 2006,1; and U.S. Department of Commerce National Oceanic and Atmospheric Administration (NOAA) National Weather Service, *Service Assessment: Hurricane Katrina August 23–31, 2005*, by David L. Johnson et al., National Weather Service (Silver Spring, MD, June 2006), 1 n. This report includes only "direct" Mississippi fatalities the day of the storm and does not estimate deaths among Mississippi evacuees in the storm's immediate aftermath.

Chapter Two

1. Chief Pat Sullivan, interview by James Pat Smith, June 4, 2008 (USM KOH).

2. William Barry Jones, interview by Deanne Nuwer, November 14, 2005 (USM KOH).

3. FEMA News Release, May 7, 2009, "Hurricane Katrina Mississippi Recovery Update," http://www.fema.gov/news/newsrelease.fema?id=48257 (accessed August 4, 2009).

4. Dr. Brian W. Amy, written testimony, *Hearing of the House Select Bipartisan Committee to Investigate the Preparation for and Response to Hurricane Katrina: Preparedness and Response by the State of Mississippi*, December 7, 2005, 6 and 11.

5. Chief Pat Sullivan, interview by James Pat Smith, June 4, 2008 (USM KOH).

6. Mayor Billie Skellie, interview by James Pat Smith, March 19, 2008 (USM KOH).

7. FEMA News Release, May 7, 2009, "Hurricane Katrina Mississippi Recovery Update," release number 1604–714. http://www.fema.gov/newsreleast.fema?id=48257 (accessed July 1, 2009).

8. Vincent Creel, interview by James Pat Smith, March 19, 2008 (USM KOH).

9. Former Harrison County Deputy Alfred Alfonso, statement to the author.

10. Chief Pat Sullivan, interview by James Pat Smith, June 4, 2008 (USM KOH); Constance "Connie" Rockco, interview by James Pat Smith, June 23, 2008 (USM KOH); and Marlin R. Ladner, interview by James Pat Smith, June 24, 2008 (USM KOH).

11. On the Friday after the storm, Brian Martin, an aide to Congressman Gene Taylor, witnessed a vigorous debate between FEMA officials and General Cross about the fire hazards the massive debris fields presented in Harrison County. See Brian Martin, interview by James Pat Smith, December 27, 2007 (USM KOH); see also Vincent Creel, interview by James Pat Smith, March 18, 2008 (USM KOH); and Chief Pat Sullivan, interview by James Pat Smith, June 4, 2008 (USM KOH).

12. Ibid.

13. Mayor Brent Warr, interview by James Pat Smith, June 29, 2008 (USM KOH).

14. Ibid.

15. Ibid.

16. Reverend Guss Shelly, interview by James Pat Smith, June 6, 2007 (USM KOH).

17. John Hairston, interview by James Pat Smith, September 4, 2008 (USM KOH).

18. Ibid.

19. Ibid.

20. United States House of Representatives, *A Failure of Initiative*, 8; and United States Geographical Survey, "Hurricane and Extreme Storm Impact Research: Post-Storm Quick Response Photos—Long Beach Area," photos 5 and 17, http://coastal.er.usgs.gov/hurricanes/katrina/quickphotos/longbeach (accessed November 17, 2008).

21. Coasts, Oceans, Ports, and Rivers Institute of the American Society of Civil Engineers, *Hurricane Katrina Damage Assessment: Louisiana, Alabama, and Mississippi Coasts*, ed. Stephen A. Curtis, P.E. (Reston, VA: American Society of Civil Engineers, 2007), 7–10; and Anita Lee, "Avoiding Another Katrina: Port Evacuation Will Be Mandatory," *Sun Herald* (Biloxi-Gulfport), July 12, 2009, A1 and A15.

22. Gross casino revenues for calendar year 2004 for the entire state came to $2.777 billion, of which coast casinos produced $1.227 billion, or 44.2 percent of the state total. Coast casino tax estimates presented here for fiscal year 2005 are estimated at 44.2 percent of the total tax income for state and local entities. Mississippi State Tax Commission Miscellaneous Tax Bureau, "Casino Gross Gaming Revenues," 2004, and Mississippi State Tax Commission Miscellaneous Tax Bureau, "Tax Revenues from Gaming," fiscal year 2005, www.mstc.state.ms.us (accessed July 12, 2008).

23. Congressman Gene Taylor, interview by Dariusz Grabka and Alanna Tobia, February 21, 2008 (USM KOH).

24. Coasts, Oceans, Ports, and Rivers Institute of the American Society of Civil Engineers, *Hurricane Katrina Damage Assessment: Louisiana, Alabama, and Mississippi Coasts*, ed. Stephen A. Curtis, P.E., 58–61.

25. Ibid.

26. Mississippi State Tax Commission Miscellaneous Tax Bureau, "Casino Gross Gaming Revenues," 2005, www.mstc.state.ms.us (accessed July 12, 2008).

27. Governor Haley Barbour, oral testimony, *Hearing of the House Select Bipartisan Committee to Investigate the Preparation for and Response to Hurricane Katrina: Preparedness and Response by the State of Mississippi*, December 7, 2005, 8.

28. Eric Lipton, "FEMA Is Eager to Show It Learned From Katrina," *New York Times*, September 1, 2008, A-11, http://www.lexisnexis.com (accessed November 8, 2008).

29. FEMA, News Release, September 3, 2005, "National Search and Rescue Teams Deployed," http://www.fema.gov/news/newsrelease.fema?id=18582 (accessed August 4, 2009).

30. Chief Pat Sullivan, interview by James Pat Smith, March 19, 2008 (USM KOH).

31. Robert Latham, oral testimony, *Hearing of the House Select Bipartisan Committee to Investigate the Preparation for and Response to Hurricane Katrina: Preparedness and Response by the State of Mississippi*, December 7, 2005,11.

32. Ellen Knickmyer, "Scores Denied Leave Time to Aid Displaced Families," *Washington Post*, September 11, 2005, http://www.lexisnexis.com (accessed August 11, 2008).

33. Governor Haley Barbour, oral testimony, *Hearing of the House Select Bipartisan Committee to Investigate the Preparation for and Response to Hurricane Katrina: Preparedness and Response by the State of Mississippi*, December 7, 2005, 19; and James A. Wombell, *Army Support During the Hurricane Katrina Disaster: The Long War Series, Occasional Paper 29* (Fort Leavenworth: Combat Studies Institute Press, 2009), 114–120.

34. Dark Kam and Alan Gomez, "Lack of Plan Hurt Katrina-Hit States' Response," *Palm Beach Post*, September 10, 2005, http://palmbeachpost.com (accessed August 12, 2009).

35. Michael Newsom, "FEMA Pulls Together Search-and-Rescue Teams," *Sun Herald* (Biloxi-Gulfport), August 31, 2005, http://www.lexisnexis.com (accessed November 8, 2008).

36. Chief Pat Sullivan, interview by James Pat Smith, June 4, 2008 (USM KOH); Robert Weaver, interview by James Pat Smith, September 23, 2009 (USM KOH); Constance "Connie" Rockco, interview by James Pat Smith, June 23, 2008 (USM KOH); and Marlin R. Ladner, interview by James Pat Smith, June 24, 2008 (USM KOH).

37. Robert Weaver, interview by James Pat Smith, September 23, 2009 (USM KOH).

38. United States Senate, *Hurricane Katrina: A Nation Still Unprepared*, 386.

39. Robert Weaver, interview by James Pat Smith, September 23, 2009 (USM KOH).

40. Dave Vincent, interview by James Pat Smith, August 28, 2009 (USM KOH).

41. Thomas Korosec, "Katrina's Aftermath: Life and Property Tolls Climb; Relief Efforts Speed Up, But Shortages Abound," *Houston Chronicle*, September 3, 2005, http://www.lexisnexis.com (accessed November 8, 2008).

42. James A. Wombwell, *Army Support During the Hurricane Katrina Disaster* (Fort Leavenworth, Kansas: US Army Combined Arms Center Combat Studies Institute Press, 2009), 123.

43. Robert Weaver, interview by James Pat Smith, September 23, 2009 (USM KOH).

44. Ibid.

45. Councilman William "Bill" Stallworth, interview by James Pat Smith, May 22, 2008 (USM KOH).

46. Ibid.; and Coasts, Oceans, Ports, and Rivers Institute of the American Society of Civil Engineers, *Hurricane Katrina Damage Assessment: Louisiana, Alabama, and Mississippi Coasts*, ed. Stephen A. Curtis, P.E., 44–45.

47. Councilman William "Bill" Stallworth, interview by James Pat Smith, May 22, 2008 (USM KOH).

48. Ibid.

49. Ibid.

50. Ibid.; and James W. Crowell, interview by James Pat Smith, May 28, 2008 (USM KOH).

51. Robert Gavagnie, interview by Rachel Swaykos, June 12, 2007 (USM KOH); Scott Marshall, "When the Cavalry Didn't Come. . . ," *Sun Herald* (Biloxi-Gulfport), September 16, 2005, B-2; and Shepard Smith, "Live Report from Waveland, Mississippi," in *Fox On the Record With Greta Van Sustern,* Fox News Network, September 7, 2005, http://www.lexisnexis.com (accessed December 2, 2008).

52. Scott Marshall, "When the Cavalry Didn't Come. . . ," *Sun Herald* (Biloxi-Gulfport), September 16, 2005, B-2.

53. Audra D.S. Burch, "Forgotten: The Poorest Residents of the Coast Seem to Wait the Longest for Supplies, Assistance," *Sun Herald* (Biloxi-Gulfport), September 6, 2005, 8.

54. Robert Weaver, interview by James Pat Smith, September 23, 2009 (USM KOH).

55. Ibid.

56. FEMA News Releases October 6, 7, and 9, 2005, http://www.fema.gov/news/newsrelease.fema?id=19550, 19503, and 19580 (accessed November 2, 2008).

57. Councilman William "Bill" Stallworth, interview by James Pat Smith, May 22, 2008 (USM KOH).

58. Douglas Brinkley, *The Great Deluge: Hurricane Katrina, New Orleans and the Mississippi Gulf Coast* (New York: HarperCollins, 2006), 273–274.

59. United States Government Accountability Office, *Hurricanes Katrina and Rita: Provision of Chartable Assistance*, written statement of Cynthia Fagnoni before the Subcommittee on Oversight, Committee on Ways and Means, House of Representatives, GAO-06-297T, December 13, 2005.

60. Professor Paul Light, interview by Margaret Warner, "American Red Cross Troubles," *PBS Online NewsHour*, December 14, 2005, http://www.pbs.org/newshour/bb/health/july-dec05/redcross (accessed November 2, 2008).

61. Bill Nichols, "Hard Lesson Learned at Red Cross; Charity Alters Preparations After Katrina," *USA Today*, Final Edition, June 6, 2006, http://www.lexisnexis.com (accessed August 11, 2008).

62. Brinkley, *The Great Deluge*, 273–274.

63. Florida Emergency Response Team, "Situation Report No.25: Katrina's Aftermath," September 5, 2005, 3–4, http://www.floridadisaster.org/eoc/update/Katrina.asp (accessed November 8, 2008).

64. John Ritter, Tom Weir, and Thomas Frank, "Evacuees Are Moving Out of Shelters," *USA Today*, Final Edition, September 16, 2005, http://www.lexisnexis.com (accessed August 11, 2008); and Brinkley, *The Great Deluge*, 274.

65. American Red Cross, "Challenged by the Storms: The American Red Cross Response to Hurricanes Katrina, Rita and Wilma," http://www.redcross.org. (accessed August 18, 2009); and Relief Web, "USA Challenged by the Storms—The American Red Cross Response to Hurricanes Katrina, Rita and Wilma," http://www.reliefweb.int/rw/rwb.nsf/db900SID/ETOA-6MF3AU?OpenDocument (accessed August 18, 2009).

66. Donna Harris, "Red Cross Seeking More Local Volunteers," *Sun Herald* (Biloxi-Gulfport), June 11, 2007, A-1; and Bill Nichols, "Hard Lesson Learned at Red Cross; Charity Alters Preparations After Katrina," *USA Today*, Final Edition, June 6, 2006, http://www.lexisnexis.com (accessed August 11, 2008).

67. James W. Crowell, interview by James Pat Smith, May 28, 2008 (USM KOH); and Rev. S. V. Adolph and Virginia Adolph, interview by James Pat Smith, June 12, 2008 (USM KOH).

68. Congressman Gene Taylor, interview by Dariusz Grabka and Alanna Tobia, February 21, 2008 (USM KOH).

69. Ibid.

70. Ibid.

71. Susan Stevens, interview by Cameron Klapwyk and Bethany Klapwyk, February 20, 2008 (USM KOH).

72. United States Senate, *Hurricane Katrina: A Nation Still Unprepared*, 26–27.

73. Congressman Gene Taylor, interview by Dariusz Grabka and Alanna Tobia, February 21, 2008 (USM KOH); and Robert Gavagnie, interview by Rachel Swaykos, June 12, 2007 (USM KOH).

74. Congressman Gene Taylor, interview by Dariusz Grabka and Alanna Tobia, February 21, 2008 (USM KOH).

75. Robert R. Latham, Jr., written testimony, *Hearing of the House Select Bipartisan Committee to Investigate the Preparation for and Response to Hurricane Katrina: Preparedness and Response by the State of Mississippi*, December 7, 2005.

76. Quoted in United States Senate, *Hurricane Katrina: A Nation Still Unprepared*, 377.

77. Ibid., 384–85.

78. Mississippi Emergency Management Agency (MEMA), Press Release, "Hurricane Katrina Update," 10 p.m. August 30, 2005, http://www.disastercenter.com/katrina%20Mississippi.html (accessed August 18, 2009).

79. Quoted by Lara Jakes Jordan, "FEMA Admitted Broken Katrina Response, Feared Mississippi Riots, Letters Show," Associated Press State and Local Wire, December 6, 2006, http://www.lexisnexis.com (accessed November 9, 2008).

80. As a result of Florida's commitment of over 2,000 emergency response personnel to Mississippi shortly after Katrina struck, Florida's emergency management agency held twice

daily conference calls with its own emergency management officials deployed in Mississippi and with Mississippi's state-level emergency operations center and produced twice daily and much more detailed reports on the situation in Mississippi than the overwhelmed MEMA and FEMA information systems could produce. Florida Emergency Response Team, "Situation Report No. 25: Katrina's Aftermath," September 5, 2005, 3–4, http://www.floridadisaster.org/eoc/update/Katrina.asp (accessed November 8, 2008).

81. Thomas Korosec, "Katrina: The Aftermath, Mississippi Coastal Crises," *Houston Chronicle*, 3 Star Edition, September 2, 2005, A-12, http://www.lexisnexis.com (accessed November 8, 2008).

82. Editorial, "South Mississippi Needs Your Help," *Sun Herald* (Biloxi-Gulfport), September 1, 2005, A-1.

83. Ibid.; and Scott Dodd, Tom Wilemon, and Scott Hawkins, "Long Lines Await Aid," *Sun Herald* (Biloxi-Gulfport), September 2, 2005, http://www.lexisnexis.com (accessed November 8, 2008).

84. Quoted by Lara Jakes Jordan, "FEMA Admitted Broken Katrina Response, Feared Mississippi Riots, Letters Show," Associated Press State and Local Wire, December 6, 2006, http://www.lexisnexis.com (accessed November 9, 2008.).

85. E-mail, Carwile to Fenton, September 1, 2005, quoted in transcript of *Hearing of the House Select Bipartisan Committee to Investigate the Preparation for and Response to Hurricane Katrina: Preparedness and Response by the State of Mississippi*, December 7, 2005, 35–36, http://www.lexisnexis.com (accessed July 29, 2009).

86. William Carwile, e-mail, September 1, 2005, ibid.

87. United States House of Representatives, *A Failure of Initiative*, 321.

88. FEMA, News Release, January 29, 2007, http://www.fema.gov/news/newsrelease.fema?id=33531 (accessed August 16, 2009).

89. United States Senate, *Hurricane Katrina: A Nation Still Unprepared*, 385.

90. Quoted in ibid., 377.

91. William Carwile, oral testimony, *Hearing of the House Select Bipartisan Committee to Investigate the Preparation for and Response to Hurricane Katrina: Preparedness and Response by the State of Mississippi*, December 7, 2005, 35–36.

92. United States Senate, *Hurricane Katrina: A Nation Still Unprepared*, 377; and Hope Yen, "FEMA Official Says Boss Ignored Warnings," Associated Press Online, October 20, 2005, http://www.lexisnexis.com (accessed November 9, 2008).

93. United States Senate, *Hurricane Katrina: A Nation Still Unprepared*, 377.

94. Adjutant General Harold A. Cross, testimony, *Committee on House Government Reform Subcommittee on Select Katrina Response Investigation*, October 27, 2005.

95. United States Government Accountability Office, Report to Congressional Committees, *Catastrophic Disasters: Enhanced Leadership, Capabilities, and Accountability Controls Will Improve the Effectiveness of the Nation's Preparedness, Response, and Recovery System*, GAO-06-618, September 2006, 47; and United States Senate, *Hurricane Katrina: A Nation Still Unprepared*, 385.

96. Congressman Gene Taylor, interview by Dariusz Grabka and Alanna Tobia, February 21, 2008 (USM KOH).

97. Ibid.; and Wombwell, *Army Support During the Hurricane Katrina Disaster*, 120.

98. United States Senate, *Hurricane Katrina: A Nation Still Unprepared*, 30 and 385.

99. Ibid., 386.

100. Quoted in United States Senate, *Hurricane Katrina: A Nation Still Unprepared*, 180.
101. Ibid., 385.
102. Editorial, "We Need More Than 'A Few Good Men,'" *Sun Herald*, September 3, 2005, 26.
103. Reverend Charles "Chuck" Leon Register, Sr., interview by James Pat Smith, July 11, 2007 (USM KOH); and Reverend Guss Shelly, interview by James Pat Smith, June 6, 2007 (USM KOH).
104. Congressman Gene Taylor, interview by Dariusz Grabka and Alanna Tobia, February 21, 2008 (USM KOH).
105. Ibid.
106. Ibid.
107. Mayor Tommy Longo, oral testimony, *Hearing of the House Select Bipartisan Committee to Investigate the Preparation for and Response to Hurricane Katrina: Preparedness and Response by the State of Mississippi*, December 7, 2005, 41–43, http://www.lexisnexis.com (accessed July 29, 2009).
108. Ibid.
109. Congressman Gene Taylor, statement, *Hearing of the House Select Bipartisan Committee to Investigate the Preparation for and Response to Hurricane Katrina: Preparedness and Response by the State of Mississippi*, December 7, 2005, 3 and 17.
110. Robert Latham, oral testimony, *Hearing of the House Select Bipartisan Committee to Investigate the Preparation for and Response to Hurricane Katrina: Preparedness and Response by the State of Mississippi*, December 7, 2005, 17; and U.S. Senate, *Hurricane Katrina: A Nation Still Unprepared*, 30.
111. Dave Vincent, interview by James Pat Smith, August 28, 2009 (USM KOH).

Chapter Three

1. Quoted by Emily Wagster Pettus, "Katrina Hands Mississippi Governor His Toughest Political Test," Associated Press State and Local Wire, September 3, 2005, http://www.lexisnexis.com (accessed September 24, 2008).
2. Editorial, *Sun Herald* (Biloxi-Gulfport), September 6, 2005, 16.
3. Michael Grunwand and Susan B. Glasser, "Brown's Turf Wars Sapped FEMA's Strength: Director Who Came To Symbolize Incompetence In Katrina Predicted Agency Would Fail," *Washington Post*, December 23, 2005, http://www.lexisnexis.com (accessed December 16, 2009); and "Brown Joked In E-Mail As Katrina Churned: Ex-FEMA Head's Correspondence Shows Banter, Trivialities Before Storm," MSNBC, November 3, 2005, http://www.rss.msnbc.msn.com/id/9912186/ns/us_news-katrina_the_long_road_back/ (accessed December 16, 2009).
4. WLOX-TV Documentary, *Katrina: South Mississippi Heroes*, CD version (RAYCOM Media, 2007).
5. David Elliot, interview by James Pat Smith, August 31, 2009 (USM KOH).
6. Geoff Pender, "Flawed Plans Didn't Account for Storms Worse Than Camille," *Sun Herald* (Biloxi-Gulfport), September 5, 2005, 1.
7. Brandon M. Bickerstaff, "Dark Side: Looters Add Insult to Injury," *Sun Herald* (Biloxi-Gulfport) August 30, 2005, 3; Kate Magandy, "House Survives Storm, But Not

Looters," *Sun Herald* (Biloxi-Gulfport), September 1, 2005, 3; and Brandon Bickerstaff, "Crime, Looting Unabated In Katrina's Wake," ibid., 3.

8. Pam Firman, "Strength in Neighbors," *Sun Herald* (Biloxi-Gulfport), September 5, 2005, 17; George Pawlaczyk, "Eight Gulfport Neighbors Organize to Make Sure Each Makes It Through OK," ibid., 17; Robin Fitzgerald and Brandon Bickerstaff, "Work for the Weary: Emergency Personnel Remain On The Job Despite Devastations of Their Own,"ibid., 18; Jim Mashek, "O'Gwin Family Has Limited Options, Plenty of Faith," ibid., 22; Kymberli Hagelberg, "Bonded by Destruction Neighbors Become Friends and Allies following Hurricane," ibid., September 6, 2005, 17; Stephen Majors, "They're Survivors: Hancock County Residents Look Out for Each Other While Waiting for Help," ibid., 9; and Dan Duffy, "We're A Real Tight Community: Hard-hit Gautier Neighbors Are Supporting Each Other Through Rough Times," ibid., 11.

9. Father Louis Lohan, interview by James Pat Smith, June 11, 2008 (USM KOH).

10. Ibid.

11. Kate Magandy, "A Little Football Laughter Helps," *Sun Herald* (Biloxi-Gulfport), September 5, 2005, 5.

12. Ibid.

13. Kat Bergeron, "Faith Survives the Storm: Churches Plan Services, Survey Damage," *Sun Herald* (Biloxi-Gulfport), September 3, 2005, 2; and Scott Hawkins, "Diocese Suffers, Will Hold Mass," ibid., 2.

14. "Spreading God's Word: Congregations Seek Solace and Rejoice at Sunday Services," *Sun Herald* (Biloxi-Gulfport), September 6, 2005, 5.

15. Rev. Lee J. Adams, interview by James Pat Smith, June 23, 2008 (USM KOH); Rev. S. V. Adolph and Mrs. Virginia H. Adolph, interview by James Pat Smith, June 12, 2008 (USM KOH); and Rev. Zachary Beasley, interview by James Pat Smith, June 16, 2008 (USM KOH).

16. Ibid.

17. Ibid.; and Kevin Fee, "Volunteers To Turn Long Beach, Miss. Roller Rink Into Temporary Church, School," *Sun Herald* (Biloxi-Gulfport), September 16, 2005.

18. Stephen Peranich, interview by James Pat Smith, December 28, 2007 (USM KOH).

19. U.S. Government Accountability Office, "Coast Guard: Observations On the Preparation, Response, and Recovery Missions Related To Hurricane Katrina," statement of Stephen L. Caldwell, July 31, 2006, GAO-06-903.

20. Hal G. Rainey and Paula Steinbauer, "Galloping Elephants: Developing Elements of a Theory of Effective Government Organizations," *Journal of Public Administration Research and Theory: J-Part*, 9 (January, 1999), 3–12, 20, and 26; Karlene H. Roberts, "Some Characteristics of One Type of High Reliability Organization," *Organizational Science*, 1 (1999), 166–76; and John R. Harrald, "Agility and Discipline: Critical Success Factors for Disaster Response," *The ANNALS of The American Academy Of Political and Social Science*, 2006, 256–72.

21. Stephen Peranich, interview by James Pat Smith, December 28, 2007 (USM KOH); and Brian Martin, interview by James Pat Smith, December 27, 2007 (USM KOH).

22. Southern Company, news release, March 22, 2006, http://southerncompany.mediaroom.com/index.php?s=43&item=173 (accessed August 5, 2008).

23. U.S. Department of Energy Office of Electricity and Energy Reliability, Hurricane Katrina Situation Report #10, August 30, 2005, and #11, September 1, 2005.

24. Geoff Pender, "A Powerful Success Story: Electric Companies Lead the Way In Coast's Recovery," *Sun Herald* (Biloxi-Gulfport), December 7, 2005; and Michael Newsom, "MS Coastions Still Lack Housing: Insurance, Rent Increases Hit Hard," *Sun Herald* (Biloxi-Gulfport), May 11, 2008, http://www.lexisnexis.com (accessed September 6, 2008).

25. Southern Company, news release, "Mississippi Power's Plant Watson Fully Restored, Ready For Summer Peaking Season," June 16, 2006, http://southerncompany.mediaroom.com/index.php?s=43&item=167 (accessed August 5, 2008).

26. Laura Jakes Jordan (AP), "Private Sector Got Preparedness Right," *Sun Herald* (Biloxi-Gulfport), November 17, 2005, B-10; and Geoff Pender, "A Powerful Success Story: Electric Companies Lead the Way In The Coast's Recovery," ibid., B-10, December 7, 2005.

27. Alfred John Peranich, interview by James Pat Smith, July 13, 2007 (USM KOH); and Kirt Brautigam, interview by David Tisdale, December 18, 2006 (USM KOH).

28. U.S. Department of Energy Office of Electricity and Energy Reliability, Hurricane Katrina Situation Report #10, August 30, 2005, and #11, September 1, 2005

29. U.S. Department of Energy Office of Electricity and Energy Reliability, Hurricane Katrina Situation Report #15, September 1, 2005, and #18, September 3, 2005.

30. "Mississippi Utilities Spent $361M To Restore Infrastructure Documents Show," *Electric Utility Weekly*, December 26, 2005, 13; and Mississippi Power news release, March 2006, http://www.mississippipower.com/news/iframe-pressroom.asp (accessed August 5, 2008).

31. Priscilla Frulla, "Safety and Beauty: Mississippi Power Renovated HQ," *Sun Herald* (Biloxi-Gulfport), June 13, 2007, B-10.

32. "Hurricane Recovery," *Electric Utility Week*, December 26, 2005, 13.

33. Kirt Brautigam, interview by David Tisdale, December 18, 2006 (USM KOH).

34. Alfred John Peranich, interview by James Pat Smith, July 13, 2007 (USM KOH); and Kirt Brautigam, interview by David Tisdale, December 18, 2006 (USM KOH).

35. Ibid.

36. Kirt Brautigam, interview by David Tisdale, December 18, 2006 (USM KOH); and U.S. Department of Energy Office of Electricity and Energy Reliability, Hurricane Katrina Situation Report #14, September 1, 2005.

37. Ibid.

38. U.S. Department of Energy Office of Electricity and Energy Reliability, Hurricane Katrina Situation Reports #28, September 8, 2005, and #29, September 9, 2005; Kirt Brautigam, interview by David Tisdale, December 18, 2006 (USM KOH); and Geoff Pender, "A Powerful Success Story," *Sun Herald* (Biloxi-Gulfport), December 7, 2005.

39. Ibid.

40. "Mississippi Utilities Spent $361M To Restore Infrastructure Documents Show," *Electric Utility Weekly*, December 26, 2005, 13; and U.S. Department of Energy Office of Electricity and Energy Reliability, Hurricane Katrina Situation Report #32, September 11, 2005.

41. U.S. Congress, Congressional Budget Office, *The Federal Government's Spending and Tax Actions in Response to the 2005 Gulf Coast Hurricanes* (August 1, 2007), 4–5.

42. Southern Company, news release, "Mississippi Power's Plant Watson Fully Restored, Ready for Summer Peaking Season," June 16, 2006, http://www.southerncompany.mediaroom.com/index.php?s=43&item=167 (accessed August 5, 2008).

43. Editorial, "Thank You, Thank You, Thank You," *Sun Herald* (Biloxi-Gulfport), September 6, 2005, 15.

44. Bill Minor, "This Little Radio Station Saved Lives," *Sun Herald* (Biloxi-Gulfport), September 6, 2007, C2; Dave Vincent, testimony before the Federal Communications Commission Regional Hearing, March 7, 2006; and Governor's Office of Recovery and Renewal, *eNewsletter*, May 15, 2006.

45. Wanda Comello, letter to the editor, "Post-Katrina Heroes Can't Be Thanked Enough," *Sun Herald* (Biloxi-Gulfport), September 25, 2007, B-2.

46. Dave Vincent, testimony before the Federal Communications Commission Regional Hearing, March 7, 2006; Dave Vincent, interview by James Pat Smith, August 28, 2008 (USM KOH); and Ricky Mathews, interview by David Tisdale, August 25, 2006 (USM KOH).

47. "Weekly Newspaper Brings Sense of Normalcy in Hurricane Area," Associated Press State and Local Wire, September 12, 2005, www.lexisnexis.com (accessed January 12, 2010).

48. Dave Vincent, interview by James Pat Smith, August 28, 2008 (USM KOH).

49. Kat Bergeron, "A Bittersweet Return To St. Charles," *Sun Herald* (Biloxi-Gulfport), August 31, 2005, 15; and Lisa Monti, "We Ask Only To Be Who We Are," *Sun Herald* (Biloxi-Gulfport), September 7, 2008, G-3 and 4.

50. Ibid.; David Elliot, interview by James Pat Smith, August 31, 2009 (USM KOH); Ricky Mathews, interview by David Tisdale, August 25, 2006 (USM KOH); and Dave Vincent, "Tough Calls—Lessons Learned from Hurricane Katrina," *RTNDA News Leadership*, http://www.rtnda.org/pages/media_items/tough-calls–lessons-learned-from-hurricane-katri . . . (accessed August 10, 2009).

51. Chevis Swetman, interview by James Pat Smith, October 19, 2009 (USM KOH).

52. Ibid.

53. Ibid.

54. Ibid.

55. John Hairston, interview by James Pat Smith, September 4, 2008 (USM KOH).

56. George Schloegel, inteview by James Pat Smith, August 14, 2008 (USM KOH); and John Hairston, interview by James Pat Smith, September 4, 2008 (USM KOH).

57. Sidney L. Rushing, unrecorded interview by James Pat Smith, June 4, 2009.

58. George Schloegel, inteview by James Pat Smith, August 14, 2008 (USM KOH); and John Hairston, interview by James Pat Smith, September 4, 2008 (USM KOH).

59. John Hairston, interview by James Pat Smith, September 4, 2008 (USM KOH).

60. Ibid.

61. George Schloegel, interview by James Pat Smith, August 14, 2008 (USM KOH); and John Hairston, interview with James Pat Smith, September 4, 2008 (USM KOH).

62. Ibid.

63. Ibid.

64. Ibid.

65. Chevis Swetman, interview by James Pat Smith, October 19, 2009 (USM KOH).

66. John Dubuisson, interview by Claire Gemmill and Jocelyn Wattam, February 19, 2009 (USM KOH); George Schloegel, interview by James Pat Smith, August 14, 2008 (USM KOH); and John Hairston, interview by James Pat Smith, September 4, 2008 (USM KOH).

67. Ibid.; and Chevis Swetman, interview by James Pat Smith, October 19, 2009 (USM KOH).

68. Ibid.

69. George Schloegel, interview by James Pat Smith, August 14, 2008 (USM KOH)

70. Fax, Chevis Swetman to James Pat Smith, February 3, 2010.

71. George Schloegel, interview by James Pat Smith, August 14, 2008 (USM KOH); John Hairston, interview by James Pat Smith, September 4, 2008 (USM KOH); and Chevis Swetman, interview by James Pat Smith, October 19, 2009 (USM KOH).

72. John Hairston, interview by James Pat Smith, September 4, 2008 (USM KOH).

Chapter Four

1. Ted Koppel, *Nightline*, "Closing Thoughts: Preparing for the Unexpected," ABC News, September 15, 2005, http://www.abcnews.com/id=1130955 (accessed June 9, 2008).

2. Robert R. Latham, Jr., written testimony, *Hearing of the House Select Bipartisan Committee to Investigate the Preparation for and Response to Hurricane Katrina*, December 7, 2005, 1 and 8.

3. United States Senate, *Hurricane Katrina: A Nation Still Unprepared*, Executive Summary, 3.

4. Marlin Ladner, interview by James Pat Smith, June 24, 2008 (USM KOH).

5. Holbrook Mohr, "Fema Director Calls State Katrina Response A Model," Associated Press State and Local Wire, September 28, 2005. http://www.lexisnexis.com (accessed January 3, 2009).

6. Ted Koppel, *Nightline*, "Closing Thoughts: Preparing for the Unexpected," ABC News, September 15, 2005.

7. John Hairston, interview with James Pat Smith, September 4, 2008 (USM KOH)

8. Robert S. McElvaine, editorial, "Mississippi Myth Spins Faster Than Katrina," *Times-Picayune* (New Orleans), October 15, 2005.

9. Charges of dictatorial tactics in the Mississippi governor's mansion were hurled in emotional fights over public education and Medicaid funding in the spring and summer of 2005 and later. See Emily Wagster Pettus, "Barbour Calls Session Within a Session On Medicaid Budget," Associated Press State and Local Wire, March 11, 2005, http://www.lexisnexis.com (accessed January 3, 2009).

10. Jill Lawrence, "Governors Handle Crisis In Own Ways," *USA Today*, September 13, 2005, 5A; and Governor Haley Barbour, oral testimony, *Hearing of the House Select Bipartisan Committee to Investigate the Preparation for and Response to Hurricane Katrina,* December 7, 2005, 30.

11. Governor Haley Barbour, oral testimony, *Hearing of the House Select Bipartisan Committee to Investigate the Preparation for and Response to Hurricane Katrina,* December 7, 2005, 30.

12. William L. Carwile, written testimony, *Hearing of the House Select Bipartisan Committee to Investigate the Preparation for and Response to Hurricane Katrina,* December 7, 2005, 3.

13. Emily Wagster Pettus, "Tale Of Two Politicians: One Governor's Stock Rises Post Katrina, Another's Falls," Associated Press, November 3, 2005, http://www.lexisnexis.com (accessed November 8, 2008).

14. Jill Lawrence, "Governors Handle Crisis In Own Ways," *USA Today*, September 13, 2005, 5A; and Emily Wagster Pettus, "Katrina Hands Mississippi Governor His Toughest

Political Test," Associated Press State and Local Wire, September 3, 2005, http://www.lexisnexis.com (accessed September 24, 2008).

15. William L. Carwile, oral testimony, *Hearing of the House Select Bipartisan Committee to Investigate the Preparation for and Response to Hurricane Katrina,* December 7, 2005, 12; and William L. Carwile, written testimony, *Hearing Before the Senate Committee on Homeland Security and Governmental Affairs*, December 8, 2005, 3–4.

16. Scott Shane, "After Failure, Government Officials Play Blame Game, *New York Times,* September 5, 2005, http://www.nytimes.com/2005/09/05/national/nationalspecial (accessed November 4, 2008).

17. Federal Emergency Management Agency, "National Incident Command System," http://www.fema.gov/emergency/nims/AboutNIMS.shtm (accessed December 24, 2009).

18. William L. Carwile, "Unified Command and the State-Federal Response to Hurricane Katrina in Mississippi," *Homeland Security Affairs*, I (2005): 12–13.

19. William Carwile, testimony, *Hearing Before the United States Senate Committee on Homeland Security and Governmental Affairs*, December 8, 2005.

20. William L. Carwile, "Unified Command and the State-Federal Response to Hurricane Katrina In Mississippi," *Homeland Security Affairs*, I (2005): 5; and William Carwile, oral testimony, *Hearing of the House Select Bipartisan Committee to Investigate the Preparation for and Response to Hurricane Katrina,* December 7, 2005, 32.

21. Robert R. Latham, written testimony, *Hearing of the House Select Bipartisan Committee to Investigate the Preparation for and Response to Hurricane Katrina,* December 7, 2005, 4.

22. William L. Carwile, "Unified Command and the State-Federal Response to Hurricane Katrina in Mississippi," *Homeland Security Affairs*, I (2005): 5.

23. Ibid.; Kay Kell, interview by Stephen Sloan, January 11, 2007 (USM KOH); and Brian Martin, interview by James Pat Smith, December 27, 2007 (USM KOH).

24. William L. Carwile, "Unified Command and the State-Federal Response to Hurricane Katrina in Mississippi," *Homeland Security Affairs*, I (2005): 6–7; statements by Wayne Payne, Alan Weatherford, Robert Weaver, and Pat Sullivan, Ghosts of Katrina Conference, Long Beach, MS, June 5, 2009; Kay Kell, interview by Stephen Sloan, January 11, 2007 (USM KOH); and Brian Martin, interview by James Pat Smith, December 27, 2007 (USM KOH).

25. Kay Kell, interview by Stephen Sloan, January 11, 2007 (USM KOH).

26. Statements by Joe Spraggins, Wayne Payne, Alan Weatherford, Robert Weaver, and Pat Sullivan, Ghosts of Katrina Conference, Long Beach, MS, June 5, 2009.

27. Kay Kell, interview by Stephen Sloan, January 11, 2007 (USM KOH); and Donna Harris, "Kell Advises Ike-affected Cities About Recovery," *Sun Herald* (Biloxi-Gulfport), February 2, 2009, A-3.

28. Dara Kam and Alan Gomez, "Lack Of Plan Hurt Katrina-hit States' Response," *Palm Beach Post*, September 10, 2005, http://palmbechpost.com/storm/content/state/epaper/2005/09/10 (accessed August 16, 2009).

29. Brian Martin, interview by James Pat Smith, December 27, 2007 (USM KOH).

30. Dara Kam and Alan Gomez, "Lack Of Plan Hurt Katrina-hit States' Response," *Palm Beach Post*, September 10, 2005, http://palmbechpost.com/storm/content/state/epaper/2005/09/10 (accessed August 16, 2009).

31. Supervisor Marlin Ladner, interview by James Pat Smith, June 24, 2008 (USM KOH).

32. Robert "Bobby" Weaver, interview by James Pat Smith, September 23, 2009 (USM KOH).

33. Ibid.

34. Chief Pat Sullivan, interview by James Pat Smith, June 4, 2008 (USM KOH); Supervisor Constance "Connie" Rockco, interview by James Pat Smith, June 23, 2008 (USM KOH); and Supervisor Marlin Ladner, interview by James Pat Smith, June 24, 2008 (USM KOH).

35. Supervisor Constance "Connie" Rockco, interview by James Pat Smith, June 23, 2008 (USM KOH).

36. Florida State Emergency Response Team, Situation Report No. 25, Katrina's Aftermath, September 5, 2005, 3–4, http://www.floridadisaster.org/eoc/update/Katrina.asp (accessed November 8, 2008).

37. Federal Emergency Management Agency, "FEMA Helps Mississippi Pay Florida For Disaster Aid," September 12, 2006, news release number 1604-439, http://www.fema.gov/news/newsrelease.fema?id=29761 (accessed August 16, 2009).

38. Governor Haley Barbour, oral testimony, *Hearing of the House Select Bipartisan Committee to Investigate the Preparation for and Response to Hurricane Katrina: Preparedness and Response by the State Of Mississippi*, December 7, 2005, 7.

39. James A. Wombwell, *Army Support During the Hurricane Katrina Disaster* (Fort Leavenworth, Kansas: US Army Combined Arms Center Combat Studies Institute Press, 2009), 114–118.

40. Robert Latham, written testimony, *Hearing of the House Select Bipartisan Committee to Investigate the Preparation for and Response to Hurricane Katrina: Preparedness and Response by the State Of Mississippi*, December 7, 2005. Latham's figures on the cost of EMAC assistance vary considerably from the numbers quoted on page 72 of the U.S. House of Representatives report, *Failure of Initiative: Final Report of the Select Bipartisan Committee to Investigate the Preparation for and Response to Hurricane Katrina.* That report quoted an October 10, 2005, Mississippi EMAC Cost Tracker estimate of $327 million. The author has accepted the later estimates which Latham prepared for his December testimony as the more accurate. The total of the piecemeal reimbursement checks which FEMA issued over several years were not available at this writing.

41. Chief Pat Sullivan, interview by James Pat Smith, June 4, 2008 (USM KOH); Mayor Gregory "Brent" Warr, interview by James Pat Smith, June 20, 2008 (USM KOH); Supervisor Constance "Connie" Rockco, interview by James Pat Smith, June 23, 2008 (USM KOH); and Supervisor Marlin Ladner, interview by James Pat Smith, June 24, 2008 (USM KOH).

42. John Hairston, interview by James Pat Smith, September 4, 2008 (USM KOH).

Chapter Five

1. John Simerman, "In Mississippi, Pride Gives Way To Tales of Survival," *Contra Costa Times* (California), September 11, 2005, F4.

2. Editorial, *St. Louis Post-Dispatch*, September 28, 2005, quoted in *Knight Ridder/Tribune*, "Editorials On Aftermath of Hurricanes," September 29, 2005, http://www.lexisnexis.com (accessed March 8, 2010).

3. U. S. Senate, *Hurricane Katrina: A Nation Still Unprepared*, 37–38.

4. S. Heather Duncan, "Removing Debris in Southern Mississippi Could Take 5 Years," *Knight Ridder Washington Bureau*, September 10, 2005, http://www.lexisnexis.com. (accessed April 12, 2010).

5. Jim Johnson, "Katrina Cleanup May Take 2 Years: Operation Will Be Nation's Largest," *Waste News*, September 26, 2005, 1.

6. Betty N. Smith, statements to the author, September 1, 2005, and November 20, 2008.

7. Trudy Fisher, "Report on Mississippi Department of Environmental Quality Disaster Debris Management Efforts After Hurricane Katrina," *Mississippi Law Journal* 77.3 (March 18, 2008): 844–845.

8. Ibid., 845–850.

9. Ibid.; and Jim Johnson, "Mississippi Employs 'Emergency Landfills,'" *Waste News*, January 30, 2006, 13.

10. Reverend Guss Shelly, interview by James Pat Smith, June 6, 2007 (USM KOH).

11. Ibid.

12. Ibid.

13. White House Press Release, "A New Mississippi: Rebuilding In Wake of Hurricane Katrina," *States News Service*, August 28, 2006, http://www.lexisnexis.com (accessed April 13, 2010).

14. Ibid.

15. James Walke, director, FEMA Public Assistance Division, written testimony, *Hearing of the United States Senate Governmental Affairs Committee Subcommittee On Disaster Recovery*, July 10, 2007, 2–3.

16. Robert T. Stafford Disaster Relief and Emergency Assistance Act of 1974, Public Law 93-288, [May 22, 1974], 88 Stat. 143 (42 U.S. Code 5173).

17. Mayor Leo "Chipper" McDermott, interview by James Pat Smith, March 14, 2008 (USM KOH).

18. Marlin Ladner, interview by James Pat Smith, June 24, 2008 (USM KOH); Constance "Connie" Rockco, interview by James Pat Smith, June 23, 2008 (USM KOH); Michael Newsom, "Cleanup Moves to Private Property," *Sun Herald* (Biloxi-Gulfport), September 15, 2005; and Eric Lipton, "On Gulf Coast, Cleanup Differs Town to Town," *New York Times,* December 26, 2005, National Desk A-1.

19. Gordon Russell and James Varney, "From Blue Tarps to Debris Removal, Layers of Contractors Drive Up the Cost of Recovery, Critics Say," *Times-Picayune* (New Orleans), December 29, 2005, National Section A-1; and Leslie Eaton, "After Huricanes Come Tempests Over Cleanups," *New York Times*, February 24, 2006, A-1.

20. Larry Margasak, "Report: Katrina Contractors Bilk Taxpayers," Associated Press Online, May 4, 2006, http://www.lexisnexis.com (accessed November 11, 2008).

21. Eric Lipton and Ron Nixon, "Many Contracts For Storm Work Raise Questions," *New York Times*, September 26, 2005, A-1; and Michael Kunzelman "Coastal Communities Complain About FEMA," Associated Press Online, May 7, 2007, http://www.lexisnexis.com (accessed April 13, 2009).

22. Jeffrey Sparshott, "Businesses Assess Harm, Start Fixes," *Washington Times*, September 9, 2005, A-1.

23. Adam Geller, "AP Centerpiece: At Bottom of Contract Food Chain, Haulers Scramble for a Share," Associated Press, October 23, 2005, http://www.lexisnexis.com (accessed November 11, 2008).

24. Ibid.

25. Gordon Russell and James Varney, "From Blue Tarps to Debris Removal, Layers of Contractors Drive Up the Cost of Recovery, Critics Say," *Times-Picayune* (New Orleans), December 29, 2005, National Section, 1.

26. Hope Yen, "Katrina's Big Contracts Go to Companies in Political Loop," Associated Press, October 19, 2005; and Hope Yen, "A Month After Pledge, FEMA Has Yet To Reopen No-Bid," Associated Press, November 11, 2005, http://www.lexisnexis.com (accessed November 8, 2008).

27. Renae Merle and Griff Witte, "Katrina Recovery Officials Unsure What's Been Spent; Lack of Detail Irks House Panel Members," *Washington Post*, November 3, 2005, D-1.

28. Associated Press report, no byline, "Army Corps to Require Contracts to Be Awarded to Miss. Companies," Associated Press State and Local Wire, December 28, 2005, http://www.lexisnexis.com (accessed April 10, 2010).

29. Hope Yen, "Political Ties Are Linked To Contracts," *Sun Herald* (Biloxi-Gulfport), October 20, 2005, B-6 and B-10.

30. Adam Geller, "AP Centerpiece: At Bottom of Contract Food Chain, Haulers Scramble for a Share," Associated Press State and Local Wire, October 21, 2005, http://www.lexisnexis.com (accessed April 10, 2010).

31. Leslie Eaton, "After Hurricanes Come Tempests Over Cleanups," *New York Times*, February 24, 2006, A-1; and "Corps Cancels Necaise's New Mississippi Debris Contract," Associated Press, undated copy posted at Construction Equipment Guide.Com., http://www.constructionequipmentguide.com (accessed June 4, 2009).

32. Debbie Burt Meyers, "William Yates Discusses Company's Role During, After Katrina," *Neshoba Democrat* (Mississippi), October 25, 2006, 2, http://www.neshobademocrat.com (accessed May 31, 2008); Michael Newsom, "Cleanup Moves to Private Property," *Sun Herald* (Biloxi-Gulfport), September 15, 2005; "Shallow Waters Show Debris Lining Mississippi Coastal Beach, Associated Press State and Local Wire, November 23, 2005, http://www.lexisnexis.com (accessed June 4, 2009); and Michael Bell, "County Seeks Allies vs. FEMA, *Sun Herald* (Biloxi-Gulfport), November 28, 2007, A-6.

33. Eric Lipton, "On Gulf Coast, Cleanup Differs Town to Town," *New York Times*, December 26, 2005, National Desk, A-1.

34. Karen Nelson, "October 28 Deadline Nears On Trash Removal," *Sun Herald* (Biloxi-Gulfport), October 18, 2005, A-3; Karen Nelson and Geoff Pender, "Barbour Lobbies Washington On Trash, *Sun Herald* (Biloxi-Gulfport), October 19, 2005, A-9; and FEMA Press Release, "On-Going Debris Removal Mounts Up," October 22, 2005, release number 1604-088.

35. Ibid.

36. Ibid.

37. Ibid.

38. Renae Merle, "4 Firms Hired to Clear Debris in Gulf Coast," *Washington Post*, September 16, 2005, A-20.

39. Kevin McCoy, "Contracts for Recovery Work Raise Controversy," *USA Today*, September 15, 2005, 4-B.

40. Edward Epstein, "Peninsula Firm Wins Cleanup Contract; Environmental Chemical of Burlingame Could Collect $1 Billion During Next Two Years," *San Francisco Chronicle*, September 20, 2005, A-10.

41. Renae Merle, "4 Firms Hired to Clear Debris in Gulf Coast," *Washington Post*, September 16, 2005, A-20.

42. Edward Epstein, "Peninsula Firm Wins Cleanup Contract; Environmental Chemical of Burlingame Could Collect $1 Billion During Next Two Years," *San Francisco Chronicle*, September 20, 2005, A-10.

43. Eric Lipton and Ron Nixon, "Many Contractors for Storm Work Raise Questions," *New York Times*, September 26, 2005, A-1; and Hope Yen, "Katrina's Big Contracts Go To Companies in Political Loop, *Associated Press Business News*, October 19, 2005, http://www.lexisnexis.com (accessed November 11, 2008).

44. Emily Wagster Pettus, "Barbour Cuts Ties With Lobbying Firm," Associated Press State and Local Wire, January 14, 2004, http://www.lexisnexis.com (accessed April 29, 2010).

45. Charlie Mitchell, "Is Barbour Profiting From Katrina?" *Sun Herald* (Biloxi-Gulfport), September 12, 2007, C-5.

46. Emily Wagster Pettus, "Miss. Governor Under Fire Over Holdings," Associated Press Online, October 4, 2007; and "Mississippi Governor Ready to Take Off?" *The Hotline*, September 28, 2007, http://www.lexisnexis.com (accessed April 29, 2010).

47. Tory Newmyer, "For Gov. Barbour, D.C. Ties Are Proving Vital," *Roll Call*, October 24, 2005, http://www.lexisnexis.com. (accessed October 31, 2008).

48. Eric Lipton and Ron Nixon, "Many Contractors for Storm Work Raise Questions," *New York Times*, September 26, 2005, A-1.

49. Editorial, "A Hurricane Of Peculation In the Gulf," *St. Louis Post-Dispatch*, September 28, 2005, B-8.

50. Tom Engelhardt and Nick Turse, "The Reconstruction of New Iraq," Thenation.com, September 13, 2005, reprinted in Betsy Reed et al., *Unnatural Disaster: The Nation on Hurricane Katrina* (New York: Basic Books, 2006), 100–106.

51. Hope Yen, "Katrina's Big Contracts Go To Companies In the Political Loop," Associated Press, October 19, 2005, http://www.lexisnexis.com (accessed April 10, 2010).

52. Edward Epstein, "FEMA Plans To Reopen $1.5 Billion in No-Bid Contracts," *San Francisco Chronicle*, October 7, 2005, A-6.

53. Lara Jakes Jordan, "FEMA Pledges to Reassess Contracts Awarded Without Competitive Bidding," *Associated Press Business News*, October 6, 2005, http://www.lexisnexis.com (accessed November 8, 2008).

54. FEMA News Release, "Another Milestone in Recovery: FEMA Completed Marine Debris Operations In Harrison, Hancock Counties," March 9, 2009, release number 1604-704.

55. "FEMA Assistance," *Mobile Register*, January 4, 2010, A-4.

56. Marlin Ladner, interview by James Pat Smith, June 24, 2008 (USM KOH).

57. Vincent Creel, interview by James Pat Smith, March 19, 2008 (USM KOH).

58. Ibid.

59. Mayor A. J. Holloway, interview by Stephen Sloan, January 18, 2007 (USM KOH).

60. Ibid.

61. Michael Kunzelman, "Coastal Counties Complain About FEMA," Associated Press Online, May 7, 2007, http://www.lexisnexis.com (accessed April 13, 2009).

62. Constance "Connie" Rockco, interview by James Pat Smith, June 23, 2008 (USM KOH).

63. Ibid.

64. Ibid.; and Marlin Ladner, interview by James Pat Smith, June 24, 2008 (USM KOH).

65. Michael Kunzelman, "Coastal Communities Complain About FEMA," Associated Press Online, May 7, 2007, http://lexisnexis.com (accessed April 13, 2009).

66. Ibid.; and Michael A. Bell, "County Appeals FEMA's Decision," *Sun Herald* (Biloxi-Gulfport), October 4, 2007, A-4.

67. Constance "Connie" Rockco, interview by James Pat Smith, June 23, 2008 (USM KOH).

68. Marlin Ladner, interview by James Pat Smith, June 24, 2008 (USM KOH).

69. Ibid.; Constance "Connie" Rockco, interview by James Pat Smith, June 23, 2008 (USM KOH); and Michael Kunzelman, "FEMA Won't Reimburse $12M, Debris Removal: Quality, Cost Doubted," *Sun Herald* (Biloxi-Gulfport), September 12, 2007, A-1 and A-8.

70. Ibid.; Michael A. Bell, "County Appeals FEMA's Decision," *Sun Herald* (Biloxi-Gulfport), October 4, 2007, A-4; and Michael A. Bell, "County Seeks Allies Vs. FEMA," *Sun Herald* (Biloxi-Gulfport), November 28, 2007, A-6.

71. Ibid.

72. Constance "Connie" Rockco, interview by James Pat Smith, June 23, 2008 (USM KOH).

73. Eric Lipton, "On Gulf Coast, Cleanup Differs Town To Town," *New York Times*, December 26, 2005, A-1.

74. Jim Johnson, "Much Work Remains in Katrina Cleanup," *Waste News,* September 11, 2006, 1; and Department of Homeland Security, "Hurricane Katrina Mississippi Recovery Update: November, 2008," http://www.lexisnexis.com (accessed April 10, 2010).

Chapter Six

1. Stan Tiner, editorial, "We're Still Standing," *Sun Herald* (Biloxi-Gulfport), September 2, 2005.

2. Corporation for National and Community Service, *National Service Responds: The Power of Help and Hope After Katrina* (Washington, D. C.: USA Freedom Corps, 2006).

3. Councilman William "Bill" Stallworth, interview by James Pat Smith, May 22, 2008 (USM KOH).

4. Ibid.

5. Ibid.

6. Federal Emergency Management Agency, "Hurricane Katrina by the Numbers: Four Years of Rebuilding a Better Mississippi," August 25, 2009, release number 1604-731; Quincy Collins Smith, "Healing Touch," *Sun Herald* (Biloxi-Gulfport), August 28, 2006, "The Volunteers Special Edition"; Corporation for National and Community Service, *National Service Responds: The Power of Help and Hope after Katrina* (Washington, D. C.: USA Freedom Corps, 2006); and *Sun Herald* (Biloxi-Gulfport), September 8, 2009, 2A.

7. Alise G. Bartley, "Confronting the Realities of Volunteering for a National Disaster," *Journal of Mental Health Counseling* 29 (January 2007): 4–6; and Wendy Frost, interview by Deanne Stephens Nuwer, October 22, 2005 (USM KOH).

8. Alise G. Bartley, "Confronting the Realities of Volunteering," 4–6.

9. Wendy Frost, interview by Deanne Stephens Nuwer, October 22, 2005 (USM KOH).

10. Councilman William "Bill" Stallworth, interview by James Pat Smith, May 22, 2008 (USM KOH).

11. Ibid.

12. Councilman George Lawrence, interview by Deanne Stephens Nuwer, July 13, 2010 (USM KOH).

13. Johan Jaffry, interview by Deanne Stephens Nuwer, April 19, 2009; and Valerie Fraser Luesse, "Faces of Hope," *Southern Living*, May 2006.

14. Corporation for National and Community Service, *National Service Responds: The Power of Help and Hope After Katrina* (Washington, D. C.: USA Freedom Corps, 2006).

15. Terry Tingle, interview by Deanne Stephens Nuwer, January 37, 2008 (USM KOH).

16. Robert Stacy McCain, "Legends of Mississippi: Nation's Poorest State Spreads Richness of Character," *Washington Times*, December 5, 2006, A2.

17. United States Government Accountability Office, *Hurricanes Katrina and Rita: Provision of Chartable Assistance*, written statement of Cynthia Fagnoni before the Subcommittee on Oversight, Committee on Ways and Means, House of Representatives, December 13, 2005, GAO-06-297T.

18. Megha Satyanarayana, "Qatari Emir Visits Coast: Sees His $100M Donation at Work," *Sun Herald* (Biloxi-Gulfport), May 1, 2008, A-2.

19. Anita Lee, "Charity, Volunteers Slowly Reviving Mississippi Coast," Associated Press State and Local Wire, August 27, 2007, LexisNexis Academic: Document, http://www.lexisnexis.com (accessed August 14, 2008).

20. Federal Emergency Management Agency, "Mississippi Recovery Update: August, 2007," August 29, 2007, release number 1604-591.

21. Stan Tiner, editorial, "Mississippi's Invisible Coast," *Sun Herald* (Biloxi-Gulfport), December 14, 2005, 1A.

22. Timothy H. Warneka, *Healing Katrina: Volunteering in Post-Hurricane Mississippi* (Cleveland, OH: Asogomi Publishing International, 2007), 30.

23. Judith Lowe, interview by Deanne Stephens Nuwer, October 20, 2005 (USM KOH). Lowe lived in Long Beach, Mississippi, prior to Hurricane Katrina. Before retiring, she worked as a full-time Red Cross employee in Washington, D.C. She was well suited to her role in Katrina.

24. Ibid.; Alise G. Bartley, "Confronting the Realities of Volunteering for a National Disaster," *Journal of Mental Health Counseling* 29 (January 2007): 4-6; and Wendy Frost, interview by Deanne Stephens Nuwer, October 22, 2005 (USM KOH).

25. Ibid.

26. Wendy Frost, interview by Deanne Stephens Nuwer, October 22, 2005 (USM KOH).

27. Ibid.

28. Stan Tiner, editorial, "Mississippi's Invisible Coast," *Sun Herald* (Biloxi-Gulfport), December 14, 2005, 1A.

29. "American Red Cross Response to Hurricane Katrina, Update 10," *Medical News Today*, September 9, 2005, http://www.medicalnewstoday.com/newsid=30401 (accessed November 18, 2008); and "Facts at a Glance—American Red Cross Response to Hurricanes Katrina and Rita," ReliefWeb, November 28, 2005, http://www.reliefweb.int/rw/RWB.NSF (accessed November 18, 2008).

30. Melissa Scallan, "Welcome Wagon," *Sun Herald* (Biloxi-Gulfport), September 1, 2005, 4.

31. Doug Barber and Mike Woten, "Red Cross Supply Truck a Welcome Sight," *Sun Herald* (Biloxi-Gulfport), August 31, 2005, Special Edition, 17.

32. "Katrina Impact Is Unprecedented Says Salvation Army Leader," *Medical News Today*, September 2, 2005, http://www.medicalnewstoday.com/newsid-30087 (accessed November 18, 2008); and Scott Dodd, "Help Us Now," *Sun Herald*, (Biloxi-Gulfport), September 1, 2005, 1 and 10.

33. "Important Information From Emergency Officials," *Sun Herald*, Sept. 3, 2005, Special Edition, 22.

34. Salvation Army Gulf Coast Command, http://www.uss.salvationarmy.org. (accessed Feb. 23, 2009); and "Salvation Army Distribution Centers," *Sun Herald*, January 1, 2006, A2.

35. Corporation for National and Community Service, "History, Legislation, and Budget," and Corporation for National and Community Service, *National Service Responds: The Power of Help and Hope after Katrina*, http://www.Americorps.org/about/ac/history.asp (accessed May 20, 2009).

36. Marcus J. Littles, "The Potential Role for Philanthropy in Mississippi's Long-Term Recovery," in *Envisioning a Better Mississippi: Hurricane Katrina and Mississippi One Year Later, A Report of the Mississippi State Conference of the National Association for the Advancement of Colored People*, ed. Roland V. Anglin, prepared by Rutgers University Initiative for Regional and Community Transformation (New Brunswick, N.J.: Rutgers University, Bloustein School of Planning and Public Policy, 2006), 51. See also Anita Lee, "Mississippi Sixth on List of Where Money Went," *Sun Herald* (Biloxi-Gulfport), August 28, 2007, C-8.

37. Corporation for National and Community Service, "National Service Agency Announces Three Grants to Bring Skilled Volunteers to Gulf Coast," http://www.nationalservice.gov/about/newsroom/releases_detail.asp?tbl-pr-id=715 (accessed April 19, 2009).

38. Steve Devane, "A Job Well Done: Dedicated Gulfport Volunteers Leave Lasting Impression," *Baptists Today*, March 2008, 36.

39. Eddie Williams, interview by Deanne Stephens Nuwer, January 4, 2006 (USM KOH).

40. Ibid.

41. Ibid.

42. Steve Devane, "A Job Well Done: Dedicated Gulfport Volunteers Leave Lasting Impression," *Baptists Today*, March 2008, 36.

43. Quoted in Ben Greenberg, "Gone to Mississippi: A Journey Along the State's Devastated Coast," *Dollars and Sense: The Magazine of Economic Justice*, March/April 2006, http://www.dollarsandsense.org/archives/2006/0306greenberg.html (accessed Sept. 7, 2009).

44. Martha Williams, interview by Rachel Swaykos, June 22, 2007 (USM KOH).

45. Steve Devane, "A Job Well Done: Dedicated Gulfport Volunteers Leave Lasting Impression," *Baptists Today*, March 2008, 36.

46. Ibid.

47. Ibid.; and Reverend Charles "Chuck" Register, interview by James Pat Smith, July 11, 2007 (USM KOH).

48. Mark Jones, interview by Rachel Swaykos, June 22, 2007 (USM KOH).

49. Ibid.; and Councilman George Lawrence, interview by Deanne Stephens Nuwer, July 13, 2010 (USM KOH).

50. Ibid.

51. Reverend Charles "Chuck" Register, interview by James Pat Smith, July 11, 2007 (USM KOH).

52. Mary Louise Coyne, interview by James Pat Smith, September 31, 2008 (USM KOH).

53. Father Sebastian Myladiyil, interview by Dariusz Grabka and Allana Tobia, February 21, 2008 (USM KOH).

54. Mary Louise Coyne, interview by James Pat Smith, September 31, 2008 (USM KOH).

55. Sister Rebecca Rutkowski, interview by Rachel Swaykos, June 12, 2007 (USM KOH).

56. Karen Nelson, "Help Keeps Coming," *Sun Herald* (Biloxi-Gulfport), August 29, 2007, A-8; and Bay St. Louis City Comptroller David Kolf, prepared statement for the community panel, Returning to Katrina Conference, University of Southern Mississippi, Long Beach, Mississippi, June 4, 2010.

57. Renee Skalij, "The Inside-Out Church," *Sun Herald* (Biloxi-Gulfport) October 17, 2008, B-1.

58. "Sustaining Survivors' Long-Term Recovery—United Methodists' Response to the Hurricanes of 2005," Relief Web, August 19, 2005, http://www.reliefweb.int (accessed August 18, 2009).

59. Rev. Zachery Beasley, interview by James Pat Smith, June 16, 2008 (USM KOH).

60. Rev. Lee Adams, interview by James Pat Smith, June 6, 2008 (USM KOH).

61. Sara Hamilton, interview by Rachel Swaykos, June 19, 2007 (USM KOH).

62. Mayor Leo "Chipper" McDermott, interview by James Pat Smith, March 14, 2008 (USM KOH).

63. Molly Seymore, interview by Rachel Swaykos, June 28, 2007 (USM KOH).

64. Mark Huseth, testimony before U.S. House of Representatives Committee on Transportion and Infrastructure Subcommittee on Economic Development, Public Buildings, and Emergency Management, July 18, 2008, *Congressional Quarterly*, http://www.lexisnexis.com (accessed June 16, 2009).

65. Peter Whoriskey, "Volunteers Fill in Gaps On Coast," *Sun Herald* (Biloxi-Gulfport), January 28, 2007, B7.

66. Karen Nelson, "Help Keeps Coming," *Sun Herald* (Biloxi-Gulfport), August 29, 2007, A-8.

67. Federal Emergency Management Agency, "Hurricane Katrina by the Numbers: Four Years of Rebuilding a Better Mississippi," news release August 25, 2009, release number 1604-731; Quincy Collins Smith, "Healingtouch," *Sun Herald*, August 28, 2006, "The Volunteers Special Edition"; Corporation for National and Community Service, *National Service Responds: The Power of Help and Hope after Katrina* (Washington, D. C.: USA Freedom Corps, 2006); and *Sun Herald*, September 8, 2009, 2A.

68. Melissa Scallan, "Volunteer Vacation," *Sun Herald* (Biloxi-Gulfport), March 26, 2007, A-1 and A-6.

69. Reilly Morse, interview by James Pat Smith, March 12, 2008 (USM KOH).

70. Ibid.

71. Ibid.; and John Jopling, "The Value of Philanthropic Research Efforts in Influencing Public Policy," Returning to Katrina Conference, University of Southern Mississippi, Long Beach, Mississippi, June 5, 2010.

72. Reilly Morse, interview by James Pat Smith, March 12, 2008 (USM KOH).

73. Ibid.

74. Ibid.

75. "Burning Man and Hurricane Katrina," Afterburn Report: 2005, http://www.afterburn.burningman.com/05 (accessed April 2, 2009).

76. Jim Puzzanghera, "Relief Efforts Slow to Reach Immigrants: Illegal Status, Lack of Translators Hamper Delivery," *San Jose Mercury News* (California), September 30, 2005, A-3; Jacqueline L. Salmon, "Rebuilding Lives After Katrina: Group Focuses on Vietnamese," *Washington Post,* February 9, 2006, T-1; and Joshua Norman, "Boat People SOS Offers Aid Navigating Post-Storm Chaos," *Sun Herald* (Biloxi-Gulfport), July 21, 2006, http://www.lexisnexis.com (accessed July 3, 2009).

77. Editorial, "On the Good News Front: Bucks-Mont Samaritans to the Rescue," *Philadelphia Inquirer*, March 20, 2007, A-14.

78. Jay Hughes, "Playground Group Close to Its Goal," *Sun Herald* (Biloxi-Gulfport), February 28, 2008, A-3.

79. Doug Barber, "Humane Society Employees Work to Save Animals," *Sun Herald* (Biloxi-Gulfport), September 4, 2005, Special Edition, 19.

80. Humane Society of the United States, "National Disaster Animal Response Team: Volunteer Opportunities," http://www.hsus.org/hsus_field/hsus_disaster_center/volunteer_for_the_hsus_disaster_anim (accessed September. 6, 2009); and Nancy Marano, "Hurricane Katrina: The Faces of Animal Rescue," *Petroglyphs*, Winter 2006, http://www.petroglyphsnm.org/covers/katrina.html (accessed Sept. 6, 2009).

81. Laura Bevan, "HSUS Responds to Katrina," DentalPlans.com, September 6, 2005, http://www.dentalplans.com/articles/2034/hsus-responds-to-katrina.htm (accessed September 7, 2009). Bevan was appointed the incident commander with the HSUS National Disaster Animal Response Team headquartered in Jackson, Mississippi, within weeks after Hurricane Katrina struck Mississippi.

82. "Outreach After Katrina," *Carolina Public Health*, The University of North Carolina at Chapel Hill, March 24, 2006, http://www.sph.unc.edu/carolina_publix_health_magazine/outreach_after_katrina_6456_19 (accessed September 6, 2009).

83. Quoted in Allen and Linda Anderson, *Rescued: Saving Animals from Disaster: Life-changing Stories and Practical Suggestions* (Novato, CA: New World Library, 2006), 17. See also Susan Moyer, *Hurricane Katrina: Stories of Rescue, Recovery, and Rebuilding in the Eye of the Storm* (New York: Spotlight Press, 2005).

84. Rita Duffus, letter to the editor, *Sun Herald* (Biloxi-Gulfport), November 19, 2007, B-2.

85. Mary Ashlyn Alderman, interview by Deanne Stephens Nuwer, November 12, 2008 (USM KOH).

86. Martha Williams, interview by Rachel Swaykos, June 22, 2007 (USM KOH).

87. Rod Dickson-Rishel, interview by James Pat Smith, June 16, 2008 (USM KOH).

88. Rene Rosencrantz, "Gulf Coast Mission Was 'Life-Changing,'" *Flint Journal* (Michigan), Flushing Observer Edition, March 19, 2006, F3.

89. Mark Jones, interview by Rachel Swaykos, June 22, 2007 (USM KOH).

Chapter Seven

1. Brian W. Sanderson, written testimony, Hearing of the U.S. House of Representatives Financial Services Committee, Subcommittee on Housing and Community Opportunity, February 22, 2007.

2. Governor Haley Barbour, written testimony, *Hearing Before the U.S. Senate Homeland Security and Governmental Affairs Committee*, Subcommittee on Disaster Recovery, May 20, 2009.

3. American Red Cross, "Disaster Operations Summary Report," September 27, 2005; Mark Bernstein et al., *Rebuilding Housing Along the Mississippi Coast: Ideas for Ensuring an Adequate Supply of Affordable Housing*, Rand Gulf States Policy Institute Occasional Paper (Santa Monica, CA: Rand Corporation, 2006), xi; Mississippi Renewal Forum, "Three Years After Katrina: A Special Report," http://www.mississippirenewal.com/index.html (accessed November 4, 2008); U.S. Department of Homeland Security, Office of the Federal Coordinator for Gulf Coast Rebuilding, *Current Housing Unit Estimates, Hurricanes Katrina, Rita, and Wilma*, February 12, 2006, 12; the University of Southern Mississippi Bureau of Business and Economic Research, "The Impact of Hurricane Katrina on South Mississippi," 2007, 10; the Compass Group, LLC, and Southern Mississippi Planning and Development District, *Mississippi Housing Data Project Detailed Report: Mississippi Gulf Coast*, January 30, 2009, 60; and the Compass Group, LLC, and Southern Mississippi Planning and Development District, *Mississippi Housing Data Project June 2009 Update: Mississippi Gulf Coast*,1 and 5, http://www.smpdd.com/data-center/mississippi-housing-data-project.htma (accessed July 18, 2009).

4. Federal Emergency Management Agency, "Hurricane Katrina Mississippi Recovery Update: September 2008," October 8, 2008, release number 1604-681.

5. In the one-year anniversary summary of its programs, FEMA reported that it had provided 48,000 travel trailers and mobile homes to Mississippi residents. Extrapolations from other FEMA reports indicate that occupancy rates hovered at or above 2.7 people per unit from December of 2005 through May of 2006. A figure of 2.7 persons per unit multiplied by 48,000 units deployed gives a total of 129,600 people who spent some time in temporary housing. This does not account for victims given rent vouchers or put up in hotel rooms who never lived in a FEMA trailer or camper. See Federal Emergency Management Administration, "Hurricane Katrina: One Year Anniversary Mississippi by the Numbers," August 17, 2006, release number 1604-424; FEMA, "Weekly Response Update for Mississippi," December 22, 2005, release number 1604-187; ibid., January 27, 2006, release number 1604-230; and FEMA Hurricane Recovery Updates: Week 25 and Week 37, February 27 and May 29, 2006, release numbers 1604-259 and 1604-356.

6. Federal Emergency Management Agency, "Current Housing Unit Damage Estimates, Hurricanes Katrina, Rita, and Wilma," February 12, 2006.

7. U.S. Government Accountability Office, "Federal Assistance for Permanent Housing Primarily Benefitted Homeowners; Opportunities Exist to Better Target Rental Housing Needs," January 14, 2010, GAO-10-17, 13.

8. Laura Clare Thompson Creel, interview by James Pat Smith, May 19, 2008 (USM KOH).

9. Ibid.

10. Ibid.

11. Ibid.

12. Ibid.

13. Constance "Connie" Rockco, interview by James Pat Smith, June 23, 2008 (USM KOH).

14. Kay Kell, interview by Stephen Sloan, January 11, 2007 (USM KOH).

15. Jonathan Weisman, "$236 Million Cruise Ship Deal Criticized," *Washington Post*, September 28, 2005, A-1.

16. Carolyn Said, "Oil Giant to Open Mississippi Tent City for Workers," *San Francisco Chronicle*, September 2, 2005, C-1.

17. No byline, "Pascagoula FEMA Trailers Down from 7000 to 850," Associated Press State and Local Wire, December 6, 2007, http://www.lexisnexis.com (accessed November 19, 2008).

18. Ibid.

19. Eric Lipton, "In Mississippi, Canvas Cities Rise Amid Hurricane's Rubble," *New York Times*, December 20, 2005, A-28.

20. Vicky Taylor, "Seabees Aid in Hurricane Cleanup," *Public Opinion* (Chambersburg, PA), December 13, 2005, 3; Colleen McCain Nelson, "Bored and Weary, Evacuees in Tent City Look for a Way Out: Months After Katrina, Many Still Waiting for Trailers in Mississippi," *Dallas Morning News*, January 22, 2006, 1-A; Colleen McCain Nelson, "Tent City Evacuees Look for Way Out," *Dallas Morning News*, January 25, 2006, 2-B; and Eric Lipton, "In Mississippi, Canvas Cities Rise Amid Hurricane's Rubble," *New York Times*, December 20, 2005, A-28.

21. Eric Lipton, "In Mississippi, Canvas Cities Rise Amid Hurricane's Rubble," *New York Times*, December 20, 2005, A-28.

22. Patrick Jonsson, "Tent Cities Spur Frustration on Gulf Coast," *Christian Science Monitor*, April 11, 2006, 3.

23. Constance "Connie" Rockco, interview by James Pat Smith, June 23, 2008 (USM KOH).

24. Joy E. Stodghill, "FEMA: Trailers Coming Slowly, But Surely" (from *The Mississippi Press*, Pascagoula), Associated Press State and Local Wire, October 28, 2005, http://www.lexisnexis.com (accessed November 11, 2008).

25. Patrick Jonsson, "Tent Cities Spur Frustration on Gulf Coast," *Christian Science Monitor*, April 11, 2006, 3; and Jonathan B. Hooks and Trisha B. Miller, "The Continuing Storm: How Disaster Recovery Excludes Those Most in Need," *California Western Law Review*, 43 (Fall 2006), 1–4, http://www.lexisnexis.com (accessed November 11, 2008).

26. Louise Perkins, interview by James Pat Smith, March 13, 2008 (USM KOH); and Elizabeth Marks Doolittle, interview by Rachel Swaykos, June 28, 2007 (USM KOH). For the first few weeks after the storm, the author worked with Ray Scurfield, a social work professor at USM, to keep university employees updated about housing options. On three separate occasions we were forced to call through our list of homeless employees to distribute the news that FEMA had lost the USM housing paperwork. FEMA's loss of paperwork was quite common in 2005. A number of university employees wound up housed in dormitory rooms at USM's Gulf Coast Research Lab in Ocean Springs.

27. Constance "Connie" Rockco, interview by James Pat Smith, June 23, 2008 (USM KOH).

28. Ibid.; and Marlin R. Ladner, interview by James Pat Smith, June 24, 2008 (USM KOH).

29. Ibid.

30. Joy E. Stodghill, "FEMA: Trailers Coming Slowly, But Surely" (from *The Mississippi Press*, Pascagoula), Associated Press State and Local Wire, October 28, 2005, http://www.lexisnexis.com (accessed November 11, 2008).

31. Anita Lee, "FEMA Teams to Tackle Long-Term Rebuilding," *Sun Herald* (Biloxi-Gulfport), November 23, 2005, A-12; and FEMA, "Weekly Response Update for Mississippi," December 22, 2005, release number 1604-187.

32. Elizabeth Marks Doolittle, interview by Rachel Swaykos, June 28, 2007 (USM KOH); and Elizabeth Marks Doolittle, *The Fabulous FEMA Females and Their Trailer Life*, unpublished memoir, 2007, University of Southern Mississippi Gulf Coast Library, 3–9.

33. Ibid.

34. Ibid.

35. Ibid.

36. Federal Emergency Management Agency, "Additional FEMA Temporary Sites Closing: More Information on Mississippi Hurricane Katrina," March 26, 2008, release number 1604-638.

37. Elizabeth Marks Doolittle, interview by Rachel Swaykos, June 28, 2007 (USM KOH).

38. Ibid.

39. Joy E. Stodghill, "FEMA: Trailers Coming Slowly, But Surely" (from *The Mississippi Press*, Pascagoula), Associated Press State and Local Wire, October 28, 2005, http://www.lexisnexis.com (accessed November 11, 2008).

40. Ray Scurfield, "Post-Katrina Storm Disorder and Recovery in South Mississippi Over Two Years Later," *Traumatology* 14 (June 2008), 101.

41. Laura Clare Thompson Creel, interview by James Pat Smith, May 19, 2008 (USM KOH); and Diane C. Peranich, interview by James Pat Smith, May 15, 2008 (USM KOH).

42. Elizabeth Marks Doolittle, interview by Rachel Swaykos, June 28, 2007 (USM KOH); Elizabeth Marks Doolittle, *The Fabulous FEMA Females and Their Trailer Life*, unpublished memoir, 2007, University of Southern Mississippi Gulf Coast Library, 26–32. Dr. Richard Tilley shared the anecdote about showering techniques.

43. Jeff Bennet, interview by Rachel Swaykos, June 4, 2007 (USM KOH); and Elizabeth Marks Doolittle, interview by Rachel Swaykos, June 28, 2007 (USM KOH).

44. David Abramson, Richard Garfield, and Irwin Redlener, *The Recovery Divide: Poverty and the Widening Gap Among Mississippi Children and Families Affected by Hurricane Katrina: A Report of the Mississippi Child and Family Health Study of Displaced and Impacted Families Living in Mississippi* (New York: Columbia University Mailman School of Public Health, 2007), 2–3; Joshua Norman, "Study: Displaced Are Suffering," *Sun Herald* (Biloxi-Gulfport), March 29, 2007, A-1; Kat Bergeron, "Study Shows Coast Still in Need of Help," *Sun Herald* (Biloxi-Gufport), February 3, 2007, A-2; Joshua Norman, "Mental Health on the Coast Making Strides: Children May Face A Long Road," *Sun Herald* (Biloxi-Gulfport), May 8, 2007, A-7; Steve Phillips, "Katrina Still Causing Mental Health Problems," *WLOX News* (Biloxi), August 1, 2008; and Jeff Bennet, interview by Rachel Swaykos, June 4, 2007 (USM KOH).

45. Jeff Bennet, interview by Rachel Swaykos, June 4, 2007 (USM KOH).

46. Frederik Tombar, written testimony, *Hearing of U.S. House of Representatives Transportation and Infrastructure Subcommittee on Economic Development, Public Buildings, and Emergency Management*, May 22, 2009.

47. Becky Gillette, "Dangers of Formaldehyde Have Been Known for Decades," *Sun Herald*, January 7, 2009, C-5; Amanda Spate, "Toxic Trailers," *The Nation*, article posted in full on *Sun Herald* Web site on February 22, 2007; David Paulison, oral statement, *Hearing on FEMA Trailers, U.S. House Committee on Oversight and Government Reform*, July 19, 2007;

Henry Falk, written testimony, U.S. House Committee on Homeland Security, January 29, 2008; and Megha Satyanarayana, "Trailers Unsafe CDC Says: Officials Suggest FEMA Move Residents by June 1," *Sun Herald* (Biloxi-Gulfport), March 4, 2008, A-1.

48. Mary Judice, "Katrina Unleashes Flood of Past-Due Mortgages: But Foreclosures in La., Miss. Are Fewer Than in the Past," *Times-Picayune* (New Orleans), March 15, 2006, Money, 1.

49. Rick Klein, "Gulf Coast's Rebuilding Bills Expose GOP Split," *Boston Globe*, September 22, 2005; Carl Hulse, "Louisiana Lawmakers Propose $250 Billion Recovery Package," *New York Times*, September 23, 2005, A-12; Michael Grunwald and Susan B. Glasser, "Louisiana Governor Presses for Hurricane Relief Aid," *National Post* (Canada), September 29, 2005, A-19.

50. Ibid.; and Shailagh Murray and Dan Morgan, "House GOP Leaders Propose Vote on Reductions in Spending," *Washington Post*, October 20, 2005, A-6.

51. Elana Schor, "Two Months After Katrina, Politics Tightens Purse Strings," *The Hill* (Washington, D.C.), November 2, 2005, 22.

52. Brian P. Nanos, "Shift FEMA Money to Gulf Coast Bush Asks: Mississippi Would Receive $6 Billion," *Sun Herald* (Biloxi-Gulfport), October 26, 2005, A-1; and Andrew Taylor, "White House Requests New Hurricane Relief Projects," Associated Press, October 28, 2005, http://lexisnexis.com (accessed November 8, 2008).

53. Brian Martin, interview by James Pat Smith, December 27, 2007 (USM KOH).

54. Taylor remarks, November 17, 2005, *Congressional Record—House*, H10543-44.

55. Terry M. Neal, "Hurricane Recovery: A Forgotten Priority?," *Washington Post*, November 30, 2005; editorial, "Waiting for Action," *Daily Journal* (Tupelo), November 28, 2005; editorial, "Whole State Baffled by Fed Inaction," *Clarion-Ledger* (Jackson), December 1, 2005, http://www.lexisnexis.com (accessed November 8, 2008).

56. Governor Haley Barbour, written testimony, *Hearing of the House Select Bipartisan Committee to Investigate the Preparation for and Response to Hurricane Katrina*, December 7, 2005.

57. Eric Lipton, "Leaders In Congress Agree on Aid for Gulf Recovery," *New York Times*, December 19, 2005, A-29; James Dao, "Using a Lobbyist's Pull From the Governor's Seat," *New York Times*, February 26, 2006, A-1; and Brian Martin, interview by James Pat Smith, December 27, 2007 (USM KOH).

58. Reilly Morse, interview by James Pat Smith, March 12, 2008 (USM KOH); and e-mail, Johnson, Bergmark, Morse, Evans et al., to Mississippi Development Authority, "Comments on Partial Action Plan for Katrina Homeowner Grant Program—Fair Housing Concerns and Absence of Basis to Seek Waiver of CBDG Low/Moderate-Income Targeting Requirements," March 17, 2006, 1–11.

59. Representative Diane C. Peranich, interview by James Pat Smith, May 15, 2008 (USM KOH).

60. E-mail, Johnson, Bergmark, Morse, Evans et al., to Mississippi Development Authority, "Comments on Partial Action Plan for Katrina Homeowner Grant Program—Fair Housing Concerns and Absence of Basis to Seek Waiver of CBDG Low/Moderate-Income Targeting Requirements," March 17, 2006, 1–11.

61. Reilly Morse, interview with James Pat Smith, March 12, 2008 (USM KOH).

62. Congressman Taylor to Governor Barbour, January 12, 2006, shared by Taylor's staff; Congressman Gene Taylor, interview by Dariuz Grabka and Alanna Tobia, February 21,

2008 (USM KOH); and Brian Martin, interview by James Pat Smith, December 27, 2007 (USM KOH).

63. Governor's Office, "HUD Approves Homeowner Assistance Program, Application Process Begins April 17," press release, April 4, 2006.

64. E-mail, Reilly Morse to James Pat Smith, May 20, 2008; and Reilly Morse, interview by James Pat Smith, March 12, 2008 (USM KOH).

65. Governor's Commission on Recovery, Rebuilding and Renewal, *Summary Report: Recommendations for Rebuilding the Gulf Coast*, November 2005, 11.

66. "Governor Barbour Taking Heat On Housing," *Clarion-Ledger* (Jackson), October 19, 2006.

67. Keith Burton, "Governor and HUD Secretary Announce New Components in Homeowner Grant Programs," GulfCoastNews.com, December 20, 2006, http://www.gulfcoastnews.com/GCNarchive/2006-2005/GCNnewsKatrinaHomeowner2ann (accessed August 3, 2009).

68. Mark A. Bernstein, Julie Kim, Paul Sorensen et al., *Rebuilding Along the Mississippi Coast: Ideas for Ensuring an Adequate Supply of Affordable Housing* (Santa Monica, CA: Rand Corporation, 2006), xv–xvi.

69. American Red Cross, "Disaster Operations Summary Report," September 27, 2005.

70. Federal Emergency Management Agency, "Current Housing Unit Damage Estimates, Hurricanes Katrina, Rita, and Wilma," February 12, 2006, 10–12 and 28–30.

71. Bureau of Business and Economic Research, University of Southern Mississippi, "The Impact of Hurricane Katrina on South Mississippi," Fall 2007, 10–11.

72. Jack Norris, written testimony, U.S. House of Representatives Committee on Financial Services, May 8, 2008, 5.

73. Reilly Morse, interview by James Pat Smith, March 12, 2008 (USM KOH); James Crowell, interview by James Pat Smith, May 28, 2008; and Bill Stallworth, interview by James Pat Smith, May 22, 2008 (USM KOH).

74. Editorial, "We Need Numbers About Housing That We Can Crunch," *Sun Herald* (Biloxi-Gulfport), December 19, 2007, C-4.

75. Steps Coalition press releases September 19, 2007, September 25, 2007, and September 28, 2007, available at http://www.stepscoalition.org/news/article (accessed October 23, 2008); editorial, "Mississippi's Misplaced Priorities," *New York Times*, June 26, 2008, A-22; "Congressional Leaders Attempt to Block HUD Money From Port of Gulfport," *Gulf Shipper*, July 7, 2008; and Shelia Byrd, "Miss. Residents Sue Over Katrina Housing Funds," Associated Press, December 10, 2008, http://www.lexisnexis.com (accessed November 30, 2009).

76. The Compass Group, LLC, and Southern Mississippi Planning and Development District, *Mississippi Housing Recovery Data Project*, January 30, 2009.

77. Mark A. Bernstein, Julie Kim, Paul Sorensen et al., *Rebuilding Along the Mississippi Coast: Ideas for Ensuring an Adequate Supply of Affordable Housing* (Santa Monica, CA: Rand Corporation, 2006), xiii–xiv.

78. United States Government Accountability Office, "Disaster Assistance: Federal Assistance for Permanent Housing Primarily Benefitted Homeowners; Opportunities Exist to Better Target Rental Housing Needs," January 2010, GAO-10-17, 27,32, and 44.

79. Shelia Byrd, "Mississippi Sends Out Homeowner Grants," Associated Press, August 28, 2006, http://www.lexisnexis.com (accessed August 14, 2008).

80. Federal Emergency Management Agency, "Current Housing Unit Damage Estimates Hurricanes Katrina, Rita, and Wilma," February 12, 2006, 12.

81. Natalie Chandler, "Legalities Slow Miss. Housing Grant Relief," Associated Press State and Local Wire, January 4, 2007, http://www.lexisnexis.com (accessed November 19, 2008).

82. Kathy Chu, "For Katrina Victims, Financial Pain Endures: Delays In Insurance Pay Outs, Grants Put Homeowners At Risk," *USA Today*, May 7, 2007, 1-A.

83. Reilly Morse, interview by James Pat Smith, March 12, 2008 (USM KOH).

84. Michael Schroeder, "Katrina Compensation Plan in Mississippi Is Criticized as Too Lax," *Wall Street Journal*, April 29, 2006, A-4.

85. Governor Haley Barbour, "Governor Barbour Updates Lawmakers On Recovery, Rebuilding and Renewal," press release, June 22, 2006.

86. Natalie Chandler, "Legalities Slow Miss. Housing Grant Relief," Associated Press State and Local Wire, January 4, 2007, http://www.lexisnexis.com (accessed November 19, 2008); Congressman Gene Taylor, statement, "Federal Housing Response to Hurricane Katrina," *Hearing of the U.S. House Committee On Financial Services*, February 6, 2006; and "HUD Official Denies Blame For Slow Housing Grants," Associated Press State and Local Wire, December 2, 2006, http://www.lexisnexis.com (accessed April 15, 2010).

87. Federal Emergency Management Agency, "Katrina Recovery Update: Week 69," release number 1604-496, December 21, 2006.

88. Stanley Gimot, acting director, Office of Block Grant Assistance, U.S. Department of Housing and Urban Development, written testimony, *Hearing of the U.S. House Financial Services Committee Subcommittee on Housing and Community Opportunity*, May 8, 2008; and Jack Norris, written testimony, *Hearing of the U.S. House Financial Services Committee Subcommittee on Housing and Community Opportunity*, May 8, 2008.

89. Norris testimony, May 8, 2008.

90. Ibid.

91. Ibid.

92. Ibid.

93. Federal Emergency Management Agency, "Current Housing Unit Damage Estimates, Hurricanes Katrina, Rita, and Wilma," February 12, 2006, 28–30. This total includes major damage or destruction of rentals from both wind and water.

94. Press Release, "Wayne Dowdy Statement On Hurricane Katrina Grant Program," Mississippi Democratic Party, June 19, 2007.

95. Melissa M. Scallan, "Rent Makes 40% Rise on Coast," *Sun Herald* (Biloxi-Gulfport), December 9, 2008, A-2; and Priscilla Frulla, "Average House Passes $180,000," *Sun Herald* (Biloxi-Gulfport), September 22, 2007.

96. Brian W. Sanderson, written testimony, U.S. House Financial Services Committee Subcommittee on Housing and Community Opportunity, February 23, 2007.

97. Priscilla Frulla, "Housing Chief Named: Davis Will Lead Renaissance Corp.," *Sun Herald* (Biloxi-Gulfport), February 7, 2007.

98. Tish H. Williams, written testimony, *Hearing of the Special Ad Hoc Katrina Recovery Committee of the U.S. House of Representatives Led by Speaker Nancy Pelosi*, Bay St. Louis, Mississippi, August 13, 2007.

99. Kevin F. McCarthy and Mark Hanson, "Post-Katrina Recovery of the Housing Market Along the Mississippi Gulf Coast" (Santa Monica, CA: Rand Corporation, 2007),

xiv–xvi; Priscilla Frulla, "Recovery Sqeeze: Low Income Renters Feel It, Katrina Housing Study Says," *Sun Herald,* September 28, 2007, C-7 and 10.

100. Federal Emergency Management Agency, "Hurricane Katrina Mississippi Recovery Update: July 2007," release number 1604-567, July 26, 2007.

101. Priscilla Frulla, "Group: Put Housing First," *Sun Herald* (Biloxi-Gulfport), September 19, 2007, B-10.

102. Editorial, "Housing Advocates Raise a $600 Million Question That Deserves An Answer," *Sun Herald* (Biloxi-Gulfport), September 23, 2007, C-2.

103. Michael Newsome, "Housing Money Diversion Denied. Barbour: Port Always in Plan," *Sun Herald* (Biloxi-Gulfport), October 10, 2007, A-1.

104. Secretary Alphonso Jackson to Governor Haley Barbour, January 25, 2008, electronic copy provided by Congressman Gene Taylor's staff.

105. Editorial, "Editorial Observations On Gov. Haley Barbour's Question-and-Answer Session With the Sun Herald," *Sun Herald* (Biloxi-Gulfport), February 24, 2008.

106. Reilly Morse, interview by James Pat Smith, March 12, 2008 (USM KOH).

107. Jimmie Bell, "South Mississippi Short About 40,000 Homes: New Apartment Complexes, Planned Communities Begin to Take Shape," *Journal of South Mississippi Business*, February 2008, 20-21.

108. "Barbour: $100M More for Housing, 76,000 Still Need Homes," *Sun Herald* (Biloxi-Gulfport), March 7, 2008, A-9; and Jack Norris, written testimony, *Hearing of the U.S. House Financial Services Committee Subcommittee on Housing and Community Opportunity*, May 8, 2008.

109. The Compass Group, LLC, and Southern Mississippi Planning and Development District, *Mississippi Housing Data Project: Detailed Report, Mississippi Gulf Coast*, January 2009, 3.

110. Federal Emergency Management Agency, "By The Numbers: FEMA/MEMA Mississippi Recovery Effort, Aug. 2008," release number 1604-670, August 25, 2008.

111. "Special Sun Herald Housing Editorial Board 07.24.08," summary available at the Web site of the Mississippi Renewal Forum, http://www.mississippirenewal.com (accessed November 4, 2008).

112. Editorial, "Coast Needs a Czar To Correct the Course of Its Recovery," *Sun Herald* (Biloxi-Gulfport), August 17, 2008, B-8; Karen Nelson, "Governor Likes Idea of Housing Czar: Coalition Suggests A Local Should Head Effort," *Sun Herald* (Biloxi-Gulfport), August 15, 2008; and "Blessey to Work On Miss. Coast Housing Recovery," Associated Press State and Local Wire, August 28, 2008, http://www.lexisnexis.com (accessed April 13, 2010).

113. Anita Lee, "MDA Moves More Money To Housing," *Sun Herald* (Biloxi-Gulfport), September 4, 2008, A-7.

114. "MDA To Close Housing Program: 26,900 Grants Awarded," *Sun Herald* (Biloxi-Gulfport), C-8.

115. Mary Perez, "Housing Czar Blessey Plans Meetings," *Sun Herald* (Biloxi-Gulfport), October 16, 2008, B-10.

116. Reilly Morse, "Community Resilience and the Legal System: Has Mississippi Turned the Corner?," paper delivered at the Returning to Katrina Conference, University of Southern Mississippi Gulf Park Campus, June 4, 2010.

117. Editorial, "Coast Needs a Czar To Correct the Course of Its Recovery," *Sun Herald* (Biloxi-Gulfport), August 17, 2008, B-8.

118. "Special Sun Herald Housing Editorial Board 07.24.08," July 24, 2008, summary available at the Web site of the Mississippi Renewal Forum; and John C. "Clark" Griffith, interview by James Pat Smith, June 25, 2007 (USM KOH).

119. Ryan LaFontaine, "Leaders Accused of Income Discrimination," *Sun Herald* (Biloxi-Gulfport), April 2, 2007, A-8; and Ryan LaFontaine, "Housing Authority Suing the City Over Tax-Credit Denials," *Sun Herald* (Biloxi-Gulfport), June 21, 2008, A-3.

120. Governor Haley Barbour, written testimony, *Disaster Recovery Subcommittee of the U.S. Senate Homeland Security and Governmental Affairs Committee*, May 20, 2009.

121. Governor Haley Barbour, written testimony, *Hearing of the Ad Hoc Subcommittee on Disaster Recovery of the U.S. Senate Committee on Homeland Security and Governmental Affairs*, May 20, 2009.

122. Anita Lee, "One Last Chance for Recovery," *Sun Herald* (Biloxi-Gulfport), November 14, 2010, A-1 and A-13; and Anita Lee, "Housing Help Coming for Katrina's Neediest Survivors," *Sun Herald* (Biloxi-Gulfport), November 16, 2010, A-1 and A-4.

123. Anita Lee, "One Last Chance for Recovery," *Sun Herald* (Biloxi-Gulfport), November 14, 2010, A-13.

124. Anita Lee, "Housing Help Coming for Katrina's Neediest Survivors," *Sun Herald* (Biloxi-Gulfport), November 16, 2010, A-1 and A-4; and Shaun Donovan, interview by Doug Walker, WLOX-TV, November 15, 2010, http://www.wlox.com (accessed November 17, 2010).

125. Ibid.

126. Editorial, "For Katrina Victims, Relief at Last," *New York Times*, November 17, 2010, A-32; and editorial, "A Fine Final Effort to Meet Housing Needs," *Sun Herald* (Biloxi-Gulfport), B-8.

Chapter Eight

1. Rucks Robinson, interview by Rachel Swaykos, June 4, 2007 (USM KOH).

2. Glen East, interview by Rachel Swaykos, May 30, 2007 (USM KOH).

3. Mississippi Department of Education, "Hurricane Katrina Public School Facility/Operational Impact," news release, September 20, 2005, http://www.mde.k12.ms.us/Extrel/news/05advisory9_20_05.html (accessed July 21, 2009); Melissa Scallan, "Schools Work Together To Get Ready For Classes," *Sun Herald* (Biloxi-Gulfport), September 15, 2005, A-7; Kim Stasny, interview by Rachel Swaykos, June 7, 2007 (USM KOH); Sue Matheson, interview by Rachel Swaykos, June 8, 2007 (USM KOH); Carolyn Reeves Hamilton, interview by Rachel Swaykos, June 5, 2007 (USM KOH); Glen East, interview by Rachel Swaykos, May 30, 2007 (USM KOH); Paul Tisdale, interview by Rachel Swaykos, May 31, 2007 (USM KOH); Henry Arledge, interview by Rachel Swaykos, May 31, 2007 (USM KOH); Robert Hirsch, interview by Rachel Swaykos, June 8, 2007 (USM KOH); Rucks Robinson, interview by Rachel Swaykos, June 4, 2007 (USM KOH); and Mark Ladner, interview by Rachel Swaykos, June 4, 2007 (USM KOH).

4. Mississippi Department of Education, "Hurricane Katrina Public School Facility/Operational Impact," news release, September 20, 2005, http://www.mde.k12.ms.us/Extrel/news/05advisory9_20_05.html (accessed July 21, 2009); Mark Ladner, interview by Rachel

Swaykos, June 4, 2007 (USM KOH); Steve Suitts et al., *Education After Katrina: Time for a New Federal Response* (Atlanta: Southern Regional Education Foundation, 2007), 15; and Evelyn Patricia Conner Joachim, interview by Rachel Swaykos, June 1, 2007 (USM KOH).

5. "Schools Welcome FEMA Aid, But Not Without Frustration," *Education Week*, vol. 44, no. 7 (October 12, 2005), 11.

6. Glen East, interview by Rachel Swaykos, May 30, 2007 (USM KOH).

7. David Abramson, Richard Garfield, and Irwin Redlener, *The Recovery Divide: Poverty and the Widening Gap Among Mississippi Children and Families Affected by Hurricane Katrina: A Report of the Mississippi Child and Family Health Study of Displaced and Impacted Families Living in Mississippi* (New York: Columbia University Mailman School of Public Health, 2007), 2–3; Joshua Norman, "Study: Displaced Children are Suffering," *Sun Herald* (Biloxi-Gulfport), October 29, 2007; Kat Bergeron, "Study Shows Coast Still in Need of Help," *Sun Herald* (Biloxi-Gufport), February 3, 2007; Joshua Norman, "Mental Health on the Coast Making Strides: Children May Face A Long Road," *Sun Herald* (Biloxi-Gulfport), May 8, 2007, A-7; Steve Phillips, "Katrina Still Causing Mental Health Problems," *WLOX-News* (Biloxi), August 1, 2008; and Jeff Bennet, interview by Rachel Swaykos, June 4, 2007 (USM KOH).

8. Glen East, interview by Rachel Swaykos, May 30, 2007 (USM KOH).

9. Mississippi Department of Education, "Hurricane Katrina Public School Facility/Operational Impact," news release, September 20, 2005, http://www.mde.k12.ms.us/Extrel/news/05Advisory9_20_05.html (accessed August 14, 2009).

10. Ibid.

11. Sue Matheson, interview by Rachel Swaykos, June 8, 2007 (USM KOH); and Kim Stasny, interview by Rachel Swaykos, June 7, 2007 (USM KOH).

12. Federal Emergency Management Agency Region VI news release, "Hurricane Katrina By The Numbers: Four Years Of Rebuilding A Better Mississippi," August 25, 2009.

13. Mississippi Emergency Management Agency, "Five Years After Katrina, Billions in Federal Assistance Has Helped Mississippians Recover and Rebuild Safer," news release, August 25, 2010.

14. Kim Stasny, interview by Rachel Swaykos, June 7, 2007 (USM KOH).

15. Ibid.

16. Ibid.

17. Ibid.

18. Ibid.

19. Ibid.

20. Ibid.

21. Ibid.

22. J. R. Welsh, "FEMA Funding For New Schools in Doubt," *Sun Herald* (Biloxi-Gulfport), July 10, 2007, A-1; J. R. Welsh, "$32.5M Bid Awarded to Build New Schools," *Sun Herald* (Biloxi-Gulfport), June 1, 2007; and Mark Ladner, interview by Rachel Swaykos, June 4, 2007 (USM KOH).

23. Kim Stasny, interview by Rachel Swaykos, June 8, 2007 (USM KOH).

24. Ibid.

25. Ibid.

26. Melissa Scallan, "Schools Work Together To Get Ready For Classes," *Sun Herald* (Biloxi-Gulfport), September 15, 2005, A-7; Kim Stasny, interview by Rachel Swaykos,

June 7, 2007 (USM KOH); Sue Matheson, interview by Rachel Swaykos, June 8, 2007 (USM KOH); Carolyn Reeves Hamilton, interview by Rachel Swaykos, June 5, 2007 (USM KOH); Glen East, interview by Rachel Swaykos, May 30, 2007 (USM KOH); Paul Tisdale, interview by Rachel Swaykos, May 31, 2007 (USM KOH); Henry Arledge, interview by Rachel Swaykos, May 31, 2007 (USM KOH)); Robert Hirsch, interview by Rachel Swaykos, June 8, 2007 (USM KOH); and Rucks Robinson, interview by Rachel Swaykos, June 4, 2007 (USM KOH).

27. The University of Southern Mississippi Department of Marketing and Public Relations, *The University of Southern Mississippi One Year Post-Katrina: A Report of the University's Response and Recovery*, August 2006, 4–8; Dr. Shelby F. Thames, interview by David Tisdale, January 31, 2006 (USM KOH); and Evelyn Patricia Conner Joachim, interview by Rachel Swaykos, June 1, 2007 (USM KOH).

28. Bill Hawkins, statement at the Ghosts of Katrina Conference at the University of Southern Mississippi, Long Beach, June 5, 2005.

29. Melissa M. Scallan, "William Carey Unveils Plan for New Campus: School to be Built at Tradition," *Sun Herald* (Biloxi-Gulfport), November 14, 2007, B-10; Becky Gillette, "William Carey University, USM Gulf Coast Surge Back to Meet Student Needs," *Mississippi Business Journal* (Jackson), August 25, 2008; and "William Carey Reopens at New Campus," Associated Press State and Local Wire, July 31, 2009, http://www.lexisnexis.com (accessed August 30, 2009).

30. Peter Baker, "Bush Addresses Gulf Coast Graduates: At Mississippi College Commencement, President Praises Students' Resilience," *Washington Post*, May 12, 2006, A-9; Mississippi Gulf Coast Community College, "Enrollment Numbers Going Back Up At MGCCC," *In Touch*, September 2006, http://www.mgccc.edu/InTouch/September2006/IT0906 (accessed June 30, 2010); and Mississippi Gulf Coast Community College, *2009 President's Report*, 15, http://www.mgccc.edu.Documents/President/2009Pr (accessed June 30, 2010).

31. In the wake of Katrina, the author was assigned responsibility for overseeing and crafting the recovery of the teaching schedule for USM Gulf Coast. The University of Southern Mississippi Department of Marketing and Public Relations, *The University of Southern Mississippi One Year Post-Katrina: A Report of the University's Response and Recovery*, August 2006, 4–8; Dr. Shelby F. Thames, interview by David Tisdale, January 31, 2006 (USM KOH); and Evelyn Patricia Conner Joachim, interview by Rachel Swaykos, June 1, 2007 (USM KOH).

32. Ibid.

33. Ibid.; and Kay Kell, interview by Stephen Sloan, January 11, 2007 (USM KOH).

34. Ibid.

35. Kim Stasny, interview by Rachel Swaykos, June 7, 2007 (USM KOH); Sue Matheson, interview by Rachel Swaykos, June 8, 2007 (USM KOH); Carolyn Reeves Hamilton, interview by Rachel Swaykos, June 5, 2007 (USM KOH); and Henry Arledge, interview by Rachel Swaykos, May 31, 2007 (USM KOH).

36. Ibid.

37. Rucks Robinson, interview by Rachel Swaykos, June 4, 2007 (USM KOH).

38. Mike Ladner, interview by Rachel Swaykos, June 4, 2007 (USM KOH).

39. Rucks Robinson, interview by Rachel Swaykos, June 4, 2007 (USM KOH).

40. Ibid.; Glen East, interview by Rachel Swaykos, May 30, 2007 (USM KOH); and Carolyn Reeves Hamilton, interview by Rachel Swaykos, June 5, 2007 (USM KOH).

41. Peggy Sullivan, interview by James Pat Smith, May 31, 2008 (USM KOH); Carolyn Reeves Hamilton, interview by Rachel Swaykos, June 5, 2007 (USM KOH); and Henry Arledge, interview by Rachel Swaykos, May 31, 2007 (USM KOH).

42. Kim Stasny, interview by Rachel Swaykos, June 7, 2007 (USM KOH); and Sue Matheson, interview by Rachel Swaykos, June 8, 2007 (USM KOH).

43. Sue Matheson, interview by Rachel Swaykos, June 8, 2007 (USM KOH).

44. Shelia Byrd, "Congressional Delegation Pledges Aid During Tour of Katrina-Damaged Areas," Associated Press, August 14, 2007, http://www.lexisnexis.com (accessed August 30, 2009); Diane Peranich, interview by James Pat Smith, May 15, 2008 (USM KOH); and Albert E. Roughton, interview by James Pat Smith, May 28, 2008 (USM KOH).

45. Peggy Sullivan, interview by James Pat Smith, May 31, 2008 (USM KOH).

46. Ibid.

47. Robert Hirsch, interview by Rachel Swaykos, June 8, 2007 (USM KOH).

48. Peggy Sullivan, interview by James Pat Smith, May 31, 2008 (USM KOH).

49. Ibid.

50. Ms. Sullivan's Seventh Grade Students, *Katrina Poetry, D'Iberville Middle School* (D'Iberville, Mississippi: D'Iberville Middle School privately printed booklet, 2007).

51. Peggy Sullivan, interview by James Pat Smith, May 31, 2008 (USM KOH).

52. Sue Matheson, interview by Rachel Swaykos, June 8, 2007 (USM KOH).

53. Albert E. Roughton, interview by James Pat Smith, May 28, 2008 (USM KOH).

54. Ibid.; and Sue Matheson, interview by Rachel Swaykos, June 8, 2007 (USM KOH).

55. Kim Stasny, interview by Rachel Swaykos, June 7, 2007 (USM KOH); Sue Matheson, interview by Rachel Swaykos, June 8, 2007 (USM KOH); Carolyn Reeves Hamilton, interview by Rachel Swaykos, June 5, 2007 (USM KOH); Glen East, interview by Rachel Swaykos, May 30, 2007 (USM KOH); Paul Tisdale, interview by Rachel Swaykos, May 31, 2007 (USM KOH); Henry Arledge, interview by Rachel Swaykos, May 31, 2007 (USM KOH); Robert Hirsch, interview by Rachel Swaykos, June 8, 2007 (USM KOH); and Rucks Robinson, interview by Rachel Swaykos, June 4, 2007 (USM KOH).

56. Ibid.

57. David Abramson, Richard Garfield, and Irwin Redlener, *The Recovery Divide: Poverty and the Widening Gap Among Mississippi Children and Families Affected by Hurricane Katrina, A Report of the Mississippi Child and Family Health Study of Displaced and Impacted Families Living in Mississippi* (New York: Columbia University Mailman School of Public Health, 2007), 2–3; Joshua Norman, "Study: Displaced Are Suffering," *Sun Herald* (Biloxi-Gulfport), March 29, 2007; Kat Bergeron, "Study Shows Coast Still in Need of Help," *Sun Herald* (Biloxi-Gufport), February 3, 2007; Joshua Norman, "Mental Health on the Coast Making Strides: Children May Face A Long Road," *Sun Herald* (Biloxi-Gulfport), May 8, 2007, A-7; and Steve Phillips, "Katrina Still Causing Mental Health Problems," *WLOX News* (Biloxi), August 1, 2008.

58. Albert E. Roughton, interview by James Pat Smith, May 28, 2008 (USM KOH).

59. Schooldigger.com, "Mississippi High School Rankings 2005-2010" (based on data from the Mississippi Department of Education and the U.S. Department of Education), http://www.schooldigger.com/go/MS/schoolrank.aspx (accessed June 30, 2010).

60. Steve Suitts et al., *Education After Katrina: Time for a New Federal Response* (Atlanta: Southern Regional Education Foundation, 2007), 11.

61. PAK12.com, "Ethnicity Data, Pass Christian District," http://psk12.com/rating/USindivphp/SchID_307540 (accessed June 30, 2010).

62. Ibid.; and Melissa Scallan, "South Mississippi Schools Raise the Bar," *Sun Herald* (Biloxi-Gulfport), September 10, 2010, 1-A, 8-A, and 10-A.

63. Melissa M. Scallan, "Group Protests Closing of Blue Ribbon School," *Sun Herald* (Biloxi-Gulfport), September 11, 2010, 8-A.

64. Rucks Robinson, interview by Rachel Swaykos, June 4, 2007 (USM KOH).

Chapter Nine

1. Mayor Tommy Longo, written testimony, "Hearing of U.S. House of Representatives, Committee on Transportation and Infrastructure, Subcommittee on Economic Development, Public Buildings and Emergency Management, June 19, 2008," *Congressional Quarterly*, Congressional Testimony, http://www.lexisnexis.com (accessed June 16, 2009).

2. Kay Kell, interview by Stephen Sloan, January 11, 2007 (USM KOH).

3. Editorial, "Like Rocky, We Must Never Lose Sight of the Goal," *Sun Herald* (Biloxi-Gulfport), September 9, 2007, C-2.

4. J. R. Welsh, "Bush Gets an Earful: Pullman Tells It Like It Is," *Sun Herald* (Biloxi-Gulfport), September 6, 2007, A-2.

5. Editorial, "Like Rocky, We Must Never Lose Sight of the Goal," *Sun Herald* (Biloxi-Gulfport), September 9, 2007, C-2.

6. Federal Emergency Management Agency, "Five Years After Katrina, Billions in Federal Assistance Has Helped Mississippians Recover and Rebuild Safer," August 25, 2010, release number 1604-748.

7. J. R. Welsh, "Bush Gets an Earful: Pullman Tells It Like It Is," *Sun Herald* (Biloxi-Gulfport), September 6, 2007, A-2.

8. Brian Martin, interview by James Pat Smith, December 27, 2007 (USM KOH).

9. Ibid.

10. Ibid.

11. Ibid.

12. Ibid.

13. Jack W. Stark, FEMA Assistant Director for Gulf Coast Recovery, written testimony, U.S. House Transportation and Infrastructure Committee, Subcommittee on Economic Development, Public Buildings, and Emergency Management, February 25, 2009.

14. Brandon Parker, "Change in FEMA Program Sought," *Sun Herald* (Biloxi-Gulfport), July 11, 2007, A-7.

15. James Walke, director, FEMA Public Assistance Division, written testimony, *Hearing of the U.S. Senate Homeland Security and Governmental Affairs Committee, Subcommittee on Disaster Recovery*, July 10, 2007.

16. David Kolf, Bay St. Louis City Clerk, statement presented at the Returning to Katrina Conference at the University of Southern Mississippi, Gulf Park Campus, June 4, 2010; Sue Matheson, interview by Rachel Swaykos, June 8, 2007 (USM KOH); and Kim Stasny, interview by Rachel Swaykos, June 7, 2007 (USM KOH).

17. Mayor Tommy Longo, written testimony, U.S. House of Representatives, Committee on Transportation and Infrastructure, Subcommittee on Economic Development, Public Buildings and Emergency Management, June 19, 2008, *Congressional Quarterly*, Congressional Testimony, http://www.lexisnexis.com (accessed June 16, 2009).

18. Ibid.

19. Mike Womack, written testimony, U.S. House of Representatives, Committee on Transportation and Infrastructure, Subcommittee on Economic Development, Public Buildings and Emergency Management, June 19, 2008, *Congressional Quarterly*, Congressional Testimony, http://www.lexisnexis.com (accessed June 16, 2009).

20. U.S. Representative Gene Taylor, written testimony, *Hearing Before the U.S. House of Representatives, Committee on Transportation and Infrastructure, Subcommittee on Economic Development, Public Buildings and Emergency Management*, May 10, 2007; Brian Martin, interview by James Pat Smith, December 27, 2007 (USM KOH); and Stephen Peranich, interview by James Pat Smith, December 28, 2007 (USM KOH).

21. Ibid.

22. Ibid.

23. Ibid.

24. Ibid.

25. Ibid.

26. Mary Perez, "Bay-Waveland Schools Are Awarded $7 Million in Katrina Arbitration," *Sun Herald* (Biloxi-Gulfport), February 2, 2010, A-1 and A-5.

27. Shelia Byrd, "Congressional Delegation Pledges Aid During Tour of Katrina Damaged Areas," Associated Press, August 14, 2007, http://www.lexisnexis.com (accessed August 28, 2009).

28. J. R. Welsh, "Pearlington To Lose Charles Murphy School," *Sun Herald* (Biloxi-Gulfport), March 28, 2007, A-3; J. R. Welsh, "$32.5M Bid Awarded to Build Schools: Officials Want '08–'09 Opening," *Sun Herald* (Biloxi-Gulfport), June 1, 2007, A-6; and J. R. Welsh, "FEMA Funding For New Schools In Doubt," *Sun Herald* (Biloxi-Gulfport), July 10, 2007, A-1.

29. Billie Skellie, interview by James Pat Smith, March 19, 2008 (USM KOH).

30. Stephen Peranich, interview by James Pat Smith, December 28, 2007 (USM KOH).

31. Billie Skellie, interview by James Pat Smith, March 19, 2008 (USM KOH).

32. Ibid.

33. Ibid.

34. Brian McDonald, director of the Mississippi Office of Recovery and Renewal, written testimony, U.S. House of Representatives Homeland Security Committee, May 22, 2007, *Congressional Quarterly*, http://www.lexisnexis.com (accessed June 16, 2010).

35. Mayor Ray Nagin, written testimony, Disaster Recovery Subcommittee of the U.S. Senate Homeland Security and Governmental Affairs Committee, July 10, 2007, *Congressional Quarterly*, http://www.lexisnexis.com (accessed June 16, 2010).

36. Stanley Czerwinski, oral testimony, U.S. House of Representatives, Committee on Homeland Security, Subcommittee on Emergency Communications, Preparedness, and Response, March 3, 2009, *Congressional Quarterly*, http://www.lexisnexis.com (accessed June 16, 2010).

37. Nikki Wittner, "Expected Repair Funds Detailed: FEMA Should Reimburse $7M," *Sun Herald* (Biloxi-Gulfport), April 3, 2007, A-5; "County Waits For FEMA Money," *Sun Herald* (Biloxi- Gulfport), March 2, 2009, A-4; and Mary Perez, "D'Iberville Cuts Remain In Effect," *Sun Herald* (Biloxi-Gulfport), July 21, 2010, A-7.

38. Mayor Ray Nagin, written testimony, Disaster Recovery Subcommittee of the U.S. Senate Homeland Security and Governmental Affairs Committee, July 10, 2007, *Congressional Quarterly*, http://www.lexisnexis.com (accessed June 16, 2010).

39. Lisa Mclean, "New D'Iberville High School Dedicated," *Sun Herald* (Biloxi-Gulfport), March 16, 2009, A-3; Melissa M. Scallan, "Two High Schools Planned: D'Iberville, West Harrison Groundbreaking Set For Next Week," *Sun Herald* (Biloxi-Gulfport), June 16, 2007, A-3; Melissa M. Scallan, "A Moving Experience: D'Iberville High Will Be in a Whole New Place Soon," *Sun Herald* (Biloxi-Gulfport), February 17, 2009, A-1 and A-5; Elmer Mullins, "From the Principal: D'Iberville High Opens Today," *Sun Herald* (Biloxi-Gulfport), February 25, 2009, A-6 and A-7; and Melissa M. Scallan, "A Fresh Start: Lost Students, Staff Only Bumps For New School," *Sun Herald* (Biloxi-Gulfport), February 26, 2009, A-1.

40. Ibid.

41. Christopher Cooper, "In Katrina's Wake: Where Is the Money?" *Wall Street Journal*, January 29, 2007, reprinted in the *Sun Herald* (Biloxi-Gulfport), January 30, 2007, C-3.

42. Ibid.

43. Guy Taylor, "States Ranked As Most Corrupt: Mississippi Is Tops, Study Finds," *Washington Times*, January 19, 2004, A-6. The weekly Washington, D.C.-based newsletter *Corporate Crime Reporter* provided the basis for this story and also inspired a January 16, 2004, story by Matt Volz for the Associated Press State and Local Wire.

44. General Russel Honoré, statement to the author, September 7, 2010, on the occasion of his visit for a public lecture at the University of Southern Mississippi's Gulf Park Campus.

45. Christopher Cooper, "In Katrina's Wake: Where Is The Money?," *Wall Street Journal*, January 29, 2007, reprinted in the *Sun Herald* (Biloxi-Gulfport), January 30, 2007, C-3.

46. Editorial, "Unmatched Destruction," *New York Times*, February 13, 2007, A-22.

47. Representative Diane Peranich stated that more than one local official was warned not to complain and "not to criticize the king when . . . you're asking him for money." Diane C. Peranich, interview by James Pat Smith, May 15, 2008 (USM KOH).

48. *Title IV—Additional Hurricane Disaster Relief and Recovery, U.S. Troop Readiness, Veterans' Care, Katrina Recovery, and Iraq Accountability Appropriations Act of 2007*, Public Law 110-28, 110th Cong., 1st sess. (May 25, 2007), 47–48, U.S. Government Printing Office, http://www.gpo.gov/fdsys/pkg/PLAW-110publ28/html (accessed June 25, 2009).

49. Christopher Cooper, "In Katrina's Wake: Where Is The Money?," *Wall Street Journal*, January 29, 2007, reprinted in the *Sun Herald* (Biloxi-Gulfport), January 30, 2007, C3.

50. Mike Womack, written testimony, U.S. House of Representatives, Committee on Transportation and Infrastructure, Subcommittee on Economic Development, Public Buildings and Emergency Management, June 19, 2008, *Congressional Quarterly*, Congressional Testimony, http://www.lexisnexis.com (accessed June 16, 2009).

51. David Kolf, Bay St. Louis city clerk, statement presented at the Returning to Katrina Conference at the University of Southern Mississippi, Gulf Park Campus, June 4, 2010.

52. "MEMA Misspent Almost $18M, Say Auditors," *Sun Herald* (Biloxi-Gulfport), March 15, 2010, A-1.

53. Geoff Pender, "Legislature Questions MDA's Katrina Contracts," *Sun Herald* (Biloxi-Gulfport), September 23, 2010, A-1 and A-7.

54. Christopher Cooper, "In Katrina's Wake: Where Is The Money?," *Wall Street Journal*, January 29, 2007, reprinted in the *Sun Herald* (Biloxi-Gulfport), January 30, 2007, C-3.

55. Donald E. Powell, written testimony, U.S. House of Representatives Budget Committee, August 7, 2007, *Congressional Quarterly*, http://www.lexisnexis.com (accessed June 19, 2009).

56. Ryan LaFontaine, "CEO's Advice: 'Kill The Snake,'" *Sun Herald* (Biloxi-Gulfport), April 15, 2008, C-8.

57. Ibid.

58. Billie Skellie, interview by James Pat Smith, March 19, 2008 (USM KOH).

59. Robert Bass, interview by James Pat Smith, May 14, 2008 (USM KOH); and Diane C. Peranich, interview by James Pat Smith, May 15, 2008 (USM KOH).

60. Ibid.

61. Ibid.; and Melissa M. Scallan, "Board Begins Analyzing Sites For USM," *Sun Herald* (Biloxi-Gulfport), February 15, 2007, A-3.

62. Melissa M. Scallan, "Cross Creek Makes USM Cut: Land Will Be Site of Second Campus," *Sun Herald* (Biloxi-Gulfport), April 19, 2007, A-1; Melissa M. Scallan, "College Board Eyes New USM Land," *Sun Herald* (Biloxi-Gulfport), November 15, 2007, A-5; Melissa M. Scallan, "Search For USM Campus Land Done Quietly," *Sun Herald* (Biloxi-Gulfport), February 16, 2008, A-8; Melissa M. Scallan, "South Mississippi Rounds Learning Curve: William Carey, USM Plans In Motion," *Sun Herald* (Biloxi-Gulfport), April 7, 2008, A-1; and Melissa M. Scallan, "USM Tries to Fit Right In: Gathering Will Consider Possibilities," *Sun Herald* (Biloxi-Gulfport), May 19, 2008, A-1.

63. Diane C. Peranich, interview by James Pat Smith, May 15, 2008 (USM KOH).

64. Ibid.

65. Ibid.

66. Sean Reilly, "Storm Disputes On Slow Track," *Mobile Register* (Alabama), October 26, 2009, A-1; and "Panel Created For FEMA Disputes," *Sun Herald* (Biloxi-Gulfport), August 7, 2009, A-8.

67. Federal Emergency Management Agency, "Mississippi Recovery Efforts Five Years After Katrina," and "Rebuilding Lives, Revitalizing Communities: Mississippi Five Years After Katrina," news releases, August 23, 2010; Anita Lee, "FEMA Funding Disputes Going to Arbitration: Five Public Entities See More Money For Recovery," *Sun Herald* (Biloxi-Gulfport), December 3, 2009, A-1 and A-5; and Anita Lee, "MEMA: Arbitration Process for FEMA Disputes Working," *Sun Herald* (Biloxi-Gulfport), September 23, 2010, A-5.

68. Ibid.

69. USM Gulf Coast Vice President Frances Lucas, statement to the author, September 1, 2010.

70. Donald E. Powell, written testimony, U.S. House of Representatives Budget Committee, August 7, 2007, *Congressional Quarterly*, http://www.lexisnexis.com (accessed June 19, 2009).

71. J. R. Welsh, "Cities Eager for Debt Forgiveness," *Sun Herald* (Biloxi-Gulfport), April 6, 2009, A-1 and A-6; and Federal Emergency Management Agency, "Mississippi Recovery Efforts Five Years After Katrina," news release, August 23, 2010.

72. Buddy Zimmerman, statement presented at the Returning to Katrina Conference at the University of Southern Mississippi Gulf Park Campus, June 4, 2010.

73. Brian Martin, interview by James Pat Smith, December 27, 2007 (USM KOH); and Kim Stasny, interview by Rachel Swaykos, June 7, 2007 (USM KOH).

74. Melissa M. Scallan, "School Leader Headed for Oxford," *Sun Herald* (Biloxi-Gulfport), March 6, 2009, 3-A.

75. Melissa M. Scallan, "Five Vacant Seats: Katrina Takes Its Toll On Coast Mayors," *Sun Herald* (Biloxi-Gulfport), March 12, 2009, 1-A.

Chapter Ten

1. Emily Wagster Pettus, "Mammoth Rebuilding Effort From Katrina Alters Mississippi Politics," Associated Press State and Local Wire, September 12, 2005, http://www.lexisnexis.com (accessed August 14, 2008).

2. Quoted by correspondent Rick Lyman in the *New York Times*, September 28, 2005.

3. Mary Perez, "Margaritaville Sailing Away? Let's Hope Not," *Sun Herald* (Biloxi-Gulfport), June 12, 2009, http://www/lexisnexis.com (accessed December 16, 2009).

4. John C. "Clark" Griffith, interview by James Pat Smith, June 25, 2007 (USM KOH).

5. Coasts, Oceans, Ports, and Rivers Institute of the American Society of Civil Engineers, *Hurricane Katrina Damage Assessment: Louisiana, Alabama, and Mississippi Coasts*, ed. Stephen A. Curtis, P.E., 58–61.

6. Leigh Coleman, "Keesler Building 1,067 Homes," *Sun Herald* (Biloxi-Gulfport), March 31, 2007, A-2.

7. John C. "Clark" Griffith, interview by James Pat Smith, June 25, 2007 (USM KOH).

8. Ibid.

9. Ibid.

10. The author saw this broadcast on the day that he began mucking out the flooded house of a family member who had lost everything.

11. Emily Wagster Pettus, "Mammoth Rebuilding Effort From Katrina Alters Mississippi Politics," Associated Press State and Local Wire, September 12, 2005, http://www.lexisnexis.com (accessed August 14, 2008).

12. Steve Quin, "Mississippi Shipyard Toils to Restart While Searching for Employees," Associated Press, September 7, 2005, http://www.lexisnexis.com (accessed January 9, 2010).

13. E. Ray Walker, "Optimism Reborn On Mississippi's Gulf Coast," *Knight Ridder/Tribune*, October 24, 2005, http://www.lexisnexis.com (accessed April 10, 2010); and Alberto Ibarguen, "I Saw Something Bigger Than The Storm; I Saw The Spirit Of The People," *Sun Herald* (Biloxi-Gulfport), August 29, 2010, B-2.

14. Quoted by Emily Wagster Pettus, "Katrina Hands Mississippi Governor His Toughest Political Test," Associated Press State and Local Wire, September 3, 2005, https://www.lexisnexis.com (accessed September 24, 2008).

15. I Corinthians 13:13; and Mississippi Legislature, "Katrina Day of Remembrance," Senate Bill 2069, regular session, 2007.

16. Spencer S. Hsu, "In Mississippi, Katrina Yields Bitter Harvest; Farmers, Fishermen Are Storm's Forgotten Victims," *Washington Post*, March 12, 2006, A-3.

17. Julie Schmit and Elliot Blair Smith, "Katrina Turned Lush Forests Into Wastelands," *USA Today*, September 14, 2005, B-1.

18. U.S. Labor Department Bureau of Labor Statistics, "The Labor Market Impact of Hurricane Katrina," *Monthly Labor Review*, August 2006, 9; and Mississippi Department of Employment Security, *Annual Labor Force Report*, 2005 and 2006, 23, 24, and 30, available at http://www/mdes.state.ms.gov/Home/docs/LMI/Publications (accessed November 20, 2008, and December 20, 2010).

19. Yvonne Abraham, "Casino Workers Wary of Future," *Boston Globe*, September 10, 2008, A-12.

20. Ricky Mathews, interview by David Tisdale, August 25, 2006 (USM KOH).

21. Emily Wagster Pettus, "Mammoth Rebuilding Effort From Katrina Alters Mississippi Politics," Associated Press State and Local Wire, September 12, 2005, http://www.lexisnexis.com (accessed August 14, 2008).

22. Michael Newsom, "Air Force Does Keesler About-Face," *Sun Herald* (Biloxi-Gulfport), September 17, 2005, http://www.lexisnexis.com (accessed November 8, 2008).

23. City of Biloxi, *Biloxi General Market Analysis, 2008*, 19; and Maryann Pelland, "Mississippi Coast Is 'Blessed' With Military Presence," *Journal of South Mississippi Business*, October 2007, 21.

24. Gross casino revenues for calendar year 2004 for the entire state came to $2.777 billion, of which coast casinos produced $1.227 billion or 44.2 percent of the state total. Mississippi State Tax Commission Miscellaneous Tax Bureau (renamed Department of Revenue in 2010), "Casino Gross Gaming Revenues," 2004, and Mississippi State Tax Commission Miscellaneous Tax Bureau, "Tax Revenues from Gaming," fiscal year 2005, www.mstc.state.ms.us (accessed July 12, 2008).

25. These figures represent totals for Harrison and Hancock counties, the only coast counties where casinos were permitted and where almost 90 percent of the coast hospitality industry was concentrated. Mississippi Department of Employment Security, *Annual Labor Force Report*, 2005 and 2006, 23,24, and 30, http://www/mdes.state.ms.gov/Home/docs/LMI/Publications (accessed November 20, 2008, and December 20, 2010); and Mississippi Gaming Commission, *Directory of Current Operators*, July 2005–January 2006, http://mgc.state.ms.us/monthly-archives-year.html (accessed November 20, 2008, and December 12, 2010).

26. Jeff Bailey, "Casino Owners Look Toward Rebuilding," *New York Times*, August 31, 2005, C-5.

27. Howard Stutz, "Changes May Be Sought In Mississippi Gaming Law Before Rebuilding," *Las Vegas Review-Journal*, September 1, 2005, http://www.lexisnexis.com (accessed November 8, 2008).

28. Geoff Pender and Tom Wilemon, "Official: Loss of Casino Revenue Could 'Paralyze State,'" *Sun Herald* (Biloxi-Gulfport), September 1, 2005; and editorial, "Casinos Must be Convinced To Again Bet On South Mississippi," *Sun Herald* (Biloxi-Gulfport), September 2, 2005, http://lexisnexis.com (accessed November 8, 2008).

29. Ibid., Pender and Wilemon; Scott Cannon and Tom Wilemon, "Beau Says No, Casino Opposes Move to Land-Based Gambling," *Sun Herald*, September 13, 2005, D-6; Tom Wilemon, "Copa Casino Employees Disgruntled, Fired The Day The Hurricane Hit," *Sun Herald* (Biloxi-Gulfport), September 20,2005, http://lexisnexis.com (accessed November 8, 2008); Tom Wilemon, "Land Casinos To Be Proposed," *Sun Herald* (Biloxi-Gulfport), September 16, 2005, C-9; and Michael Bradford, "Casinos Consider Moving To Guard Against Storms," *Business Insurance*, September 26, 2005, 29.

30. Geoff Pender, "Special Session On Katrina Relief Set Sept. 27," *Sun Herald* (Biloxi-Gulfport), September 20, 2005, A-3.

31. "Barbour Calls Special Session On Katrina," *USA Today*, September 19, 2005, http://www.usatoday.com/news/nation/2005-09-19 (accessed December 3, 2009).

32. William H. Perkins, Jr., *The Baptist Record*, online edition, September 29, 2005, http://www.bpnews.net/bpnews (accessed November 8, 2008); and Bobby Harrison, "Some Say Issue of Land-Based Casinos Complex," *Northeast Mississippi Daily Journal* (Tupelo), September 23, 2005, http://www.lexisnexis.com (accessed November 8, 2008).

33. Rick Lyman, "Mississippi May Move Its Casinos Ashore," *New York Times*, September 28, 2005, http://www.nytimes.com/2005/09/28/business/28gamble.html (accessed November 8, 2008).

34. Ibid.

35. Geoff Pender, "House Passes Onshore Bill, Holds Breath," *Sun Herald* (Biloxi-Gulfport), October 2, 2005, A-8; and "Onshore Casino Bill Going to Mississippi Governor," Associated Press State and Local Wire, October 3, 2005, http://www.lexisnexis.com (accessed November 8, 2008).

36. Adam Goldman, "Mississippi Governor Signs Laws Allowing Casinos Devastated To Rebuild On Land," Associated Press State and Local Wire, October 17, 2005, http://www.lexisnexis.com (accessed November 8, 2008).

37. E. Michael Powers, "Relaxed Casino Siting Rules Prime Gulf Building Boom," *Architectural Record*, 194, no. 2 (February 1, 2006), 28.

38. Ricky Mathews, interview by David Tisdale, August 26, 2006 (USM KOH); Ricky Mathews, "Together, We'll Draw A Blueprint For Rebuilding," *Sun Herald* (Biloxi-Gulfport), B-5; and editorial from the *Delta Democrat Times* quoted in "What Others Are Saying About The Mississippi Renewal Forum," *Sun Herald*, October 14, 2005, A-4.

39. David Tortorano, "Hundreds Will Brainstorm For 6 Days," *Sun Herald* (Biloxi-Gulfport), October 13, 2005, A-1; Anita Lee, "The Recovery Process," *Sun Herald* (Biloxi-Gulfport), October 10, 2005, A-1; and Anita Lee, "Renewal On The Horizon, Forum Begins Wednesday On How To Rebuild 11 Coast Areas," *Sun Herald* (Biloxi-Gulfport), October 11, 2005, A-1.

40. Quincy C. Collins, "Team Wants To Capture Unique Style In Rebuilding: Experts Stress Importance of Maintaining Coast's History," *Sun Herald* (Biloxi-Gulfport), October 12, 2005, A-4.

41. The Mississippi Renewal Forum, *Mississippi Renewal Forum—Summary Report*, November 2005, 2–4.

42. Gavin Smith, interview by Linda Van Zandt, January 10, 2007 (USM KOH).

43. Judy Stark, "The House That Katrina Built," *St. Petersburg Times* (Florida), January 28, 2006, 1-F.

44. Mark Bernstein et al., *After Katrina: Building Back Better Than Ever: A Report to the Honorable Haley Barbour, Governor of Mississippi, from the Governor's Commission on Recovery, Rebuilding and Renewal* (Jackson, MS: Mississippi Governor's Commission on Recovery, Rebuilding and Renewal, 2005), 1–178 with itemized list of recommendations on pages 165–178; see also "Commission Report Recommendations," *Sun Herald* (Biloxi-Gulfport) January 12, 2006, Section A.

45. Geoff Pender, "It's OK to Dream of Doing It Right," *Sun Herald* (Biloxi-Gulfport), October 23, 2005, A-12.

46. Dick Polman, "Two Steps Forward, One Step Back, A Report To The Knight Foundation," June, 2008, 5–8, http://www.knightfoundation.org/news/stories_of_transformation (accessed August 18, 2008).

47. David Tortorano, "We Are Looking For Big Ideas: Developers Urged To Fashion A New Look," *Sun Herald* (Biloxi-Gulfport), October 19, 2005, A-1; and David Tortorano, "Rebuild Report Released Online: Flood Maps May Cause A Ruckus," *Sun Herald* (Biloxi-Gulfport), January 11, 2006, B-10.

48. Mississippi Department of Employment Security, *Annual Labor Force Report*, 2005–2010, 23, 24, and 30, available at http://www/mdes.state.ms.gov/Home/docs/LMI/Publications (accessed November 20, 2008, and December 20, 2010).

49. Amber Craig, "Refinery Named Top Big Business in the State," *The Mississippi Press* (Pascagoula), July 26, 2008, A-1 and A-12.

50. U.S. Department of the Interior Minerals Management Service News Release, "Impact Assessment of Offshore Facilities from Hurricanes Katrina and Rita," release number 3418, January 19, 2006; Melton Harris, interview by James Pat Smith, June 11, 2008 (USM KOH); and "Chevron Restarts Mississippi Refinery Closed by Katrina," Associated Press, October 13, 2005, http://www.lexisnexis.com (accessed November 8, 2008).

51. Jeffrey Sparshott, "Businesses Assess Harm, Start Fixes," *Washington Times*, September 9, 2005, A-1; Alex Veiga, "Defense Giant Northrop Cuts Outlook, Citing Hurricanes," Associated Press, October 10, 2005; and Holbrook Mohr, "Damages to Shipyard Exceeds $1 Billion, Northrop Grumman Official Says," Associated Press, November 8, 2005, http://www.lexisnexis.com (accessed November 8, 2008).

52. Steve Quinn, "Mississippi Shipyard Toils to Restart While Searching For Employees," Associated Press, September 7, 2005; and Northrop Grumman Media Advisory, "Update For Gulf Coast Employees," September 11, 2005, http://www.lexisnexis.com (accessed January 9, 2010).

53. Leslie Wayne, "Northrop Grumman Seeks $2 Billion to Fix Shipyards Hit by Hurricane," *New York Times*, November 17, 2005, C-2; Gary Holland, "Ingalls in Pascagoula," *Sun Herald* (Biloxi-Gulfport), May 5, 2006, A-10; and "Shipyards Recovering Quickly From Hurricane Katrina," Associated Press State and Local Wire, December 19, 2005, http://www.lexisnexis.com (accessed November 19, 2008).

54. Loren C. Scott, *Advancing in the Aftermath of Katrina II: Tracking the Recovery from Katrina and Rita*, summary and results published on *Business Wire*, June 16, 2006, http://www.lexisnexis.com (accessed January 9, 2010); and Chad Calder, "Industrial Expansion Vital for Recovery: N.O., Gulfport Slower to Rebound Than Other Areas," *The Advocate* (Baton Rouge), June 22, 2006, D-1.

55. Veto F. Rolley, "Chevron Expansion: Chevron Announces $500 Million Project," *The Mississippi Press* (Pascagoula), October 16, 2007, A-1; and Karen Nelson, "Chevron Expanding Again: Pascagoula Pumped Up About Base Oil," *Sun Herald* (Biloxi-Gulfport), August 22, 2008, C-10.

56. Observation by LSU economist Loren C. Scott reported in "Gulf Coast Economic Recovery Remains Mixed," *Business Wire*, October 9, 2006, http://www.lexisnexis.com (accessed July 24, 2010).

57. Geoff Pender and Tom Wilemon, "Mississippi Economy Hit Hard by Casino Losses," *Sun Herald*, September 1, 2005, http://www.lexisnexis.com (accessed December 10, 2009).

58. The authoritative R. L. Polk Motor Vehicle Resistration Survey showed that in 2004, a total of 26,003 new and used cars and trucks were registered for the first time in the three Mississippi Gulf Coast counties. In the twelve months following Katrina the number skyrocketed to 81,249. The difference of 55,246 between these pre- and post-Katrina numbers provides a rough estimate of the number of vehicles Katrina destroyed in Mississippi.

59. Erin Robinson, "Dealing With the Winds of Change," *Automotive News*, August 28, 2006, 6.

60. Lisa M. Krieger, "Down on the Farm Despair: Loss of Power Hurt Dairy Farmers," *Sun Herald* (Biloxi-Gulfport), September 17, 2005, B-10.

61. Federal Emergency Management Agency, "Mississippi Fishermen Get, Give Help to Stay Afloat," August 8, 2007, release number 1604-569.

62. Megha Satyanarayana, "Long, Steep Climb: Recovery Especially Tough for Coast Vietnamese," *Sun Herald* (Biloxi-Gulfport), September 30, 2007, A-1 and A-17.

63. Sue Nguyen-Brown, interview by Deanne Stephens Nuwer, January 8, 2006 (USM KOH); and Amy Worden, "Scattered Immigrant Community Poised to Change Again, *Philadelphia Inquirer*, August 28, 2006, http://www.lexisnexis.com (accessed July 7, 2010).

64. Charles (Chuck) B. Benvenutti, interview by James Pat Smith, February 13, 2008 (USM KOH)

65. Ibid.

66. Ibid.

67. Ibid.; Tish Haas Williams, written statement, "Testimony to Members of Congress," Town Hall Meeting, Bay St. Louis, Mississippi, August 13, 2007; Shelia Byrd, "High Rates Keep Habitat Homes Unoccupied," *Sun Herald* (Biloxi-Gulfport), November 18, 2008, A-1; Rick Jervis, "Habitat Homes Going Empty in Mississippi: Soaring Insurance Rates Keep Houses Out of Reach," *USA Today*, November 25, 2008; and Jay Hughes, "Insurance Costs Hurt Residents: Many Could Leave Coast," *Sun Herald* (Biloxi-Gulfport), March 30, 2008, A-8.

68. Jack Norris, written testimony, *Hearing Before the Committee on Financial Services, U.S. House of Representatives*, May 8, 2008.

69. Ibid.; and Tish Haas Williams, "Testimony to Members of Congress," Town Hall Meeting, Bay St. Louis, Mississippi, August 13, 2007.

70. Anita Lee, "State Farm Suspends New Policies in Mississippi," *Sun Herald* (Biloxi-Gulfport), February 15, 2007; A-1; Anita Lee, "Wind Coverage a Moving Target, Almost No Major Insurers Offer It," *Sun Herald* (Biloxi-Gulfport), June 7, 2007, A-6; Anita Lee, "The Perfect Insurance Storm," *Sun Herald* (Biloxi-Gulfport), February 18, 2007, A-1; editorial, "The Good Neighbor Policy: Punishing Mississippi," *Sun Herald* (Biloxi-Gulfport), February 18, 2007, A-1; Anita Lee, "No Carriers Will Cover New Customers," *Sun Herald* (Biloxi-Gulfport), February 14, 2008, http://www.lexisnexis.com (accessed March 4, 2009); and Anita Lee, "State Farm to Hike Rates About 13% and Drop Some Policy Holders," *Sun Herald* (Biloxi-Gulfport), June 12, 2008, A-1.

71. Leslie Wayne, "Northrop Grumman Seeks $2 Billion to Fix Shipyards Hit by Hurricane," *New York Times*, November 17, 2005, C-1; and Geoff Fein, "Northrop Grumman's Ingalls Shipyard Still 18 Months From Fully Recovering From Katrina," *Defense Daily* 231, no. 91 (November 14, 2006), http://www.lexisnexis.com (accessed January 9, 2010).

72. Kathy Chu, "State Farm Retreats In Gulf: Won't Offer New Policies in Miss.," *USA Today*, February 15, 2007, A-1; and Anita Lee, "Katrina Propels Insurance Factor, Costs Skyrocketed After the Storm," *Sun Herald* (Biloxi-Gulfport), August 19, 2007, B-4.

73. DeWayne Wickham, "Democrats Should Put Victims of Katrina Front and Center," *USA Today*, December 26, 2006, A-13. Pelosi visited in August of 2006 and August of 2007.

74. Gene Taylor, interview by Dariusz Grabka and Alanna Tobia, February 21, 2008 (USM KOH); Gene Taylor, "The Insurance Crisis: The Need for Immediate Reform," public lecture, University of Southern Mississippi Gulf Coast, February 29, 2008; Brian Martin, interview by James Pat Smith, December 27, 2007 (USM KOH); editorial, "Opponents of

Multi-Peril Insurance Offer No Alternative for Storm Victims," and "Representative Gene Taylor's Response To the Chamber's Letter," *Sun Herald* (Biloxi-Gulfport), August 15, 2010, B-8; Geoff Pender, "Insurance Industry Blocked Support for My Bill, Says Taylor," *Sun Herald* (Biloxi-Gulfport), September 11, 2010, A-4.

75. State Representative Brandon Jones, interview by Dave Elliot and Doug Walker, *WLOX Newswatch This Week*, December 18, 2010; "Lawmakers Discuss Upcoming Legislative Session," *Sun Herald* (Biloxi-Gulfport), December 12, 2010, A-1 and A-16; Gulf Coast Business Council Research Foundation, "The Critical Need for Wind Pool Funding: Mississippi Economic Impact Study," February 19, 2009; editorial, "Imagine Where Coast Would Be if Insurance Were Not a Problem," *Sun Herald* (Biloxi-Gulfport), April 30, 2009, B-2; and editorial, "How High Will Insurance Rates Be Allowed to Go?" *Sun Herald* (Biloxi-Gulfport), December 2, 2009, C-2.

76. J. R. Welsh, "FEMA Maps May Wipe Bay Off Map: Much of City Now in Hazard Zone," *Sun Herald* (Biloxi-Gulfport), January 27, 2008, A-3; J.R. Welsh, "Bay May Fight FEMA Maps: Others Dispute New Flood Zones," *Sun Herald* (Biloxi-Gulfport), February 3, 2008, A-8; J. R. Welsh, "Officials Resist Flood Elevations," *Sun Herald* (Biloxi-Gulfport), February 5, 2008, A-5; Jenny Jarvie, "Future of Pass Could Play Out At Treetop Level: They're Not Going to Run People Off the Water, Mayor Says," *Sun Herald* (Biloxi-Gulfport), March 6, 2008, B-1 and B-3; and J. R. Welsh, "Bay Feels Hit Twice: FEMA Elevations Seem Impossible," *Sun Herald* (Biloxi-Gulfport), March 5, 2008, A-2.

77. Two years after the storm, Tish Williams told reporter Jimmie Bell, while 300 companies were operating in Hancock County, in that county alone hundreds of businesses that were destroyed in Katrina would probably never reopen. See Jimmie Bell, "Hancock Businesses Get Back Up and Running," *Journal of South Mississippi Business*, September 2007, 6; and Priscilla Frulla, "Blue Rose Blues: High Cost of Insurance May Close Business," *Sun Herald* (Biloxi-Gulfport), April 4, 2007, C-12.

78. David Tortorano, "Hundreds Will Brainstorm For 6 Days," *Sun Herald* (Biloxi-Gulfport), October 13, 2003, A-1.

79. Mississippi State Tax Commission (renamed Department of Revenue in 2010) Miscellaneous Tax Bureau, "Casino Gross Gaming Revenues," 2005–2010, www.mstc.state.ms.us (accessed December 12, 2010); Mary Perez, "Best August Ever For Casinos," *Sun Herald* (Biloxi-Gulfport), September 18, 2007, B-8; Kathy Chu and Tali Yahalom, "Gulf Coast Casinos Hit Revenue Jackpot, Mississippi Sites Make More Now Than Before The Storm," *USA Today*, August 2, 2007, 3-B; and Mississippi Gaming Commission, *Directory of Current Operators*, July 2005–July 2010, http://mgc.state.ms.us/monthly-archives-year.html (accessed November 20, 2008, and December 12, 2010).

80. Roger Yu, "Casinos Flush With Cash In Mississippi," *USA Today*, May 15, 2006, 1-B; and Mississippi State Tax Commission (renamed Department of Revenue in 2010), Miscellaneous Tax Bureau, "Casino Gross Gaming Revenues," 2005–2006, www.mstc.state.ms.us (accessed July 12, 2008).

81. Ibid.; and multiyear historic data from the Mississippi Department of Employment Security quoted in Nicole Dow, "Coast Unemployment Rises in November," *Sun Herald* (Biloxi-Gulfport), December 23, 2010, C-8.

82. Stan Tiner, "So Much More Than a Bridge," *Sun Herald* (Biloxi-Gulfport), November 1, 2008, A-1 and A-8; and Melissa Scallan, "Coast's Christmas Gift May be a New U.S. 90," *Sun Herald*, June 23, 2008, A-1.

83. "Coming 2010: Margaritaville Casino and Resort at Grand Biloxi," http://www.harrahs.com (accessed September 14, 2010).

84. Mary Perez, "Casinos Spell Recovery With a B," *Sun Herald* (Biloxi-Gulfport), August 19, 2007, Business-6; and Mary Perez, "Casinos Prove Invaluable In Mississippi's Recovery," *Washington Post*, September 16, 2007, A-3.

85. Editorial, *Clarion-Ledger*, quoted in "What Other Publications Are Saying About the Mississippi Renewal Forum," *Sun Herald* (Biloxi-Gulfport), October 14, 2005, A-4.

86. Gulf Coast Business Council Research Foundation, "Mississippi Gulf Coast 3.0: Three Years After Katrina," August 2008, 3 and 5.

87. Kathy Chu and Gtali Yahalom, "Gulf Coast Casinos Hit Revenue Jackpot," *USA Today*, August 2, 2007, 3-B.

88. Mary Perez, "Casino Financing Turns Tough Due To Slowdown," *Sun Herald* (Biloxi-Gulfport), May 10, 2008, C-5.

89. Mary Perez, "Don't Worry. Margaritaville Will Be Built, Work Just Slowing Down," *Sun Herald* (Biloxi-Gulfport), July 23, 2008, A-1; and Mary Perez, "Biloxi May Land New Casino, Hotels," *Sun Herald* (Biloxi-Gulfport), May 20, 2010, http://www.lexisnexis.com (accessed August 3, 2010).

90. Mississippi State Tax Commission (renamed Department of Revenue in 2010) Miscellaneous Tax Bureau, "Casino Gross Gaming Revenues," 2005 –2010, www.mstc.state.ms.us (accessed December 12, 2010); and Mississippi Gaming Commission, *Directory of Current Operators,* July 2005–July 2010, http://mgc.state.ms.us/monthly-archives-year.html (accessed November 20, 2008 and December 12, 2010).

91. Mary Perez, "Tavoli Casino Approval Facing Challenge," *Sun Herald* (Biloxi-Gulfport), April 15, 2007, A-3; Mary Perez, "South Beach Rising," *Sun Herald* (Biloxi-Gulfport), October 4, 2007, D-8; and Mary Perez, "Holloway Shows Impatience With Idle Casino," *Sun Herald* (Biloxi-Gulfport), July 15, 2010, http://www.lexisnexis.com (accessed August 3, 2010).

92. Mississippi Department of Employment Security, *Annual Labor Force Report*, 2005–2010, http://www/mdes.state.ms.gov/Home/docs/LMI/Publications (accessed November 20, 2008, and December 20, 2010).

93. Ibid.

94. Mary Perez, "Margaritaville Sailing Away? Let's Hope Not," *Sun Herald* (Biloxi-Gulfport), June 12, 2009, http://www/lexisnexis.com (accessed December 16, 2009).

Chapter Eleven

1. Romans 5: 3–4 (NIV).

2. Mary Perez, "44 Percent of East Biloxi Still Vacant From Katrina," *Sun Herald* (Biloxi-Gulfport), January 8, 2011, A-9.

3. Gulf Coast Business Council Research Foundation, "Mississippi Gulf Coast Regional Brief: Third Quarter 2009," 10; and Gerald Blessey, "We Must Have Strong Legs to Take the Bold Steps," *Sun Herald* (Biloxi-Gulfport), August 25, 2010, Opinion, C-3.

4. Stan Tiner, editorial, "So Much More Than a Bridge," *Sun Herald* (Biloxi-Gulfport), November 1, 2007, A-1 and A-8; Ryan LaFontaine, "Together Again: The People of South Mississippi Are Reunited By the Biloxi Bay Bridge," *Sun Herald* (Biloxi-Gulfport), November 1, 2007, A-1.

5. Mary Perez, "Rebirth of the Coast: Silver Linings Emerge From the Rubble," *Sun Herald* (Biloxi-Gulfport), August 26, 2010, A-1 and A-6.

6. Michael Newsom, "Recession, Insurance Costs Hamper Ideas From Governor's Commission Report," *Sun Herald* (Biloxi-Gulfport), August 27, 2010, A-9.

7. Editorial, "Faith and Hope Go Only So Far in Rebuilding Effort," *Sun Herald* (Biloxi-Gulfport), February 1, 2007, B-4.

8. Joshua Norman, "Study Overlap Sparks Debate: Methods May Now Improve," *Sun Herald* (Biloxi-Gulfport), August 25, 2007; Raymond Scurfield, "Post-Katrina Storm Disorder and Recovery in South Mississippi Over Two Years Later," *Traumatology*, prepublication copy, 2008; and Mary Foster, "Some Say Katrina's Death Toll Still Rising: Psychological, Physical, Financial Problems 'Killing' Storm Victims," *Sun Herald* (Biloxi-Gulfport), June 3, 2007, B-2; Steve Phillips, "Katrina Still Causing Mental Health Problems," *WLOX News*, August 1, 2008.

9. Ronald C. Kessler et al., "Mental Illness and Suicidality After Hurricane Katrina," *Bulletin of the World Health Organization,*" 84, no. 12 (December 2006), 8.

10. Kat Bergeron, "Storm Brought Out Survivor's Spirit," *Sun Herald* (Biloxi-Gulfport), August 29, 2009, A-1.

11. Louise Perkins, interview by James Pat Smith, March 13, 2008 (USM KOH).

12. Ibid.

13. Ibid.; and e-mail, Louise Perkins to James Pat Smith, August 13, 2010.

14. Ibid.

15. Ibid.

16. Ibid.

17. E-mail, Louise Perkins to James Pat Smith, August 13, 2010.

18. Louise Perkins, interview by James Pat Smith, March 13, 2008 (USM KOH).

19. Anita Lee, "An Enduring People," *Sun Herald* (Biloxi-Gulfport), August 29, 2010, A-1.

Index